P9-DNB-843

PUBLIC LIBRARY
ASSOCIATION
A division of the American Library Association

2002–03 Edition
GUIDE TO INTERNET JOB SEARCHING

Margaret Riley Dikel | Frances E. Roehm

VGM Career Books

Chicago   New York   San Francisco   Lisbon   London   Madrid   Mexico City
Milan   New Delhi   San Juan   Seoul   Singapore   Sydney   Toronto

OUACHITA TECHNICAL COLLEGE

VGM Career Books

A Division of The **McGraw·Hill** *Companies*

Copyright © 2002 by The McGraw-Hill Companies, Inc. All rights reserved. Printed in the United States of America. Except as permitted under the United States Copyright Act of 1976, no part of this publication may be reproduced or distributed in any form or by any means, or stored in a database or retrieval system, without the prior written permission of the publisher.

1 2 3 4 5 6 7 8 9 0 VLP/VLP 1 0 9 8 7 6 5 4 3 2

ISBN 0-07-138310-7
ISSN 1527-7410

This book was set in Stone Serif
Printed and bound by Vicks Lithograph and Printing

Cover design by Jennifer Locke
Interior design by Precision Graphics

McGraw-Hill books are available at special quantity discounts to use as premiums and sales promotions, or for use in corporate training programs. For more information, please write to the Director of Special Sales, Professional Publishing, McGraw-Hill, Two Penn Plaza, New York, NY 10121-2298. Or contact your local bookstore.

This book is printed on acid-free paper.

HF
5382.7
.R557
2002

Contents

FOREWORD — v

PREFACE — vii

ACKNOWLEDGMENTS — ix

1   Pounding the Virtual Pavement: Using the Internet in Your Job Search — 1

2   Your Resume on the Internet — 33

3   The Great Job-Lead Banks — 49

4   Jobs in Business, Marketing, and Commercial Services — 63

5   Jobs in the Social Sciences and the World of Nonprofits — 79

6   Jobs in the Humanities, Recreation, Hospitality, and Personal Services — 99

7   Jobs in the Natural Sciences, Health, and Medicine — 119

8   Jobs in Engineering, Mathematics, Technology, and Transportation — 139

9   Opportunities in Government, Public Policy, and Public Service — 173

10   Entry-Level and Summer Employment, Internships, and Co-ops — 189

11   State and Local Resources for the United States — 199

12   International Opportunities — 275

13   Resources for Diverse Audiences — 307

14   Lifelong Career Planning — 323

15   Executive Job Searching Online — 349

Index of Cited Resources — 360

Subject Index — 372

Foreword

According to *BusinessWeek* Online (July 30, 2001) Dow Chemical no longer accepts paper resumes from professionals. Accenture (formerly Andersen Consulting) hires 20 percent of its midcareer recruits through online sources. Dole Foods, ADP, and Pitney Bowes have found a number of senior-level professionals through the Web. Corporate sites now outrank the mega job boards in number of hires. Job boards, however, are still useful for companies without name recognition.

How times have changed! Do you remember sending resumes via snail mail and dithering over what size envelope to use? Should you use a number 10 and fold the resume or use a larger one so it would lie flat? No more. Technology has revolutionized job hunting . . . for some. There are still too many people who try an online job hunt but give up after a few—or many—hours of frustration. They suspect there is a wealth of information and opportunity out there in the ether, but they don't know how to find it. Online job hunting—from simple research on industry salary ranges or details on individual companies to websites offering more esoteric information—shouldn't mean random surfing and prayers for a lucky hit. That's why Margaret Riley Dikel and Frances Roehm put together the fourth edition of *Guide to Internet Job Searching*—to help the job hunter get and stay on target.

Both Margaret and Frances are librarians. Margaret created The Riley Guide (rileyguide.com) while a librarian at Worcester Polytechnic Institute. Richard Bolles (*What Color Is Your Parachute?*) has called this website the best gateway site for job hunters. It represents extensive research and is comprehensive, well organized, and easy to use. If Margaret is the grandmother of Internet searching, Frances is one of the foremost practitioners. She's also a career librarian at the Skokie (Illinois) Public Library where she's much in demand by job hunters. I should know. I refer many of my career-consulting clients to Fran every year.

How long do you want to spend finding the right job? As little time as possible, right? This user-friendly guide can help you do the kind of extensive job search that would be impossible if you had to start from scratch and learn on your own. In addition to listing general recruiting sites, the book has chapters that list job sites within specific industries such as engineering, health care, and hospitality. There are chapters focusing on nonprofits, government sites, and international opportunities. There is also a chapter on preparing your resume and cover letter for E-mail. Some things never change: a job-specific job objective on your resume is still a must. It shows prospective employers that you are focused. (It also helps you narrow down your targets.) Use this book as a tool to help you define that job objective. As your search progresses, the resources listed in the *Guide to Internet Job Searching* will allow you to identify opportunities and specific jobs that you may not have been aware of when you started. You can then fine-tune your job objective.

Think of *Guide to Internet Job Searching* as a road map, whether you are a novice in Web surfing or a techie whiz. As any casual surfer knows, often the website that was your original destination will offer links that can lead to unexpected places. Use this book to help you follow your personal road.

Marilyn Moats Kennedy
Managing Partner, Career Strategies

Preface

It's hard to believe that we first embarked on the original *Guide to Internet Job Searching* in 1994! Information technology in today's world is much different than it was even those few years ago, and it continues its evolution at an increasingly frantic pace. At the time, the public was just catching on to the wonders of the Internet and the enormous promise offered by connectivity and the information highway.

In that initial volume we included many resources accessible via gopher, which has long since been overtaken by the World Wide Web; Usenet newsgroups, which were one of the first uses of the Internet and have now been greatly diminished in importance by the use of E-mail lists and message boards; and telnet, which continues to play a role, though relatively minor, in today's Internet. Since the publication of the first *Guide*, the World Wide Web and its easy-to-use browsing and searching features have caused a shift in the way we find information and communicate with one another and have rapidly made the Internet an integral part of our information environment.

According to figures compiled by the American Library Association, 94.5 percent of the nation's public libraries now offer a connection to the Internet along with their more traditional services. In addition, schools are wired, folks are connected to the Internet at home, and people are shopping, communicating, and finding information online as they would not have dreamed even five years ago. Traditional information providers are finding that these services are not only user-friendly but also cost-effective—they are saving paper, staff time, and long-distance charges—essentially giving all parties involved more bang for the buck.

Job and career information is perfectly suited to this online environment. In electronic format, information can be accessed from anywhere, by anyone, and at any time! Job postings can be scanned in very quickly, making the information available almost as soon as a position is open. Resumes can be electronically matched to companies or suitable job listings. Folks can access advice from respected career specialists such as Dick Bolles or Carol Kleiman any hour of the day. Job candidates can research prospective employers or obtain information about a company prior to the interview.

Public libraries have traditionally played a vital role in the job search, providing local and national newspapers, career guides, business directories, and knowledge of the community and its agencies to direct individuals to the information they need. Today's public library is more important than ever! Skilled librarians are better than search engines when it comes to helping individuals find the information they need, whether it is online, at a local agency, or in print resources or databases in the library.

Your public library can help point the way, with books about the job search or resume writing, career guides, other print resources, and databases. It can also provide you with access to the Internet and offer links to some helpful Web-based career resources. For your convenience, many libraries now offer access to their databases from home as well. Call your local public library to find out how the librarians can assist you, and take advantage of the wealth of information available to you.

This Public Library Association (PLA) guide will show you how to access job and career information found on the Internet, and it offers some of the best places to look for it. It will also give you the guidelines you need to manage this interactive, ever-changing environment. Users of the previous guides will notice changes in this edition of the book. For one thing, this volume continues to reflect the movement toward smaller sites that are focused on only one occupational discipline, industry, or location. You'll find too that several of the major job sites are following the same trend and in addition to maintaining their large websites are creating smaller focused web pages or portals for specific geographic regions or job categories. A tremendous number of sites have closed, a trend that will continue, but many others are coming along to try to stake a claim in the field.

We have continued to expand our listing of resources for even more occupations and industries that were not online previously. The Internet is an increasingly vital tool for individuals navigating the world of work, and as this virtual environment evolves, we encourage you to take advantage of the research and networking opportunities accessible to you twenty-four/seven.

Use the *Guide* with our best wishes for success in your job search!

Acknowledgments

It's been several years since we lost our close friend and coauthor Steve Oserman, and yet we continue to be inspired by his warmth and good works on behalf of job seekers and career changers. Steve came up with the idea for this project initially and early on provided much of the perspiration behind its success. His vitality and energetic personality were wonderfully inspiriting, and we only hope we can continue to uphold his vision for the book and to follow his example of service to the community.

We also owe a debt of gratitude to the following librarians who helped with this edition of the book. They have all been longtime supporters of our work and the work of the Job and Career Information Services Committee, and their assistance at this time made all the difference.

Mary Grace Desidero, manager, Job and Career Education Center, Carnegie Library of Pittsburgh (Pennsylvania)

Norman Eriksen, division chief, Education and Job Information Center, Brooklyn (New York) Public Library

Vera Green, member of the Library Committee, Academy of Senior Professionals, Eckerd College, St. Petersburg, (Florida) (and the former manager, Job and Career Education Center, Carnegie Library of Pittsburgh)

Jan Maas, assistant division chief, Education and Job Information Center, Brooklyn (New York) Public Library

Frank McKenna III, M.L.I.S., assistant manager, Special Services/Job Information Center, Queens Borough (New York) Public Library

Joe McNair, librarian, Brooklyn (New York) Public Library

Sue Schlaf, reference librarian, Schaumburg Township (Illinois) District Library

Ruth S. Schwab, career information consultant and former Education/Job Information Center librarian, Ossining (New York) Public Library

Barbara Vlk, business specialist, Arlington Heights (Illinois) Memorial Library

We'd also like to thank Susan Joyce, president of NETability and owner of Job-Hunt.org, and Susan Ireland, professional resume writer and author, for allowing us to quote their work in our book.

From Frances:

Good projects don't just happen. It takes work, generally lots of it, and this edition of the *Guide* has required the support of many good friends and colleagues—you know who you are! There are some who have provided so much in the way of inspiration or encouragement that I must extend a public thank-you.

Leonard J. Cotter keeps the home fires burning.

Carolyn Anthony and members of the board, staff, and volunteers of Skokie Public Library offer continuing encouragement and moral support.

Sarah Long and the North Suburban Library System provide technical assistance and ongoing support.

Dick Bolles, Joan Durrance, Carol Kleiman, Janet Shlaes, Katherine Sopranos, Jane Hagedorn, Lola Lucas, and others inspire me in my efforts at providing the information and assistance my customers deserve.

Christopher Roehm, family, and friends make my world a better place.

And Wulfy reminds me to make time for fun.

From Margaret:

Until you work on something like this you never know how many people it takes to really create it. To those who volunteered their time and energies to make this work, I can only say thank you. And to all those who were set aside until I completed this, thank you for your patience.

Friends and colleagues such as Dick Bolles, Joyce Lain Kennedy, Tony Lee, Fran Quittel, Mary-Ellen Mort, Susan Joyce, Steve Hoffman, and Craig Morton are priceless. They not only keep an eye on what I'm doing, they introduce me to so many more good people just like them.

Family is even more important, and my family is one of the true blessings I have.

I must also acknowledge Drake Beam Morin, Inc., for their continued sponsorship of The Riley Guide.

And finally, many thanks go to my husband, David Dikel, for his patience and love.

And Misty, too.

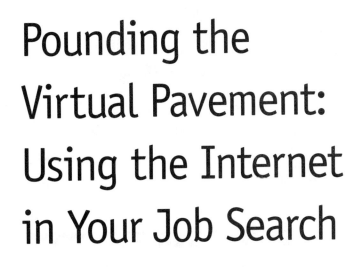

Pounding the Virtual Pavement: Using the Internet in Your Job Search

Using the Internet in your job search is not necessarily easy. The online job search crosses a variety of services and information resources. No single website, online service, or electronic resource will contain everything you need for a fully effective online job search.

What Is a Complete Job Search?

Many people think they are working hard on their search for a new job when they religiously scan the Sunday classifieds each week. Unfortunately, what they are really doing is expending 100 percent of their effort on only 25 percent of the possibilities.

A complete job search involves four activities:

1. Researching and contacting employers about possible opportunities

2. Reviewing job leads

3. Networking

4. Preparing a resume and distributing it

Each of these activities has two facets—offline and online:

Job Search Activity	Offline	Online
Research and contact employers	Print telephone books/ business directories/ employer pamphlets	Online telephone books/ business directories/ association links/industry sites/employer web pages/etc.
Review job leads	Print newspapers/journals/etc.	Online job banks/recruiters/ newspapers/journals/ associations/etc.
Network	Meeting with anyone you can through associations/friends/ colleagues (a.k.a. "pressing the flesh")	Participating in appropriate mailing lists and chat forums, as well as turning off the computer to make calls and attend meetings (a.k.a. "face time")
Prepare a resume for distribution	A nicely designed copy for distribution	A plain-text copy ready to post or E-mail on demand

However you approach your job search, you cannot put all your eggs in only one of the available baskets. A successful job search means spreading your assets across a variety of baskets, combining as many search activities as possible. While you are the only one who can determine your level of comfort with any given activity, you need to use at least one facet of each activity (research, job leads, networking, and the resume) to get the best results from all your effort. Look at it this way:

- If you don't have your resume in plain text, it won't be easy to respond to job leads found online.

- If you don't network by attending local association meetings, you could be missing a chance to meet the people best positioned to help you with your search.

- If you don't look at the jobs posted online, you could be missing lots of local opportunities that you've missed in other places.

- If you don't call the employers you've found, you can't speak with them about possibilities and convince them how much they need you.

Each of these activities is discussed separately later in the chapter.

Going Online: Why Bother?

If the job search is already hard, you may be thinking, why make it any more difficult by adding the Internet? Here are seven good reasons:

1. You can access current information at all hours of the day or night, when it's convenient for you, even if that is at 10 P.M. after getting the kids to bed.

2. The Internet doesn't take holidays, and the whole network won't go down all at once for maintenance. One site may be down, but there are always others you can use.

3. There are no geographic limits online, so you can take your job search far beyond your regular boundaries. There may be employers who would prefer to hire from their local area, but that doesn't mean you can't talk them into giving you the job, since you'll pay for your own move. It could be the best investment you've ever made.

4. You can dig down deeper into your local area, finding the smaller employers within walking distance from your house who are dying to find someone just like you.

5. Using the Internet in your search demonstrates leading-edge skills to employers. You not only know how to use a computer, but you also know

how to navigate this online morass. If you use the Internet for any job-search activity, make sure you tell the employer.

6. The Internet lets you meet new people and initiate new relationships with others in your profession or region without the usual "first date" stress. On the Internet, no one can see you sweat. You don't have to worry about looking OK or wonder if everyone can see that your hands are shaking. Take your time, and relax. Find the groups and folks that feel best to you and are discussing things that interest you, and then take your time getting to know them before putting your best electronic face forward.

7. The Internet can help you explore career alternatives and options that you might not have considered. Not quite happy with your current job? Is it the job or the career path you've chosen? Not sure how to answer? Explore! What sounds like fun? Are there any ways to apply your current skills in a new direction? You can find some self-assessment tools online, loads of occupations and disciplines to explore, and even lists of local career counselors and career centers to help you if you feel you need it.

But Before You Go Online . . .

You need to answer some questions before you can start your online search. Make a list of your responses in these three principal areas:

1. What do you want to do? What can you do? (Skills and Occupations) What skills do you have, what interests, what abilities? For instance: *I can type seventy words per minute; I like working with my hands; I'm licensed to drive a forklift.* Along with your list of specific skills, put down general occupations that interest you. Don't worry about specific job titles like chief medical officer or vice president of international sales. Think "doctor" or "sales" instead.

2. Whom do you want to work for? (Industries and Employer Preferences) What industry interests you, what type of employer? For instance: *I've always wanted to work for a Fortune 500/Inc. 500/high-tech start-up/family-friendly/ environmentally conscious organization. . . .* If you have some specific companies you want to target, great! Put them on the list, too.

3. Where do you want to live and work? (Location, Location, Location) Is there a particular city, state, region, or country you are targeting? For instance: Southern California, Maryland, someplace with good golf courses and very little snow. If you are thinking about a particular city, find out what other cities and municipalities surround it, the name of the county it's in, and if the region has a geographic nickname like "Silicon Valley" or "Silicon Alley," and add all this to your list. An atlas can help you here, as can the online telephone books and map services (see Chapter 14 for a short list). Your local librarians can point you toward even more useful materials.

JOB SEARCH TIP:

Narrowing the Field. If you are saying to yourself, "I'll go anyplace I can find a job," then you need to stop and find out where the jobs are so you can target employers in that area. There are too many employers and too many newspapers to read for you to just look everywhere. You can use labor market information (LMI) available from each state and the Bureau of Labor Statistics to help with this. Information on this along with other resources can be found in Chapter 14.

Why is this exercise necessary? Your responses will help you begin building the list of keywords you'll use in your job search. After all, most of the online job banks allow you to search their listings using keywords, but if you don't know the words you want to search, how can you effectively use any of the job banks? You can't, so take the time to work through your list before you start.

Having trouble thinking of keywords? Here are some tips:

- Ask a friend. Friends can frequently see things in you that you can't see yourself. They might also have some good ideas and interesting options for you to consider.

- Ask a librarian. Librarians are usually very good at this kind of exercise, but try to ask for some help when the reference desk isn't busy so the librarian can concentrate on your request. He or she can probably point you to books and other resources that can also help with this.

- Scan some online job banks. Search some of the big job-lead banks listed in Chapter 3, such as Monster.com (monster.com) or America's Job Bank (ajb.org), for jobs that interest you. Read the job descriptions, note the skills and kinds of experience the employers are seeking, and then use these words in your search.

- Read some good books. Check your local bookstore or library for a copy of *What Color Is Your Parachute?* by Richard Bolles (Ten Speed Press), *Cool Careers for Dummies* by Marty Nemko and Paul and Sarah Edwards (IDG Books), or *Career Change: Everything You Need to Know to Meet New Challenges and Take Control of Your Career* by David P. Helfand (VGM Career Books). These all contain exercises and information designed to help you identify your skills and interests. Your local career center, public library, or employment service center will have even more good resources you can use.

- Talk to a career counselor. If you have a lot of trouble figuring out what you want to do, you might want to get some help from a career counselor. He or she can help you learn more about yourself and your interests and guide you through the process of deciding where to go. You'll find some resources to help you find career counselors in Chapter 14.

Learning to Swim Before You Surf: How to Find Information on the Internet

There is a method to controlling this madness, and it's not as hard as you might think. There are actually only two ways to find information online, and there's only one good way to approach your search:

- Look for information by browsing or searching, or using a combination of the two.

- Approach your search by moving from general to specific.

Sounds simple, doesn't it? And it is simple! Maybe it's from general sites and sources to more specific ones, or from general job banks to specific ones targeted to your location, occupation, or industry, but always think about moving from general to specific. And as you move along, everything you encounter will let you browse through things or do a quick search. As the following sections explain, there are times when browsing is better than searching, and vice versa.

BROWSING

When you are unsure of where to start or what to look for, browsing is the way to go. It's also helpful in cases in which you've already started looking online but aren't finding what you want. Maybe it's just a matter of "knowing it when you see it." Browsing is like window shopping or scanning the shelves at the library or bookstore: you have a basic idea of what you want, but you could use some suggestions or pointers to move you in the right direction.

Browsing is actually a general "search and scan" process. You use very broad terms from your keyword list to search Internet libraries or directories for information and resources on your choice of occupations or industries, and then you scan the resulting list to see what came up. It's like searching the catalog in your local library: you find a book that looks promising and go to the correct shelf to pull it, but while there, you look around to see what else might catch your eye. You don't rely on just the list of links to other sites and resources; you're more interested in the categories of information produced so you can scan the shelves and see what you might find. In most cases, you should start finding information and resources almost immediately, along with suggestions for more paths to explore. It's highly unlikely that you'll find job leads immediately, but you can find potential employers, links to industry or occupational information, or pointers to online resource guides.

Another advantage to browsing is the process of testing your keywords. While browsing, you are learning which words from your list point you in the right direction, maybe even giving you better keywords to use. You are also learning which words don't work as well but might have some promise in certain areas and which words are taking you in the wrong direction and should be removed from your list. In any case, it is not a wasted activity.

SEARCHING

Searching comes into play when you have your objectives identified, you've worked your keyword list and settled on the very best terms defining your needs and objectives, and you have your resume already prepared. Searching is like running into the grocery store for a jar of spaghetti sauce with mushrooms that you know is in aisle three near the front of the store on the bottom shelf. You run in, grab the sauce, go right to the express checkout with exact change in hand, and get out again before your favorite song on the radio has finished playing. Think "tactical search-and-retrieval."

When you are finally ready to search, you are going to use very specific terms that define your skills, the types of jobs for which you are looking, and the companies or organizations for which you want to work. You've selected these words because in previous browse-and-scan sessions they produced the best results. This does not mean the largest list of possibilities, but rather the most specific and best-matched ones.

The advantages of searching are speed and accuracy. You can cover more ground online because you can move faster and with more determination. You can get in and out of the major job-lead banks in ten minutes or less, you're able to review loads of information about an employer in preparation for an interview in twenty minutes or less, and you aren't wasting time scanning hundreds of job leads. Your searches produce a limited number of highly qualified leads and highly qualified employer lists with very little mismatched "job-lead spam."

So, through browsing and searching, you have already begun to move from general data to specific information. Now you can start expanding this approach to the online resources needed for your search.

Stepping Through the Internet Research Process

STEP 1: BROWSE THOSE VIRTUAL LIBRARIES AND INTERNET DIRECTORIES (VERY GENERAL)

Virtual libraries and Internet directories are large collections of information arranged by broad topics. Because they cover many subjects, they act as general guides to the Internet morass. They are useful for identifying the best terms for searching and to begin finding helpful resources. Start out by browsing their main categories, and then use their search features, scanning the resulting lists for ideas.

Try this: search *education* or *finance* in the following libraries and directories to find information on these topics. Make a note of employers you find and topics you discover.

Yahoo!	yahoo.com
W3O Virtual Library	http://vlib.org/Overview.html
Librarian's Index to the Internet	lii.org
LookSmart	looksmart.com
Search.com	search.com
About.com	about.com

Many of the search engines listed under Step 3, coming up, also maintain directories of information you can browse.

STEP 2: BROWSE AND SEARCH ONLINE RESOURCE GUIDES (BECOMING MORE SPECIFIC)

Online resource guides are sites or online documents dedicated to a specific topic or industry. Like print directories or encyclopedias that focus on only one topic, they are much more specific in identifying industry and employer information and are usually more inclusive of resources. The virtual libraries and Internet directories will begin pointing you toward online resource guides (look for the indexes or directories under any topic). Also, some virtual libraries, such as The Clearinghouse and Britannica, are dedicated to maintaining pointers to these highly useful resources.

When you are looking for online resource guides, remember that organizations or specialists in a particular subject or topic usually compile the best ones. Many of the most respected reference books found in libraries are now online, so these will be particularly useful. To help evaluate a resource guide you find for the topic that interests you, look for information on who has compiled it, what his or her background is (or the organization's background), and why the guide was created.

Try this: search *education* or *finance* in the following guides to find websites and sources dedicated to these topics. Note any employers or associations you come across.

Libraries of Online Resource Guides

The Clearinghouse	clearinghouse.net
Britannica	britannica.com
The Scout Report	http://scout.cs.wisc.edu
University of Delaware Access to Internet and Subject Resources	http://www2.lib.udel.edu/subj
Research Guides from the Melvin Gelman Library, George Washington University	gwu.edu/gelman/guides

Sample List of Online Resource Guides

Hoover's Online (business information)	hoovers.com
Scholarly Societies Project (professional and scholarly associations)	scholarly-societies.org
The Riley Guide (employment information)	rileyguide.com
Editor & Publisher Interactive (newspapers worldwide)	editorandpublisher.com

STEP 3: SEARCH THOSE SEARCH ENGINES (VERY SPECIFIC)

Search engines are searchable databases of keywords retrieved from Internet documents, and these databases are huge. For this reason, it's best to not use the search engines until you are very specific about what you want to find. Use search engines to locate hidden information on any topic (occupation or industry) or employer. You can find these through the virtual libraries and Internet directories; in fact, many of the directories are associated with certain search engines, such as Excite and Lycos.

One thing to be aware of is that each search engine is different in how it works and what it indexes, so you should use two or three in your search and compare the results. Try them all, but choose the ones you like best to use as a real part of your search. Don't feel obliged to use the ones that your friends, the local librarians, or even this book might recommend. It's a personal choice. Then, once you select the ones you like the best, learn all the advanced commands so you can improve your searching even more.

We've included some metacrawlers in our list of search engines. These are like search engines on steroids, going out and searching four or five engines with the click of a single button. They can help you combine and compare the results of many stand-alone search engines, but when you really want to dig up some nitty-gritty, you should go directly to a stand-alone search engine and use its advanced features to target your desired data.

Try this: use the following engines to search the names of employers you found in your previous searches or specific topics and occupations you found.

Search Engines

AltaVista	altavista.com
Google	google.com
HotBot	http://hotbot.lycos.com
Excite	excite.com

Lycos	lycos.com
AskJeeves	ask.com
Webcrawler	webcrawler.com
Metacrawlers	
MetaCrawler	metacrawler.com
Dogpile	dogpile.com
Ixquick	ixquick.com

Frequently Asked Questions About the Online Search Process

Why are search engines the third step? Shouldn't they be first, because they are the fastest?

The advantage of search engines is that they scour a lot of pages of data online. The disadvantage is that they scour a lot of pages of data online. Don't you hate doing a search and coming up with 300,000 hits? All that stuff just slows you down. By putting search engines last, you are not turning to them until you are very, very specific about what you want them to find, thereby (we hope) cutting down on the number of false hits and unreasonable responses you get and actually increasing your speed.

Why bother with online resource guides when there are big-time sites like Yahoo!?

Because the directories are dedicated to one or two specific topics, they are much more in-depth and up-to-date than Yahoo! and similar sites. They also pull in a lot of related information and smaller bits and pieces that the big sites might be tempted to overlook. These nuggets of information are especially useful when you need to dig deeper into an idea or industry.

Why go to places like Yahoo! first? Isn't Yahoo! a search engine?

No, it really isn't. Look at Yahoo!'s front page. It's a catalog of topics, and each breaks down into more topics. Try a search in Yahoo! and look at your result. It starts with a listing of the Yahoo! categories that match your search request. Then it gives you a list of Yahoo! sites that match your search, again organized according to Yahoo! categories. Only if Yahoo! does not find anything within its own collection will it stretch out to the general Internet to try to answer your request, using one of the search engines to go beyond its own confines.

Why is the foregoing distinction important?

Yahoo! acts like a subsection of the Internet, meaning you are dealing with a lot less data. This makes Yahoo! a great place for testing your keywords. You can try searches on occupations and disciplines, on industries, and on skills. Then review the results to answer these questions:

- Am I still too general? (lots and lots of resulting categories in Yahoo!)

- Am I already too specific? (very few results in Yahoo!, or it's already tapping the Internet)

- Am I using the wrong words to describe what I'm looking for? (the results are not right, or Yahoo! immediately hits the Internet and still doesn't find anything)

Yahoo! and similar sites can also be helpful in exploring options in careers and industries. For instance, if you search Yahoo! for the word *finance*, the results include personal finance, corporate finance, finance and banking, and on and on. Lots of options, don't you think?

Now that you've learned how to "swim" online, you can start surfing for employment opportunities! Remember that there are four activities in the job search—researching, reviewing job leads, networking, and preparing a resume—and you'll need to work through each one separately.

INTERNET TIP:

URLs. If you ever have trouble connecting to a web page, try cutting the address, or url (for "uniform resource locator"), back one slash mark, so http://www.dbm.com/jobguide/manuf.html becomes http://www.dbm.com/jobguide and even www.dbm.com. The file or directory you are seeking may have moved, and by backing up one level at a time, you may be able to find the new location easily.

Research—Finding Information on Employers, Opportunities, and Options

The Internet is a huge collection of databases just waiting to be used. Tap the resources provided by the thousands of companies, colleges and universities, governments, and news and information services to do extended research into your target occupations, industries, and employers.

Have you ever gone into a hardware store and asked the manager if there were any job openings for day care providers? Probably not, because you know it is pretty unlikely a hardware store would have any need for someone with those skills. However, many employers do offer day care on-site, but you may not know if a company does, or if it has a potential need for someone with your skills, unless someone tells you. This is why you research employers, to find those that have a need that you can fill. You want to know what they do, how they function, and how you might fit into the organization.

In the same vein, if you are invited for an interview based on your resume, you can't just walk into an employer's office and say, "So, what is this job you are interviewing me for, and how do I fit into your organization?" Most employers expect you to know who they are, what they do, what the job entails, and how you fit into the company structure and culture before you come in. Researching the employer will get you past the small talk and into the real purpose of your interview, convincing the employer that he or she needs you and that you will be a valuable addition to the team.

Think of a job interview as a sales pitch: you have a product to sell (yourself), but you need to know who is buying (the employer) and what he or she is looking for (what skills are required in what jobs). Once you've determined the situation, you send in your marketing brochure (the resume and cover letter), highlighting the company's needs and specifying how your product fills those needs. If you've done it right, you'll be invited to make a live presentation (job interview), and possibly make the sale (be offered a position). All it takes is some advance research. You probably know the conventional wisdom: 80 percent of all jobs are never advertised, not even on the Internet. Well, researching the employers and contacting them is one way to get connected to that "hidden market."

Here's the three-stage procedure:

1. Start your employer research at the employer's website. The company website is a book about the employer by the employer. Read it "cover to cover," and print out the pages that interest you or have information you want to double-check.

- Look at anything that says "News" or "What's New." This will give you the latest information on what is happening and possible clues on new areas or projects where you might be able to help.

- Read any mission statements or description of services to learn how this organization describes itself. Use this to customize your cover letter to the company's interests.

- Look for an annual report or strategic plan, and read it carefully. These will tell you where the company is going and where it's coming from.

- Check out the human resources area for more information on current or ongoing job openings and the benefits offered by this company. It's possible that there are many job openings not posted online, but read over the instructions given on the website for applying, and use this as a guide to the application procedures.

- Look over the whole site. What does the design of these pages say to you about this organization? Is the design conservative or freewheeling? Are the pages well organized or difficult to follow? Most companies want their websites to reflect the business's corporate image, so the site can say a lot about the institution with very few words.

- Refer to the website during your interview. It will reinforce your efforts to convey your knowledge and skills regarding the Internet. Some company representatives aren't aware of what their pages say or haven't seen them recently, so it could be useful to take some clean copies of certain pages with you to the interview. Just don't point out any spelling errors.

The virtual libraries and Internet directories can help you find employer websites, as can many of the online resource guides dedicated to business information, such as those on the following list. If these aren't working for you, then try the search engines.

Online Business Directories

Hoover's (also has a European list)	hoovers.com
CorporateInformation (worldwide listings)	corporateinformation.com
WSRN.com: Wall Street Research Net	wsrn.com

2. Check business directories and other employer information sources for outside profiles of the employers. This could include a brief profile with financial information, as you'll find in Hoover's, a copy of a 10K report from the U.S. Securities and Exchange Commission's Edgar database, or insider profiles like those from The Vault Report and WetFeet.com. The reference librarians in your local library can point you toward even more print and electronic resources to help you with your research.

You'll need to find online resource guides for business and industry information for this step. The Clearinghouse and Britannica can help, as can "Tell Me About This Employer" from The Riley Guide. Along with its many links to business research resources, The Riley Guide includes a section on how to research employers, with links to online tutorials that you'll find helpful.

Online Resource Guides

Hoover's (company profiles)	hoovers.com
Edgar (10K reports)	sec.gov/edgar.shtml
Vault.com (insider reports)	vault.com
WetFeet.com (insider reports)	wetfeet.com
Tell Me About This Employer: The Riley Guide (more guides, plus tutorials on doing business research)	rileyguide.com/employer.html

3. Fire up the search engines. Look for more information on an employer anywhere you can find it. Search the employer's name, the company's products, the names of any people in the organization, and so forth. Why? Well, as one job seeker put it: "The employer's website told me what they wanted me to know, but I found what I wanted to know by doing more searching online." Anything you find can be useful in your initial search, your sales pitch, or even your decision on whether it's even worth contacting this employer about opportunities.

JOB SEARCH TIP:

That's not all, folks. The Internet can also be used to find information on industries, career options, salaries, and much more. We have resources at the end of this chapter plus even more in Chapter 14.

Job Listings and Recruiting Sites

While searching for employers and opportunities, look for job listings at several levels, again always thinking about moving from general to specific.

- Start with the large recruiting sites to get the broadest overviews and largest database searches you can.

- Review the online journals, newspapers, and job banks for your target location, industry, and occupation or discipline. Look for recruiters who specialize in a particular industry or occupational group, or who concentrate on one geographic area.

- Scan through appropriate websites and online journals for the various professional or trade associations to find job listings marketed to your particular job areas, occupational fields, industries, and geographic location. There are also websites for many of the diversity and affinity groups with which you might identify yourself, and many times these will carry job announcements.

- Visit employer websites, even if you found their jobs listed in other locations. Many now use the major job-lead banks to advertise "generic" jobs they are always looking to fill but post the specific openings, along with even more job categories, on their own sites. It's also likely you will find a way to contact their human resources departments to learn about any opportunities they haven't posted.

JOB LISTINGS 101: START WITH THE INTERNET JOB GUIDES

Online resource guides for job and career information contain links to hundreds of Internet employment resources. Using these, you can quickly identify places to begin your job search. The Employment or Jobs/Careers sections of the virtual libraries might also be useful, but you'll likely find these guides better organized and more in-depth. We've included a short list here to get you started. You'll find a more complete list of resources with descriptions at the end of Chapter 3.

The Riley Guide	rileyguide.com
JobHuntersBible.com	jobhuntersbible.com
JobHunt	job-hunt.org
JobStar	http://jobstar.org

JOB LISTINGS 102: THE GREAT JOB-LEAD BANKS

Job-lead banks feature hundreds or even thousands of job announcements in numerous fields and occupations. The online classifieds of most major newspapers fall under this category (smaller regional and local papers are generally considered targeted sources, the next category). Almost all of these sites and sources have a keyword searching capability, allowing you to scan all the job listings in a few minutes instead of a few hours. A sample listing follows; a more complete list of the great job-lead banks along with descriptions can be found in Chapter 3.

America's Job Bank	ajb.org
Monster.com	monster.com
NationJob	nationjob.com
CareerBuilder.com	careerbuilder.com

JOB LISTINGS 103: TARGETED SOURCES

Many sites are set up to serve a particular industry, occupation, geographic location, or group of people. Professional and trade associations along with all trade and industry publications fall into the category of targeted sources. This book contains hundreds of these sites, so select the chapters that address your needs, and also scan the index for topics you hadn't thought of. Here is just a small example of the kinds of resources you'll find online:

InfoMine (mining industry)	infomine.com
Asia-Net (Asian-language specialists)	asia-net.com
SaludosWeb (persons of Hispanic descent)	saludos.com
American Zoo and Aquarium Association	aza.org
ComputerWorld (IT trade journal)	computerworld.com

| ChicagoJobs
(leads for jobs in the Chicago area) | chicagojobs.org |
| New Mobility's Interactive Café
(disabled people) | newmobility.com |

Within this book, we've listed a few of the hundreds of mailing lists that can also carry targeted job announcements. These online services are discussed in the upcoming section on networking.

JOB LISTINGS 104: EMPLOYER WEBSITES

As we outlined in "Stepping Through the Internet Research Process" earlier in the chapter, you'll need to identify lists of employers in any given industry, filter the list to just those in your local area, and make contact. Business directories and telephone directories can be useful in this part of your job search, as can your local public library or job service office. The Riley Guide's "Tell Me About This Employer" also will help you find many resources. Here are five places to head:

Yahoo! (start identifying employers)	yahoo.com
Hoover's (business research)	hoovers.com
AltaVista (search engine)	altavista.com
SuperPages.com (find businesses in a certain area)	superpages.com
Tell Me About This Employer: The Riley Guide	rileyguide.com/employer.html

Top Six Online Job-Search Mistakes

You now know where to go and what to look for, but we want to warn you about common mistakes made by many who use the Internet as a job-search tool. Susan Joyce, manager of Job-Hunt.org (job-hunt.org), has put together this list of common errors she sees as she works with both job hunters and hiring managers.

1. Failing to protect your privacy or your identity. You can, and must, protect your contact information (name, address, E-mail address, and phone number) during your search. Many employers do search for the resumes of their own employees in the job site resume/applicant database and/or the search engines. Those employees' jobs are at risk when their resumes are found! People do lose their jobs this way! And, an identity thief doesn't need much more than your resume and your social security number to steal your identity!

2. Using your employer's assets (computer, software, network, etc.) and E-mail account for your job search. Over 25 percent of employers (maybe more, depending on which report you read) say that they are "monitoring" employee E-mail traffic. So, don't assume that your E-mail is private, even if the company hasn't told you that they monitor your E-mail. Again, it may cost you your job, if you have one, by inappropriately using company assets, by violating a company's "Internet acceptable use policy," and/or by revealing to your employer that you are job hunting.

3. Sending a resume through E-mail as an attachment to the E-mail. Unless specifically directed otherwise by an employer, use a plain-text resume copied into the body of your E-mail when sending your resume to a potential employer. [See Chapter 2 for information on how to create and send a plain-text resume.] Attachments frequently get detached as the E-mail message transits through the various segments of the Internet. In addition, many computer viruses are spread as Word attachments to E-mail messages, so attachments may be either blocked by network managers or ignored by the recipient.

If a resume attachment has been requested or specified by the employer, by all means send one as directed. Otherwise, send plain text copied into the message body.

4. Using a crazy or weird name on your E-mail account. Recruiters and potential employers are looking for someone who is qualified for their job opening and who will fit into their group, working well with the other employees or team members. If your E-mail name is "WeirdAl," "WildWoman," "BoyWonder," "HackerKing," or something similar, you are not exactly putting your best foot forward in your job search. Keep the crazy names for amusing your family and friends. Don't undermine your job search by using them in correspondence with potential employers. If you don't already have one, establish an E-mail account with a "grown-up" name. Use a variation of your real name or a (restrained) marketing/descriptive name like MJJones231@hotmail.com or CalTechEngineer@excite.com.

5. Providing too much or inappropriate information on your resume. In general, it is not a good idea to include a photograph of yourself on your HTML resume page or to include it when you mail a resume. By including a photograph of yourself and/or your family, you are providing the answers to the questions that employers cannot, by law, ask you! They will know (or have a good indication of) your race, age, and sex by looking at your photograph. If you include a nice photograph of yourself and your family, they will also know your marital status, number and ages of your children, even your sexual orientation. Keep the contents of your resume focused on the opportunity you want, and the skills and experience you have that will benefit the employer. This is not the time to throw a lot of extraneous information on your resume, just because you have the space and a gift for putting it into words.

6. Dressing up your HTML resume with inappropriate graphics and multimedia. Just because you have the technical skill (or software) to add the music from your favorite artist or musical to your personal resume web page does not mean it's a good idea. Certainly the dancing rubber ducks and kittens are cute, but "cute" is probably not what a potential employer is looking for. It may cost you an opportunity if there is too great a disconnection between the requirements of the job and the fluffiness of your resume web page. Even online, a resume is a business communications document. Employers are looking for the same things they have always wanted on a resume—an understanding of what you have to offer so that they can determine if there is a good fit between your skills and experience and the requirements of their opportunity. Don't distract from the marketing message of your resume.

Online Networking

If you access the Internet through the public workstations at your local library, you might be tempted to skip this section. *Don't!* Even though most libraries can't give you an E-mail address, there are ways for you to participate in these services through the Web. Keep reading to find out how!

If you ever have the chance to speak with one of the great job-search gurus such as Richard Bolles or Joyce Lain Kennedy, ask him or her the best way to find a new job. We can almost guarantee you the answer will be "networking," and we can also testify to many successful situations, including firsthand experience, in which networking made the difference in a job search. However, networking can be the most stressful of the four activities in the job-search process, so it is used the least. This is a case in which the Internet can make a difficult situation a bit easier.

JOB SEARCH TIP:

Networking. We can't possibly give you enough information on networking in this short section, so we suggest you check the following books and online resources for more information and help with this activity.

- Baker, Wayne E. *Networking Smart: How to Build Relationships for Personal and Organizational Success.* iUniverse.com, 2000.
- Job Hunting Advice: Networking, CareerJournal (careerjournal.com).
- Kramer, Marc. *Power Networking: Using the Contacts You Don't Even Know You Have to Succeed in the Job You Want.* VGM Career Books, 1997.
- Marler, Patty, and Jan Bailey Mattia. *Networking Made Easy.* VGM Career Books, 1997.
- Tullier, L. Michelle. *Networking for Everyone: Connecting with People for Career and Job Success.* Jist Works, 1998.

Advantages to Online Networking

- There are thousands of discussion groups covering hundreds of subjects.

- You can "break the ice" before meeting someone in person.

- You can listen, engage, or be engaged as you wish. No one can see you sweat, and you don't have to feel like an oddball wallflower, because no one can see you standing off by yourself.

- Many employers and recruiters use subject-specific groups to post jobs targeting a defined segment of potential applicants.

- Many recruiters follow the discussions to help locate interesting and highly qualified candidates for positions they are trying to fill.

And the Disadvantages

- Networking online is just as difficult as networking in person! In fact, it may be harder because you can't establish a true personal relationship online. The only thing that is easier is making first contact.

- First impressions count more than ever, so be very careful with your first public posting.

- Your online behavior counts much more than you think. You must be even more professional and polite than in person. Rude or obnoxious behavior online will get you "blacklisted" faster than you can imagine.

- Not all groups carry job announcements. Very few allow resume postings. Don't rely on these discussion groups for just those purposes.

THE FINE ART OF NETIQUETTE

To repeat, because you aren't face-to-face with the other person, the stress of making new connections is greatly alleviated through the Internet, but this isn't a fast track to the hidden job market. It is important that you begin these relationships in the right way and maintain them properly. Because you can't use your voice or body language to express yourself, you are limited to making sure the words used and the ways they are presented properly represent your intentions. In other words, don't make a mess of a great opportunity to connect with people in hiring places!

This caveat doesn't apply to just the new Internet users, aka "newbies." A lot of Internet oldie-moldies need a reminder that there are real people behind the electrons, and real people make real decisions based on your electronic communication blunders. So, we humbly offer these few words of advice: *Do not go boldly where you have never gone before!*

Take the time to learn the rules of Netiquette, otherwise known as the Fine Art of Correct Behavior on the Internet. These simple rules can mean the difference between stepping out in style or stumbling off the online block.

- Stop and learn the respective rules of conduct and desirable topics of discussion for any particular mailing list, and then follow them!

- Look for a list of Frequently Asked Questions (FAQs) so you don't ask the same questions that everyone else has and frustrate the other users of the list.

- Listen patiently to the groups you have joined and learn the tone, language, and culture of the group before you start posting.

- Never post your resume or ask if anyone can help you find a job in your first, second, or third message to the list. In fact, you should never post your resume or make this kind of request unless you are doing so in a mailing list dedicated to these types of postings.

INTERNET TIP:

Flaming. Make sure you know what you are doing before you post so you do not become a victim of those nasty messages called "flames." Flaming can be particularly degrading and insulting and can make many veterans of the Internet turn off the computer for months. Think of each mailing list as an association meeting or an office party where you are the new person in the crowd who must introduce yourself. You want to make a good impression your first time out there, so don't get burned!

Here are three principles to remember as you begin exploring online networking options. First, public participation is necessary to get networking contacts. If you don't make yourself visible, no one will know you are there, including recruiters and potential employers. Second, it's always best to monitor your chosen mailing lists for a few weeks without posting. Follow the discussions and learn what they are talking about. Do not participate in the discussions until you are comfortable with the group and know how members speak to each other and what they talk about. Third, networking is a two-way relationship that must be beneficial to both parties. You must give in order to receive. If you aren't helping others on the list, then it is unlikely they will be willing to help you.

The following articles are (or certainly should be) required reading before you start strutting your stuff online:

- Agre, Phil. "Networking on the Network," (http://dlis.gseis.ucla.edu/people/pagre/network.html). Although the author intended this guide for his graduate students, the principles apply widely to anyone considering using the Internet as a networking tool.

- Halpern, Nancy. "E-Networking," (rileyguide.com/enetwork.html). This article contains strategies on how to develop new business contacts via networking on the Internet. It also includes sites to visit and techniques to make your E-networking efforts more effective.

- Rinaldi, Arlene H. "The Net: User Guidelines and Netiquette," (fau.edu/netiquette/).This is a complete introduction to appropriate online behavior.

MAILING LISTS

The Internet is a great way to begin those casual relationships that can later turn into wonderful opportunities. This is where mailing lists come in. In the same way, you can use the various "chat" rooms and forums available on a number of websites and in services such as America Online. The advantage of mailing lists is their availability to all users of the Internet instead of just those who subscribe to individual online providers.

Many experienced workers use mailing lists as a networking tool, discussing recent developments in their occupation or industry and asking questions of one another. Anyone involved in career exploration can benefit from following these online, public discussions, learning about current trends and developments and the interests and concerns of those involved. Once you identify the mailing lists that carry discussions for your field or industry, it's also possible that you'll find job announcements crossing these groups, making these yet another targeted service for your job search. If you are not already familiar with these services, you will find them to be a powerful addition to your job-search toolbox.

Mailing lists are discussion groups that operate through E-mail. A central computer sometimes called the *listserv*, *listproc*, or *majordomo* runs the list. The name varies according to which list manager software the computer is using. To participate in a mailing list, you must first subscribe to the list, a very simple process. You send a message to the computer hosting the mailing list in which you are interested and ask to be added to that particular list. The computer will then send you back a message to let you know your status. Once it says you are successfully added, you will automatically begin receiving the messages from that mailing list in your E-mail account.

Mailing lists cover a broad variety of topics and fields. They carry occasional job postings, usually in advance of print announcements, and they are a good resource for networking contacts, industry trends, and other developments. However, the main advantage to mailing lists is their ease of use. If you have E-mail, you can participate in mailing lists.

If you don't have an E-mail account available where you access the Internet, you can register for one of the Web-accessible free E-mail services and then sign up with any relevant mailing lists you find. Here are some services to look into:

HotMail	hotmail.com
Yahoo! Mail	http://mail.yahoo.com
USA.Net	usa.net

INTERNET TIP:

Read On. To learn more about the basics of mailing lists, along with the rest of the Internet, we suggest the following books:

- Kent, Peter. *The Complete Idiot's Guide to the Internet*. MacMillan.
- Levine, John R., Carol Baroudi, and Margaret Levine Young. *The Internet for Dummies*. IDG Books.

Both of these are updated frequently, so look for the most recent editions you can find. Ask your local librarian for suggestions on books and other resources to help you learn more about using the Internet.

Excite's Free eMail	excite.com
Email.com	email.com
IName.com	iname.com

To find mailing lists that could be useful to you, you'll need to review a list of them. While the list is constantly changing, it will give you a good idea of what is available. Visit the online resource guides for mailing lists, and search them using some of the keywords on your own list that describe the subject or occupational area in which you are interested. Some mailing lists are archived online. This makes it easier for you to get the feel of a list without having to actually subscribe to it. The archives are fairly limited in the number of groups they cover, but it's worth taking a look to see what might be helpful. Here are some good possibilities for list directories and archives:

Topica	topica.com
Yahoo! Groups	http://groups.yahoo.com
eScribe	escribe.com
Google Groups	http://groups.google.com

There's one more feature you must remember about mailing lists, and that is how to control them. When you are first added to a list, you should receive a brief message with explanatory commands, including the ones you need in order to suspend mail while you are on vacation or to unsubscribe to the list should it not be right for you. You should save this message somewhere, but if you happen to hit the delete key by mistake, Jim Milles wrote a handy guide listing all commands you need to control your mailing list participation titled *Discussion Lists: Mail List Manager Commands*. A copy of this can be found in The Riley Guide at rileyguide.com/mailser.html.

IDENTIFYING THE GOOD CONTACTS AND MAKING THAT FIRST CALL

Now that you are in a discussion group, how can you identify the people who might be your best contacts? Look for postings by someone who seems knowledgeable about the topic being discussed. You can do this only by knowing the topic yourself, but beyond that, look for people not only who seem authoritative, but also about whom others say, "Yes, listen to this person." Note the person's E-mail address at the top of his or her E-mail message, and then look for a signature at the bottom citing any organizational affiliation, position in the organization, and more complete contact information. While such signature information is not a guarantee that this person is very good, it's at least a statement that the writer is not afraid to identify him- or herself and the affiliate organization.

Once you have selected some mailing list participants you want to contact, prepare your approach carefully. Because you know them from the Internet, your first contact should be through the Internet. Be sure your E-mail message is professional and especially polite, and double-check for grammar and spelling errors before sending it. A few more pointers:

- Be sure to contact the person or persons directly and not through the list. Do not post a general message to the list asking if anyone is willing to talk to you.

- Be concise, identify yourself, state why you are contacting the person, and list some of your interests and where you noticed some correlation with his or her postings.

- Request a follow-up to your message, via phone or E-mail. Give your contact the choice of how to continue.

- If you are contacting more than one person, do not copy the same message to each of them. Send each person a separate E-mail message. It not only looks better but also avoids the possibility of fueling any hidden rivalries that might work against you.

Posting Your Resume Online

IF YOU POST IT, WILL THEY COME?

Like taking out a "Position Wanted" ad, you can post your resume in hundreds of databases online with the hope that you will be "discovered" by a great employer and offered your dream job. *Yessiree, it's job-search Utopia! By simply placing your resume online, you are guaranteed to be overwhelmed by the job offers that will come pouring in. . . .* Sorry to burst your bubble, but it is highly unlikely that this will ever happen to you unless you have the hottest, latest, greatest combination of technology and programming skills on the planet according to *ComputerWorld* and the business world.

But that's not to say that posting your resume is not worth your effort. Many people have posted their resumes online and gotten calls that have turned into successful new jobs. Articles about such people have appeared in various national publications, and many have even sent us accounts of personal experiences or events they have witnessed, but these cases are a small percentage of all those who are posting.

In the second edition of his book *Job-Hunting on the Internet* (Ten Speed Press, 1999), Richard Bolles gives the job-search activity of posting a resume online an effectiveness rating of less than one-half of 1 percent if you are not seeking a computer-related job, and 20 percent if you are. However, he also goes on to state that if he were job hunting, he would post his resume online, but then he would get right back to his other activities of networking, researching, and reviewing job leads. We agree with him 100 percent. No, posting your resume online is not the best way to find a job, but yes, we want to encourage you to post your resume. It's one of the four primary job-search activities, so you should do it, but you should not concentrate most of your effort nor place most of your hope on this one task. But if you do it, we want you to do it right, not only considering the form and format but also the ramifications of your decision to pursue this activity. This discussion requires a lot of attention, so we have devoted all of Chapter 2 to how, why, where, and what to do about posting your resume online.

Information Overload: How to Select Only the Right Stuff

Now that you've found them, how do you decide which resources are the best and will fit your needs? You will have to make the final decision yourself based on your own needs and preferences, but following are questions to ponder as you review everything you find.

What are you finding here?

- Is it advertising, or is there useful information for your search? A site that is merely advertising its services isn't giving you any help right now.

- Is it more formal (written by an expert in this field) or informal (comments submitted by others)? While some lay users may contribute useful tips, articles from experts will have more authoritative and reliable information.

- Are there lists of employers, including maybe businesses, colleges and schools, or nonprofit associations? These can be very helpful for targeting key firms or linking you to organizations of which you were unaware.

- Are there job listings, job-search tips, and other helpful items? While job listings are always good to find, you may prefer a site with cover letter– and resume-writing articles at a time when you are struggling through this process.

About those job listings . . .

- Are there real jobs listed here, or just "sample lists of jobs we are currently trying to fill"? Samples are always fine, but when you're ready to "buy," pay for only the real thing, even when it comes to "free" job listings.

- Are the job listings dated so you know when they were added? It is frustrating to you and to the employer to waste time on a job that was filled six months ago.

- If you don't see any dates, can you find any relevant information under the section for employers who want to post jobs? For instance, how much do they pay for the service, and how long will their jobs remain here? Most sites will tell an employer that a job will be posted for a limited amount of time for a specific fee. If you can't find this information anywhere, put this site at the bottom of your attention list.

- In cases in which you can't find any date-related information, is there contact information so you can send an E-mail message to the site's webmaster and ask how long the site retains position listings in the database? In an ideal situation, you'll get a response like "We post jobs for sixty days." If the reply is, "We post them until the employer removes it," then keep the site at the bottom of your list. If you get no response at all, cross this particular site off your list.

How old is the other information posted here?

- Are articles dated so you know the last time someone reviewed and revised them? Articles can become dated the same way job leads can.

- Are the site's owners updating and adding new materials on a regular basis (daily, weekly, monthly)? If they are not posting anything new, how can you be sure they're working on maintaining anything else on this site, like the job listings?

- Do the articles or other information posted here remain for an extended amount of time, or are they deleted when new material is added? While it's not necessarily a mark of higher quality, an archive of the older articles is a nice touch.

Who runs this service?

- Is there information for you to read about the people who run this site? A simple profile is not hard to write, especially for a group with nothing to hide from visitors.

- What are their backgrounds (recruiters, industry specialists, librarians, etc.)? There are many online job-search services now being run by people who have no background in what they are doing. They are just looking for some fast money and are hoping you'll give it to them.

- Is there a name, address, or phone number for contacting them with questions? At the very minimum, there should be an E-mail address for questions. Again, legitimate services will provide this information. They want to hear from you.

Do you know anyone who has used this service?

- What did your acquaintances use the service for (posted a resume, reviewed job leads, worked through the career exploration exam)? How well did it work for them (got calls from recruiters, found good job leads, got some interesting insight from the exam)?

- Did they like what they found? Were the recruiters who called nice? Did they feel comfortable with this service?

- Do they feel it was helpful and worth the time spent here?

If there's a fee for this service, is it worth the cost?

- Can you find other sites and services that offer an equal service at no cost? Don't just pay for this service; be a careful shopper and compare it with others.

- What will your money get you? If you are paying to have your resume forwarded to employers, how many employers, in what industries, and can you have a list of those who will be receiving it? Are these employers people who have registered with this service as interested parties, or is it a spam list cobbled together from other sources?

- What is the refund policy if you're not satisfied? Again, look for who is running this site, where they are located, and how to contact them.

What promises are they making, and are these promises reasonable?

- If they say anything about "guaranteed results," then the Federal Trade Commission will want to speak with them. Nothing in a job-search process is guaranteed. There's no exclusive access to the "hidden job market," and there's no guarantee that shooting hundreds of copies of your resume to employers through E-mail will result in your getting an interview, let alone a job.

If you send these people an E-mail message asking for more information on who they are and what services they are selling, do they actually respond?

- If they never contact you, consider this a warning that saved you some money.

- If they contact you by E-mail or phone, then judge them using your own criteria based on the information they provide. Be sure to ask them all the questions that are important to you, and don't let anyone bully you into buying.

INTERNET TIP:

When you pay for any service online, use a credit card. Never send a check or money order, and we don't recommend using a debit card either. With a credit card, you have some recourse if you do not receive the services or products advertised by contacting the issuer of your credit card and challenging the charges. If you don't want to "transmit" your credit card information over the Internet, call the company from whom you want to purchase the goods and/or services and give them the information over the phone. If they will not accept your payment information in this way, take your business elsewhere.

As we said at the beginning of this section, the final decision for using any site or service online (or off) is yours and yours alone. Be a careful consumer and buy wisely. And, if you get lousy service somewhere or pay for services that are not provided in the manner that was promised (or do not produce the promised results), don't take it lying down. Complain to the Better Business Bureau (bbb.org), the Federal Trade Commission (ftc.gov), and the Internet Fraud Complaint Center (https://www.ifccfbi.gov/). And after you notify all of them, please send an E-mail to Margaret Riley Dikel (webmaster@rileyguide.com) because we want to know about it too!

Managing Your Time Online

People are always telling us that every night, they start searching online in the same place, and well, heck, they spend so much time in those pages that they never get anywhere else. To this, we respond, "So, why are you doing that?"

Every time you connect, start someplace new. Pick out a select list of general resources, use them to find more specific resources, and keep moving. Things change, but not so rapidly that you will miss something important if you check there only twice a week. Plan your online job-search strategy so you don't get stuck in one place and waste time and money.

Here's an outline of what we think is your best plan for spending your time online wisely. It's based on a simple idea: remember to move from general to specific, but always remember to move!

1. Visit the large information databases first. These include virtual libraries and large recruiting sites such as CareerBuilder (careerbuilder.com) and all the other sites listed in Chapter 3. Look for links to information in your chosen field or industry. Repeat this search every few days—for example, Monday and Thursday.

2. Move on to the smaller, more exclusive resources and services, including online resource guides and sites dedicated to your field or industry. You want to find links to employers or collected information in your field that can give

you leads or networking contacts. Repeat this search every few days—say, Tuesday and Friday.

3. Use the search engines to locate new and hidden resources specific to your occupation and field. If you are interested in a certain company, search on the company name, any variations or nicknames by which it is known, and names of its major products. Repeat this search every few days—maybe Wednesday and Saturday.

4. Finally, shut off the computer and spend some time with your family, your friends, and yourself. Take the seventh day and relax, do some reading, walk outside, and remind yourself that there is a world out there and people to talk to. You can even update your resume or prepare some cover letters, but don't go onto the Internet. Play with your dog or scratch the cat, and if you don't have a dog or cat, substitute whatever pets you have. All work and no play just stresses us out more and makes everything, even our job search, much harder. Your health and well-being are important at this juncture, so take some time to recover.

PROBABLY THE MOST IMPORTANT STATEMENT IN THIS ENTIRE BOOK . . .

The Internet cannot be the only resource you use for your job search!

You must continue to utilize all contacts, information resources, and services available to you for the most effective and efficient search for employment. Continue to attend meetings, pick up the telephone and call people, and use the reference books in your local library. Remember, there are four activities— researching, reviewing job leads, networking, and preparing a resume—and each has two facets.

Limit your time online to one-quarter (25 percent) of the total time you can dedicate to your job search . . . unless you are a techie who is working in any area related to computer networks or programming. In that case, move it up to one-half (50 percent) of your time, but make sure your skills are current in order for you to be your most competitive.

Suggested Reading for Your (Internet) Job Search

Following are only a few of the many books available to help you learn how to take your job search online. Your local public library or career service center may have these in its collection along with other titles. Ask librarians for their recommendations. If you'd like your own copy to tear apart, mark up, or personalize in other ways, then check your local bookstore or any of the online bookstores.

Many of these titles are updated every year or two, so always look for the most recent editions.

- Bolles, Richard. *Job-Hunting on the Internet* (The Parachute Library). Ten Speed Press (updated regularly).

- ————. *What Color Is Your Parachute?* Ten Speed Press (updated annually).

- Crispin, Gerry, and Mark Mehler. *CareerXRoads*. MMC Group (updated annually).

- Dixon, Pam. *Job Searching Online for Dummies*. IDG Books, 2000.

- Gurney, Darrell W. *Headhunters Revealed! Career Secrets for Choosing and Using Professional Recruiters!*. Hunter Arts Publishing, 2000.

- Ireland, Susan. *The Complete Idiot's Guide to Cool Jobs for Teens*. Alpha Books, 2001. Includes information on resumes, internships, and laws governing the employment of young persons.

- Weddle, Peter D. *Weddle's Job-Seekers' Guide to Employment Web Sites*. Amacom, 2001.

Job-Search Guidance Online

JobHuntersBible.com from Richard Bolles

jobhuntersbible.com

This is the newest addition to the many guides from the author of *What Color Is Your Parachute?* It incorporates his Net Guide (megalist of job resources online) with many of the self-assessment exercises and job-searching advice from *Parachute*. You'll love it.

Joyce Lain Kennedy's Careers

sunfeatures.com

If you don't know Kennedy, you haven't been around. She's the author of the Los Angeles Times Syndicate's column "Careers," which has been around for more than thirty years and appears in more than one hundred newspapers. She has also written many books on careers and job search that have influenced the way thousands of us think of this process. You can find her latest series of books, *Cover Letters for Dummies, Resumes for Dummies, Interviews for Dummies*, and *Financial Aid for Dummies*, in most libraries and bookstores.

Career Resource Library from the New York State Department of Labor

labor.state.ny.us/working_ny/finding_a_job/career_resource.html

The New York Department of Labor has several good guides and tools to help you through your job search on its website.

OUACHITA TECHNICAL COLLEGE

JobWeb from the National Association of Colleges and Employers

jobweb.com

JobWeb refers to itself as a "complete guide to the job search." Users will find information and articles to help with all activities in their job search. Most of the articles and resources are targeted to the new college graduate, but many apply to users at all experience levels.

CareerJournal from the *Wall Street Journal*

careerjournal.com

At the risk of repeating ourselves ad infinitum, you will find hundreds of articles and information resources covering all aspects of your job search at this site, and they cover all experience levels from entry-level to chief executive. You'll see we mention this site many times throughout the book as a great source because it is the absolute truth.

Interviewing and Networking Advice

Believe it or not, these two activities are actually fairly similar. The same rules of etiquette apply in both cases, as do the same rules of caution. Don't forget the networking resources listed earlier in this chapter.

Interview Tips from Monster.com

http://content.monster.com/jobinfo/interview

Among other offerings from this popular job site, you'll find a script to follow for making phone calls, a virtual interview to help you prepare for the real thing, a sample of tough questions to practice answering in advance, and a list of questions to ask a headhunter.

Handling Questionable Questions in a Job Interview

rileyguide.com/dob.html

How do you respond when an interviewer asks you an improper question, like "what is your date of birth"? This article asked several career and job-search professionals as well as recruiters for their advice.

Networking Dos and Don'ts

rwn.org/network.html

Set up by the Rochester (New York) Women's Network, this site offers a nice summary of the best things to do and not do when networking and meeting new contacts.

Job Offers

You'll find many more articles on evaluating and negotiating job offers in The Riley Guide (rileyguide.com). We have information on salary guides in Chapter 14.

Evaluating a Job Offer, from the *Occupational Outlook Handbook*

bls.gov/oco/oco20046.htm

This is a detailed article on the many issues to consider when assessing a job offer.

Counter Offer, from Fristoe & Carleton

adjob.com/counter.htm

The experts at this executive search firm say you should always think twice before accepting a counteroffer, and they tell you why.

The Negotiation Clinic from Salary.com

salary.com

Select "Salary Advice" and then "Negotiation" to review this ten-part online clinic on negotiating everything from the job you really want to salary and benefits and even promotions and pay reviews.

Job-Search Support Groups

Check your local newspaper or public library for notices of job-search groups that meet in your community.

Live Online from the *Washington Post*

http://washingtonpost.com

You do not need to live in the Washington, DC, area to participate in and benefit from the many discussions taking place through this site. Some are specific to careers and jobs, including @Work, Career Track, and On the Job, but you may see other areas that interest you. To access LiveOnline, connect to the *Washington Post* website and click on the Live Online tab at the top of the screen. To participate in a discussion, you will need to register, a free process that takes only a few moments.

Forty Plus of Northern California

fortyplus.org

Forty Plus of Northern California is a nonprofit self-help group of executives and professionals over age forty who are currently in career transition. There is a fee to use this service. From this site, you can find other Forty Plus chapters around the United States and in Canada.

The Layoff Lounge

layofflounge.com

This is an online and offline destination for support and networking. Online, you'll find resources to help you with your search, including a resume database, career and business news, chat rooms, and announcements of the offline meetings. Yes, real face-to-face time with others. They are currently operating in several locations across the United States.

2

Your Resume
on the Internet

When talking about the job-search process, the action of distributing a resume is rated the least effective of the four activities that make up a complete search. And while we noted how little emphasis you should place on posting your resume online, we don't want you to ignore the resume itself. Writing your resume, actually creating the one that employers and others will review, is one of the most important tasks in a job search, the one place where you need to take the time to do it right, really thinking about what you want to do before you can start pounding the pavement. Even with our statements on how ineffective it is to post your resume in the many databases online, if you are going to do it, and we think you should do it, you must do it right.

Your resume is your product brochure, that piece of paper that summarizes all the benefits of you and why the employer should "buy" you. A great resume can help you win the position you want. A bad one will knock you out of consideration, no matter how qualified you are. You must have a great resume, but we are not the ones to help you with this. At the end of this chapter you'll find a list of good books and online workshops offered by great experts in this field. They are the ones to help you write a resume. Your local librarians, career counselors, and bookstore managers can recommend even more books and resources, so don't be afraid to ask should you not find something you like here.

What we're good at is helping you take that resume and get it online, so that is what this chapter will cover. We'll also address the problems associated with posting a resume, how to format it so posting it in websites and E-mailing it to employers is fast and easy, and how to select where to post it. We encourage you to read this before you create your resume and then come back to it when you have your resume ready to go online. Consider the issues and advice we present here, and think about them as you are working on your resume. And remember, you do not need to limit yourself to just one resume. You can have several presented in different ways and including or removing your contact information. If you have access to a computer with word-processing software, you are limited only by the available space on your disk or diskette.

The Myth About the Internet Resume

Many people think that the advancement of resume databases, resume management systems, and keyword searching requires you to produce one resume for paper but an entirely different resume for online. This is not true!

When done correctly, your well-written, well-prepared resume will contain all of the necessary keywords to attract attention whether it is being read by a hiring manager or scanned and searched in any database, online or off. You still need only one resume, but now you want to have it in several formats, ready to produce in the proper form as needed, including these:

1. A designed or hard-copy version—a good looking printed resume with bulleted lists, bold and italicized text, and other highlights, ready to send to contacts through the mail

2. A scannable version—a neat word-processed and printed resume without bullets, bold, italics, or other design highlights, written in a standard font and printed on white paper to send to employers who use scanning systems

3. A plain-text version—a no-frills plain-text file you keep on a diskette for copying and pasting into online forms and posting in online resume databases

4. An E-mail version—another no-frills plain-text file you keep on disk, but one formatted to meet the length-of-line restrictions found in most E-mail systems, making it easy to copy and paste into an E-mail message and forward to an employer or recruiter in seconds

Information on both plain-text and E-mail resumes is included in this chapter under "Preparing a Perfect Plain-Text Resume," but while we are talking about formats, there is one more you may want to consider—an HTML version of your resume. This can be posted on a personal website or with any site offering this kind of service.

Many job seekers are creating "webbed" resumes in the hopes of being discovered or as a place to refer an employer who might want to see more than just that flat resume. This format works particularly well for anyone in a visual arts field, but it could serve anyone who wants to present more than what is usually found on a resume, provided it is done right and for the right reasons. Doing it right means creating a simple HTML version of your designed resume, not a hip-hop page of spinning-whirling gizmos, dancing gerbils, and accompanying audio files that takes more than two minutes to download over a 56K modem. Doing it for the right reasons means turning your resume into an employment portfolio, complete with links to former employers or projects that are already online. And if you do this, you must be sure you are not violating any copyright or confidentiality clauses by putting project information online.

The main problem with HTML resumes is the "too-much-information" factor. Many job seekers make the resume a part of their personal website where there is all kinds of information an employer does not need to know before you are hired, such as your marital status, your ethnic background, or your personal interests. Allowing an employer to learn so much about you can lead to all kinds of problems, including unknown discrimination against you for your physical appearance, political beliefs, religious practices, or even just the image you present. When you place your professional image online by posting your resume, it is important that you keep your presence entirely professional by never linking it to personal information of any kind. So, if you decide to add an

HTML resume to your campaign, post it in a location separate from your personal website, and do not link between the two.

Rules for Responding Online

The fastest way to respond to Internet job listings is by E-mailing your cover letter and resume to the person or organization indicated. Yes, your resume and cover letter are still your best bet for winning an interview, but if you mess up the application process, those great documents won't get you where you want to be. The rules are short and simple, so take a couple of minutes to review them before you hit the "send" key.

1. You need a correctly formatted E-mail resume. If you try to copy and paste the text of your designed resume into the body of an E-mail message and then just send it without preparation, by the time it reaches the intended recipient the formatting will be such a mess it may be unreadable. (See "Preparing a Perfect Plain-Text Resume" later in this chapter.)

2. Send your resume in the body of the E-mail message. Never send it as an attachment. You have only about twenty seconds to catch the eye of a recruiter or employer and to get him or her to read your resume. If you send your resume as an attachment, the recruiter has to find it and open it before he or she can read it. Zip! Your twenty seconds are over before they even start. Put the resume right in the message so the reader will see it immediately upon opening the mail. This also helps you bypass E-mail systems that refuse attachments in this day of rampant computer viruses.

3. Always include a cover letter, whether or not you are responding to an advertised opening. Make that cover letter specific to the person or organization you are contacting, and make it interesting. If you are responding to an advertisement, note where you found the advertisement and any relevant job codes. You can create and store a "standard" cover letter in text, but remember to customize it for each job listing for which you are applying, checking the format before you send it.

4. Use the advertised job title or job code as the "Subject" of your E-mail message. This makes it easy for the recipient to sort everything coming in and route your resume and letter to the appropriate person. If you are "cold calling," trying to get your resume into someone's hands without an advertised position to note, put a few words stating your objective in the "Subject" line.

5. Read all of the application instructions included in the announcement, and follow them exactly. Sometimes employers want applications sent to a specific E-mail address according to the job location. Sometimes they want everything submitted via fax. They may even say you must apply through

their website, using a specific code. And once in a while they will even ask you to send your resume in Word as an attachment, but this is quite rare. Whatever they say, do it. You don't want your application to be delayed because you sent it to the wrong address or person, and you don't want to be perceived as someone who cannot follow directions.

Always remember this as you prepare to E-mail your resume to an employer: it takes only a couple of seconds for someone to delete an E-mail message. Don't let that happen to you. Read and think before you respond!

E-Resumes Are Not Just for E-mail

Besides the need to have a well-done plain-text resume for E-mailing, there are hundreds more reasons to take the time to create an E-resume, namely all those places online where you can post your resume. Yes, almost all sites have a copy-and-paste option for getting your resume online. Some even offer to let you build your resume right on the site, but resume experts like Susan Ireland don't recommend using these forms for the following reasons:

1. It's very easy to have typos if you type directly into the site's form. Working first in your word-processing program (with its spellcheck) can greatly improve your chances of having a perfect resume.

2. The form may force you to use a resume format that you don't like. Most online resume builders insist on a chronological resume, a format that focuses on work history. This will put career changers at a disadvantage because the system doesn't allow you to build a functional resume, a format that focuses on skills.

3. You cannot easily save your resume for other uses because the resume bank is on a website. That means you'd have to repeat your resume-building efforts on each site where you want to post your resume.

The best way to post your resume online is to copy and paste it from a prepared copy you have already formatted to look great online. For the best results, that means transforming the hard-copy version of your resume before you copy and paste it into the website's resume form.

JOB SEARCH TIP:

Protect Your Privacy when Cutting and Pasting! Susan Joyce from Job-Hunt.org notes that people frequently sabotage their own privacy by unknowingly copying the top of their resume (with all of their contact information) into the "body of the resume" blocks on web forms. So, while the job site blocks access to the contact information input into specific labeled fields, the job seeker accidentally reveals the information in the text block fields of the resume form. Be careful with the copy-and-paste process!

Preparing a Perfect Plain-Text Resume

Preparing a resume for electronic mail is an easy process, and anyone creating a resume should take the extra few minutes needed to generate a plain-text version while still at the computer. Most word processors and resume-writing programs will let you save a file to plain text. The next step, altering the format, is simple. The following instructions prepared by Susan Ireland will help you take that hard-copy resume and turn it into a perfect plain-text document for posting online. Ireland even talks you through an easy way to format it for E-mailing. Why is this a separate process, and why do we suggest you have two different plain-text copies of your resume? Because E-mail has more formatting restrictions than most online resume databases, but we know what those restrictions are. To find even more complete instructions on creating resumes, cover letters, and even various formats for your E-resume, visit Susan's website (susanireland.com).

Please note that these instructions assume that your resume is in MS Word for Windows. If your resume is in another word-processing application or on a different computer platform like Macintosh, you may need to consult your word-processing manual for specific instructions.

Step 1: Save your resume as a Text Only document. A Text Only document works best for an electronic resume because you can adjust the margins and formatting to suit the database or E-mail system in which you are working. To convert your MS Word resume to Text Only, do the following:

A. Open the MS Word document that contains your resume.

B. Click File in your toolbar and select Save As.

C. Type in a new name for this document in File Name, such as "ResTextOnly."

D. Under this is the Save As Type pull-down menu. From this list, select "Text Only (*.txt)."

E. Click Save to perform the conversion.

F. Now close the document but stay in MS Word.

G. Reopen the document you just closed by going to File in the toolbar, click Open, select the file named "ResTextOnly.txt," and click Open. **Warning:** if you exit MS Word and then open the resume document by clicking on its icon in the directory, it will be opened in Notepad—not what you want if you intend to use this version to prepare an E-mailable resume (see below)!

After converting your resume to Text Only, what appears in your document window is your resume stripped of any fancy formatting. You are now ready to make a few final adjustments before posting it online:

Step 2: Check keywords. Be sure your resume has all the keywords that define your job qualifications.

Step 3: Delete any references to "page two." If your resume is more than one page, delete any indications of page breaks such as "Page 1 of 2," "Continued," or your name or header on page 2. You are making your resume appear as one continuous electronic document.

Step 4: Use all CAPS for words that need special emphasis. Since Text Only stripped your resume of all bolds, underlines, and italics used for highlighting words, use all capitalized letters to draw attention to important words, phrases, and headings. For the best overall effect, use all caps sparingly and judiciously.

Step 5: Replace each bullet point with a standard keyboard symbol. Special symbols such as bullet points, arrows, triangles, and check marks do not transfer well electronically. For example, bullet points sometimes transfer as "&16707," ")," or a little graphic of a thumbs-up. Therefore, you must change each to a standard keyboard symbol. Suggested replacements are:

> Dashes (—)
>
> Plus signs (+)
>
> Asterisks (*)
>
> Double asterisks (**)

Use the Space Bar to place a single space immediately after each symbol (and before the words). Do not use the Tab key for spacing as you may have done in your original resume. Also, allow the lines to wrap naturally at the end of a line. Don't put a forced return (don't push the Return or Enter key) if it's not the end of the statement and don't indent the second line of a statement with either the Tab key or Space Bar.

Step 6: Use straight quotes in place of curly quotes. Like bullet points and other special symbols, curly or "smart" quotes do not transfer accurately, and in fact, may appear as little rectangles on the recipient's screen. So you should replace curly quotes with straight quotes. To do this, select the text that includes the quotes you want to change. Click Format in your toolbar and select AutoFormat. Click the Options button, and make sure Replace Straight Quotes with Smart Quotes is not selected under both the AutoFormat and AutoFormat As You Type tabs. Then click OK to exit the AutoFormat box, and your curly quotes will be changed to straight quotes.

Step 7: Rearrange text if necessary. Do a line-by-line review of your document to make sure there are no odd-looking line wraps, extra spaces, or words scrunched together in the body. Make adjustments accordingly. This may require inserting commas between items that were once in columns and are now in paragraph format because tabs and tables disappeared when the document was converted to Text Only.

Now that you have the plain-text resume for posting, it takes just a few more steps to create a perfect plain- text resume for E-mailing. Again, if you take the time to do this now, you will save yourself a lot of time later.

Step 8. Limit line lengths. Because each type of E-mail software has its own limit for the number of characters and spaces per line, your E-mail may have longer line lengths than the receiver of your E-mail allows. This can cause the employer to see line wraps in unusual places, making your resume document look odd and even illogical. To avoid this problem, limit each line to no more than sixty-five characters (including spaces). Here's an easy way to make line length changes in your document:

A. Open MS Word, click Open, select the file named "ResTextOnly.txt," and click Open. **Warning:** if you open the resume document by clicking on its icon in the directory, it will be opened in Notepad—not what you want right now.

B. Select the entire document and change the font to Courier, 12 point.

C. Go to Format in your toolbar; select Page Setup; set the left margin at 1 and your right margin at 1.75.

With the font, size of font, and side margins set, each line of your document will be no more than sixty-five characters and spaces. Don't worry about whether you want the employer to see your resume in Courier font—his or her E-mail software will convert it to the font set on his or her system.

Step 9: Save as Text Only with Line Breaks. In order to save the line length changes you made in Step 8, you need to convert your Text Only document one more time by doing the following:

A. With your Text Only resume document open, click File in your toolbar and select Save As.

B. Type in a new name for this document in File Name, such as "ResTextBreak."

C. Directly under this is the Save As Type pull-down menu. From this list, select "Text Only with Line Breaks (*.txt)."

D. Click Save to perform the conversion.

E. Now close the document but stay in MS Word.

F. Reopen the document you just closed by going to File in the toolbar, click Open, select the file named "ResTextBreak.txt," and click Open. **Warning:** do not open the resume document by clicking on its icon in the directory. That would open it as a Notepad document—not what you want!

Don't worry that the margins will automatically reset when you reopen your Text Only with Line Breaks document. Your line lengths are safely preserved by paragraph returns that were inserted by the conversion.

Once you have redone your resume in the E-mail format, E-mail it to yourself and to a friend to see how it looks after going through the Internet. This will help you identify any additional formatting problems you need to correct before you start sending it out to possible employers.

RESUME TIP:

Never use your current office address, E-mail address, or phone number on your resume. This is considered stealing from your current employer, using company time for your own purposes instead of business, and using the company's resources for your own advancement. The thinking goes that if you'll do it to that employer, you'll do it to the next one, too. Always use personal contact points, like a post office box, cell phone, and a personal E-mail account. This will also help you avoid possible monitoring by your current employer.

Where, Oh, Where Should That Resume Go?

With the hundreds, if not thousands, of possible posting sites now available online, you have ample opportunity to saturate the Internet with your resume. After all, don't you want to get your resume in front of every recruiter or employer you can, regardless of who they are? No, you don't.

Recruiters are tired of finding the same resumes for the same people in every database they search. They are even starting to ignore these "resume spammers," refusing to give them any consideration for possible job openings. There is also the danger that the farther your resume spreads, the less control you can exert over it. To make sure you don't encounter these problems, limit your resume exposure by limiting your postings.

- Post it on only one or two of the large online databases, preferably ones attached to popular job sites. This will give you maximum exposure to many employers and recruiters.

- Post it on one or two targeted resume databases specific to your industry, occupational group, or geographic location. This will give you a targeted exposure to employers and recruiters looking for a smaller yet more highly qualified candidate pool.

If you don't get any responses to your resume within thirty days, remove your resume from its current locations and place it elsewhere.

Limiting the number of locations is a good way to protect your resume, but it is also important to select those few sites with care. Susan Joyce, manager of Job-Hunt.org, encourages job seekers to carefully evaluate the job sites you use, because if you aren't careful, you risk a total loss of privacy. Not only could your resume become visible to anyone who comes across it, your personal information might be sold to people who have products and services to sell you. Her article "Choosing a Job Site" (job-hunt.org/choosing.shtml) outlines several criteria designed to help you evaluate a site before you trust it with your resume.

1. Does the site have a privacy policy posted? Carefully read the job site's privacy policy. Don't depend on a third party, like BBBOnline or TRUSTe to protect your privacy. Read the policy yourself, if there is one!! If you don't like the site's privacy policy, or if it doesn't even have one, don't register! Move on to the next site.

2. Can you search for an interesting job opportunity without registering your resume or profile? Most sites allow job searches without registering your resume or profile first. Of course, if you want to apply for any of the jobs, you'll probably be required to register, but postpone registering as long as reasonably possible. Assuming that you have read the privacy policy and don't have any issues with it, then register when you must, providing the minimum of information required (particularly your contact information). Be suspicious of sites that require registration before allowing you to do a job search or ask for information like date of birth or gender. It may not be worth it to you!

3. What kind of control do you have over access to your resume or profile? The best sites offer several methods for you to use, and you choose the one that fits your needs at the time:

The most control: Potential employers see your resume only after you have decided that they have a job that interests you, and you authorize the site to send your information to that specific employer, on a case-by-case basis.

Good control: Your resume is in the database, but the site automatically blocks access to your contact information until you authorize its release to specific employers on a case-by-case basis.

Some control: Your resume with visible contact information is available to employers and/or agency recruiters searching through the database. However, you may block access to your resume for specific employers (your current company, for example).

No control: The site requires you to give it all of your contact information and then permits anyone (or any employer who pays a fee) to search the database.

4. What kind of access will you have to your resume after you post it? At a minimum, you should be able to edit your resume whenever you feel it necessary (like every time you apply for a different job). You should also be able to delete your resume (or profile) from the database whenever you want to get out of the job market, for whatever reason you decide. Questions to ask include

Is there a set time frame when your resume will be "active" after which it will be removed from the applicant database, can you "renew" your resume if you want it to remain in the database after the normal expiration date, and how easy is it to renew?

5. Do you like the job-search capability? If they list jobs, do you like the search capability? If not, then move on to another site.

6. Does the site have the kind of jobs that interest you? You won't find many marketing jobs on a site for computer technical people, and vice versa, so do a little research to see what the site offers. Skip any site that does not already list your field or interests or where you cannot find jobs that match your desires.

7. Check out the employers listed at the site. Look for a listing of employers, or do a search with very few (or very broad) criteria to get the maximum number of results and then look at the employers listed. Are these companies or organizations that interest you?

Are they real employers, or are they staffing agencies? Do you like the employers listed here, or are they companies you would rather not work for? If that is the case, move on to another site."

JOB SEARCH TIP:

Why should you care if they are staffing agencies? Isn't that good? Not necessarily, for a couple of reasons. First, ethically challenged agency recruiters may take the resume that you submit for one employer's job and send that resume to other employers. Good agencies won't do this, but not all are good. Second, agencies charge employers a fee for each applicant placed. This raises the "cost-of-hire" of the agency candidate to the employer over the cost of a candidate who goes directly to the employer. If a company is closely watching its budget, all other things being equal, the choice will often be to hire the less-expensive candidate. There are many cases where employers have hired agencies to act as their representatives posting listings online, so an agency is not always a bad sign, but you should pay attention.

---

8. Will they distribute your resume? As a "benefit" to job seekers, some sites offer to "cross-post" resumes on other websites or even "blast" your resume to thousands of employers and recruiters. You will not necessarily be told who will receive it or where it will be distributed, and you will have no control over who reads it or how long it stays in circulation. If you cannot decline the distribution offer, choose another site.

9. Where and how does the site get its job listings? The best situation is one where employers place their own job postings at the site. This should ensure the "freshness" of the postings and reduce the number of agency postings. In some instances, the job postings have been "cross-posted" by one site to other sites (sometimes hundreds of other sites). This expands the number of opportunities for you to see, but it may also indicate a site having difficulty getting enough postings from employers and/or agencies to survive.

The bottom line is **You Rule**. Many sites want your resume in their database. You can afford to be choosy about where you will place it and which sites you will use in your search.

Before You Post, Something to Think About

For some people, posting a resume online has been a great way to find new opportunities. For others, there is a very real fear that their address and phone number will fall into the wrong hands, or that the wrong organizations—such as their current employer—will see it and problems will arise. We are also all familiar with news reports about stolen identities. You are the only one who can say how comfortable you are with this decision and how you want to approach the idea of posting your resume. Before you begin, review our list of Job-Search Mistakes in Chapter 1 one more time, and then consider the following questions very carefully:

1. Do you want your resume public? Once you have posted it, no matter where you place it, you should consider your resume to be a public document and out of your control. Anyone can look in the public databases and see what is there. Even the private resume databanks as well as those offering "confidential handling" of your resume may not let you dictate who can and cannot look at your resume. So what do you do to protect yourself?

Don't just strip your name and all personal contact information from your resume, leaving nothing by a cryptic E-mail address for recruiters to use if they want to contact you. Consider renting a post office box and a cell phone for the duration of your search. Many employers and recruiters still prefer to contact you by phone and will skip over resumes without a phone number. As one recruiter said, "If this candidate looks like a good fit for a job I have to fill, I want to speak with him or her now, not in several hours or days when he or she gets around to checking the E-mail." Yes, they might get voice mail instead of you, but they still feel they've connected with you.

2. Are you prepared for the consequences if that electronic resume comes back to haunt you? It is a real possibility. Some job seekers are falling victim to aggressive recruiters who grab their resumes from the Internet and unwittingly feed them back to the job seekers' current employers, with very bad results for the employee. Others are finding their resumes posted in places they never put them, the victims of unprofessional resume services who copy the documents from other open venues. Some employees have even been confronted by current employers brandishing copies of their resumes which they found online, not realizing that the documents were more than a year old and part of the campaign to get the current job. You should always go back and delete any resumes you posted during your search as soon as your search is over, but you might not be able to get to every electronic copy out there. How do you fight this?

Many job seekers are putting dates at the very end of their resumes as a record of when it was posted. Some have even made slight changes to the wording of each copy they've posted, creating a code identifying where a copy originated. These small alterations will give you some ammunition should your resume float into the wrong hands at the wrong time. There are also ways to "scrub" a resume to make it even harder for your current employer to not only find you but also recognize you. You don't have to be scared off the Internet, but you should be aware of what can go wrong. Take a look at "Your Cyber-Safe Resume" by Susan Joyce for tips on creating a very confidential resume (job-hunt.org/resumecybersafe.shtml).

Resume Blasters: The Wave of the Future or a New Form of Spam?

Resume-distribution services, sometimes called resume broadcasters, are proliferating online. While you may think this is a great way to get your resume seen, we disagree. In reference to your privacy, Susan Joyce feels that "such wide distribution may offer little, if any, control on where a copy of your resume could end up. Your name, address, and phone number, in addition to your education and work experience, could become completely public for a very long time." But there are other problems too.

For one thing, not all those who are on the lists of these services actually requested they be placed on the list. Both authors have received resumes broadcasted by these services, and neither requested such a service. Then there may be problems with the resumes that are sent out, problems that the job seekers may not be aware of because they were not allowed to review their resumes before they were broadcast. One hiring manager sent us the following E-mail commenting on her experience with a resume-broadcasting service.

A recruiting site for IT and technical professionals started bombarding me with forwarded resumes two days ago (I must have received twenty or so). They told us it was a free service, which I believe to be true.

Because I had no positions open, and because we respond to every resume we receive, this put a burden on us that we don't really have time to handle, so I asked them to stop sending the resumes. In addition, a large number of the forwarded resumes did not contain contact information for the applicants, which made it impossible for us to let them know we had received the resume, or to contact them in case we might be interested in them. Two of the resumes did not even contain the candidates' names.

I received an E-mail today saying they had complied with the request to remove my E-mail address from their system. Well and good.

It went on to say, however, that these were 'current resumes of candidates presently in the job market and who have paid to have their resumes reviewed by recruiters, right now.'

That outraged me. If an organization is going to collect money from candidates to forward their resumes, then it has (I believe) an obligation to make the process of reaching a promising candidate possible. Resumes without names or contact information are useless to a recruiter, as you can well imagine. I think these candidates should know that they are paying (a) for recruiters without jobs, or (b) to have their resumes forwarded in a way that cannot be responded to. They should use their money for something else.

In this instance, resumes were being sent out without any regard as to whether or not the employer requested it. While the chances of a successful match through this activity are already low, broadcasting resumes to employers who have no expressed interest in receiving them is almost guaranteed to eliminate even the slimmest possibility those resumes will be given any consideration. Then there is the contact information problem on some resumes. This makes it difficult, if not impossible, for the employer to even contact these candidates. If you are going to cold call an employer, you must give the employer a way to call you back. But the worst part of all this is job seekers actually paid for this service, using their hard-earned and probably limited funding to pay for a service that will provide almost no return on their investment. It is a losing proposition for both the job seeker and the employer. The only winner was the blasting service because it got the money.

Help with Resumes and Cover Letters

Each of the following books and Internet services has good information and guidance for preparing your resume. Almost all will also walk you through the process of translating your designed resume into the necessary scannable and E-mail formats, and a couple will even take you into web resumes. We've also included titles covering resumes for teenagers, international variations, and resumes for positions with the U.S. federal government. New editions of any of these may have been released between the time we created the list and when you are reading it, so check your local library or bookstore for the most recent edition.

- Bolles, Richard Nelson. *What Color Is Your Parachute?* Ten Speed Press (updated annually).

- Criscito, Pat. *Resumes in Cyberspace: Your Complete Guide to a Computerized Job Search.* Barrons, 2001.

- Frank, William S. *200 Letters for Job Hunters*. Ten Speed Press, 1993.

- Ireland, Susan. *The Complete Idiot's Guide to the Perfect Cover Letter*. Alpha Books, 1997.

- ———. *The Complete Idiot's Guide to the Perfect Resume*, 2nd ed. Alpha Books, 2000.

- Kennedy, Joyce Lain. *Cover Letters for Dummies*, 2nd ed. IDG Books, 2000.

- ———. *Resumes for Dummies*, 3rd ed. IDG Books, 2000.

- Parker, Yana. *The Damn Good Resume Guide*. Ten Speed Press, 1996.

- Smith, Rebecca. *Electronic Resumes and Online Networking*, 2nd ed. Career Press, 2000.

- Thompson, Mary Anne. *The Global Resume and CV Guide*. John Wiley & Sons, 2000.

- Troutman, Kathryn Kraemer. *Creating Your High School Resume*. Jist, 1998.

- ———. *Electronic Federal Resume Guidebook*. The Resume Place Press, 2001.

- ———. *The Federal Resume Guidebook*, 2nd ed. Jist, 1999.

- Weddle, Peter D. *Internet Resumes*. Impact Publications, 1998.

Online Guides and Guidance

Susan Ireland

susanireland.com

Susan Ireland is the author of *The Complete Idiot's Guide to the Perfect Resume* and other books, and her website has terrific information and samples for the job seeker. You will enjoy her online workshops for resume writing, E-resumes, and cover letters, along with the many samples of resumes, cover letters, and thank-you letters.

Rebecca Smith's eResumes & Resources

eresumes.com

Rebecca Smith has been promoting the electronic resume since 1995. Her website is not about writing a resume, it is about taking that resume and turning it into the best tool it can be for your online search. She also looks at online networking and how to make it work for you.

The Resume Place

resume-place.com

The Resume Place is the resume writing service operated by Kathryn Troutman, author of *The Federal Resume Guidebook* and *Creating Your High School Resume*.

On her website you'll find free articles and advice on preparing what you'll need in order to create your resume, including some nice short articles on quantifying your experience and summarizing your accomplishments. If you are considering applying for a job with the federal government, then you must review Troutman's information, as she is the expert in the federal resume (which is not like the resume you need for the private sector).

OWL—Online Writing Lab, Purdue University

http://owl.english.purdue.edu

This online information resource was set up to help with writing all types of documents. Under "Student/Teacher Handouts," the section called "Resume and Business Writing" includes help on writing resumes, cover letters, offer acceptance and refusal letters, personal statements, references, and postinterview letters.

Resumania

resumania.com

"Resumania" is a term coined by Robert Half, found of Robert Half International, Inc. (RHI), to describe errors made by job seekers on resumes, applications, and cover letters. Yes, this is an entire site dedicated to typos, grammatical errors, spelling errors, and other faux pas by job seekers for whatever reason. The idea here is that if they see these errors, others will not make the same mistakes, thereby improving not only the appearance of their resume but also the chance they will get an interview and a job.

The Portfolio Library by Martin Kimeldorf

http://amby.com/kimeldorf/portfolio

Sometimes a resume just doesn't work because it can't tell the whole story. This is where a portfolio comes in. Martin Kimeldorf has written several articles on this topic as well as a book titled *Portfolio Power* (Peterson's, 1997). His website includes articles introducing you to portfolios and discussing how to create one. Sample portfolios are also included.

200 Free Cover Letters for Job Seekers

careerlab.com/letters

Compiled by Bill Frank, a career management consultant in Colorado, this impressive collection of samples for all occasions in your job search is taken directly from his book of the same title.

3

The Great
Job-Lead Banks

Job-lead banks are the sites and services on the Internet known for their collected job listings. They cover multiple fields, industries, and occupations, providing leads for almost every job you can think of. Most are based in the United States but do not necessarily limit themselves to job listings for just this country.

This chapter is divided into two categories of resources:

1. Online recruiting services: these are recruiters and other organizations posting job announcements on the Internet.

2. Online guides to the job hunt: these are tips and pointers, along with lists of resources. Most, but not all, cover just Internet resources.

JOB SEARCH TIP:

Save some time and effort in online applications. If you use one Internet job service frequently and have had good luck finding positions advertised there, consider registering your resume with that service. Some job databases automate the application process, letting those with a registered resume at the site forward it in response to a job announcement with a single mouse click. It's also likely the same recruiters who post their jobs here also search the resume database, increasing your chances of being found. Look over our information on E-resumes and posting in Chapter 2.

Online Recruiting Services

Online recruiting services offer job listings in multiple fields, industries, and occupations. While many cover U.S. and international opportunities, the job banks primarily serving non–U.S. audiences are included in Chapter 12.

Abracat

http://abracat.com/abracat/index.jsp

This is a compilation of searchable classifieds from various sources and newspapers across the United States, including jobs. Select a zip code or city and state to narrow your search. All announcements are dated, but some have very sketchy contact info.

AdSearch

adsearch.com

Here you'll find all kinds of classified ads, including employment opportunities. Select a job category from the list, and add in any keywords that you want to use to further refine the search. You also have the option of selecting All Jobs to browse. The date of listing is posted on the job announcements, which appear in order from oldest to most recent.

America's Job Bank (AJB)

ajb.org

This site is a joint effort of the two thousand offices of the state employment service and the U.S. Department of Labor. You can search the database by occupation or keyword, and transitioning military personnel can search by military specialty codes. This is a great way to match your skills to jobs in the public sector. AJB is one of the largest job sources online and is not limited to the continental United States. You can also search the databases of the individual state, district, and territorial employment services. We suggest you search both the local state job bank and the main AJB site to review all available jobs in any given area.

Asia-Net

asia-net.com

Asia-Net is a clearinghouse for jobs that require bilingual fluency in English and Asian languages, specifically Japanese, Korean, and Chinese.

BestJobsUSA.com

bestjobsusa.com

This site includes job listings plus articles from *Employment Review*, a publication of Recourse Communications, Inc. Job seekers will benefit from the many additional resources, services, and information links found here.

The Black Collegian

black-collegian.com

The online site of the magazine dedicated to college students and professionals of color has wonderful position announcements. Search by keywords and target a location, or scan the list of employers.

Career.com

career.com

You can search this site, one of the oldest commercial recruiters on the Internet, by company name, discipline, location, or keywords. Their "Hot Jobs," entry-level opportunities, and international listings are also featured in their own lists.

Career Magazine

http://vertical.worklife.com/onlines/careermag

This online magazine includes job listings, employer profiles, and news and articles related to the job hunt today.

CareerBuilder

careerbuilder.com

CareerBuilder has evolved into one of the larger and more dynamic sites for job and career information. Registering with them allows you to store your resume online without posting it in their database, and you can create up to five personal search profiles to track new jobs added to the database and E-mail you when something is found.

CareerCity

careercity.com

Provided by Adams Media Corporation, this site hosts a job bank with all varieties of jobs. You can also opt to search other job banks from this site.

CareerExchange

careerexchange.com

This service covers the United States, Canada, and international jobs and allows you to search for jobs by category or keyword and narrow your choices to postings from particular dates. You can easily apply for jobs by pasting your plain-text resume into the form provided.

CareerJournal.com from the *Wall Street Journal* Interactive Edition

http://careerjournal.com

This free site features articles, information, and jobs. While some of the articles are from the *Wall Street Journal*, many are written specifically for CareerJournal.com. They have a great job bank to go with their terrific job and career content. Be sure to look at the "Salary and Hiring Info" with all the salary profiles and hiring trends listed by industry. This site has something for job seekers at all levels of experience.

CareerMart

careermart.com

CareerMart lets you search for jobs in the usual way, or you can review their list of employers and see all positions posted. If you find a job you want to apply for but are not a registered member of the service, you can still paste your plain-text resume into the form. That's very nice.

Careersite

careersite.com

This site has a lot to offer. You can start with a very simple quick search by selecting a region (United States or Canada) and an occupation. You must select the job title to see the full announcement, including application information. The date of posting is not noted on the job announcements.

CareerWeb

careerweb.com

This site includes job listings from the regional Employment Guide magazines as well as the many employers that are customers of this service. The site has good career and job-search information for all job seekers.

College Grad Job Hunter

collegegrad.com

Don't let that title fool you! This website, based on the book of the same title, is a cornucopia of resources and information to guide you through a complete job search. It has job databases for internships, entry-level job seekers, and experienced job seekers, along with a searchable database of more than eight thousand employers. And to top it all off it offers great advice on careers, the job search, resume preparation, and more.

Comforce Corporation

comforce.com

Comforce is a leading provider of staffing, consulting, and outsourcing solutions focused in several fields. The jobs can be searched by industry or location.

Cool Jobs

cooljobs.com

At first glance, Cool Jobs doesn't look like much, but when you review the resources you will find links to contact information and news regarding many diverse industries. Check it out!

Employers Online

employersonline.com

You'll find diverse job offerings here, including professional, medical, and clerical. Post your resume for free for up to six weeks.

Excite Careers

http://directory.excite.com/careers

Excite has done a tremendous job of developing useful career-related content on its website. You'll find job leads, career articles, and info to help you check out the best employers.

Excite Classifieds

classifieds2000.com

This site features classified ads for everything, including employment opportunities. The domestic jobs are separated from the other listings, but at the time of review almost everything posted here was a work-at-home or start-your-own-business listing. These are free ads, where the other job opportunities are not, so job seekers should be cautious when reviewing and responding to any of these.

FlipDog

flipdog.com

FlipDog uses "crawler" technology to crawl over employer websites and copy those listings to its site. Employers can also list themselves here voluntarily, and they have the option of paying to have their job postings featured in a more prominent position.

4Work

4work.com

4Work, part of the About.com network, is a searchable source of job listings from all over the United States.

Futurestep from Korn/Ferry

futurestep.com

Futurestep is a search service for midlevel management professionals brought to you by Korn/Ferry International, the world's largest executive search firm, and the *Wall Street Journal*. Registering with Futurestep is a free and confidential process and will cover more than just your standard resume. You will be considered for searches they are doing, but your information will never be given to hiring companies without your express approval.

Home Page of Malachy

execpc.com/~maltoal

This is a service of Mal Toal, a recruiter in Wisconsin with outreach to all locations and industries. Several candidates who have been successfully placed through positions listed here recommend the site highly. It's not a fancy site by any means, but it has some interesting listings.

HotJobs

hotjobs.com

Search for jobs by keyword, company, or location, or select a career channel and limit your search to just the postings in this area. In 2001, HotJobs was acquired by Yahoo!. There is a chance this site will be integrated into theirs in the not-so-distant future.

The Huntington Group

hgllc.com

The Huntington Group, a subsidiary of Hall Kinion, specializes in the emerging technology industries. This does not mean the only positions they work to fill are for technology specialists. You can review a partial list of their open searches online, each of which includes instructions on how to submit your resume for consideration.

Imcor

imcor.com

Imcor, a division of Spherion, is "America's Leading Supplier of Portable Executives," specializing in short- to midterm placement in senior management positions. Current assignments are posted on the web page with date, title, and location information. If you see a position for which you are qualified, you can submit your resume for consideration. If you don't see anything at this time but wish to be added to their network, your resume is also welcome. Please read the instructions for submitting resumes on their page.

IMDiversity

imdiversity.com

IMDiversity is the one-stop career and self-development site devoted to serving the cultural and career-related needs of all minorities. Sponsored by *The Black Collegian*, this is an excellent resource for all minority and diversity candidates. The many "villages" include resources and information specific for each group, and those without a separate village will find information in the global village. These folks are committed to serving minority/diversity groups and are doing a great job.

Internet Career Connection

iccweb.com

The Internet Career Connection is a service from Gonyea and Associates, the developers of Help Wanted USA and the former America Online Career Center. This group is also one of the earliest groups to consider job searching and career consulting online. This site includes job listings, information on careers, a career-guidance service, and a resume database. You can take a free career-interest survey online and learn what careers might be best for you based on what you like most.

Job Sleuth

jobsleuth.com

Job Sleuth is a metasearch tool that searches several online job sites and compiles the results into a single list for you to review. A nice feature here is they group the results by the site where they were found and tell you how many were found there, making it easy for you to see which sites are good for you and which aren't. As with any metasearch, the best results are actually found by going directly to the host site, but this one helps you figure out which those might be. Registered users can store search profiles to be executed on a regular basis with the results sent to you via E-mail. Users of public computers should note that Job Sleuth uses cookies to store your registration data. You can read about this plus learn how to remove them by reviewing their privacy policy.

JobBankUSA.com

jobbankusa.com

A good site for many jobs in all kinds of fields, JobBankUSA.com offers information organized and accessible through a variety of means. You can search the job database by keyword search, refining your search by location and position type (full time, contract, etc.). You can also scan the list of featured employers and connect to their websites. Their Job Metasearch allows you to access the searchable databases of several of the major job resources.

jobfind.com

jobfind.com

This site includes searchable ads and a list of employer profiles. You can also create an HTML resume to post here. While the job listings can be freely searched and most have some kind of application information included, registered users who post their resume on jobfind.com can activate a "one-button" application process to have their resumes forwarded to the employer. Based in the Boston area, most of their listings come from this region, but it is certainly not limited to this area.

JobOptions

joboptions.com

Formerly known as E-Span, this site is still a leader in the online recruiting market. It provides a searchable database of job openings as well as a wide variety of resources for the job seeker. Posting dates are clearly marked, and the database is updated daily. JobOptions offers a "Search Employer" feature that is good for building a list of target companies in a select industry in a desired geographic region. There is lots of great information here.

Jobpilot.com

jobpilot.com

This is an international job market with offices in several countries plus the United States. The services offered through the website include job listings (search by keyword or country and discipline, and limit the search to the most recent listings or all), a resume database, company listings, and an E-mail service. International job seekers wanting to work in the United States will appreciate the additional information covering their needs.

Kforce.com

kforce.com

Kforce is a professional staffing firm with openings and opportunities in many job areas covering the United States as well as some international locations. This site includes several good articles on career, transition, and work.

LeadersOnline

leadersonline.com

LeadersOnline was started by Heidrick & Struggles to help today's management professionals. Their clients range from Fortune 100 companies to dot-com start-ups, and they're looking for top professionals in the $75K–$180K salary range. After registering with LeadersOnline, your profile and resume are matched against available positions, and if a match is found, you'll be contacted with details about the position. You then decide whether you're interested in further pursuing the opportunity. If you are interested, LeadersOnline will do a more extensive evaluation of your qualifications, but you are kept informed of the progress, from initial evaluation to interviews and offers of employment.

LucasCareers.com

lucascareers.com

A division of Lucas Group, a national recruitment firm, LucasCareers.com offers a nice database of job positions for you to search. They also offer a specific division, Lucas Group Military, designed to facilitate the transitioning of military officers into civilian positions. Register to post and edit your resume. When you find a job you like, place a check mark in the box next to it, click on the "Send me more Info" button at the bottom of the page, and fill out the registration. Have your resume ready to paste into the box.

Manpower

manpower.com

Manpower is the largest employer in the United States today, and not just through placing secretaries and receptionists in offices. The world of the temp has opened up all the way to the chief executive's office. Assignments are searchable by location, and you can submit resumes by E-mail, fax, or the online form provided.

Monster.com

monster.com

Monster.com is probably the most recognized name in the online job-search industry. They offer an enormous variety of job and career resources for everyone from college students to contractors to chief executives, and most are served with their own communities that include job listings and career advice. They also offer several industry/job-field communities, including health care, human resources, and finance.

MonsterTRAK

monstertrak.com

Formerly known as JobTrak, this site has joined the Monster.com community. Your college or university must be a member of MonsterTRAK for you to gain access to the job postings on this site. See if your institution is listed, and if it is, call your career center and ask for the password. This site has been cited as an excellent resource for executive as well as entry-level opportunities, so it is worth it for alumni to take some time to look at this.

MRI's PrioritySearch.Com

http://prioritysearch.com

A service of Management Recruiters International, this site comprises several special areas, including agriculture/horticulture, educational publishing, plastics, manufacturing, and financial publishing. Resumes can be submitted online to the appropriate account manager noted on each page.

NationJob Network

nationjob.com

This site features an impressive collection of job openings, company info, and a variety of ways to find what you are looking for. It divides into many sources of occupational and industry-related resources, creating an excellent source of information for all.

Net-Temps

http://net-temps.com

This site features a searchable company database of temporary and full-time job listings, which can be searched by geographic location and keyword. You can also search a specific job category by job type (contract or full time) and location. Persons living in or wanting to work in Canada can check the Net-Temps Canada site for opportunities there.

Randstad North America

us.randstad.com/index.html

Randstad provides a wide variety of opportunities for talented people with primarily office, industrial, technical, creative, and professional skill sets. It also offers strategic client-related employment services, outsourcing, and training. Select the most appropriate area and set up a free account. Once registered, you can create a resume or use other helpful resources in the "Career Tool Box" provided for each section.

Recruiters Online Network

recruitersonline.com

This network is "an association of executive recruiters, search firms, and employment professionals around the world who have created a virtual organization on the Internet." Job seekers can search the database of openings posted by the participating recruiters, post their resume for consideration by all members, and search for recruiters working with a particular industry or occupational field for direct contact. This site also includes tips on job hunting and articles on using recruiters in the job search.

Saludos.com

saludos.com

This website, dedicated exclusively to promoting Hispanic careers and education, is supported by *Saludos Hispanos* magazine. Information here includes a Career Pavilion with job listings and other good career information and an Education Pavilion with announcements of internships, mentoring programs, and scholarship opportunities.

Snelling Personnel Services

snelling.com

Snelling is one of the world's largest providers of personnel services for business and industry. Job seekers can review the hundreds of current openings that Snelling is working to fill in numerous categories and apply online, or they can see which office is handling the search and contact them directly. Persons who don't immediately see jobs for their fields can register for future consideration.

Top Echelon

topechelon.com

Top Echelon is a cooperative network of more than twenty-five hundred recruiters. It has some good listings ranging from entry level well into the six-figure range. You can also search the recruiter listings and contact some of the recruiters directly.

WantedJobs

wantedjobs.com

WantedJobs offers a metasearch capability, allowing you to search more than three hundred U.S. sites online from a single location. Select a job category and a location (if desired), and enter keywords to help refine your search. Registered users can set up a Job Agent to run each time they visit the site. WantedJobs also offers metasearches for the United Kingdom (more than 20 sites), Canada (more than 160 sites), and Quebec (more than 40 sites, and everything is in French).

Winter, Wyman, and Co.

winterwyman.com/boston/index.asp

Winter, Wyman is one of the largest recruitment firms in New England, and it also has offices in Atlanta, Metro (Washington) DC, and New York. Select a target office to view the current searches each is handling. If you find a position for which you feel qualified, you can forward a resume to the appropriate search consultant as noted in the listing.

Yahoo! Careers

http://careers.yahoo.com

This section of Yahoo! features job postings from all over the United States organized by geographic region. While you can start your search with keywords or by choosing from a list of job families, you will be asked to target your search to a specific location. It does make a pretty good match from your local town to the closest major metropolitan area. If your local area doesn't include listings for your chosen field, it will default to a nationwide search.

Online Guides to the Job Hunt

These Internet guides for the online job search, sometimes referred to as "metaguides," gather information and resources to help you use the Internet to find employment. Some will give you notes about the resources, some will give you articles on the job search, but all will take you to more online information for your search.

Career Paradise's Colossal List of Links

emory.edu/CAREER/Main/CareerLinks.html

Supported by the career center at Emory University, this is a nice list of resources for career information, job leads, and industry research.

The Career Resource Homepage

careerresource.net

Started by Jasmit Singh Kochhar, this site is a metalist of career-related resources for the online job search. All categories are arranged alphabetically, be they titles or topics, but you can browse and hit hundreds of interesting sites.

Careers.Org, Career Resource Center

careers.org

Here are more than seventy-five hundred links to employers, recruiters, magazines and newspapers, and other resources for your job search. They have also compiled links of regional resources for the United States and Canada.

The Catapult on JobWeb, the Career Service Professionals Homepage

jobweb.com/catapult

Originally developed by Leo Charette to guide career counselors in the use of the Internet, this service is now supported by the National Association of Colleges and Employers (NACE). The Catapult provides numerous quality links to information and resources that can help anyone in the job search. This site is especially good for entry-level job seekers but also has very good information for more experienced workers.

Job Finders Online

http://jobfindersonline.com

This site is provided by the publishers of the Job Finders books to give them a place to post updates for the series. We particularly like the free update sheets for each book, which allow you to see what's happening in the areas and topics. If you own the books or they are in your library, office, or career center, then you are in luck. If you don't have the books, there is still good information here.

Job-Hunt.org

job-hunt.org

One of the earliest guides to the Internet job search, Job-Hunt.org still offers numerous well-selected links to job-search resources for the world. You can search for job sites by location, profession, industry, or job type.

JobHuntersBible.com

jobhuntersbible.com

This online guide to the job search comes from the Dean of Career Counseling himself, Richard Bolles! The Job Hunter's Bible is a supplement to Bolles's bestseller *What Color Is Your Parachute?* and is spiced with his comments and observations on the job search and your decision-making process. Part of this site is his Net Guide to the best job-search and career-information sites online. Only the best get his stamp of approval.

JobStar

http://jobstar.org

JobStar began as a "California Job Search Guide," but it has always been a highly useful resource for everyone. Now it is purposely expanding to new regions in the United States. JobStar is one of the best places online to find out how and where to look for employment, both online and offline. Among the wealth of information included here are articles on the hidden job market, negotiating salaries, and numerous other topics that work to enhance the choice resources listed, selected because they are the best.

Purdue University Center for Career Opportunities Job Search Sites on the World Wide Web

cco.purdue.edu/student/jobsites.htm

Purdue's award-winning list has more than a thousand resources, divided into several categories. It is huge, maybe even a bit overwhelming, but you should definitely pay it a visit. Be wary of broken links, as it is difficult to check a site this large with regularity.

The Riley Guide: Employment Opportunities and Job Resources on the Internet

rileyguide.com

The first guide to the Internet as a tool for finding new employment, this resource started in January 1994 and has been going strong ever since. The Riley Guide links you to hundreds of sources of information for job leads, career exploration, and potential employers. It even has information to help you explore new careers, new places to live, and new education and training options.

Yahoo! Employment and Work

http://dir.yahoo.com/business_and_economy/employment_and_work

Yahoo! links to more than fifteen hundred sites for job leads and other sources of employment information. Don't limit yourself to just this list, though. Almost every category on Yahoo! has a separate employment category, so browse the shelves frequently.

Jobs in Business, Marketing, and Commercial Services

The resources covered in this chapter point to job information in business fields and commercial services. Commercial services are services provided to a company, such as janitorial services, event management, and equipment leasing.

We have not included names of specific companies or organizations that are recruiting in these fields, although many of the links listed will take you to those companies. Use the procedures and resources outlined in Chapter 1 to look for prospective employers on your own. For example, if you are interested in working for a medical firm, use search terms or follow links that relate to the medical field. You can use the virtual libraries to identify organizations or employers of interest. Keep in mind that even high-tech companies cannot do business without a team of accountants, sales representatives, and managers to help them run efficiently. The opportunities are endless, and this list is just the beginning!

Great Business Starting Points

Careers in Business

careers-in-business.com

This site is designed to help you find a job in the business world. Careers in Business includes information on career areas to explore, starting with an overview of each area, and then goes through the skills and talents needed for the work, very basic salary information, links and resources for more information, facts and trends in the field, and, if available, a link to job listings from jobsinthemoney.com.

Job-Search Links, Columbia Business School

columbia.edu/cu/business/career/links

Created by the Office of M.B.A. Career Services at the Columbia Business School, this is a good guide to online resources for job and industry information for the M.B.A.

Accounting and Finance

AAFA: The American Association of Finance and Accounting

aafa.com

AAFA is an alliance of executive search firms specializing in the recruiting and placement of finance and accounting professionals. Search their Careers area for searches posted by member firms, and submit your resume for consideration.

Accountemps

accountemps.com

Accountemps, a division of Robert Half International, Inc., specializes in placing qualified temporary accounting and finance professionals.

Accounting.com

accounting.com

Accounting.com includes all kinds of positions in accounting and finance for all levels of experience. The site also provides great links to industry and professional information.

AICPA Online: American Institute for Certified Public Accountants

aicpa.org

AICPA is "the national, professional organization for all Certified Public Accountants. Its mission is to provide members with the resources, information, and leadership that enable them to provide valuable services in the highest professional manner to benefit the public as well as employers and clients." Job listings are publicly accessible on the website under "Career Opportunities."

American Banker.com

americanbanker.com

This is the magazine of the financial industry, featuring daily updates and industry news. The CareerZone is operated in conjunction with bankjobs.com (see entry later), but you need a free password to search the database, and to get the password you must submit your resume. American Banker.com has good industry news and information. There is a substantial amount of free information here, but those who want to subscribe will get two weeks free and can cancel within that time without paying anything.

American Society of Payroll Managers

aspm.org

This association website includes news and information for payroll, tax, and human resources professionals as well as jobs for those seeking new careers in these fields.

Association for Finance Professionals (AFP)

afponline.org

Formerly known as the Treasury Management Association, AFP's membership is made up of individuals representing a broad spectrum of financial disciplines. Their Career Services area offers terrific resources for association members, including networking groups. The Online Job Center is also offered through

Career Services, and while the full site is open only to members, visitors may browse a sample listing of the jobs posted here. At the time of review, we saw jobs from cash managers to business analysts to senior executives, some posted by search firms.

Bankjobs.com

bankjobs.com

Bankjobs.com includes job and career information for banking and financial services candidates. A password seems to be required to search the job database, but at the time of review we were able to bypass this using their "QuickSearch" on the front page. Otherwise, to get a free password, you must post your resume in their database. Please note that this service is limited to U.S. residents and job seekers who meet the educational or experience requirements. Resumes are limited to sixty-five hundred characters, and they do give you tips on posting an "anonymous" resume. There are some nice industry links for you to use.

Bloomberg Online

bloomberg.com

Bloomberg Online is an extensive site for financial information online. And, under the Life category, you'll find the Career Center, complete with a nice database of jobs for brokers, traders, analysts, and others in the financial industry worldwide. The job database is operated in conjunction with CareerBuilder.

CFO.com

http://cfo.com

CFO Publishing's website features content from *CFO Magazine*, CFO Europe, and CFO Asia. The site includes international news, articles, resources, and featured jobs for chief financial officers (CFOs), treasurers, and other senior financial executives in the United States and Canada. You'll also want to review the "CFO Compensation Survey."

Execu|Search Group

execu-search.com

This is a recruiting and placement firm in New York City, specializing in accounting, finance, brokerage, graphics, and information technology jobs.

Financial Job Network

fjn.com

This international site lists job opportunities for actuaries, controllers, auditors, chief financial officers, and many more finance professionals.

FinancialJobs.com

financialjobs.com

These are jobs for accounting and financial professionals throughout the United States.

Fincareer.com

fincareer.com

Fincareer, another international financial site, links job seekers to the global players in the banking and finance markets.

International Market Recruiters

goimr.com

This group specializes in permanent and consultative placements exclusively in the financial services arena. You can review some of their current searches and submit your resume for consideration in the search.

JobsintheMoney.com

jobsinthemoney.com

This site offers job and career information for financial professionals. Check the Company Gallery for a list of employers/firms posting here, review the Job Resources for employer profiles from Wetfeet.com and lists of good books to review, and go through the News and Links to keep up with the latest news or connect to more financial info. They list many good financial jobs covering an extensive international market. You can search the jobs without registering, but registering and storing your resume here will make it easier to apply for jobs. They want you to add a "cover letter" to each application, so have a template available that you can cut, paste, and customize.

National Banking and Financial Services Network

nbn-jobs.com

This is a large association of recruiting firms with nationwide job listings. This site includes jobs in finance, banking, and credit as well as many more opportunities within this industry. Jobs are listed by region or specialty function. You must register, but you can do so anonymously and it is free.

RHI Management Resources

rhimr.com

This division of Robert Half International provides senior-level accounting and financial professionals on a project basis. You can easily search for projects that might interest you.

Robert Half Financial Recruiting

roberthalf.com

Founded in 1948, Robert Half is the world's first accounting, financial, banking, and information systems staffing service. The company specializes in recruiting for finance, accounting, treasury, and information systems positions. You can search this site by job title or geographic location.

Rutgers Accounting Web (RAW)

http://accounting.rutgers.edu/raw

Within this enormous site, you will find links to information on taxation, finance, auditing, professional associations, and information on accounting firms in the United States. We suggest reviewing the Site Map to get more information on each area before you start exploring.

Tax-Jobs.Com

tax-jobs.com

This site features job listings for tax professionals.

Actuaries

The Berry List of Actuarial Resources

geocities.com/wallstreet/1602

This is an excellent source of online information for actuaries compiled and maintained by Pete Berry, an associate of the Society of Actuaries and a member of the American Academy of Actuaries. The site includes links to employment information, recruiters, and industry information online.

Rollins Search Group

rollinssearch.com

Rollins specializes in recruiting in actuary (actuarial) and insurance systems technology specialists.

Advertising/Communication/Public Relations

AdAge.com's Career Center

adagespecials.com/jobbank/careercenter.html

Advertising Age is placing its classified ads online with the help of Monster.com. There are hundreds of current leads.

AdWeek

adweek.com

The AdWeek Career Network is a leading classified resource in the advertising, marketing, and media professions. At the time of review, the site was undergoing revision, but according to the posted information, it will be offering free and fee-based services. Those who subscribe to the new service will receive access to current job listings, full-text articles from *AdWeek*, and free resume posting. Those who wish to use the free service will receive access to archived job listings (seven days old), access to headlines and abstracts of articles, and free resume posting.

Commarts.com Network

commarts.com

This site includes information for those engaged in the communication arts: graphics, marketing, artwork, and other visual methods for communicating with others. It hosts an impressive collection of resources for the industry and the individual and a job bank featuring lots of openings for graphic designers, web project managers, and writers.

Fristoe & Carleton, Inc.

adjob.com

Fristoe & Carleton is an executive search and recruiting firm specializing in placement of advertising and public relations executives in the Midwest and South. A sample list of current searches is available and updated frequently.

International Association of Business Communicators

iabc.com/homepage.htm

The IABC represents writers, editors, public relations directors, and other advertising and communications specialists. The job bank is open for all to review and may include jobs for webmasters, public relations specialists, technical writers, editorial staff, and directors of corporate communications. Many chapters also maintain individual job banks.

Public Relations Society of America (PRSA) Career Resources

http://prsa.org/career

The PRSA Career Resources area includes information on starting your own PR firm, a reading room with information on this career area, a salary survey, a resume database, and a job-lead bank. The job leads are updated every Friday, and postings are retained online for about a month. Job seekers will also want to check the list of local chapters found on the main website, because many also maintain job lists on their individual websites.

Church Business Administration

National Association of Church Business Administration

nacba.net

This is "an interdenominational, professional, Christian organization which exists to train, certify, and provide resources for those serving in the field of church administration." They offer training toward certification as a Fellow in Church Business Administration (FCBA) along with a number of workshops and conferences to assist others in this work. The website features some terrific resources, including job listings and links to additional sources, and the association does a compensation survey of church administrators every couple of years.

Customer Relations/Call Centers

CallCenterCareers.com

callcentercareers.com

CallCenterCareers.com is an online job site for the call center and customer relationship management (CRM) industries. The site includes job postings, a resume bank, industry news, and specialized career services. Registration is not required to search the database or apply for the jobs.

Equipment Leasing

Equipment Leasing Association Online

elaonline.com

The Equipment Leasing Association provides industry information as well as limited job postings. The job postings can be found in the Career Exchange area of the website.

Monitor Daily

monitordaily.com

Monitor Daily features industry news and information for the equipment leasing and finance industry. A service of Molloy Associates, recruiters for this industry, this site also hosts two different listings of job opportunities. The Career Showcase includes listings of current searches being handled by Molloy Associates, and the Classified Ads are listings posted by various employers in this industry.

Human Resources

BenefitsLink

benefitslink.com

This site includes good information for anyone dealing with benefits, from the human resources manager to the actuary trying to figure it all out. You can read the latest news, check the industry links, and review the employment opportunities as well as employment-wanted ads.

BenefitNews.com

benefitnews.com

BenefitNews.com is the online companion of *Employee Benefit News* magazine, covering health care, retirement planning, compensation, and other employee benefits. This site carries job listings and good information for benefits managers. It is a free site, but registration is required.

HR Careers from TCM.com

tcm.com/hr-careers

This site combines job listings with job-search tips and a resume database.

HR Opportunities from Shaker Advertising

shaker.com/hropps.html

Shaker Advertising is a recruitment advertising firm, but it maintains a database of jobs for HR professionals.

International Foundation of Employee Benefit Plans

ifebp.org

The International Foundation of Employee Benefit Plans, the largest association for employee benefit plans, provides good resources for those in this field, including job postings. Jobs can be reviewed by posting date, location, or job title, and you can sign up for their free daily E-mail bulletin of new jobs posted. Resumes can be posted here for a fee.

Jobs4HR

jobs4hr.com

This site features jobs for HR professionals at all levels. Registration is not required to search or apply for jobs, but the free registration will allow you to customize certain features of the site.

MonsterHR

monsterhr.com

MonsterHR is Monster.com's contribution to the careers of HR professionals. Along with a more streamlined job search, it offers several career and professional resources for persons in this field.

Society for Human Resource Management (SHRM)

shrm.org/jobs

The SHRM has one of the largest databases of new jobs. You can also find a very well-organized collection of human resources links at this noteworthy site.

WorldatWork

worldatwork.org

Formerly known as the American Compensation Association, this professional association website includes information and jobs for compensation and benefits specialists.

Insurance

Insurance National Search, Inc.

insurancerecruiters.com

This association of recruiting firms specializes in the insurance industry. The site includes searchable databases of job listings and recruiters. Each job listing is less than sixty days old, and you contact the specific recruiter handling the placement directly.

Jacobson Associates

jacobson-associates.com

Jacobson Associates is an executive search firm for the insurance industry. It has divisions for actuarial, general insurance professionals, and interim insurance staffers, and all three divisions list opportunities or openings for which they are accepting inquiries.

National Association of Insurance Commissioners (NAIC)

naic.org

NAIC is an organization of insurance regulators from the fifty states, the District of Columbia, and the four U.S. territories. Jobs with the state commissions are posted here. To view them, select "General Information" on the front page. Some of the job listings are in Word, some are in Adobe PDF format, and some are on web pages. You will see notes identifying the format of each.

Rollins Search Group

rollinssearch.com

Rollins specializes in jobs in the insurance industry, especially for actuaries and information systems personnel.

Meeting and Event Management

International Association of Assembly Managers, Inc.

http://iaam.org

The International Association of Assembly Managers comprises leaders who manage or provide products and services to such public assembly facilities as arenas, amphitheaters, auditoriums, convention centers/exhibit halls, stadiums, and university complexes.

Professional Convention Management Association

www.pcma.org

This professional association website includes industry information, a job bank (under Industry Toolbox), checklists, continuing education opportunities, and scholarship information. Some great bonuses to this site are descriptions of the roles that meeting managers play and information about how to prepare for a career in this field.

Office Support Services

AdminExchange

adminexchange.com

AdminExchange specializes in listings for administrative and support personnel. All announcements are dated, and all have full contact information on where to apply. You can also fill in the Hotlist Sign-Up form to have your credentials forwarded to clients with jobs matching your areas of expertise.

Champion Personnel System

championjobs.com

Through its website, Champion, a staffing agency based in Cleveland, Ohio, offers limited job postings for temporary and permanent office support. The site is updated weekly and also includes useful information on job searching, resume preparation, and interview techniques, along with a salary guide for office support staff.

Packaging

Executive Search International

esihbc.com

This is a search firm specializing in the placement of sales and marketing professionals within the consumer packaged goods industry (beauty care, cosmetics, nutritionals, and over-the-counter pharmaceuticals). The website includes a brief list of current searches, a list of recent placements, and a nice list of questions that you should ask a headhunter along with some you should expect to answer.

PackagingBusiness.com

packagingbusiness.com

PackagingBusiness.com has information, news, and resources for the packaging industry. Jobs can be found in its Job Fair, not in the classifieds.

PackagingInfo.com

packaginginfo.com

You must register to use this site, but it is free and worth it! PackagingInfo.com is a gateway to articles and other good industry information offered by the print publications *Food and Drug Packaging*, *BrandPackaging*, and *Flexible Packaging*. The offerings include searchable product information, industry news, and jobs listed under Classified.

Packinfo-World

packinfo-world.com/WPO

PackInfo-World gives you news and events from all over the world and includes a worldwide list of packaging institutions. Look under PackInfo-World/US to find PackJobs, a list of links to resources for opportunities in this industry, including the Institute of Packaging Professionals (IoPP) Employment Resources. A direct link to this particular resource can also be found on the front page.

Purchasing and Procurement

BuyingJobs.com

buyingjobs.com

BuyingJobs.com is a site for purchasing and supply chain professionals. Scroll past the surveys, advertisements, and client list to get to the list of feature jobs.

International Purchasing Service Staffing

ipserv.com

This is a recruiting and temporary services firm providing professional purchasing management on a temporary basis. A short list of job openings is available.

National Association of Purchasing Management (NAPM)

napm.org

The professional association for purchasing management operates a site that features its publications, information on careers and courses in the field, and links to related resources, including local chapters. The NAPM job and resume databases are available only to members, but the list of additional career resources is available to nonmembers. Those curious about a career in this field will find good information here. Many chapters have employment opportunities on their web pages.

Quality Control

American Society for Quality (ASQ)

asq.org

ASQ is the leading quality-improvement organization in the United States, with more than 130,000 members worldwide. This website is a prime resource for those in this field. You must be a member to have access to the employment listings and resume database services, but nonmembers should check the many section websites for open listings.

Real Estate and Relocation

Employee Relocation Council (ERC)

erc.org

ERC is "a nonprofit professional membership organization committed to the effective relocation of employees worldwide." This extensive website includes job listings in the relocation industry, a great online research library to help you find the answers to legal and other questions, articles from *Mobility* magazine, and the Worldwide Relocation Services Directory.

NACORE International, the International Association of Corporate Real Estate Executives

nacore.com

This is an organization for business leaders engaged in the strategic management of real estate for major corporations worldwide. Check out select articles from their magazine *Corporate Real Estate Executive*, and browse the job listings for real estate managers as well as facility planners and managers, lease negotiators, and facility designers. At the time of review, NACORE International was preparing to merge with a similar association to form a new organization called CoreNet Global in 2002.

Real Estate Job Store

realestatejobstore.com

The Real Estate Job Store offers numerous job listings for the real estate industry, as well as valuable links to openings in related fields, such as facilities management and finance. We suggest searching its main integrated job database unless you find so many postings in your area that it is easier to search the individual, specialized databases.

Sales and Marketing

American Marketing Association

ama.org

The American Marketing Association's job bank, part of its Career Center, is open to all users regardless of member status. However, to apply for any jobs found here, you must register, a free process that takes about five minutes and includes storing your resume on the site. You do have the option of not posting your resume in its searchable database. While a plain-text resume is required for application and posting, you have the option of adding a designed resume to the database for employers to download.

Ludwig & Associates, Inc.

ludwig-recruit.com

This is an executive search firm specializing in the placement of sales and marketing professionals for consumer packaged goods companies. Individuals in this industry are invited to review the list of current searches and contact them at any time.

MarketingJobs.com

marketingjobs.com

MarketingJobs.com lists marketing, sales, and advertising employment opportunities in the United States. To make your search a little easier, they offer some location subcategories so you can target major regions faster and you can also search for jobs by employer. You can register your profile here for free, meaning you can store your resume in its database for employers to search and for you to use when applying to jobs found here.

Training and Development

American Society for Training and Development (ASTD)

astd.org

ASTD is the premier professional association for the training and development community. Along with all the other excellent resources, a public job bank is available to all visitors.

Instructional System Technology Jobs

http://education.indiana.edu/ist/students/jobs/joblink.html

This site lists opportunities in all areas of training, including academic faculty, media developers, and corporate trainers. It is a service of the Department of Instructional Systems Technology in the School of Education at Indiana University, Bloomington, and it will reject any job posting that appears to be unrelated to instructional technology. The listings are divided into corporate, nonprofit, and internships.

5

Jobs in the Social Sciences and the World of Nonprofits

The areas surveyed in this chapter have been grouped together for their interest in society and the public. The social sciences cover many fields, including education and academe, and many of these organizations cross into the nonprofit field. Opportunities with the many nonprofit organizations are not easy to locate because they do not have the money to recruit like for-profit companies. We have provided you with a few job databases for this area as well as information to help direct you to these organizations.

Anthropology

American Anthropological Association

aaanet.org

Anthropology is "the study of humankind, from its beginnings millions of years ago to the present day. . . . Anthropologists may study ancient Mayan hieroglyphics, the music of African Pygmies, and the corporate culture of a U.S. car manufacturer." The website from this association includes information on meetings, publications, and careers, as well as job listings. Many, but not all, are in academic institutions.

Arbitration

American Arbitration Association

adr.org

If you are interested in arbitration, this is the group to look to for help. This organization is available to resolve a wide range of disputes through mediation, arbitration, elections, and other out-of-court settlement procedures. The group also provides training for people interested in this field.

Archaeology

Archaeological Fieldwork Server

cincpac.com/afos/testpit.html

Individuals seeking archaeology fieldwork opportunities can browse through postings for volunteers, positions in field schools, full-time and contract jobs, and other archaeological openings that are submitted or found on mailing lists and in newsgroups. Positions are categorized by geographic location of the site or school. This service also links to additional resources that may list more positions.

The Archaeological Institute of America (AIA)

archaeological.org

AIA is the oldest and largest archaeological organization in North America, with more than eleven thousand members around the world. You'll find lots worth looking at here, including information on fellowships, along with myriad publications targeted at anyone from children up to scholars.

Economics

E-JOE

inomics.com/query/show?what=ejoe

This European version of JOE is loaded with links and international jobs. Inomics, the host for this service, also maintains information on conferences and other good economics resources.

International Economic Development Council (IEDC)

iedconline.org

Formed by the merger of the American Economic Development Council (AEDC) and the Council for Urban Economic Development (CUED), IEDC serves economic and community development professionals and those in allied fields. The merged website was still under development at the time of review, but it includes information on professional development, certification, and resources for funding and financial assistance. The Career Services area offers job listings for IEDC members and information on internships with the association.

JOE—Job Opportunities for Economists

eco.utexas.edu/joe

This is the electronic version of *Job Opportunities for Economists (JOE)*, now published by the University of Texas at Austin. This lists jobs as reported by the members of the American Economic Association. *JOE* is published every month except January and July. The online version is generally available on the fifth of the month. The listings are grouped into U.S. academic, international, and nonacademic positions, and each grouping is then arranged alphabetically by the name of the posting institution ("University of" is ignored). Each month's listing contains only new postings, but several months are available online.

Education and Academe

We have divided this heading into major sections based on the types of positions offered, but many of the resources overlap categories. We suggest you review the entire list to find all that fit your needs.

COLLEGE AND UNIVERSITY POSITIONS

Academic Employment Network

academploy.com

The Academic Employment Network features job listings by state for colleges and kindergarten through twelfth-grade institutions. You can post your resume for a nominal fee. A nice feature here is it will list only those states with actual job openings. Select your state to see all positions listed, or just view all listings. Jobs are generally posted for thirty days.

Academic Position Network (APN)

apnjobs.com

The APN is an online position announcement service for academic institutions all over the world. Job listings include faculty, administration, and staff positions, as well as announcements for research fellowships and graduate assistantships.

Academic360.com

academic360.com

Formerly know as Jobs in Higher Education, this site provides more than fifteen hundred links to colleges and universities advertising their position announcements online in the United States, Canada, Australia, and the United Kingdom.

The AERA Bulletin Board

aera.net/anews

The American Educational Research Association (AERA) is concerned with improving the educational process by encouraging scholarly inquiry related to education and by promoting the dissemination and practical application of research results. Its members include educators; administrators; directors of research, testing, or evaluation in federal, state, and local agencies; counselors; evaluators; graduate students; and behavioral scientists. The Bulletin Board includes grant and fellowship opportunities, job announcements posted with AERA and on the AERA listserv, miscellaneous opportunities in other research areas, and much more.

ASEE's National Engineering Information Center (NEIC)

asee.org/neic

ASEE, the American Society for Engineering Education, has put together the NEIC as a list of hyperlinks and resources pertaining to engineering and engineering education. It includes general engineering information, information about engineering education, engineering societies, issues of interest to engineers, and careers in engineering. This last section includes the CareerScope with its information on projects, funding, conferences, companies, fellowships, and engineering faculty openings in various colleges and universities. The listings to be published in the next month's *ASEE Prism* are open to members only, but nonmembers can read them once they are published in print.

Chronicle of Higher Education's Career Network

http://chronicle.com/jobs

This site includes career articles and job listings from the *Chronicle of Higher Education*, the weekly publication of higher education worldwide. Many international institutions and companies with research divisions advertise here also. The job listings are updated daily and are free for all users. If you are considering a teaching or administrative position with a college or university, you should be looking here!

Employment Opportunities in Women's Studies and Feminism

inform.umd.edu/EdRes/Topic/WomensStudies/Employment

This directory is part of the Women's Studies Database at inforM, the University of Maryland, College Park Campus's online information system. Job postings include the closing date on the menu, so you can easily see application deadlines. There is an occasional nonacademic position listed here, but most are faculty positions.

HigherEd Jobs

higheredjobs.com

This website lists jobs in more than five hundred member academic institutions for both faculty and staff. You can view the postings by category, location, or keyword.

NISS Vacancies Service

vacancies.ac.uk

This service from National Information Services and Systems displays employment opportunities at the many universities in the United Kingdom. There are several fields from which to choose, and links to additional job resources for these areas are also included. NISS has provided comprehensive, professionally maintained online information services for the U.K. education sector since 1988.

Positions in Christian Higher Education

cccu.org/jobs

This site posts faculty and administrative positions at the member and nonmember affiliate institutions of the Coalition for Christian Colleges & Universities. According to the sponsor, "Position listings are generally posted within twenty-four hours of submission and are posted here for ninety days when no application deadline is specified in the listing." The most recent notices are listed first. Browse the faculty or administrative/nonteaching lists, or search the text. The full list of member and nonmember affiliate colleges participating in this association is available.

THES: The Times Higher Education Supplement

thesis.co.uk

THES is a great way to find jobs in higher education worldwide. It carries lists from all categories of higher-education job vacancies worldwide as advertised in the *Times*. Jobs are sorted first into U.K. or international groups and then by their classification type—lecturers and tutors, principal/senior lecturers, professors, and readers and chairs. Listings are retained for about one month or until filled, whichever comes first.

Women in Higher Education

wihe.com

Women in Higher Education (WIHE) supports this website with news and views providing an overview of issues affecting women on college campuses. The Career Connection posts several academic openings for faculty and chief administrators, but be sure to check application deadlines. Many articles from the association's monthly magazine can be read online, and the Web Resources section will link you to many further sources of information for women.

JOB SEARCH TIP:

Looking for Work in Academe. If you are interested in teaching at a college or university, you can check an institution's web server for job listings, including assistantships, fellowships, and postdoctoral opportunities. Use Yahoo! (yahoo.com) and directories such as Peterson's (petersons.com) to find institutions, and then check the human resources departments as well as the specific department in which you are interested for job listings. Professional societies may also carry good announcements. If you are trying to find an institution with a particular specialty, use virtual libraries to target departments.

COLLEGE AND UNIVERSITY ADMINISTRATION

ACPA Ongoing Placement Listings: American College Personnel Association

http://acpant.acpa.nche.edu/onplace.nsf

These listings include jobs for resident advisers, directors of student programs, and the like at colleges and universities. The date of posting is noted on each announcement, and most also say how long the announcement will stay active.

Council for Advancement and Support of Education (CASE) Job Classifieds

case.org/jobs

Specializing in administrative positions in academe and education, the jobs listed at CASE include positions in alumni relations, communications, development/fund-raising, public relations, major gifts, annual fund, government relations, information systems and advancement services, and advancement management.

EDUCAUSE Job Posting Service

educause.edu/jobpost/jobpost.html

EDUCAUSE is "focused on the management and use of computational, network, and information resources in support of higher education's missions of scholarship, instruction, service, and administration." Jobs are posted by member institutions and include all types of academic information and management positions.

Jobs from AIR: Association for Institutional Research

airweb.org/jobs.html

AIR is dedicated to professional growth of all people who participate in decision making related to higher education via management research, policy analysis, and planning. AIR members work in many different postsecondary areas—finance, academic affairs, instruction, student services, and institutional development—and in offices at the international, state, system, and campus levels. The AIR Job Bulletin contains job listings for institutional planners and researchers that have been submitted to this organization.

The National Association of College and University Business Officers

nacubo.org

The National Association of College and University Business Officers (NACUBO) is a nonprofit professional organization representing chief administrative and financial officers at more than twenty-one hundred colleges and universities across the country. News, resources, and a link to its job service can be found on the main page.

National Association of Student Personnel Administrators

naspa.org

The National Association of Student Personnel Administrators (NASPA) is the leading national association for college and university student affairs administrators. Its JobsLink includes openings for admissions, enrollment management, student affairs, housing, health, and much more.

KINDERGARTEN THROUGH TWELFTH-GRADE TEACHING AND ADMINISTRATIVE OPPORTUNITIES

Ed Jobs U Seek

http://jobs.coled.umn.edu

Ed Jobs U Seek is a free service for educational employers, new graduates, or seasoned professionals in education and human development seeking available positions in schools, institutions, and a variety of education-related organizations in business, government, and community agencies. Jobs in administration, higher education, human development, teaching (K–12) and licensed fields (counselors, nurses, etc.) can be reviewed by category, or you can use a map to search for jobs by location. The College of Education and Human Development at the University of Minnesota run Ed Jobs U Seek.

Independent School Management Career Corner

isminc.com/pubs/mart/mm.html

This site posts opportunities for principals and other administrators in private schools around the United States.

TABS: The Association of Boarding Schools

schools.com

TABS is a nonprofit association working to support and promote independent boarding schools. Its website includes The Boarding School Directory, a list of nearly three hundred boarding schools in the United States, Canada, and abroad. The directory can be browsed by name, location, and school type (boys, girls, military, etc.).

Teacher Job Links

geocities.com/Athens/Forum/2080

This is an impressive list of links to job sites for educators and administrators set up and maintained by a former teacher. He operates this on Geocities because it is free, so you will be subjected to the Java-driven advertising that Geocities forces on you, but don't let that scare you away from this rich resource.

RECRUITING NEW TEACHERS

There is a real shortage of teachers in the United States, so there are services trying to encourage people in one career to consider the change to teaching as a profession.

Teach for America

teachforamerica.org

Teach for America (TFA) is a nonprofit organization that recruits primarily recent college graduates of all academic majors to teach for two years in an underserved urban or rural public school. However, applicants at all age and experience levels are welcome. If you've ever considered the idea of teaching others what you have learned, you might want to look more closely at this opportunity. Certification not required.

Troops to Teachers

http://voled.doded.mil/dantes/ttt

Troops to Teachers provides referral assistance and placement assistance to military personnel interested in beginning a second career in public education as a teacher. Besides employment resources and listings, the site provides information on how to obtain certification and a list of mentors. Job seekers will appreciate the information on school districts needing teachers to fill openings.

ENGLISH AS A SECOND OR FOREIGN LANGUAGE (ESL/EFL)

EFLWEB

eflweb.com

EFLWEB is an online magazine for both the teachers and the students learning English as a foreign language. It is an excellent resource for anyone interested in this field of study, and the site includes a resume bank and job vacancies board.

ESL Cafe's Job Center

http://eslcafe.com/jobs

This site, presented by Dave Sperling, provides a wonderful list of resources for ESL educators. The Job Center includes jobs wanted, jobs posted, a Korean job board, a place for ESL/EFL teachers to talk to each other, a journal of job experiences, a teacher-training forum, and links to even more resources.

Law, Paralegal, and the U.S. Judiciary

The Federal Judiciary

uscourts.gov

This website includes information on our federal courts, including employment opportunities. These are not limited to legal professionals but cover all areas supporting the U.S. courts, their services, and areas of responsibilities. You can review the listings by location, desired salary, or position title. Some announcements are in PDF format and will require the free Adobe Acrobat reader for viewing. Please note that not all of the judiciary's employment opportunities are found here; other announcements may exist on each court's website. This site links to the Federal Law Clerk Information System, which also carries job listings.

FindLaw Career Center

http://careers.findlaw.com

FindLaw is a marvelous resource for legal information as well as for job and career information for all aspects of legal work. Positions listed here include summer clerks, legal secretaries, law librarians, and attorneys in practice or academic positions. You'll also find listings here for accounting, marketing, and any other type of assistance the lawyers need to help run their practices.

Hieros Gamos, the Comprehensive Law and Government Portal

hg.org

Hieros Gamos is a wonderful source of legal information on the Internet. The Employment area includes links to legal employment centers online, sources for job listings, related Internet employment resources (including its own list of legal recruiters), publications on searching for jobs, alternatives to corporate practices, and much more.

Job Links for Lawyers

http://home.sprynet.com/~ear2ground

This site contains 720 unique links to sites that post current job openings for attorneys. The list includes sites with job listings in more than one state or jurisdiction, job listings with agencies of the United States government, and sites that generally focus on particular states or jurisdictions. For a job-seeking lawyer, this is an absolute gold mine.

The National Federation of Paralegal Associations

paralegals.org

This website offers terrific information on work as a paralegal, including information on how to get started, where to study, legal resources, and continuing education, as well as links to international associations and information. The Career Center offers a job database along with a directory of recruiters and a referral service.

Update Legal Staffing

updatelegal.com

This is a staffing firm offering permanent and temporary opportunities for attorneys, paralegal or legal assistants, and litigation-support personnel, all with varying levels of experience.

Resources for Verbatim/Court Reporters can be found at the end of this chapter.

Library and Information Sciences

American Association of Law Libraries

aallnet.org

"The American Association of Law Libraries was founded in 1906 to promote and enhance the value of law libraries to the legal and public communities, to foster the profession of law librarianship, and to provide leadership in the field of legal information," say the sponsors of this site. Services include information on the profession, professional development workshops offered by the association and other organizations, jobs, and other good resources.

American Library Association (ALA) Library Education and Employment Menu Page

ala.org/education

The ALA Employment Page has the latest job listings from association publications, including *American Libraries* and *C&RL NewsNet*, and groups like Library & Information Technology Association (LITA) combined with impressive links to other library job postings on the Internet.

ARLIS/NA JobNet

arlisna.org/jobs.html

The Art Libraries Society of North America provides vacancy announcements for art librarians, visual resources professionals, and related positions.

Association of Research Libraries (ARL) Career Resources Online Service

http://db.arl.org/careers/index.html

The Career Resources Online Service was established in 1996 to provide job hunters with an easy-to-use resource for finding positions in ARL libraries. Any visitor can review all listings currently posted, review only the entry-level positions, or search the listings by region, state/province, or job category.

BUBL Information Service

http://bubl.ac.uk

The BUBL Information Service, formerly called the BUlletin Board for Libraries, is an Internet-based information service for the U.K. higher education community. This site includes extensive international information resources for librarians, including job announcements for the United Kingdom, Europe, the United States, and worldwide.

C. Berger and Company: Library Consultants

cberger.com

C. Berger offers employment services including temporary positions for professional, paraprofessional, and clerical personnel as well as permanent professional library and information-management positions in libraries and information centers. Though it is based in the Midwest, its searches are not limited to this region.

C&RL News Classified Advertising, Association of College and Research Libraries

ala.org/acrl/advert3.html

These are primarily academic job listings from the monthly *C&RL News*, published by the Association of College and Research Libraries, a division of the American Library Association.

InfoCurrent

infocurrent.com

InfoCurrent is the online source for library and records-management opportunities from Telsec CoreStaff. These jobs are not limited to M.L.S. holders, and there are listings for direct hire, temporary-to-permanent, and temporary positions. You can review all jobs in its database, but you must fill out a free registration form to apply for any jobs. That is not the same as submitting your resume to its database, but Info Current does encourage you to do this too. If you are interested in these fields, then this is a wonderful source for jobs. While it tends to concentrate around New York City and Washington, DC, the jobs are not limited to these areas.

Job Resources from the University of Illinois at Urbana-Champaign (UIUC)

lis.uiuc.edu/gslis/resources/jobs.html

The Graduate School of Library and Information Science at UIUC has compiled a long list of links to resources for library and information professionals who are looking for new employment opportunities.

Job Search from *Library Journal*

libraryjournal.com/classifieds/index.asp

Library Journal, the trade journal of the library and information sciences profession, is now online, complete with the classified ads. You can either search the advertisements using keywords or browse them.

LIBJOBS

ifla.org/II/lists/libjobs.htm

LIBJOBS is an Internet mailing list for employment opportunities for librarians and information professionals. Information on how to subscribe can be found on this web page, and subscribers receive nothing from this list except job opportunities. This mailing list is hosted at the National Library of Canada and managed by IFLANET. Anyone may send messages to the list; the list is moderated, so resumes, misdirected E-mail, and spam will not be forwarded to subscribers. Persons who do not want to subscribe to the mailing list can review the automatically updated archives through the Web (you'll find the link on this page). These are split into various chronological sections, with a labeling scheme that suggests the year, month, and perhaps the week and even day.

Library Job Postings on the Internet

http://webhost.bridgew.edu/snesbeitt/libraryjobs.htm

This is a comprehensive list of resources compiled by Sarah Nesbeitt from the Maxwell Library at Bridgewater State College in Massachusetts. The descriptions include the update schedule for each site, scope of jobs included, and instructions for navigating the sites.

Lisjobs.com

lisjobs.com

Lisjobs.com is a comprehensive guide to online job resources for librarians and information professionals. The site is entirely designed and maintained by Rachel Singer Gordon, a librarian based in Franklin Park, Illinois. This is a marvelous site that hosts its own job and resume databases as well as providing links to many other resources for U.S. and international job leads.

Music Library Association (MLA)

musiclibraryassoc.org

MLA is the professional organization for music librarians in the United States. Among its many services is the Placement Service Job List, a monthly listing of open positions for music librarians across the United States. A nice feature of the Job List is the listing of recently filled positions as well as a review of positions posted in previous months. Several months of the Job List are available online.

Linguistics

Jobs in Linguistics

linguistlist.org/jobsindex.html

This site is updated almost daily, with mostly, but not exclusively, academic openings, and it provides links to other sources for job announcements. International job seekers are encouraged to review information on employment standards in various countries, while linguistics students who have not yet earned a Ph.D. can review a listing of fellowships, internships, research positions, and other opportunities open to them.

Jobs in Russia and the NISE

departments.bucknell.edu/russian/jobs.html

The Russian Department at Bucknell University has compiled a great list of resources for contacting potential employers and viewing job listings for people with Russian-language skills. According to Bucknell, "A little-known fact about foreign language study is that the job market is glutted with Spanish speakers while jobs for those with a knowledge of Russian go unfilled or are filled by less-than-qualified applicants."

Xlation.com, Resources for Translation Professionals

xlation.com

Xlation translates to *translation* for you and me, but to those who work in this field, this site is a wonderland of tools, resources, dictionaries, glossaries, and jobs!

Ministry

MinistryConnect

ministryConnect.org

MinistryConnect is sponsored by the Ministry Resource Center, a collaborative venture of fourteen congregations of Catholic Sisters, headquartered in Scotch Plains, New Jersey. This site exists to assist anyone interested in providing, finding, and encouraging meaningful work in the service of others. The effort embraces people of all faiths, helping to connect resources with needs in order to bring about a greater good for society. You can view the jobs by date, type of ministry, or geographic region. There is a small fee for placing your resume on the site.

MinistryLink: Employment Opportunities in Church Ministry

csbsju.edu/sot/MinistryLink/Default.htm

This online database of employment opportunities in church ministry is sponsored by Saint John's School of Theology & Seminary in Minnesota. You can search the job database by keywords to find openings for pastors, music directors, religion teachers, and others working in religious centers. Current positions are posted at the head of the list. Users can choose to search for listings added to the site since a certain date. MinistryLink also offers a free place for posting "position wanted" announcements and a searchable list of volunteer organizations.

Resources for Church Business Administration can be found in Chapter 4.

Nonprofits, Associations, and Foundations

ASAE CareerHeadquarters

asaenet.org/careers

This area of the American Society of Association Executives' website allows you to search its job database, post a resume, check on careers in associations, or request a critique of your resume for a fee. Job seekers will also want to check out the ASAE's great resources under Find Associations, People, Businesses for networking and targeting potential employers.

Boulware & Associates

boulwareinc.com

Boulware & Associates is an executive search firm based in Chicago. It has a nice list of searches for nonprofits at any time but it also handles searches for public and private institutions. Profiles for many of the searches can be reviewed online, and you can easily submit your qualifications for any that interest you.

Charity Channel

charitychannel.com

The Charity Channel includes discussion forums, book reviews, and a very nice job-lead bank for nonprofits in the United States. That job-lead bank carries postings from executive recruiters as well as direct hire postings.

Community Career Center

nonprofitjobs.org

This site lists nonprofit jobs all over the United States, from support staff to chief toxicologist to executive director.

ExecSearches.com

execsearches.com

This site features executive and senior-management positions in nonprofit, public sector, and socially conscious organizations. It is a search firm, but other search firms and recruiters from around the world also post here. Interested job seekers can also post a resume in its free Resume Registry.

International Service Agencies (ISA)

charity.org

The ISA's stated mission is "to help millions of people overseas and in the United States who suffer from hunger, poverty, and disease or from the ravages of war, oppression, and natural disasters." The organization is made up of fifty-five diverse agencies ranging from African medical relief funds to the Boy Scouts (overseas) and Catholic Charities. Information about each member agency is provided.

Internet NonProfit Center

nonprofits.org

The Internet NonProfit Center does not list jobs, but it does provide documents describing hundreds of voluntary and nonprofit organizations, including financial data about organizations.

JobLink from The Independent Sector

independentsector.org/members/job_postings.htm

The Independent Sector is a national leadership forum working to encourage philanthropy, volunteering, not-for-profit initiatives, and citizen action that help better serve people and communities. The JobLink lists jobs at member organizations across the country. All postings are active for sixty days; organizations may delete them earlier if a position is filled.

The National Civic League

ncl.org

Founded in 1894 by Theodore Roosevelt, Louis Brandeis, and other turn-of-the-century Progressives, the National Civic League (NCL) is a community-focused advocacy organization. The site highlights grassroots efforts from around the United States and covers every field, from prenatal care, parent education, and job training to school-based health clinics, affordable housing, and community-oriented policing.

Nonprofit Career Network

nonprofitcareer.com

The Nonprofit Career Network is dedicated to the nonprofit sector of today's business and economic world. The website is a good source of information on nonprofit organizations and job and volunteer opportunities in the sector.

NonProfit Times

nptimes.com

This is an online version of the monthly newspaper for the nonprofit industry, including selected articles and the classifieds. You will also find several special resources here, such as the Salary Survey and the NPT Power and Influence Top Fifty, a list of the real movers and shakers for the past year.

Nonprofitxpress

npxpress.com

This is a publication from the A. J. Fletcher Foundation with news for the nonprofit industry. It carries daily headlines, all kinds of announcements, and resources including a nice job bank.

Opportunity NOCs.org

opportunitynocs.org

Opportunity NOCs (Nonprofit Organization Classifieds) was launched by The Management Center of San Francisco in 1986 as a print newsletter of job openings in the nonprofit sector. Today, in addition to this national website, there are six regional print editions across the country in Atlanta, Dallas, New England, Northern California, Philadelphia, and Southern California. The site contains all levels of jobs in the nonprofit sector, as well as links to other nonprofit sites and job sites. Jobs listed on the website do not represent all the jobs found in the regional print editions. Information on the regional editions plus links to their sites can be found under Resources/Print.

Professionals for Nonprofits, Inc.

nonprofit-staffing.com

This is a staffing firm for the nonprofit industry, and job seekers can review many of the positions it is working to fill through its site.

FUND-RAISING

Chronicle of Philanthropy Career Network

philanthropy.com/jobs

The *Chronicle of Philanthropy* is probably the leading news source for development professionals. Its online Career Network includes employment opportunities, compensation news and trends, career information for those interested in fund-raising, and much more. The job leads from the current issue plus the immediate past issue are online, but you must be a paid subscriber to access the current listings. It also has listings for persons who are new to the field. Don't forget to check the links to online resources at the bottom of the page or you'll miss a list of links to many more good resources for nonprofit jobs.

Philanthropy News Digest from the Foundation Center

http://fdncenter.org/pnd/current/index.html

Philanthropy News Digest's website includes articles and information from its print publication. There is also a Job Corner with employment listings submitted by nonprofit foundations. Job seekers will also want to follow the links back to information resources provided by the Foundation Center for more leads to potential employers.

Philanthropy News Network

http://pnnonline.org

Information on the nonprofit world is featured here, including a nice job database.

Psychology and Counseling

APA Monitor Classified Advertising: American Psychological Association

apa.org/ads

The past two months of the jobs posted in the *American Psychological Association Monitor* are browsable by state at this location.

CTOnline Classifieds

counseling.org/ctonline/classified.htm

CTOnline is the online version of *Counseling Today*, a publication of the American Counseling Association. These classifieds include an event calendar, merchandise and services that can be purchased, and employment listings.

Mental Health Net Joblink: Openings

http://mentalhelp.net/joblink

Employers of all types can post their mental health positions free of charge at this site. Resumes can also be posted at no charge.

NACE JobWire

naceweb.org

JobWire is the job announcement section of *Spotlight*, the biweekly newsletter of the National Association of Colleges and Employers (NACE). The most recent listings with openings for career counselors and human resources professionals are made available here. Career counselors will also want to comb through the full NACEWeb server for more resources and information, and job seekers likewise will appreciate the wealth of resources available to help them.

The Society for Industrial and Organizational Psychology

http://siop.org

The Society for Industrial and Organizational Psychology website includes information on this field of psychology, current and back issues of the quarterly newsletter (*TIP*), and positions available divided into academic, industry/consulting, or internships.

Social Work

NASW: National Association of Social Workers

naswdc.org

The NASW maintains this website full of information for social workers, careers in social work, and jobs. You do not need to be a member to view the jobs, but it is encouraged to help you keep track of your job-search activities. If you do not want to register, just click on New User to gain access to the job-search area.

NASW California Jobs Bulletin

http://naswca.org/jobbulletin.html

The National Association of Social Workers, California Chapter, publishes a large list of social work positions on the fifth and twentieth of each month.

Social Work and Social Services Jobs Online

http://gwbweb.wustl.edu/jobs

This site lists jobs in academe, administration, advocacy, case management, clinical social work, community development, direct practice, fund-raising, international social development, nonprofit management, social policy, research, and other areas of interest to people in social work. The career resources include links to licensing information. Carol Doelling, director of Career Services at the George Warren Brown School of Social Work, and Violet E. Horvath, M.S.W., created this site. It is supported by the Career Services Office of the college.

Socialservice.com

http://socialservice.com

This is a great place to look for a job in social services. To increase your job-search reach, any social service organization that has a website can get a free link.

Verbatim/Court Reporters

BestFuture.com

bestfuture.com

BestFuture is here to tell you everything you wanted to know about court reporting—how it is evolving and moving from the courtroom into new jobs in business and multimedia fields and even working to assist the hearing disabled through captioning technology. The career options section covers the many career paths such as scoping, medical and legal transcriptionists, and captioning as well as the more traditional courtroom services. You will also find all the information you need on the various certification programs in this field. This information is provided by the National Court Reporters Association.

Internet Scoping School

scopeschool.com

What is a scopist? "Simply stated, a scopist's job is to edit transcripts, written by court reporters on stenotype machines, into readable, easily understood English." The official National Court Reporters Association definition is "one who edits a transcript translated by CAT (computer-aided transcription) software into English, correcting mistranslations of steno notes, employing proper punctuation, English, and format." The Internet Scoping School offers an online course in scoping along with information on this career field and how to figure out if this could be an interesting choice for you.

Scopists.com

scopists.com

"This site is dedicated to the support of the professions of the scopist and court reporter by providing reference resources, word lists, employment opportunities, and just about anything of use to court reporters and scopists all over the world!" The site includes a directory of freelance scopists, a place to post job announcements, and links to useful reference sources for scopists.

Verbatim Reporters Center

verbatimreporters.com

The National Court Reporters Association (NCRA) sponsors this website. Demand for people with these skills is expected to grow more than 300 percent in the next few years due to the Telecommunications Act of 1996 and the need for more experts to aid in captioning. Sounds like a good career to consider, and this is where you can learn about this occupation, how to get the best training, and all the places that training can take you. The online version of the job bank is available to members only, but nonmembers can request a print copy by fax or mail for a fee.

Jobs in the Humanities, Recreation, Hospitality, and Personal Services

This chapter may seem to be a rather eclectic mix of occupations and disciplines, but each category includes people who provide a service to others, whether it's entertainment or assisting someone with a need. Actual job listings in these various disciplines are not as easily found on the Internet as are jobs in programming or biology, but they do exist. More important, many of the organizations that hire people in these fields are online. As a job seeker, you should first think about your options based on what you like to do and what interests you, and then match your training to the career path that will best fit these criteria. Remember that job listings might not come right out and state that a degree in English literature or dance is necessary. You need to know where the skills and training you have will fit in, along with your interests. Examine the job-listing sites in Chapter 3 for more leads, and use your creativity to explore the options.

General Arts and Humanities Sources

H-Net Job Guide for the Humanities and Social Sciences

matrix.msu.edu/jobs

This guide covers positions in history and other fields in the humanities and social sciences. A new Job Guide is posted every Monday and includes jobs, research grants, fellowships, internships, and other scholarly opportunities. H-Net is "an interdisciplinary organization of scholars dedicated to developing the enormous educational potential of the Internet and the World Wide Web."

The Liberal Arts Job Search

http://riceinfo.rice.edu/projects/careers/students/getting-a-job/liberal-arts.shtml

The Rice University Career Services Center wants you to know that liberal arts majors have a real advantage in a job search. This helpful site covers options and job-search ideas for anyone with a liberal arts (or performing arts) background.

Art and Artists

The Art Newspaper

theartnewspaper.com

This newspaper is written for "keen exhibition viewers, museum professionals, collectors, artists," and others who want to know and show where the power lies in the art world. It reports on a wide range of events and trends in worldwide art, including significant sales, theft and destruction, important new hirings, conservation, and exhibitions. Daily stories are offered on the home page, and job openings and courses in art management are listed.

The Arts Deadlines List

xensei.com/users/adl

This service lists "competitions, art contests, calls for entries/papers, grants, residencies, auditions, casting calls, funding opportunities, art scholarships, fellowships, jobs, internships, etc., in the arts or related areas (painting, drawing, photography, etc.)." There is a free list and a fee list, so if you find a lot here to interest you, a paid subscription may be to your benefit.

Arts Wire Current

artswire.org

Arts Wire is a national computer-based communications network for the arts community. It is designed to enable artists, individuals, and organizations in arts communities across the country to better communicate, share information, and coordinate their activities. Job listings appear in every issue. The "Arts Wire Current" section is accessible for free and lists a few jobs.

WWAR: World Wide Arts Resources

http://wwar.com

This is an enormous gateway for any and all information on art—visual, performing, and other (antiques, film, etc.). WWAR includes links to art image collections, artists, education, art history, museums, arts agencies, and sources for employment and staffing opportunities.

Acting and Entertainment

Artslynx Theatre

artslynx.org/theatre

This subsection of Artslynx covers all aspects of this art and entertainment field from companies to directors to original materials and more. Yes, it has some links to employment-lead sources, but it also encourages you to look at the other resources for more connections.

BackStage Online

backstage.com

BackStage is the weekly newsmagazine for the theater business, with separate East and West Coast editions. On the *BackStage* website, you can read the reviews of East and West Coast productions, check out articles such as an interview with several New York directors on how they got where they are, and scan the Performing Arts Directory to find training and education resources. People hoping to make it big will want to look over the Callboard (directors and writers) or the Daily Casting Calls (acting, staff, technical, and other listings, divided by region and including equity as well as nonequity listings). Paying members get better access, particularly to casting calls, so serious job seekers should consider subscribing.

EntertainmentCareers.Net

entertainmentcareers.net

This site lists all kinds of jobs and internships within the entertainment industry, even reporters for TV news.

Hollywood Creative Directory Online

hcdonline.com

This site offers information to help you connect to the people you want to talk to in the entertainment industry. While some portions of this site are limited to members, and many of the online databases charge a fee, the job board is free.

Playbill

playbill.com

Playbill is a great source for listings of acting and theatrical support positions on and off Broadway and throughout the United States, London, Canada, and Brazil. While you'll see the link for Casting and Jobs in the left margin and you can even search or browse the database without registering, you will need to sign up for the free Playbill On-line Club (PBOL Club) to view the job announcements.

ShowBizjobs.com

showbizjobs.com

This site features opportunities in all occupations in the film-, television-, recording-, and attractions-industry job markets. You can search the listings by region and job field or browse them by company and date of posting.

Stagebill

stagebill.com/index.html

Stagebill is the national performing arts magazine for prestigious performing arts organizations nationwide. This site includes the Performance Finder (choose a city, a date, and a type of performance, and go), in-depth articles on the performing arts, and the Roster of Arts Organizations—the groups for which the organization publishes editions (there are more than eighty). The roster includes links to available websites, and those sites frequently include job leads.

UK Theatre Web

uktw.co.uk

The UK Theatre Web probably includes everything you could possibly want to know about the dramatic arts scene in the United Kingdom, and then some.

Going to London and want to know what's on stage? It's here. Where can you get tickets? It's here. Want to study theater in the United Kingdom? Get the lists here. Looking for work in theater or movies? It's here, and not just for the actors and actresses.

Cartooning

National Cartoonists Society

reuben.org

Are you the next Scott Adams? Well, the National Cartoonists Society wants you to know what it's really like to work as a cartoonist. Check out how to go from doodler to professional doodler from the folks who really know what it's like, and see how they got to where they are now. There are no job listings here, but there is information on how to advance in this field.

Child and Elder Care

CareGuide

careguide.com

This directory contains thousands of listings for providers of child and elder care all over the United States. While it does not contain job listings, you can use the information here to locate and then contact potential employers.

Entry-Level Jobs in Hospitality, Long-Term Care, and Child Care

urban.org/employment/brochure1/index.htm

This is a report offering information on the job market and the possibilities for advancement in hospitality, long-term care, and child care. The material is useful for anyone seeking information about job requirements, expected earnings, and potential for upward mobility in these fields.

Culinary and Baking Arts

American Culinary Federation

acfchefs.org

The American Culinary Federation calls itself "the nation's largest association of cooks and chefs." If you are interested in entering this field, this is the place to look for apprenticeship programs and accredited culinary programs. The site carries bulletins on the latest news for culinary professionals, including updates on food safety and irradiation. There is a job bank for members, so if you are job searching, membership might be advisable. The resume database is open for anyone to post in (nonmembers pay a fee).

Bakery-Net

bakery-net.com

Are you interested in baking or the baking industry? Check out these links to equipment, suppliers, associations, and (of course) jobs.

BakingBusiness.com Job Center

http://jobcenter.bakingbusiness.com/jobcenter

BakingBusiness.com is a site with industry news and resources for the baking industry. There is a very nice job database here, and you can submit your resume to the free database. It also has employer and recruiter profiles.

Bread Bakers Guild of America

bbga.org

This professional guild works to provide education in the field of artisan baking and the production of high-quality bread products. You'll find recipes, tips, information on places to buy supplies and equipment, education links, and job listings at this site.

Escoffier On Line

escoffier.com

Escoffier On Line is for all food professionals from bakers to chefs to food-service managers. This is a wonderful resource to use if you are looking for a job, for education and training information in food-service hospitality or culinary work, and for other good industry links.

FoodIndustryJobs.com

foodindustryjobs.com

This site features job listings and other information for persons interested in the food, food-service, institutional hospitality, and related industries. You can search the job leads, review the employer or recruiter directories, or post your resume. Registration is required if you want to post your resume and activate the Career Scout's automatic search-and-notification service.

StarChefs

starchefs.com

StarChefs offers recipes, wine, meal suggestions, cookbooks, links to more information on cooking, and a career center that includes jobs and resumes.

US Pastry Alliance

uspastry.org

The website for this association of pastry chefs hosts listings of open jobs, but only members or paying subscribers have access to the contact information for each employer. The site will also post "situation-wanted" ads.

Dance

Artslynx International Dance Resources

artslynx.org/dance/index.htm

This is an extensive directory for resources in the performance, history, and scholarship of dance from Artslynx, a gateway for Web-based materials on the creative and performing arts. The site provides annotated links on dance-related organizations, academies, schools, companies, magazines, international competitions, and much more. A search engine that encompasses the entire Artslynx gateway is available for users who wish to search the entire site.

CyberDance: Ballet on the Net

cyberdance.org

CyberDance is a resource guide with thirty-five hundred links to classical ballet and modern dance resources on the Internet. This list includes dance companies, news and information (featuring events, auditions, and competitions), people, international information, and more.

Voice of Dance

voiceofdance.com

Voice of Dance is a directory of resources, news and discussions, and places to find out about jobs and auditions. "Begun initially as a vehicle for dance enthusiasts to voice their opinions and thoughts about dance, it rapidly blossomed into a much broader resource, providing not just bulletin boards on which to post reviews and ideas or chats with dance celebrities, but also offering calendar listings for major dance companies around the world, quick review excerpts of dance performances from all over, as well as the latest news from the arts world." It also offers a global directory of more than twenty-five thousand dance-related companies and organizations.

Fashion and Beauty

The Apparel News

apparelnews.net

This site presents news for the industry along with loads of links to the players and buyers.

BeautySchool.com

beautyschool.com

This is a directory of beauty schools and beauty colleges. You merely select the state in which you want to go to school, and the complete listing of all schools in the area will appear! Even better, at the top of each state's listing is a summary of the licenses available, required hours of training needed to qualify for a license, minimum license requirements, reciprocity of licenses between states, and what agency in each state you need to contact for further information.

FashionCareerCenter.com

fashioncareercenter.com

The Fashion Career Center features jobs for anyone in the fashion industry—models, sales representatives, pattern makers, and more. Look over the listings, or post your resume at no cost. You'll also find a few select links to other fashion-industry career sites and industry news sources.

Hair-news.com

hair-news.com/pto.html

This online magazine is set up for both consumers and stylists to learn more about hair and its care. The Stylist's Resource Center includes good lists of professional trade organizations, shows and trade events, and commercial links.

HairWorld

hairworld.com

HairWorld appears to be based in the United Kingdom, but it has a job board with listings from many countries. At the time of review, you did not need to register to review the jobs, but most were in the United Kingdom or the United States.

JobsInFashion.com

jobsinfashion.com

This is a job site for the fashion and apparel industry. Users can search the job listings, post a resume, or utilize the resources in the career center, including links to education and training resources, recruiters for the fashion industry, and more industry resources.

Women's Wear Daily Classified Ads

http://wwd.com/classified/wwdads.htm

These are all the classifieds from the print publication, including Help Wanted and Sales Help Wanted, updated every night before they go into the print edition the next morning.

Funeral Directors

FuneralNet

funeralnet.com

FuneralNet links to extensive information on funeral homes and funeral services nationwide. Employment and internship opportunities are posted in the Classified Ads section, with the most recent ads at the end of the list.

National Funeral Directors Association (NFDA)

nfda.org

The NFDA has an excellent site with good information on education and licensing requirements for this field. Details on scholarships for people interested in this area are available here, as are job listings.

Graphics, Multimedia, and Web Design

HireKnowledge

hireknowledge.com

HireKnowledge is a staffing firm with offices around the country. While it says it does hardware/software and systems, it has several postings for graphic designers and presentation designers who can use PowerPoint, Photoshop, Quark, and other graphics programs.

Silicon Alley Connections

salley.com

Salley.com is a recruiting agency serving the new media industry of New York City. Job listings for specialists in Internet/www technology, multimedia, networking, PC programming, and technical support can be found here. These even include opportunities for art directors, web programmers and developers, and copywriters.

3DSite

3dsite.com

3DSite is a server dedicated to three-dimensional computer graphics. The job list contains information on opportunities all over the world. These are arranged alphabetically by country, with the organization that is recruiting clearly noted. You can browse or search the database for free, but for a small fee you can sign up for Job by Mail. This will send you daily updates on the job listings. Note that not all of these positions require you to know programming languages! Many organizations are looking for talented artists who can use computers. A resume database is available to which you can add your information.

Update Graphics

updategraphics.com

Update Graphics offers permanent, temporary, and freelance opportunities for graphic and design artists, including advertising folks.

You may find more resources for this field in Chapter 8 under "Computing and Technology."

Gaming

Casino Careers Online

casinocareers.com

Casino Careers Online "provides a place for experienced gaming personnel, as well as other candidates and graduating students interested in careers in the gaming industry, to create and post their resumes for free." This site is a resume database service for the gaming industry, but only people matching the required qualifications will be added to the database, and only gaming companies that are registered users of this service can search the database. Qualified job seekers can post either an "open" or a "confidential" resume, which must be updated every three months to stay active.

Casino Employment Guide

casinoemployment.com

The Casino Employment Guide includes job listings, a resume database, and some links to other sources. The job listings cover a wide variety of occupations in this industry.

Hospitality

Executive-Placement Services

execplacement.com

This executive-recruiting service specializes in the retail, gaming, health care, and hospitality industries nationwide.

Hospitality Net Virtual Job Exchange

hospitalitynet.org

This site is a great source for jobs in hotels and restaurants as well as the food and beverage industry.

Hotel Online

hotel-online.com

Hotel Online is a great information source and online directory for the hospitality industry. It includes up-to-date industry news (archived for the past four days), classified ads (employment openings, positions wanted, business opportunities, etc.), a great discussion area, product and service catalogs, and special issue and trends reports prepared by several firms consulting to the industry.

Resort Jobs

resortjobs.com

This site features jobs at resorts all over the world. While they may not be the most up-to-date postings, you can find out what talent each resort is looking for and contact them to see if these or other positions are open. Resort Jobs also includes a few links to additional resources for the industry as well as for all kinds of job resources.

Museums and Archives

Museum Employment Resource Center

museum-employment.com

The Museum Employment Resource Center (MERC) lists jobs for museums and other cultural resource institutions in the United States.

Museum Professionals Mailing List

http://hclist.de/museum/index1.html

This is a moderated mailing list for professionals in "museums, universities, and other academic institutions, as well as students of the arts, cultural sciences, museology, and history." The list focuses on questions related to museums, especially museums and the Internet, but it is also intended to be interdisciplinary and may include archaeological, historical, cultural, and artistic information. Users may read the archived messages (select Archiv on the front page) or join the list through this site. Job announcements in museums are posted here, and while some were found elsewhere and copied here, many new ones also appear. The fastest way to see these is to select Subject and look for the messages marked POS at the beginning. Users should note that the list is bilingual with messages in German and English.

Music

The American Symphony Orchestra League (ASOL)

symphony.org

ASOL operates this site as a part of its effort to provide leadership and service to American orchestras while communicating to the American public the value and importance of orchestras and the music they perform. The staff works to match qualified conductors and administrators with orchestras around the country. If you are interested in orchestra management, the Fellowship Program is a must. Other good information can be found under the Career Center. Individual membership is available and encouraged for anyone interested in pursuing music or arts management as a career. It also gets you access to a special Career Development area of the website, including jobs.

Ensemble

ensemble.org

This site "collects, stores, and redistributes information relating to subjects in all areas of music as taught in our schools, and sung or played in our churches, synagogues, and communities." If it's about music, it can be found at Ensemble, including many job postings in the Career Connection section. You'll also like the links to associations, many of which host job listings on their own pages. Guest access to the conference area and job listings is available, but full participation requires you to fill in the free registration form. The Texas Choral Directors Association sponsors this site.

MusicalOnline

musicalonline.com

This wonderful collection of resources for the performing arts community includes links to organizations, resources, and even job listings! The materials and resources cover all facets of music, from academic research links to orchestras, competitions, and managers, to help with your career.

Operissimo

operissimo.com

If it is a question about operas, the performers, the halls, or the companies, you can probably find the answer here. Go to the list of opera companies and opera houses to find schedules for many and links to any available web pages, where you might possibly find a few job openings. It's unlikely they will be looking for a Carmen or a Pagliacci, but they may have other needs you can fill.

Orchestralist

orchestralist.org

Orchestralist is a mailing list providing an international forum for conductors, composers, players, and their colleagues in the orchestra business. The mailing list covers a variety of topics, including repertory, performance practice, new compositions, conducting and playing techniques, auditions, job opportunities (professional and academic), marketing, publicity, organization, and programming. The website will give you the information needed for subscribing to the mailing list, but it also hosts a nice catalog of links to more materials. For people who want to preview the list, an archive of almost all postings from the inception is available.

Yahoo! Orchestras

http://dir.yahoo.com/Entertainment/Music/Artists/By_Genre/Classical/Orchestras

Still regarded as one of the best directories of Internet information, Yahoo! has a wonderful list of links and resources for connecting with symphony orchestras all over the world. For those seeking employment in this field, visiting each orchestra's website will help in finding contact information for the group, personnel lists including the administrative staff, and notices of job openings as well as audition opportunities (they are usually listed under two different categories by the orchestras). Note that Yahoo! maintains separate lists for chamber and symphony orchestras, and be sure to check both. You may even want to move up a category or two and check the other resources they have, like chamber music.

Philosophy

The Guide to Philosophy on the Internet

earlham.edu/~peters/philinks.htm#jobs

This guide is maintained by Peter Suber, a professor of philosophy at Earlham College in Indiana. The site links to hundreds of sources for information in this field, including a variety of resources for finding employment as a student or professional. One note of warning: this site is one very long web page (367K at the time of review). You must wait for it to fully download before you can jump to the various sections, particularly the job information.

Jobs in Philosophy

sozialwiss.uni-hamburg.de/phil/ag/jobs/main_english.html

PhilNet in Hamburg, Germany, is to be commended for this excellent worldwide list of jobs in philosophy posted in any language.

Photography/Photojournalism

National Press Photographers Association

nppa.org

The National Press Photographers Association is dedicated to the advancement of photojournalism. The membership includes still and television photographers, editors, and representatives of the businesses that serve this industry. The public side of the website includes sections with information on careers, scholarships available from the organization, and schools and colleges offering courses in this field. The Job Info Bank is open to members only.

PDN Online

pdn-pix.com

Photo District News (PDN) Online carries news, product reviews, and interesting information for and about photographers and the photography industry. The classifieds include listings of equipment and businesses for sale along with help-wanted announcements.

PPA's Photocentral

ppa.com

The Professional Photographers of America site offers certification courses for professional photographers, copyright protection assistance for your work, and many other benefits. The website also includes good information for those looking to get into this business or expand their business presence, including free classified ads.

Publishing, Printing, and Bookbinding

The Bookbinders Guild of New York Job Bank

bbgny.com/guild/jb.html

The Bookbinders Guild lists employment opportunities in all areas concerned with the publishing, printing, and purchasing of books. Its list of industry resources includes links to similar organizations around the United States along with other associations and publications of interest.

Bookbuilders of Boston

bbboston.org

This is a "nonprofit organization dedicated to bringing together people involved in book publishing and manufacturing throughout New England." Its website is an excellent resource for interested users, featuring information on education and training opportunities, resources for the industry, and a job bank.

PrintStaff

printstaff.com

This staffing agency specializes in the print, copy, and digital industries. To review job listings, select a regional office and then select a job area that interests you. At the time of review, it listed jobs in bindery, duplicating, large press, prepress digital, silk screen, and other areas.

Publishers Weekly

http://publishersweekly.reviewsnews.com

Publishers Weekly is the "international news source of book publishing and bookselling." In the online companion to the print publication, you'll find weekly updates on news affecting this industry along with other services and resources you can use. It also links to other Cahners' publications, including *Library Journal* and *School Library Journal*. Under Tools and Services you'll see jobs covering the worldwide publishing industry along with links to more industry resources and associations.

Sports and Recreation

Baseball Links

baseball-links.com

This is probably the most comprehensive collection of links to baseball resources online. There are currently 8,460 unique links covering anything and everything baseball from Little League to the majors. Areas you might want to review for potential career information include Coaching/Instruction, Rules/Umpiring, Scouting & Tryouts, and Baseball Parks.

C.O.A.C.H.

coachhelp.com

C.O.A.C.H., Comprehensive On-line Access to Coaching Help, is a service to assist athletic coaches in finding information, support, equipment, and employment. The current content includes articles, associations, links to equipment providers, a discussion group area, a job board, and a resume board. You can search the jobs by title and location or opt to view all jobs at once. Note that any job with the location "Outside" is a listing from outside of the United States.

Cool Works

coolworks.com

Cool Works is the major source for jobs in our national parks, ski resorts nationwide, and other similar opportunities. Organized by state, the listings range from summer or seasonal to year-round permanent and from the person who points out where to park your car up to the manager of the resort.

The Fitness Professional's Center

http://fitnesslink.com/fitpro

This resource center includes links to professional associations, conventions, continuing education opportunities, networking exchanges, business opportunities (including job opportunities), tips on building your fitness business, and career profiles for members of the fitness industry.

FitnessManagement.com

fitnessmanagement.com

FitnessManagement.com is the online companion of *Fitness Management* magazine. Resources here include articles, news, product listings and reviews, and a great networking section filled with job listings, a calendar of events, and a directory of clubs. Registration is required to access some sections of this site, but it is free.

OnlineSports.com Career Center

onlinesports.com/pages/CareerCenter.html

OnlineSports.com is a catalog of sports memorabilia, products, and services. It also hosts a Career Center with job opportunities in all areas of the sports and recreation industry.

The Outdoor Network

outdoornetwork.com

Did you ever wish you could take your talent at fly-fishing and turn it into a job? How about leading trips into the Central American jungles? Do you think it would be great to spend a summer leading Outward Bound seminars? If so, this may be the website for you. The Outdoor JobNet is the outdoor industry's free job and resume classified service for professionals, featuring positions in experiential education, outdoor recreation, and adventure travel. According to the site advisory, "The Outdoor Network's Outdoor JobNet is for serious job seekers with previous outdoor industry experience only."

SkiingtheNet

skiingthenet.com

Just what you always wanted, a real reason to spend the whole day at the ski resort! Here you'll find jobs in the ski, snow sports, and snowboard industries. These cover jobs with ski resorts, ski shops, restaurants, and hotels or employment opportunities with snow sports gear and clothing manufacturers, suppliers, and other support entities. The site lists seasonal as well as year-round and professional positions.

Sporting Goods Manufacturers Association (SGMA)

sgma.com

The SGMA website includes all kinds of information on the sports equipment industry. There are job listings, links to member companies and their employment listings, and links to executive recruiters for this industry.

Writing, Journalism, and Broadcast Media

TELEVISION AND RADIO BROADCASTING

Broadcast Employment Services

tvjobs.com

This site includes job listings and other information for the entire broadcast industry in all fields. Among the free resources here is the Master Station Index, a searchable database of all broadcasting stations in the United States and Canada. The Education area includes lists of college programs, professional training programs, and scholarships. Under Professional Development you'll find an agent directory. And there is the Employment area with the Freelance Database, the Resume Bank, and the Job Bank. Listings in the freelance directory are available for a small fee, as is access to the job listings. A listing in the resume database is slightly more.

RRonline.com

rronline.com

RR (Radio & Records) online calls itself "the Radio and Record Industries Information Leader." It includes industry headlines, job announcements for general managers as well as radio personalities, and loads of directory-type listings for you to peruse under "R&R Exclusives." Some portions of this site are open to paying members only.

Television and Radio News Research

http://web.missouri.edu/~jourvs

This website hosts many reports on the broadcast industry written by Vernon Stone, professor emeritus at the Missouri School of Journalism (University of Missouri at Columbia). It offers "a systematic look at the people and institutions that bring you television and radio news in the United States" and addresses such topics as newsroom profitability, salaries, staff diversity, careers, and internships. With more than twenty-five years' experience in this area, Stone can give all visitors a good view of where the industry has been, where it is going, and how and where you might fit in.

WRITING, INCLUDING JOURNALISM

Editor & Publisher Online

editorandpublisher.com

Editor & Publisher is the online companion to the weekly print newsmagazine for the newspaper industry. Its Classifieds section includes employment listings for academic, administrative, editorial, advertising, production/technology, and other facets of this industry. You'll also want to use its Media Links to connect with other international news publications and outlets for more opportunities.

J-Jobs Journalism Job Bank

journalism.berkeley.edu/jobs

This site is a service to the journalism community provided by the University of California at Berkeley Graduate School of Journalism. It is an expansion of the Jobs in Journalism service hosted by Louisiana Tech and includes links to additional job-search support and career resources for journalists. Jobs are posted once a week and are removed after about thirty days.

The Journalism and Women Symposium (JAWS) Job Bank

jaws.org/jobs.shtml

In this job bank focusing on opportunities for women journalists, no listing is more than thirty days old. Look over the list of related links for more sites on journalism.

National Diversity Newspaper Job Bank

newsjobs.com/jobs/jobs.html

Visit this site for jobs in all facets of the journalism industry. While the job bank is targeted to diversity populations, it is open to all users.

National Writers Union (NWU) Job Hotline

nwu.org

The NWU site lists writing, authoring, and multimedia jobs in the United States. While anyone can view the list of jobs, the contact information for each employer is given out only to members. (All working writers are eligible to join the union.) If you land a job with the help of a Hotline listing, you must agree to pay the Hotline a nominal finder's fee, which goes to help continue the service.

NewsLink JobLink

http://newslink.org/joblink

This searchable database features positions of all kinds in journalism, including research and communication. It includes entry- to senior-level jobs and crosses the lines between academic, traditional, and online media.

Society for Technical Communications

stc.org

The Society for Technical Communications is an individual membership organization dedicated to advancing the arts and sciences of the field. Its twenty-three thousand members include technical writers, editors, graphic designers, multimedia artists, web and intranet page information designers, translators, and others whose work involves making technical information understandable and available to those who need it. The website features a really nice job database that is open to the public, listings of internships, information on research grants and scholarships, and more information about this career.

SunOasis Jobs

sunoasis.com

SunOasis lists jobs and freelance opportunities for writers, editors, and copywriters. There are also links to additional sources and job sites. It can be a little difficult to follow, but there are a lot of good things here. Be sure to check out the Writers Guide to Finding Jobs Online, a nice tutorial on how to use the Internet to help you find work.

The Write Jobs from the Writers Write

writerswrite.com/jobs/jobs.htm

Found here are listings for all kinds of writing work, including technical writing.

7

Jobs in the Natural Sciences, Health, and Medicine

This chapter leads you through sources for the natural sciences, including agriculture and food sciences, physics, chemistry, and the earth sciences, as well as the many health and medical fields. Many of the natural science and health/medical fields overlap, so don't limit your review of this chapter to just one particular heading. You may also want to review the engineering entries in Chapter 8 for related areas of interest.

General Resources

BioSpace.com

biospace.com

BioSpace is a "global hubsite for life sciences." Persons interested in biotechnology and other life sciences will find news, trends, jobs, and career information here. The job listings can be reviewed by region, company, or job category. Avid bioscientists will want to join the GenePool, its free E-mail news list.

GrantsNet

grantsnet.org

GrantsNet is a searchable, continuously updated database of funding opportunities in biomedical research and science education. It contains programs that offer training and research funding for graduate and medical students, postdoctoral fellows, and junior faculty, as well as programs in science, math, engineering, and technology for undergraduate faculty and students. This service is supported by the Howard Hughes Medical Institute (HHMI) and the American Association for the Advancement of Science (AAAS).

MedZilla

medzilla.com

MedZilla is an established recruiting site for the biological and health care industries run by a recruiting firm with several years' experience. This site includes jobs and a resume database. All resumes are kept confidential (only your brief profile is displayed online), and matches for legitimate positions are made by the MedZilla staff, who will then contact you before forwarding your information to a prospective employer.

Nature

nature.com

Nature is the weekly international journal of science. Visitors will want to check out the latest features, sign up for the daily update, and go through the Jobs and

Career section for career and employment issues, upcoming meetings and courses, announcements, employer listings, grants, and jobs.

New Scientist Jobs

newscientistjobs.com

New Scientist, a major newspaper for the scientific community, has established this site to post its popular employment leads on the Web. The publisher explains, "This site contains every job featured in the print edition of *New Scientist* over the last four weeks. You can search for jobs by area, discipline, sector, or keyword." Data are divided into public/private/academic sectors, a variety of disciplines (you can choose all), and many international geographic regions. Users can register for this site for free if they wish to use the immediate "apply online" feature, store cover letters and CVs here, save jobs, and receive a tailored E-mail alert notice. All users can review the job listings.

Post-Docs.com

post-docs.com

This is exactly what you might guess from the name, a database of nothing but postdoctoral positions. They say that most of the job listings posted here are free for all to view, but becoming a paying subscriber will "give you full access to even more postdoc job information." Anyone can post a resume here for free, and there are other good resources to recommend persons visit this site.

Science Careers

http://recruit.sciencemag.org

Science Careers is operated by the American Association for the Advancement of Science and *Science* magazine. This site includes job and career information for persons pursuing a career in any scientific field. The jobs can be browsed by company, position title, or date posted, or they can be searched by keyword combined with several limiting factors like location, discipline, type of organization, and more. Users can also sign up for the Job Alerts, a free service providing E-mail updates of newly posted job advertisements from the database, as well as career-related information.

Sciencejobs.com

sciencejobs.com

Sciencejobs.com is owned and produced by the publishers of ChemWeb.com, BioMedNet, *Cell*, and *New Scientist*. Select either the Bioscience or Chemistry job search to begin your search for industry, academic, and government jobs in a variety of fields located all over the world. Users can register for a free jobs-by-E-mail alert to be delivered on a schedule you choose and using your search criteria.

Agriculture, Forestry, and Landscaping

AAEA Employment Service: American Agricultural Economic Association

aaea.org/classifieds

This service is dedicated to M.S./Ph.D. employment opportunities in agriculture. Most have application deadlines, but check each announcement carefully as the most recent postings are sometimes intermixed with older postings. The jobs are primarily but not exclusively academic and are not limited to the United States.

American Society of Agricultural Engineers (ASAE)

asae.org

ASAE is "the society for engineering in agricultural, food, and biological systems." This is a great site for finding information and links to agricultural, biological, and environmental sources. All users also can view the recent job listings from *Resource* magazine, the society's monthly publication, easily located in the Career Resources section. ASAE members have access to a resume database on the site.

ASA/CSSA/SSSA Personnel Listings

asa-cssa-sssa.org/personnel

This is a joint project of the American Society of Agronomy (ASA), the Crop Science Society of America (CSSA), and the Soil Science Society of America (SSSA). Users can browse the position announcements from *Crop Science, Soil Science, and Agronomy News (CSA News)* and from submissions received throughout the month. The listings include government, private, supervisory, international, and assistantship/fellowship opportunities.

College of Food, Agricultural, and Environmental Sciences Career Information, Ohio State University

http://cfaes.ohio-state.edu/career

This college offers a national database of full-time, part-time, and internship opportunities received by the college. The search is set up more for the students so others may find it easier to leave all options blank and retrieve all positions. It also links to a food science and technology job bank maintained by the OSU Department of Food Science and Technology and a national database of horticultural internships, but dates must be carefully reviewed as several very old announcements were found at the time of review.

Cyber-Sierra's Natural Resources Job Search

cyber-sierra.com/nrjobs/index.html

This is a wonderful collection of links to resources for jobs in forestry, earth sciences, and other natural resource fields. The maintainer has an excellent "read me first" file on the problems in finding work in these fields.

Farms.com AgCareers

farms.com/careers

This site is a source for jobs in all areas of agriculture, including working with animal health, teaching, natural resources management, and administration/sales. The listings cover Canada, the United States, and other international locations. The site also offers several links to additional resources.

National Arborist Association

natlarb.com

This trade association of commercial tree care firms, established in 1938, "develops safety and education programs, standards of tree care practice, and management information for arboriculture firms around the world." Postings of help-wanted announcements are updated monthly, but job seekers will also want to check the links to members and other resources under Industry Information. Those exploring this field as a career option will find information on "How to Become an Arborist" under Information for Consumers.

Positions in Weed Science (WeedJobs)

nrcan.gc.ca/~bcampbel

The WeedJobs pages, which were first published on February 6, 1995, list permanent, term, postdoctoral, graduate student, and summer positions in weed science for which applications are invited. Invitations for job swaps are also posted. This site is the official online vehicle for the placement services of the Weed Science Society of America and the Canadian Expert Committee on Weeds.

Professional Lawn Care Association of America

plcaa.org

Visit this site to learn how you can become a Certified Turfgrass Professional and start a career in this growing industry. Information at this site indicates that "more than twenty-one million households in the United States spent a record $16.8 billion on professional landscape/lawn care/tree care services." The list of links will take you to several related resources and associations, and those searching for employment opportunities will find a wealth of potential employers in the Professional Locator.

You can find related resources for landscaping and landscape architecture under "Architecture and Urban Planning" in Chapter 8. Information for farm workers is included later in this chapter.

Animal Sciences, Fisheries, and Marine Sciences

American Fisheries Society Jobs Bulletin

fisheries.org/jobs.html

From the society representing fisheries scientists, here's a job bulletin listing positions at all levels in fisheries and fisheries sciences. The site managers also provide an excellent list of links to additional job sources.

American Society of Limnology and Oceanography (ASLO) Job Announcements

http://aslo.org/jobs.html

ASLO is the society dedicated to "promoting the interests of limnology, oceanography, and related sciences." Job listings include openings for biologists, aquatic scientists, postdocs, trainers, and administrators, as well as grad fellowships. Positions are posted until approximately two weeks after their deadlines have expired, and they are shown in the order received, with newest announcements at the top.

Aquatic Network

aquanet.com

Aquatic Network includes information on aquaculture, conservation, fisheries, limnology, marine science and oceanography, maritime heritage, ocean engineering, and seafood. The employment opportunities are worldwide, and the page includes links to additional resources for career and job information.

Employment Opportunities at Northwest Fisheries Science Center (NWFSC) and in Fisheries or Related Fields

http://research.nwfsc.noaa.gov/staff/jobopportunitiesmenu.html

In the words of the site sponsor, this service includes "information concerning temporary, work-study, or student internship opportunities at NWFSC. These usually target students at the University of Washington or other area colleges. Also listed are announcements sent to the center director's office advertising employment opportunities in fisheries, chemistry, and other related areas." The listings are somewhat erratic and tend to be more active during the academic year.

Equimax—Where Jobs and Horse People Find Each Other

equimax.com

Equimax provides job listings and resume services to job seekers interested in working in the horse industry, both for a fee. What you will want to look at on the site is the free hiring and career advice, including the article on "What It's Like to Work in the Horse Industry." The list of links to interesting sites includes many more resources you will want to review.

EquiSearch.com

equisearch.com

"Where horse owners click." EquiSearch.com is a site for those interested in riding, raising, or just reading about horses from Primedia, a publisher of several magazines covering horses and riding. While the many resources can lead you to potential employers, there is an Employment section within the classifieds.

HerpDigest

herpdigest.org

HerpDigest is a "free, electronic newsletter dedicated only to reptile and amphibian science and conservation." This weekly E-mail newsletter offers the latest news from the scientific general media as well as professional information. There's also information on new legislation, job notices, and related resources. Registered users can read the full text of archived articles, and this is a free service.

Zoo and Aquarium Employment Listings

http://resource.aza.org/positions

These listings are hosted by the American Zoo and Aquarium Association. People who are interested in careers or volunteer work in zoos and aquariums will find good information in the AZA Publications section, along with other links and relevant information leads throughout the site.

You may also want to review our information on veterinary medicine later in this chapter.

Astronomy

American Astronomical Society (AAS) Career Services

aas.org/career/index.htm

The site includes links to several resources for students and job seekers in this field. Among the links are the AAS Job Register, updated monthly; Resume Posting Services/Recruiters; Fellowship and Student Opportunities; and Summer

Employment Opportunities listed with the society. Other links are Job Listings, Web Career Resources, and Articles/News of Interest.

More resources can be found under "Physics" later in this chapter.

Biology

Bio.com Career Center

http://career.bio.com/pages/index.cfm

Bio.com's Career Center is a compendium of employment listings, career forums, and great career and job-search articles by Dave Jensen, an executive recruiter from Search Masters International who specializes in the biological and health care industries. While you are here, check out BioOnline's home page for links to even more biotech industry and information sources and the career discussion forums moderated by Dave Jensen.

Employment Opportunities: Bionet.jobs.offered

bio.net/hypermail/EMPLOYMENT

Employment Wanted: Bionet.jobs.wanted

bio.net/hypermail/EMPLOYMENT-WANTED

These two archives maintained by BioSci at Stanford University provide users Web-based access to the postings from the bionet.jobs.offered and bionet.jobs.wanted Usenet newsgroups.

Listings for biotechnology and biomedical engineering can be found in Chapter 8.

Chemistry

American Association of Cereal Chemists

scisoc.org/aacc

This association is an international organization of cereal science and other professionals studying the chemistry of cereal grains and their products or working in related fields. Information on employment, internships, education, and other topics is included in the website.

Chemistry & Industry Jobs On-line

chemind.org/jobs.html

This site lists jobs in chemistry from all over the world and in all employment sectors (private industry, academe, government, etc.). Click on Vacancies at the top of the page to scroll down the list of current announcements. These postings are also published in the print edition of *Chemistry and Industry* magazine.

ChemistryJobs.com/ChEJobs.com

chemistryjobs.com

This site lists jobs in chemistry and chemical engineering. All of the jobs show the date of posting, and visitors may also find links to additional employers.

JobSpectrum.org from the American Chemical Society (ACS)

jobspectrum.org

This job and career information service for chemical professionals is not limited to ACS members. There are a few areas that are limited to ACS members, but the majority of this site, including the job listings and resume database, is open and free for all visitors.

Organic Chemistry Resources Worldwide

organicworldwide.net

This is a nice metasite for organic chemists involved in academic or industrial research. There are links to journals, databases, dissertation collections, reviews, guides, patents, and current awareness sources. The resources for laboratory work include links to chemical product databases, laboratory safety bulletins (in pdf), products and services, and much more. The site also includes a plethora of links to organic chemistry labs worldwide, as well as links to possible job sources (along with its own small job database).

Environmental and Earth Sciences

E Jobs

ejobs.org

E Jobs links to environmental opportunities in the United States and Canada, including careers in fields such as environmental engineering, nature and wetlands science, geographic information systems, chemistry, earth science/geology, policy and law, wildlife conservation, planning, education, wastewater treatment and operations, program and project management, and natural resources. It also maintains its own listings and links. You will not want to miss the list of employers in environmental fields.

Earthworks

earthworks-jobs.com

Earthworks lists jobs in geoscience, environmental science, ecology, conservation, and other related positions. It is operated by a small advertising agency based in Cambridge, England. The Earth-Ocean-Atmosphere-Space Links button will connect you to a huge list of links to more resources.

Ecological Society of America Career and Funding Opportunities

http://esa.sdsc.edu/opportunity.htm

The Ecological Society of America posts job announcements that are submitted to the *ESA NewSource*, a bimonthly publication, as well as funding opportunities. These pages provide specific listings for individuals looking for internships, employment, or additional funding to further their careers and research in ecology. The job announcements are updated on the fifteenth of each month, or the next closest business day. Student job seekers will want to review the online Careers in Ecology brochures for information about the field of ecology and for links to related websites. There are two versions available— one for high school students and one for undergraduates.

EE-Link: The Environmental Education Web Server

eelink.net

EE-Link connects you to environmental education resources online, including job and grant opportunities and links to environmental organizations and projects. There are several sources for job information here. From the front page select the link for EE Job Resources. The main part of this consists of links to other sites with job listings, but in the left menu you'll see links for their Enviro Ed Job Search, a metasearch capability that will scan for jobs on specific sites listing jobs in EE, and View EE Jobs, a link to EE-Link's own database of job announcements. However, review the entire site for information on grant opportunities, professional resources, and much more. EE-Link is a project of the North American Association for Environmental Education.

EnvironmentalCareer.com

http://environmental-jobs.com

This site from the Environmental Career Center in Virginia has comprehensive environmental and natural resources job listings that cover all experience levels

---

INTERNET TIP:

E-mail Access. You should have a personal E-mail account for your online job search. This way, you can participate in mailing lists, sign up for newsletters and job-announcement services, and even place your personal E-mail address on your resume. If you gain access to the Internet through a public workstation such as those at your local public library, if your office is your primary Internet access point, or even if you would just like a "private" E-mail address to use for your job search, you can register for free E-mail services that will allow you to send and receive E-mail through the Web. Check "Online Networking" in Chapter 1 for more information.

from entry-level to senior management. There are even listings for environmental support jobs and career changers.

Environmental Careers Organization

eco.org

This group lists paid internships in environmental areas.

Environmental Sites on the Internet

lib.kth.se/~lg/envsite.htm

Developed and designed by Larsgöran Strandberg, lecturer and information scientist in industrial ecology at the Royal Institute of Technology in Stockholm, this is a huge site with links to information on all areas of environmental work. Because of its size, users may find the site difficult to navigate, but the time spent is worth the effort.

Entomology

Entomological Society of America

entsoc.org

Among the many other resources here, the society hosts listings for jobs and internships in entomology along with a short list of links to additional sources for jobs and internships or graduate assistantships. Whether you think you might be interested in studying bugs or just want to figure out what these people really do, the Educational Resources section has guides to entomology, the work of entomologists, and how to prepare for a career in this field.

Job Opportunities in Entomology

colostate.edu/Depts/Entomology/jobs/jobs.html

The entomology department at Colorado State University hosts listings for openings in the field. The site also links to other resources that may have job openings.

Farm Workers

Migrant and Seasonal Farmworkers Sites

http://wdsc.doleta.gov/msfw/html/msfwlink.asp

This list, provided by the National Farmworkers Jobs Program of the U.S. Department of Labor, links employers and laborers to resources and organizations designed to help them with funding, housing, health, education, and work conditions.

Michigan Agriculture Migrant and Seasonal Farm Worker Program

michaglabor.org/index_agriculture2.jsp

Michigan is going online to recruit migrant workers by postings jobs on this site sponsored by the state. In addition to job openings, the site profiles growers, types of crops, living conditions, and wages for potential workers. With Internet access available in most public libraries and state job offices, migrant workers everywhere should be encouraged to log onto this website for employment and support service information.

Forensics

This field covers many disciplines and is adding areas of study all the time.

American Academy of Forensic Sciences

aafs.org

This is "a professional society dedicated to the application of science to the law. Its membership includes physicians, criminalists, toxicologists, attorneys, dentists, physical anthropologists, document examiners, engineers, psychiatrists, educators, and others who practice and perform research in the many diverse fields relating to forensic science." You can review information on a career in forensic sciences (including emerging disciplines), check the many employment opportunities covering this diverse field, look for educational institutions offering programs leading to this field, and much more. This is a very rich resource.

American Society of Crime Laboratory Directors

ascld.org

This is a nonprofit professional society devoted to the improvement of crime laboratory operations through sound management practices. The site includes information on meetings and accreditation of labs, links to additional forensic societies, and jobs.

Education in Forensic Science from Forensic DNA Consulting

forensicdna.com/index.htm

"Our goal is to provide both the professional and lay community with education resources in the field of forensic science. We provide a general framework for thinking about forensic science and integrate all the different specialties through that framework." They have a nice summary on careers in this field, a short list of classes they offer, and links to additional resources.

Forensic Resources from the Law Offices of Kim Kruglick

kruglaw.com/forensic.htm

This site features more than seven hundred links to forensic sites and information sources covering firearms, facial recognition, forensic experts, arson, chemical and toxicology, and much more.

Geospatial and Geographic Information Systems

Find Executive and Technical Search

find-gis.com

Find is a recruiter specializing in geographic information systems (GIS) and automated mapping/facilities management (AM/FM).

GeoJobSource

geojobsource.com

GeoJobSource is a great resource for spatial data professionals. You can review the jobs by date of posting or by region. Announcements at the time of review cover the United States and the Middle East. The Resource Directory links you to academic departments, professional organizations, and other resources including career and job resources.

GeoPlace

geoplace.com

GeoPlace.com calls itself "the world's leading provider of geospatial information." It is the online home for several publications in this field from Adams Business Media, and each offers several articles along with events, product news, and people news. The Geo Resource area includes links to product information, the Geo Directory with its listings of associations and employers, and a small career center.

GIS Jobs Clearinghouse

gjc.org

This clearinghouse is a great source for jobs in geographic information systems (GIS), image processing (IP), and global positioning systems (GPS). It also provides links to additional information and resources. You can post a resume here for free.

Meteorology

American Meteorological Society

ametsoc.org/ams

The American Meteorological Society promotes the development and dissemination of information and education on the atmospheric and related oceanic and hydrologic sciences. Founded in 1919, AMS has a membership of more than eleven thousand professionals, professors, students, and weather enthusiasts. The site includes publications from the association, a career guide for the atmospheric sciences, certification information, a directory of local chapters, and employment opportunities in a variety of organizations.

Physics

American Institute of Physics: Employment and Industry

aip.org/industry.html

Jobs in the academic, industry, and business worlds are updated on this site every two to three days. You should also review the great links to related sites for more employment information.

PhysicsWeb

http://physicsweb.org

PhysicsWeb is a great resource for persons in this field. It covers news, product reviews, web links, articles from *Physics World* magazine, and physics jobs. All the jobs, studentships, and courses advertised in the magazine are automatically placed on this server. You can quickly and easily search through the listings to view quality positions in academia, industry, and commerce.

PhysLink

physlink.com

PhysLink was founded to provide comprehensive research and education tools to physicists, engineers, astronomists, educators, students, and all other curious minds. Within all of the wonderful resources here is the Job Board with listings for corporate, academic, graduate, and postgraduate opportunities.

Veterinary Medicine

Association of American Veterinary Medical Colleges

aavmc.org

The Association of American Veterinary Medical Colleges represents more than four thousand faculty, five thousand staff, ten thousand veterinary students, and three thousand graduate students studying and working in veterinary colleges, departments of veterinary science, and noted animal medical centers in the United States and Canada. Visitors will find information on preparing for a career in veterinary medicine, applying for admission to a veterinary college, and job listings in member institutions plus similar institutions around the world.

VeterinaryLife.com

http://veterinarylife.com

This is a source of classified ads for veterinarians and vet techs from all over the world. These include veterinarian jobs offered or wanted, clinic jobs offered or wanted, and equipment and practices for sale. A review of the "clinic" jobs showed several jobs for vet techs and nurses, some with larger hospitals like Angell Memorial in Boston.

VetQuest

vetquest.com

VetQuest lists classified ads directed to persons in veterinary medicine. You'll want to select the "Positions Offered" listings from the right panel to search the listings. The listings here include postings for full-time and part-time D.V.M.s, vet techs, hospital and clinic managers, partners in established practices, as well as intern/extern opportunities. Persons wanting to take over an existing practice can search through the "Hospital Sale Lease Buy" listings.

Health Care and Medicine

GENERAL RESOURCES

Academic Physician and Scientist (APS)

acphysci.com

APS is a joint effort of the Association of American Medical Colleges and Lippincott Williams & Wilkins. This site lists open academic medical teaching positions and research fellowships for U.S. medical schools and affiliated institutions.

America's HealthCareSource

healthcaresource.com

This site brings you jobs in the health care industry along with good links to licensing and professional associations.

Classified Advertising for *JAMA*, *American Medical News*, and the *Archives Journals*

ama-assn.org/cgi-bin/webad

This searchable database includes the current employment listings for many of the publications of the American Medical Association. You can select a region or state and then choose as many specialties as you wish in order to collect all relevant openings for your search.

Experimental Medicine Job Listings

medcor.mcgill.ca/EXPMED/DOCS/jobs.html

This official job board of the Canadian Society of Biochemistry and Molecular & Cellular Biologists (CSBMCB) includes jobs from all around the world. The listings are primarily for placements in academic and government research facilities. You'll also find links to fellowships and even more job resources.

Health Care Job Store

healthcarejobstore.com

This site lists jobs for the health care industry. Many targeted databases within the main database cover disciplines and specialties in the field. We suggest that at first, you search both the main database and your select niche sites to be sure you find all the announcements that interest you, until you are more familiar with the site's listings and cross-posting procedures.

Health Careers Online

healthcareers-online.com

This is a source for jobs in all areas of health care, including administration and management.

HealthWeb

http://healthweb.org

HealthWeb is a collaborative project of the health sciences libraries of the Greater Midwest Region of the National Network of Libraries of Medicine and those of the Committee for Institutional Cooperation and is supported by the National Library of Medicine. The participants set out to create a site to "provide organized access to evaluated noncommercial, health-related, Internet-accessible resources." Choose an area of interest from the list of topics and take a look at the numerous resources linked within each. Several areas include a specific heading for career information, but those that don't will have information on potential employers within their resources. Searches on the keywords *career* or *employment* will take you to those areas the fastest.

MedHunters

medhunters.com

MedHunters lists jobs for all health care professionals in locations all around the world. Users can browse the listings by location or profession. One very nice feature here: each location or profession notes the number of job listings it contains.

Medimorphus.com

medimorphus.com

Medimorphus is a career and employment site for health care professionals. Do a quick job search, review employer profiles, check on continuing education opportunities, and get help with licensing, all right here. Registration is not necessary to search or apply for jobs, but if you do register, you can use its one-step online application.

Monster Healthcare

http://healthcare.monster.com

This zone of Monster.com features career and industry information targeted to health care professionals along with job announcements. While you could find these jobs in its main database, it's easier to search just the health care subset of the job listings from here and avoid the many thousands of listings that don't necessarily relate to your interest. However, don't skip over the main job database. A quick check by the reviewer found different results from the same basic search.

Physicians Employment

physemp.com

Job listings for physicians, nurses, and other allied health professionals make up the Physicians Employment site. The listings can be searched by specialty and location, and your visa status is needed. Military positions are also included.

Dental

American Dental Association (ADA)

ada.org

Job seekers will find the ADA to be a good source of information on all careers in dentistry, including dental hygiene, dental assisting, and dental laboratory technology. Select the Profession area from the front page to access the Education and Careers section, which has all you need on how to prepare for a career in dentistry, including job listings.

Hospice Care

National Hospice and Palliative Care Organization (NHPCO)

nhpco.org

This organization's website includes information on hospice care that will prove helpful to persons interested in this line of work as well as those interested in utilizing these services. NHPCO also maintains an excellent searchable directory of hospices as well as a Career Center with job and resume postings.

Mental Health

Mental Health Net

http://mentalhelp.net

This site is an excellent resource for information on all topics related to mental health. Job opportunities are available through JobLink, under the Professional Resources category. Be sure to check the date of postings, as the reviewer found many that were quite old. Users should also note that the most recent postings are found at the end of the search results page.

Also see the listings under "Psychology and Counseling" in Chapter 5.

Midwifery

MidwifeJobs.com from the American College of Nurse-Midwives

midwifejobs.com

This site holds employment opportunities as well as excellent information on a career as a certified nurse-midwife. Users can register to store a resume here at no cost, making it possible to use the Submit Resume feature found on each job announcement. Registration is not required to search the database, and contact information for each employer is noted.

Nursing

National NurseSearch

nursesearch.net

National NurseSearch is a recruiter working to fill nursing openings in many specialties and at all experience levels. You can read brief job announcements, but all are "blind" and include instructions on submitting your resume to the firm for consideration.

Nursing Spectrum

nursingspectrum.com

This is the online companion to the regional magazines, and along with good career information, it is a nice job database. Interested users can also sign up to be notified when the job database is updated, usually every two weeks or less.

Pharmaceutical

InPharm.com

inpharm.com

InPharm.com provides "executives in the pharmaceutical and health care industries with relevant information services such as news, views, jobs, directories of services, and thousands of links out into the Net." Job seekers will appreciate being able to search this international database by location, type of business, or specific recruiting firm. Jobs are not dated, but they are posted for two months.

International Pharmajobs

pharmajobs.com/index.html

At this site, you can search for jobs in the worldwide pharmaceutical and chemical industry as well as biotech. Several career and industry links keep you connected and informed about your world. All jobs are displayed for eight weeks but are not dated.

Pharmacy Week

pharmacyweek.com

Pharmacy Week's website includes job postings, articles, and links to more information from the weekly print magazine. Browse the job listings by category, search the listings for those in a particular location, or view all listings at one time.

Physical, Occupational, and Massage Therapy

American Massage Therapy Association

amtamassage.org

This site from the professional association for massage therapists presents great information on what massage therapy is and how you can become a massage therapist, along with other news and information, including select articles from the association journal. It's a great resource for people considering this career option. A job-lead bank is available to members only, but if this is your career field then membership is recommended.

RehabTime.com

rehabtime.com

RehabTime is an online resources site that is focused mostly on the "rehab team," including physical therapy, occupational therapy, and speech therapy. Users will appreciate the free job listings and continuing education information along with resources for those in this field.

Public Health

Career Espresso

sph.emory.edu/studentservice/Career.html

Career Espresso is the Career Action Center from the Rollins School of Public Health at Emory University. It is a fun yet very useful resource for professionals in the field, featuring its own source of job listings and links to several other good information sources. The Featured Menu Items are open to all visitors, and the House Specials are generally restricted access and intended for students of the school.

Public Health Resources on the Internet

lib.berkeley.edu/publ/internet.html

This guide to public health information is maintained by the Public Health Library at the University of California, Berkeley. It is a great source of information on the field of public health and includes links to associations and other resources for professionals.

Jobs in Engineering, Mathematics, Technology, and Transportation

Presented here are all the fields and occupations with any relation to engineering, technology, and transportation. These include all of the engineering specialties, as well as mathematics, construction, mining, public utilities, unions, and manufacturing. You may want to look back at Chapter 7, "Jobs in the Natural Sciences, Health, and Medicine," for some related areas.

Because of the length of the Computing and Technology section, it is at the end of the chapter.

Multiple Fields

AEJob.com

aejob.com

Hall & Company operates this site, which lists jobs nationwide for engineering, architecture, and environmental consulting firms. Jobs are available at a variety of levels.

Alpha Systems

jobbs.com

Alpha Systems is a contingency recruiter for technical, industrial, and engineering fields and industries. Top jobs are posted at the website, and resumes can be submitted for a specific job or for future consideration. While no dates are included on the announcements, the site removes a listing as soon as the search for that job closes.

ASTM International Directory of Testing Laboratories

astm.org/labs

According to the American Society for Testing and Materials site, "The ASTM International Directory of Testing Laboratories is an on-line full-text search for services and locations of testing laboratories. The information on the types of tests performed, specific tests performed, materials analyzed, or other services offered has been provided by the laboratories. ASTM has not attempted to investigate, rate, endorse, approve, or certify any laboratory. Each laboratory has paid ASTM a fee for their listing." Search by location, lab name, subject area, products, services, or keyword of your own choosing.

ContractJobHunter

cjhunter.com

This is the new website from *Contract Employment Weekly*. It specializes in job openings for contractors and consultants in engineering, IT/IS, and technical disciplines and includes all the jobs from the print publication as well as those posted here. The job listings are open only to members, but the fee is quite reasonable.

DiversiLink

diversilink.com

DiversiLink is sponsored by the Society for Hispanic Professional Engineers (SHPE), and this site is dedicated to assisting its members in finding work, preparing resumes and cover letters, and exploring their career options. The job listings, student opportunities, and virtual career fairs are open to all to view. A private resume database and a mailing list for job announcements are also available, and all users are invited to participate.

Engineering Job Source

engineerjobs.com

This free site lists jobs for engineers and technical professionals. Browse the listings by state or search by keyword. The site also hosts a resume database where you can list your resume free for ninety days.

EngineeringJobs.com

engineeringjobs.com

This site features links to company employment pages as well as to recruiters, engineering societies and organizations, and resumes of engineers seeking employment.

MentorNet

mentornet.net

MentorNet is the online presence of the National Electronic Industrial Mentoring Network for Women in Engineering and Science. "We pair women who are studying engineering or science at one of our participating universities with professional scientists and engineers working in industry, and help them form E-mail-based mentoring relationships." Potential mentors can find information on joining the program at this site. Those who want to be mentored but are not a student at a participating university can use MentorNet's links to find additional programs and services through other organizations.

National Society of Professional Engineers (NSPE)

nspe.org

The NSPE website provides excellent career information for anyone interested in any engineering specialty. Under the Employment heading is a collection of resources from career tips and job listings to salary information and lists of NSPE member firms for you to contact. Other areas of the site include more information on this career field, networking opportunities, and the PE (professional engineer) licensure. Membership is required to participate in some services like the resume board, but it will be worth the investment.

SWE: The Society of Women Engineers

swe.org

SWE's mission is to "stimulate women to achieve full potential in careers as engineers and leaders, expand the image of the engineering profession as a positive force in improving the quality of life, and demonstrate the value of diversity." The website includes tremendous information and career/employment resources for women interested in or currently pursuing engineering careers.

Tech/Aid

techaid.com

Tech/Aid is one of the TAC Worldwide Companies. It is a staffing company specializing in contract professionals for engineering and manufacturing applications, including engineers, CAD operators/technicians, lab support personnel, designers, technical writers, and technicians.

TechEmployment.com

techemployment.com

TechEmployment.com is devoted to the IT, IS, tech management, and engineering fields. You are not required to register your resume here, but it makes it easier to apply for jobs that interest you because not all those who post put direct contact information in the descriptions.

Aeronautics and Aerospace

AeroWorldNet

aeroworldnet.com

This site is a central resource for information and news on the aerospace and aviation industry. It includes classified ads along with links to industry and professional associations and aerospace companies. The jobs are not dated, and we do not know how long the listings remain active.

American Institute of Aeronautics and Astronautics (AIAA)

aiaa.org

At this site, the association rolls out loads of good information for you to review in your career or job search. Start with the Market Pulse section to find information on careers in aerospace, job listings from *Aerospace America*, industry insights, links to related resources, and a list of the AIAA corporate members. The Calendar of Events section will help you find conferences, workshops, and courses you can take to meet others as well as advance your career, and under Participate with AIAA you'll find a list of its sections so you can connect with those in your region.

Astronaut Selection from NASA

nasajobs.nasa.gov/jobs/astronauts/index.htm

Here's your chance to be a part of this exciting program. The National Aeronautics and Space Administration (NASA) has a need for pilot astronaut candidates and mission specialist astronaut candidates to support the Space Shuttle and Space Station programs. NASA is accepting applications on a continuous basis and plans to select astronaut candidates every two years, if needed. Persons from both the civilian sector and the military services will be considered. This site includes all the information you need on qualifications, applications, positions, pay, and much more.

Space Careers

spacelinks.com/SpaceCareers

Space Careers carries job listings along with links to hundreds of sources for employers, industry news, and information that spans the entire world. It is well organized and easy to review very quickly, but it is heavy on the graphics and takes time to download and display.

Space Jobs

spacejobs.com

Space Jobs connects you with employment opportunities in the aerospace industry worldwide while keeping you up-to-date with the news of the industry. Review the list of jobs currently posted, and review information on each employer so you know who they are before you apply. Job seekers will also be interested in the list of events, allowing you to easily plan your networking activities.

Architecture and Urban Planning

American Planning Association (APA)

planning.org

You will find great information on careers in planning and affiliated fields along with jobs posted with this professional organization. Check under People, Jobs & Consultant Services for employment listings, but don't skip the Educational Opportunities & Careers in Planning section, where you'll find more information about this field plus conferences and other professional development opportunities. The many chapters listed under APA will also connect you to local information and networking opportunities. APA's Jobs Online job listings are open to the public and may be listed for little as one week, so you will want to check this site weekly if it is a part of your search plan. There is also a separate *JobMart* print newsletter issued twice a month (subscription information is on the site). Ads in Jobs Online are not copied to

JobMart, nor are the *JobMart* ads copied to Jobs Online, so you'll need both to get the full list of leads.

American Society of Landscape Architects (ASLA)

asla.org

ASLA's website includes information on careers in landscape architecture and continuing education, a list of landscaping firms, notices of scholarships and internships, and job openings. In other words, it's possible to learn about this career field, find an accredited program, study the industry, and get a job all right here at this site. A resume database is available for members and nonmembers, but nonmembers pay a much higher price for posting. Jobs are listed by date of posting and appear in order from newest to oldest.

Architecture.com

architecture.com

This is the official home page of the Royal Institute of British Architects (RIBA). The heart of the site is an indexed collection of hundreds of annotated links to architecture resources from around the world, though it focuses mainly on Britain (search the links by keyword or browse them by category/subject). The Careers section is a wonderful exploration of the field, from how it affects society to the training necessary and where to get the training. While this is all wonderful for any reader, much of the really good stuff (like where to study and how to pay for it) is dedicated to the United Kingdom. Other features here include a registry of architects in the United Kingdom, information on events and competitions, site of the day, a bookshop, and a job board (riba-jobs.com).

E-Architect, the American Institute of Architects

e-architect.com

This site includes excellent career and job information along with many resources for professional development and networking with others in the field. Anyone interested in a career in architecture will learn much from what is here.

Cyburbia, the Planning and Architecture Internet Resource Center

cyburbia.org

This is an excellent starting point for your career and job search. Cyburbia is a terrific list of resources for jobs in planning, architecture, and some landscape architecture. It is operated by a single individual who doesn't always have enough time to get all the editing done, but he's been doing this since 1994 and has earned our respect for his longevity, expansive coverage of the resources in this field, and continued efforts. The Cyburbia Café contains discussion boards where anyone can read or participate in discussions, and at the bottom of this page you'll find a link to the jobs board. Please note that any "Hire Me" or resume notices will be removed from the boards immediately.

Gaines International

gainesintl.com

Gaines International is a search firm for the design and building industry (architecture, interior design, real estate, construction, engineering and landscape).

Job Hunting in Planning, Architecture, and Landscape Architecture

lib.berkeley.edu/ENVI/jobs.html

Created by the Environmental Design Library at the University of California, Berkeley, this is a selectively annotated guide to help job seekers in the professions of architecture, landscape architecture, and city/regional planning. This guide is not a resource for job listings but an outline of the complete job-search process targeted to those in these career fields and listing resources and links to job-lead sources. While many annotations and resources are specific to resources available from the University of California, all who review the site will find it useful as a guide to the many resources available to assist in a job search. Almost all resources noted can be accessed in almost any public or university library.

Automotive

JobJunction Executive Search and Recruiting Services

jobjunction.com

This firm is based just north of Detroit, and the website features many searches for automotive engineers, trim experts, and manufacturing professionals, along with the usual software, medical, and sales/marketing professionals. JobJunction does not limit searches to the Detroit area, but it is a particularly strong source for the automotive industry in this region. The job leads listed on the site may be outdated, but use them as a guide to the kinds of searches done by this firm and submit a resume if you are someone they may want to talk to for other positions.

The Society of Automotive Engineers

sae.org

The Society of Automotive Engineers includes nearly eighty thousand members in more than ninety-four countries worldwide who share a common interest in advancing mobility technology. This includes engineers, business executives, educators, and students. The website includes info on the association, its conferences and training opportunities, and job leads.

WardsAuto.com

wardsauto.com

WardsAuto.com is the online companion to many of Ward's publications covering the automotive industry, including *Ward's AutoWorld* and *Ward's Automotive Reports*. This site is packed with all kinds of news, including people, manufacturers, suppliers, and industry developments. From here you can also gain access to the websites for some of their other publications.

Aviation

Airparts.com

airparts.com

This is a terrific resource for those who need to find aircraft or aircraft parts, or those who are involved in the operation or maintenance of aircraft. The Classifieds section includes a place for employment postings, both help wanted and position wanted. The most recent posts are at the bottom of the page.

Aviation Employee Placement Service (AEPS)

aeps.com

AEPS is a source of jobs for all occupations and fields in the aviation industry, from executives to mechanics and including both general and corporate opportunities. Access to listings of current jobs requires a paid subscription, but a free trial subscription is available so you can test the database.

AVJobs.com

avjobs.com

The Airline Employment Assistance Corps (AEAC) and AVJobs.com offer an online resource that brings together employers and employees in the aviation industry. Offerings for paying members include a job database, a resume service, and other career guidance resources. Free resources found here include excellent career information covering many specific fields within this industry.

Find a Pilot

findapilot.com

This site includes public job announcements for flight instructors, corporate and other pilots, mechanics, helicopter pilots, and others. For a fee, you can post your resume here. There's also a list of links to additional aviation sites for you to use.

Biotechnology and Biomedical Engineering

Medical Device Link

devicelink.com

This service is targeted to the people who design, manufacture, and market medical devices. The Career Center includes an annual salary survey, a salary estimator work sheet, and job listings, while the rest of the site includes news, events, extensive links to suppliers and consultants, and links to even more information. Registration is required to view jobs and use some other special features on this site, but it is free.

There are many more resources for this field in Chapter 7.

Camera Repair

Fargo Enterprises Inc.: Gateway to the Camera Repair Industry

fargo-ent.com/index.html

Stop by this site, and you can search for industry news, repair shops, manufacturers, or repair manuals and also learn about the correspondence courses available for people who want to learn how to repair cameras. Moreover, Fargo will connect you to the associations for this trade.

Chimney Sweeps

Chimney Safety Institute of America

csia.org

This is "a nonprofit educational foundation that has established the only nationally recognized certification program for chimney sweeps in the United States." Visitors can check the site for great consumer information on safe chimneys and how to find a certified professional or learn how to become a certified sweep.

National Chimney Sweep Guild

ncsg.org

This guild is an organization owned and managed by chimney service professionals dedicated to making life and business better for every sweep. Persons interested in working as a chimney sweep can find information on apprentice programs here.

Civil Engineering

American Society of Civil Engineers

asce.org

The American Society of Civil Engineers (ASCE) represents more than 123,000 members of the civil engineering profession worldwide and is America's oldest national engineering society. The site is divided into Public Information and Professional Community. The Public Information side includes career information such as a description of civil engineering, how to get started in this field, and lists of colleges and universities offering degrees in the many disciplines that make up this field. The Professional Community includes a Career Development area with a job bank divided into civil engineering or university positions.

Review the sections "Construction and Public Works," "Mining, Drilling, and Offshore," and "Surveying" in this chapter, as well as "Environmental and Earth Sciences" in Chapter 7 for more information and resources.

Construction and Public Works

A/E/C JobBank

aecjobbank.com

This is a large job and resume resource for the architecture, engineering, and construction community, with thousands of postings. These are cross-posted to other building portal sites, so don't be surprised to find them elsewhere.

American Public Works Association (APWA)

apwa.net

The APWA site is a tremendous resource for information on the many fields covering public works, featuring a stellar list of links to related professional and trade associations. The association also hosts a nice job board with opportunities sorted by region.

Builder Online

builderonline.com

This extensive website for construction professionals includes features such as the searchable Builder 100, a ranking of companies in the industry with profiles and contact information for each. Users will also like the product database and industry news from the print magazine and other sources. There is also a Talk area that includes a place for folks to trade information on job openings. From this site you can also reach the online websites for other magazines from the same publisher, Hanley-Wood. This site came highly recommended from someone who said it was a good resource for project managers, purchasing agents, and other similar fields in this industry.

CLP Resources

clp.com

CLP Resources, Inc., formerly Contract Labor Pool, provides quality, skilled tradespeople to a broad range of clients. CLP maintains offices throughout the United States, making it one of the largest suppliers of skilled tradespeople and construction labor in the country. The people whom CLP hires are contracted out to work on a variety of jobs. You can review the current openings and the benefits of working for CLP and start your application right here.

ConstructionOnly.com

constructiononly.com

ConstructionOnly.com is a small but specific site for the construction industry. The job leads are divided into Management and Craft. We suggest merely using the "View All" option in each database as the fastest way to review the listings.

ConstructionWebLinks.com

constructionweblinks.com/index.html

This site bills itself as "the nation's most comprehensive guide to architecture, engineering, and construction resources on the Internet," with annotated links to more than three thousand sites. Links are organized by topic under the headings of Organizations, Industry Topics, Resources, and Prior Issues. Some of the topics break down further to help users find the relevant resources more quickly. Professionals in these fields will appreciate these sources plus the extensive links to Jobs and Careers along with the Organizations. A little tip: the list of sites under Find Personnel is only slightly smaller than the one under Jobs and Careers, and they do not necessarily have the same listings.

The Electronic Blue Book

thebluebook.com

Check in here for online access to continually updated construction industry information. The publishers of the regional editions of *The Blue Book of Building and Construction* have combined their many guides into one free and easily searched online resource. Job seekers interested in this industry can use this resource to target potential employers.

Engineering News-Record (ENR)

enr.com

The weekly publication of the construction industry provides news and resources for the industry and for the job seeker. The Career Opportunities section posts several weeks of job listings online, but don't skip the lists of ENR's top-ranked firms in various fields.

PublicWorks.com

publicworks.com

PublicWorks.com includes jobs, industry news, and resources. The jobs listed here have salary ranges from $25,000 to more than $100,000 and cover all occupations involved in public works. Have your resume ready in plain text so you can take advantage of the online application. Some positions may also require you to register your resume with PublicWorks.com in order to apply, but registration is free.

Right of Way

rightofway.com

This site, sponsored by Allen, Williford & Seale, Inc., has good information along with job listings for the industries and occupations related to this field. Jobs are posted for ninety days. If you aren't sure what is meant by "right of way," check the FAQ.

Electrical Engineering

EE Times.com

eet.com

EE Times.com is the online companion to the industry journal for electrical engineers. Check the industry news, events listings, product reviews, and career information. The careers area includes a Q&A section by Nick Corcodilos, author of *Ask the Headhunter: Reinventing the Interview to Win the Job* (Penguin/Plume, 1997); its annual salary survey; job listings from TheWorkCircuit.com; and other great resources.

Electronic News On-Line

http://electronicnews.com

News and information for electrical engineers and related industries are the focus of this site. The Employment Classifieds section is somewhat limited.

IEEE (Institute of Electrical and Electronics Engineers) Computer Society's Career Service Center

http://computer.org/careers

The Career Service Center is provided to assist members of this IEEE division in their efforts to further their careers or search for new positions in the computer science and engineering community. All users can review the job postings and most other information resources, but only members of this IEEE division will be allowed to post their resumes in the database.

IEEE (Institute of Electrical and Electronics Engineers) Job Site

http://jobs.ieee.org

Here you'll find jobs, job resources, and career advice for IEEE members and others in electrical engineering. While some services are limited to members, the job listings and employer profiles are open for the public to review.

Electrical engineers and other computing professionals may want to review other IEEE societies and councils for more information to assist with their careers and job searches. The full list of these can be found on the IEEE website (ieee.org) under "About IEEE." Even more career and employment resources can be found under "Career and Employment."

Environmental Engineering

See "Environmental and Earth Sciences" in Chapter 7.

Facilities Engineering and Maintenance

Association for Facilities Engineers (AFE)

afe.org

AFE is a professional organization of nine thousand members bringing together professionals who ensure the optimal operation of plants, grounds, and offices at Fortune 500 manufacturers, universities, medical centers, government agencies, and innovative small firms around the world. The CareerNet link connects you to Quantum Careers, a general job site listing employment opportunities in many fields and locations.

Association of Higher Education Facilities Officers

appa.org

This international association is dedicated to maintaining, protecting, and promoting the quality of educational facilities. The membership also includes specialized institutions, such as medical and law schools, seminaries, and other nonprofit organizations, such as public and private kindergarten through twelfth-grade schools and districts, military installations, and city/county governments. Job listings here are updated weekly with a few weeks being archived at any time. Industry news is also provided, and there is a separate section with information for people working in kindergarten through twelfth-grade institutions.

FacilitiesNet

facilitiesnet.com

Facility engineers and others involved in plant maintenance will want to review the news, suppliers, and other information here. If you are job searching, the Career Development section contains a nice Career Center with job announcements, a resume database, and the SalaryBase, a tool you can use to check how your pay rate stacks up to others in your area. FacilitiesNet also offers a nice Peer Networking area along with links to associations and related web resources.

Finishing

Finishing.com

finishing.com

This website is dedicated to professionals of the metal finishing industry, those who coat, anodize, plate, and otherwise cover everything. There are chat rooms and links to technical resources, events, professional societies and related organizations, job shops, consultants, and suppliers, all of which are sources of potential opportunities. The site also hosts Help-Wanted and Situation-Wanted boards.

Fluid Dynamics

CFD (Computational Fluid Dynamics) Jobs Database

cfd-online.com/Jobs

The CFD Jobs Database is filled with jobs in this field. The listings are sorted into industry, academe, postgrad, Ph.D., full time, contract, and country/continent. This is a service of CFD Online, and you should examine the entire site for even more links to potential job sources and employers.

Food and Beverage Processing

At-sea Processors Association

atsea.org

The At-sea Processors Association (APA) represents U.S.–flag catcher/processor vessels that participate in the healthy and abundant groundfish fisheries of the Bering Sea. This site lists information on the companies operating these ships and links to additional industry and related information, many of which could be used as sources for employment listings. It also includes information on the realities of working on the oceangoing processing plants, and anyone considering this work should read these descriptions carefully.

FishJobs

fishjobs.com

This site lists employment opportunities in seafood, fisheries, or aquaculture companies seeking to fill sales, marketing, management, operations, or quality control positions. Opportunities are categorized by geographic region, and postings are retained for as long as six months. Many listings include direct contact information for the employer, while others do require you to submit your resume to H. M. Johnson & Associates, the recruiters who operate this site.

Processfood.com

processfood.com

This is a service of the Food Processing Machinery and Supplies Association, a nonprofit trade association representing more than 350 suppliers of the machinery, equipment, supplies, and services used to prepare the world's beverages and processed foods. The Industry Jobs section has listings of openings posted by member companies, but you must look at the full listing to see the date it was posted. The Product Locator and Industry Directory areas can help you find potential employers and connect to more resources.

Professional Brewers' Page

http://probrewer.com

This site features a Market Guide, a Library, a section on Legal Issues, and Classifieds, along with other terrific information for people interested in the brewing industry. The entries in Classifieds include employment listings, but check the dates on postings because many are old. The Market Guide includes a Supplier Search, so you can look for vendors that supply materials, equipment, and even cleaning supplies. The Library is extensive, with both local brew news and scientific studies. Grab some demographic and market studies from the Research Center, follow the links to the industry online, chat with others in the business, and even review profiles of other visitors to these pages, including chemists, production managers, and sales and marketing pros. This is not only a handy industry resource, it is also very international!

Winejobs from WineBusiness.com

winebusiness.com/services/industryjobs.cfm

This site lists wine industry jobs from big-name wineries, distributors, universities, and more. You can search the jobs by category, location, and company. Job seekers can also post job-wanted announcements on a community board. Persons interested in even more industry information will enjoy checking out the WineBusiness.com Directory.

Footwear

Footwear Industries of America

fia.org

Footwear Industries of America is the only national association for footwear manufacturers, importers, distributors, and suppliers to the leather and allied trades. The single best thing here is SoleSource, the searchable directory of the footwear industry. You can look for companies, products, brand names, or industry category (noting that Executive Search Firms is a category).

Shoemaking.com

shoemaking.com

Shoemaking.com is a source for news, equipment, a directory of worldwide manufacturers of footwear, and jobs.

Heating/Ventilating/Air-Conditioning

HVACJob

hvacjob.com

This site serves the heating/ventilating/air-conditioning (HVAC) and controls industry employers and job seekers. Positions are for management-level, executive-level, and field-skilled industry professionals, including residential, commercial, and institutional contractors; wholesaler/distributors; manufacturers; building owners and managers; and consulting engineering firms. The jobs listed in the Job Search section cover many fields, but the Hot Jobs are specific to HVAC. There's also a list of links to employment pages of the Air Conditioning Contractors of America (ACCA), but you must access it by starting with Job Search on the front page.

House Painting

College Pro Painters

collegepro.com

College Pro Painters is painting houses all over the United States and Canada. You can review job descriptions, local franchises, and benefits through its website. You can even apply for a job or a new franchise here.

Industrial Design

Core77 Design Magazine and Resource

core77.com

Industrial designers are the people who create toys, develop new TV sets, and even redo the entire Tupperware line! This area will fill you in on the field and the benefits, offer advice for freelancers, and connect you with the education and training opportunities—and the jobs. The job board, Coroflot (coroflot.com) lets you post a portfolio as well as search for employment. Core77 also gives you a frequently updated list of design firms to contact for internships, co-ops, and employment.

Instrumentation/Control/Automation

ISAJobs.org

isajobs.org

ISAJobs.org lists employment opportunities and resume postings for vacancies in all industries that use instrumentation, control systems, and automation equipment. The job listings are open for all to review. ISA members may post a resume in the database for free. Non-ISA members are required to pay $50 to post a resume. All listings are automatically deleted after eight weeks. ISAJobs.org is a service of the ISA, the Instrumentation, Systems, and Automation Society (isa.org). The ISA website is filled with much more information on the field, including certification and training resources.

Logistics

JobsInLogistics.com

jobsinlogistics.com

JobsInLogistics.com lists jobs and hosts a resume database for people in logistics-related fields (customer service, distribution, inventory management, supply chain, transportation, warehousing, etc.).

Manufacturing

Kolok Enterprises

kolok.net

This recruiter specializes in engineering, technical, and manufacturing management. A partial list of current openings is available on the website, but you will have to contact the recruiter for more information on any that interest you.

Link Staffing Services

linkstaffing.com

Link Staffing offers temporary employment and permanent placement in the light industrial, manufacturing, and skilled crafts and trades industries through more than forty offices across the United States. Job seekers can review current searches or find the nearest office and call.

Manufacturing Marketplace

manufacturing.net

Manufacturing Marketplace is a great source for general information on the manufacturing industry. There is terrific industry news divided into sections on Design, Processing and Automation, Plant Operations/MRO, and SupplyChainLink. The Careers section includes links to training information, and the Resources list with its links to Associations and more will help you find more information and resources.

Rothrock Associates, Inc. (RAI)

raijobs.com

RAI focuses on materials and procurement, engineers for design and manufacturing, and all human resources disciplines for plant, division, and corporate locations.

Maritime

International Seafarers Exchange

jobxchange.com

Dedicated exclusively to the global cruise and maritime industry, this site sets up direct connections among cruise and maritime companies, crewing agents, maritime schools, universities, and prospective crew members. The CrewXchange area with the job listings requires a fee to view the database, but people who are considering work on the seas can review the many job descriptions for free. BlueSeas International operates this site.

The Seafarers International Union

seafarers.org

The Seafarers International Union (SIU), Atlantic, Gulf, Lakes, and Inland Waters District, AFL-CIO, represents unlicensed U.S. merchant mariners sailing aboard U.S.-flag vessels in the deep sea, Great Lakes, and inland trades. The union also represents licensed U.S. mariners in the Great Lakes and inland sectors. SIU members sail in the three shipboard departments: deck, engine, and steward. They work aboard a wide variety of vessels, including commercial containerships and tankers, military support ships, tugboats and barges, passenger ships, gaming vessels, and many more. They also sponsor the Paul Hall Center for Maritime Training and Education, located in Piney Point, Maryland, a vocational training facility operated by an SIU-affiliated entity. Information on entering a training program is available through the website.

Materials/Metallurgy

ASM International

asm-intl.org

ASM is a professional society for materials engineers. Guests can review much of their information, including journals, newsletters, and directories of suppliers, as well as discussion forums with many job postings.

MaterialsJobs.com

materialsjobs.com

MaterialsJobs.com lists jobs for materials specialists.

Mathematics

American Mathematical Society

ams.org

This association website is a great resource for all mathematicians. The employment services are for Ph.D. mathematicians and include public job listings, the Academic Job Search Booklet, articles on job searching, and links to related job resources. Others in this field should look at the Career and Education page for information on pursuing or furthering a career in mathematics.

Listings for actuaries can be found in Chapter 4.

Mechanical Engineering and CAD/CAM

ASME, the American Society of Mechanical Engineers

asme.org

This website for mechanical engineers includes information on professional development, industry news, and jobs and internships. A nice feature of the job bank is the division of jobs among internships, entry-level (zero to two years' experience), and three-plus years' experience. ASME publishes several journals and newsletters that you will want to review.

The following websites list jobs for specialists who know how to use a variety of CAD/CAM (computer-aided design/computer-aided manufacturing) software programs.

AutoCAD Job Network

acjn.com

Job listings involve AutoCAD skills.

CATIA Job Network

catjn.com

Job listings involve CATIA CAD/CAM/CAE skills.

IDEAS Job Network

ideasjn.com

Job listings involve SDRC CAD/CAM/CAE skills.

Pro/E Job Network

pejn.com

Job listings involve Pro/ENGINEER CAD/CAM/CAE skills.

SolidWorks Job Network

swjn.com

Job listings involve SolidWorks CAD skills.

UG Job Network

ugjn.com

Job listings involve Unigraphics CAD/CAM/CAE skills.

Mining, Drilling, and Offshore

Drilling Research Institute

drillers.com

This site started for the purpose of marketing a CD, but the author and organizer has expanded the site to include a place for job listings as well as links to associations, recruiters, industry suppliers, and job sites. You should definitely read his Dayrates and Warning sections. Dayrates is a survey of highest and lowest pay rates for particular jobs in specific countries, so that's a good source of information. The Warnings section includes information on bad employers as well as employment scams and other problems that drillers have reported.

InfoMine

infomine.com

This is probably the most informative mining site on the Internet. You'll find information on equipment, companies, education and training, events, countries, and much more. InfoMine's CareerMine includes many job listings from around the world along with a list of recruiters and a resume database. The problem is many of the areas (including most of the job listings) are limited to subscribers, but if this is your field, then the subscription is a wise investment.

The *Mining Journal*

mining-journal.com

This online resource links to many other publications and resources for the mining industry, including companies and projects. Abbreviated employment opportunities from the weekly print journal are posted here.

Mining USA

miningusa.com

Here you will find mining industry jobs in the United States and internationally. All of the ads carry the date of posting. Other great information on the industry is also available at this site.

Offshore Guides

offshoreguides.com

This site started as a way to let people know about a book, *The Complete Offshore Employment Handbook*, but it has expanded to include more employment information for this field. The job listings might not be the most up-to-date, so posting a resume may be a better way to connect to the employers. While you are here, look over the handbook, including rig types, employment trends, and work conditions.

Oil and Gas Online

oilandgasonline.com

This is a nice source of oil and gas industry information online. There are links to product suppliers, which can be used to target potential employers, and the News and Community section keeps you up-to-date with news, technical forums, event calendars, and much more. The site also hosts a nice job and resume database and offers a simple salary survey you can use to compare your own earnings to those posted by others.

Petroleum Place

petroleumplace.com

Petroleum Place is a source for information and resources on the worldwide oil and gas industry. If you are looking for jobs, it has a pretty nice career area with listings, links to sources, and a free public resume database.

Thomas Mining Associates

thomasmining.com

Thomas Mining is a U.K.-based recruiter specializing in the worldwide mining and quarrying industry.

Musical Instrument Repair

National Association of Professional Band Instrument Repair Technicians (NAPBIRT)

napbirt.org

This is "a nonprofit organization that supports the activities of quality professional band instrument repair technicians." NAPBIRT lists the schools that have courses in band instrument repair and related classes as part of a full-time structured program. Association membership is open only to school-trained technicians (in a NAPBIRT-approved learning situation) or technicians who have been on the job for a minimum of five years on their own or have apprenticed for a period of five years. In addition, members must be presently working in a legal, licensed operating business. There are no formal apprentice programs in place, but many repair technicians will help you learn more about training and may consider taking you on as an apprentice.

Occupational Safety and Industrial Hygiene

American Industrial Hygiene Association

aiha.org

This association represents the people who are concerned with occupational and environmental health and safety issues. This is "an organization of more than 11,500 professional members dedicated to the anticipation, recognition, evaluation, and control of environmental factors arising in or from the workplace that may result in injury, illness, impairment, or affect the well-being of workers and members of the community." Job seekers will like the employment listings and information on members and consulting groups.

NSC Crossroads, National Safety Council

crossroads.nsc.org

This search engine and news network from the National Safety Council (NSC) was created to provide safety, health, and environmental (SHE) professionals with information, tools, and contact information. Site highlights include a dedicated SHE search engine and collections of articles, expert commentary, and related online resources organized in ten categories. Featured articles are also listed on the front page. A small job bank with open positions and "job-wanted" postings is available.

Osh.Net

osh.net

Osh.Net is made up of more than thirteen hundred links to occupational safety and health information and resources. These include feature articles, FAQs, an internal search engine, a bulletin board, employment postings, and a free newsletter.

Safestyle.com

safestyle.com

Safestyle.com, focused on safety and health resources, is sponsored by an occupational safety consulting firm. The job listings here are available through paid subscription, but qualified professionals can submit a CV for inclusion at no cost in the list of Expert Witnesses. If you are a professional in this field or someone in need of more information, you can use the list of links to several online sources.

Optics and Photonics

Optics.org

http://optics.org

Optics.org is sponsored by the Institute of Physics (IOP). Within this rich resource is a great employment area with job listings and a resume database that are both free and open to the public.

Photonics Jobs

photonicsjobs.com

Photonics Jobs is an employment resource for persons in the laser, fiber-optic, and photonics industries. You can search job listings by location and category or keyword, or you can easily view all jobs in the database by clicking on

"Search by Criteria" without any criteria. If you'd prefer, you can review the jobs by categories like engineering, quality, technician, or pre-IPO.

TateWeb Optoelectronics Portal

tateweb.com

TateWeb is a source of industry and technical news for optics and photonics specialists as well as links to corporate pages and a small job site called OpticsJobs.com. "Tate Associates serves the advertising, public relations, and new-media needs of companies that sell to OEM and end-user technical markets, with our specialty the optics and photonics industry."

Plumbing

PLUMBjob.com

plumbjob.com

PLUMBJob.com "serves contractors, wholesalers, consulting engineers, building owners and managers, and municipalities needing skilled plumbers, estimators, engineers, PE, project managers, foremen, sales, sales managers, sales engineers, installers, and many more." The job database is not really specific to plumbers but does include several good listings. The Hot Jobs section lists nothing but plumbing jobs.

Public Utilities

American Gas Association

aga.org

This trade association is composed of about three hundred natural gas distribution, transmission, gathering, and marketing companies in North America. The site gives you good industry news, the current issue of *American Gas Magazine* (including the job listings), a list of member websites, a searchable handbook covering the publicly traded member companies, and more. When you review the job listings, look at the date of posting noted within each, as the publication information at the top of the page is confusing.

American Water Works Association (AWWA)

awwa.org

AWWA is an international nonprofit scientific and educational society dedicated to the improvement of drinking water quality and supply. Its more than fifty thousand members represent the full spectrum of the drinking water community: treatment plant operators and managers, scientists, environmentalists, manufacturers, academicians, regulators, and others who hold genuine interest in the water supply and public health. Membership includes more than four thousand utilities that supply water to roughly 180 million people in North America. This site is awash in job listings, links to water utility sites, links to local sections, industry and government regulation info, and much more.

ELECTRICJob.com

electricjob.com

ELECTRICJob.com "serves contractors, wholesalers, consulting engineers, building owners and managers, REC's and utility companies needing skilled electricians, linesmen, lineworkers, energy professionals, engineers, BSEE, PE, project managers, foremen, sales, sales managers, sales engineers, relay technicians, and many more." The Job Board covers several industries, but the Hot Jobs are just electric jobs.

Energyjobs.com

energyjobs.com

Energyjobs.com is a partnership between Careersite.com and Energy.com to create a source for the many energy companies to post and recruit and a place where the "energy experienced" can look for new opportunities. Free membership is encouraged but not required. If you want to browse the employers, note that it has the "preferred" list and a separate alphabetical list with all employers.

Platts Global Energy

platts.com

Platts is the specialist energy market reporting company of the McGraw-Hill Companies. Platts initially reported only on U.S. petroleum markets, but in more than seventy-five years of reporting has concentrated on covering the international energy markets. In addition, Platts also reports on oil, petrochemicals, nonferrous metals, shipping, power, and natural gas. Under "Community" in the left navigation bar you will see a link to the Job Bank containing listings from *Power Magazine* and *Electrical World T&D*.

PowerMarketers.com

powermarketers.com

Here you have news, information, and employment opportunities for people experienced in managing and marketing power, courtesy of the Power Marketing Association. This organization represents the entire spectrum of the U.S. electric power industry, including independent power marketers and brokers, regulated utilities, unregulated utility affiliates, and providers of products and services to the industry.

Semiconductors

Semiconbay.com

semiconbay.com

Semiconbay is a portal to information on the semiconductor industry. It includes links to industry reports as well as good career information found on other sites. It also supports a job-lead bank.

Surveying

LandSurveyors.com

landsurveyors.com

This is a bright, flashy, commercial page with information for all surveyors. It contains links to hundreds of resources for the surveyor, including a Surveyors Directory with listings of professional surveyors and surveying firms in the United States and Canada. There is an area for job classifieds, but the few postings were rather old at the time of review.

More information on jobs in surveying can be found in this chapter under "Construction and Public Works," "Mining, Drilling, and Offshore," and "Architecture and Urban Planning."

Telecommunications

Daily News—The Independent Source for Wireless Industry News

rcrnews.com

This is a gateway to two online resources for the wireless communications industry. Published by Crain Communications, *RCR Wireless News* is updated daily with a mix of breaking news and in-depth analysis into the issues that mold today's wireless telecommunications environment. *Global Wireless* is updated weekly and provides analysis, data, and news on international wireless markets, the wireless Internet, industry players, technology trends, and product developments. There is a Job Bank, but the age of the posted notices is not apparent.

Open System Consultants

opensystem.com

Open System is a national executive recruiting firm located in Southern California specializing in providing key engineering, marketing, and management talent to growing start-up and multinational telecommunications, wireless, and datacommunications-development companies.

Wireless Week

wirelessweek.com

This is a companion to the weekly newspaper covering all the business, technology, and regulatory news in the cellular, personal communications services, paging, specialized mobile radio, private mobile radio, wireless data, satellite, wireless local loop, and microwave fields. The JobBank includes "help-wanted" listings in several fields.

Transportation

TransportNews.com

transportnews.com

This website contains possibly all the news you could want on the transportation industry, updated daily. There are no job listings here, but the extensive resources connect you to other sources, plus numerous potential employers.

Trucking

1800Drivers.com

http://1800drivers.com

This is a good source of job leads and job information for the trucking industry. If you are new to the industry, there are many postings for companies willing to train you. You will get brief information on the jobs, but registration is required to view the full listings. No mention of fees is made on the site, but users may want to verify this. Related information at this site includes lots of good, useful links for truck drivers and others who might be interested in this industry.

Union Hiring Halls

IBEW Construction Jobs Board

ibew.org/jobs_board.htm

This is the official job network for the construction branch of the International Brotherhood of Electrical Workers. Select your country (United States or Canada), then the location, scale, and/or date of posting of the job, and go. Job calls are posted directly by the local unions themselves. All listings contain information on whom to contact for more information or to apply for the openings.

Union Jobs Clearinghouse

unionjobs.com

Union Jobs Clearinghouse lists union staffing and trade/apprenticeship positions across the United States. This site was set up to centralize these position announcements. You can review the staffing listings geographically or alphabetically by posting organization. At the time of review, very few positions were listed under Trade/Apprenticeship, and those we saw were quite old.

Computing and Technology

Job-lead and recruiting sources for this field are well established online. The entries in the following sections represent a small sample of all the information and resources available through the Internet for job seekers in these fields.

GENERAL RESOURCES

Association for Computing Machinery (ACM)

acm.org

ACM provides most of its online resources for members, but nonmembers will find several areas open for review. The chapter listings will connect you to local professionals who share your interests, and many maintain their own websites. The career opportunities are open to the public, but the majority of these listings are for academic positions. ACM members have access to an even larger array of career services, so you may want to consider joining.

Harry's Job Search Internet Hot List

http://jobinfo.freeyellow.com/index.html

Before there was the Internet, there were bulletin boards (BBS) that carried job listings for computing professionals, and Harry's Job Search BBS List was the place you went to find out where to go. Most of the BBS have disappeared, but Harry is still looking for the sources that will help you find a job. This helpful source is a gift from one computing professional to his colleagues.

STAFFING FIRMS, RECRUITERS, AND RECRUITING SITES

Alpha Systems

jobbs.com

Alpha Systems is a contingency recruiter for technical, industrial, and engineering fields and industries.

Aquent

aquent.com

Aquent supplies companies with graphic designers, web designers, production artists, presentation graphics experts, writers, illustrators, project managers, and desktop support talent on a freelance, permanent, and try-before-you-hire basis. They have been rated very highly by the designers and other talented individuals who work for them. Look over some of the current opportunities, submit your resume, and review the benefits of being a part of the Aquent team, all online.

The Beardsley Group

beardsleygroup.com

Beardsley is a recruiting and placement firm looking for professionals in the areas of IT/internetworking and biotechnology.

BrassRing.com

brassring.com

BrassRing is one of the larger and better employment sites for IT professionals. It includes job listings, career tips, and a virtual job fair.

ComputerJobs.com

computerjobs.com

This Internet-based advertising service posts technical job and career information for computer professionals. The site is divided into geographic and skill areas to make it easier for you to target the opportunities that interest you, but keyword searching is also possible. A nice feature here for non–U.S. citizens is a flag on opportunities posted by an employer willing to sponsor a work visa for you.

Computerwork.com

computerwork.com

This site offers job listings and a resume database for computing and technical professionals. Candidates can search for jobs by skill set, employment type, or location using the extensive Computerwork.com Family of Sites. In addition, when candidates post their resumes, they can choose to have their resumes E-mailed to member firms whose requirements match their qualifications and preferences.

Developers.Net

developers.net

Developers.Net lists jobs for software developers.

Dice.com

dice.com

If you wanted to search only one site online, then Dice.com should be it. This is probably the best single site for IT professionals. Dice.com has been consistently rated very highly by recruiters looking for IT talent, which means they are using this site and liking it a lot. As a job seeker, you will appreciate the job listings, online resume database, and other good career tools. Some services will require you to fill out the free registration form. Dice.com is a service of EarthWeb.

ERP Jobs

erp-jobs.com

This is a place for enterprise resource planning (ERP), supply chain management (SCM), execution management (EM), customer relationship management (CRM), business intelligence (BI), E-commerce, EDI, enterprise application integration (EAI) professionals, website developers, LINUX experts, end-user organizations, software firms, implementation service companies, and complementary software firms to advertise their career and contract opportunities and their availability. Jobs are categorized by enterprise area (SAP R/3, JDEdwards, Enterprise Asset Management, etc.). There is also a nice list of corporate subscribers for you to review. The jobs are not dated, but they remain active for only thirty days.

Hall Kinion International (HKI), Asia Pacific

tkointl.com

HKI Asia Pacific, formerly known as TKO, provides services for International (Asia-Pacific) professionals, managers, and individual contributors for the semiconductor, software, and communications industries. To this end, the company partners with North American and Asia-Pacific high-tech firms to find the key people necessary to carry out their business strategies. You can review openings they are working to fill and sign up for a free monthly newsletter with new openings.

HireKnowledge

hireknowledge.com

This staffing firm features jobs for creative, technical, and management professionals. You can search for jobs using keywords, review jobs listed with a specific office, or display the entire list for easy scanning.

Instructional Systems Technology: Employment Opportunities

http://education.indiana.edu/ist/students/jobs/joblink.html

Specialists in instructional systems technology (IST) build and test processes, products, systems, and services for use in education and training settings. In this case, "technology" is much broader than hardware and software development. IST includes analysis, design, development, evaluation, and implementation/management of instructional systems and other learning environments. Jobs you might find here include course developers, human performance researchers, usability specialists, media specialists, and much more.

ITCareers.com

itcareers.com

ITCareers.com is part of the ITWorld network of IT trade magazines, including *ComputerWorld*, *JavaWorld*, and much more. At the time of review, we saw listings for electrical and mechanical engineers included in the job database.

New Dimensions in Technology, Inc.

ndt.com

This is a fairly good job resource for engineering, marketing, sales management, consulting, and IT at all levels in the technology and computing industry, nationally and internationally. Job searching is easy, and resumes can be submitted online.

NTES: National Technical Employment Services

ntes.com

NTES lists jobs from all over for techies. Users can search the leads or scan the list of recruiters using this service and connect to the recruiters' sites for leads.

SoftwareJobs.com Home Page

softwarejobs.com

This is the home of Allen Davis & Associates, a respected search firm specializing in software and IT search and placement. Professionals will want to review the technology-specific newsletters, many of which list jobs. You can also search the entire job-lead bank using keywords.

Starpoint Solutions

http://starpoint.com

Formerly known as TIS Worldwide, Starpoint Solutions is an information technology staffing firm as well as a systems development firm. You can search the internal openings or the openings Starpoint is working to fill for its Fortune 1000 clients, or you can review contract assignments it is currently handling.

techies.com

techies.com

This site lists jobs and projects for IT professionals around the United States and also offers good career and professional development information and resource links. Registration is required in order to apply for the jobs posted here, meaning you will need to store your resume in the database, but you have the option of making it available to employers searching the database. An interesting feature is the ability to research lists of employers based on a geographic region. The site has expanded its offerings to allow headhunters (i.e., recruiters) to post jobs here, but these postings are retained in a separate database.

Volt Services Group

volt.com

Volt provides varied services to the telecommunications industry and operates a technical and temporary staffing business. Jobs available through Volt cover a broad spectrum of technical as well as administrative support positions for the industries served.

ZDNet Careers

zdnet.com/special/filters/techjobs

This career site for computer industry and information technology professionals is sponsored by Ziff-Davis, publisher of many IT and computing magazines.

TRADE PUBLICATIONS AND PROFESSIONAL SOCIETIES

AECT Placement Center

aect.org

The Association for Educational Communications and Technology provides leadership in educational communications and technology by linking professionals holding a common interest in the use of educational technology and its application to the learning process. The Career Information Center contains a Job board you can search in a variety of ways from job title to location to salary range. Not all of the jobs posted here are in academic institutions. Many are with large companies that need instructional technology professionals to develop in-house training programs.

ComputerWorld

computerworld.com

This website accompanies and expands on the weekly print IS/IT trade publication. If you are considering a career in computing, or are an experienced professional who wants to keep up with the latest developments, this is the place to learn everything you need to know about what to expect, where to go, and what to do once you get there. Most readers will want to home in on the Careers area with its job listings, surveys, and career-related articles, but the entire site has much to offer.

Computing Research Association (CRA)

http://cra.org

CRA is an association of more than 180 North American academic departments of computer science and computer engineering, industrial and government laboratories engaging in basic computing research, and affiliated professional societies. The site includes public job listings for computer science, computer engineering, and computing research professionals. Most positions listed here are with academic institutions.

DBWorld Mailing List Archives

http://groups.yahoo.com/group/dbworld

The DBWorld mailing list is intended for messages of interest to the database research community, including job postings, conferences, and journal announcements. Nonmembers can search the mailing list archive, but members will find active participation to be a great networking source. You can search the archive by keyword or review postings by date. Job announcements are frequently tagged with the subject word *job*, but you should also be prepared to look around for listings without that tag.

InternetWeek

internetweek.com

This is the information networking trade journal from CMPNet focused on information for Internet-driven enterprises. To this end, the site is an excellent resource for what's happening in the industry and how it can affect your career. For more job and career resources, *InternetWeek* links to IT Week CareerDirect, a centralized resource operated by CMPNet for all of its online trade journals. CareerDirect lists jobs, allows you to post a resume, and provides links to more career resources for computing and technology professionals.

Women in Technology International (WITI)

witi.com

The WITI Foundation, founded in 1989, is an association dedicated to advancing women in technology. The Foundation helps women develop the core competencies in demand by all levels of technology organizations and brings women to the attention of organizations and boards looking for strong talent. While the website is geared toward women of all ages and levels of experience, it offers excellent career and job information to all.

9

Opportunities in Government, Public Policy, and Public Service

This chapter covers domestic opportunities for employment in public service, as well as with government agencies and departments and the institutions that work closely with them. International governments listing employment opportunities on the Internet are included under the appropriate heading in Chapter 12.

U.S. Federal Government

The federal government is one of the largest employers in the United States and probably the most diversified. You can find listings for employment opportunities in several locations online and can examine all of them at no charge. Be sure to check the dates on the listings and to note all job code numbers. You might need specific forms in order to apply, or you might be asked to include information with your application that is not on your resume, so check for "Information on Applying" at any of the sites.

Federal Computer Week

fcw.com

This companion to the print magazine for information technology professionals in the U.S. government also includes links to job opportunities, associations, and career resources in computer, government, and related sites on the Web.

Federal Jobs Digest

jobsfed.com

Federal Jobs Digest, a private resource for listings of federal jobs, is nicely arranged by job group (science, administration, and law enforcement) and easy to use. Click on Live Jobs to reach the current vacancies, which include some blue-collar positions.

Federal Jobs Net

http://federaljobs.net

This career center provides links to federal agencies along with a Job Hunters Checklist, advice for your federal government job search, and step-by-step guidance through the process. Author Dennis Damp has made much of the material from his book *The Book of U.S. Government Jobs* (seventh ed., Brookhaven Press, 2000) about federal job hunting accessible online.

FEDIX

http://content.sciencewise.com/fedix

FEDIX (Federal Information Exchange) is an outreach tool that provides grant information to educational and research organizations from participating federal agencies. It also provides access to some employment opportunities. You'll see some crossover with MOLIS (see upcoming entry).

FedWorld Federal Job Search

fedworld.gov/jobs/jobsearch.html

FedWorld was established in 1992 to serve as the online gateway to information disseminated by the federal government. The FedWorld Federal Job Search uses files created by the Office of Personnel Management (OPM) in Macon, Georgia. These are the same files and job announcements you can find in the USAJobs website, and FedWorld links to those listings. You can search jobs by region or state and by keywords. For a more complex search, use of USAJobs is recommended, but FedWorld's search allows you to look at the database in a different way.

GovExec.com Careers

govexec.com/jobs

A service of *Government Executive* magazine, this site features a weekly Federal Career Corner, salary and training information, and OPM job listings for senior executives. The site features information for veterans and listings for positions in the labor-relations field and careers in the Washington, DC, area. There are links to job-vacancy notices for Republican organizations, Democratic organizations, and other sources.

MOLIS (Minority On-Line Information Service)

http://content.sciencewise.com/molis

MOLIS provides online services that promote education, research, and diversity on a national level for minority institutions in partnership with government, industry, and other sectors. It is a good resource for scholarships, minority research funding, and employment opportunities. You'll see some crossover with FEDIX (see earlier entry).

The Resume Place

resume-place.com

Kathryn Kraemer Troutman, author of *The Federal Resume Guidebook* (Jist), gives you great information on creating your private-sector resume as well as preparing your federal resume. She is considered the expert on the new format in use by the government to replace the SF-171 and its new electronic resume system. If you are considering the federal government as a potential employer, then you must review Troutman's information.

Studentjobs.gov

studentjobs.gov

The Office of Personnel Management (OPM) and the Department of Education's Student Financial Assistance Office support this site. "This website is designed to be your one stop for information you need to find the job you want in the federal government. Whether you're in high school, college, or graduate school, you could be eligible for a variety of special opportunities for students in the federal government." Learn about co-ops, internships, summer employment, the Outstanding Scholars Program, volunteer opportunities, and plenty of temporary and permanent part-time and full-time jobs. Visitors can search for jobs, post a profile for auto-matching, post a resume, learn about the many government agencies and departments, and link to those who aren't required to post their information in OPM's central database, USAJobs.

USAJobs

usajobs.opm.gov

USAJobs is the official site for federal employment information and jobs listed with the U.S. Office of Personnel Management. Search Current Job Listings, then fill in the online application. (Note: the application options may represent only a small part of the application process; read the job postings carefully, and follow the directions.) You can also contact the agency that posted the position for more information. There are additional links to information about applying for federal jobs and career transition assistance at the Department of Labor website. If you are researching government pay programs or are looking for the salary tables, the information can also be found here.

In addition to these many sources, individual departments and agencies usually post jobs on their own pages. You may find these easier to target. There are also a few departments and agencies that are not required to post their openings with USAJobs. The following resources will help you find the many departments, agencies, and services that make up the U.S. government.

Access America

accessamerica.gov

The Federal Web Locator from The Center for Information Law and Policy

infoctr.edu/FWL

FirstGov

firstgov.gov

Jobs on Capitol Hill

These are opportunities to work for members of the U.S. Congress, but you may also find listings for political action groups, lobbyists, and various nonprofit or educational institutions working closely with the government.

Congressional Quarterly (CQ)

cq.com

Congressional Quarterly's website offers daily bulletins of news from Capitol Hill, breaking news stories, daily and weekly columns, and indexes of the *CQ* since 1998. All items listed under News are free, including the Capitol Hill job listings and photo gallery.

RCJobs from *Roll Call*

rcjobs.com

Roll Call is the newspaper of Capitol Hill with news and information on what's happening "inside the Beltway." RCJobs is its free employment service where you can search for jobs or post a resume. Registration of your resume is not required, but it is encouraged and it is free. It will also facilitate forwarding of your information to employers.

Law Enforcement and Criminal Justice

The Blue Line: Police Opportunity Monitor

theblueline.com

The Blue Line is a resource for links to law enforcement resources and organizations and also offers a monthly newsletter featuring job openings in public service. A sample listing of job openings is available on this site, along with a discussion group. The full listings are available only to paying subscribers.

Criminal Justice Links, Florida State University School of Criminology and Criminal Justice

criminology.fsu.edu/cjlinks

This is an extensive collection of links to resources, CJ departments, CJ labs, and much more.

Department of Justice

usdoj.gov

The Department of Justice is made up of several U.S. government protective and legal entities, including the Federal Bureau of Investigation, the Bureau of Prisons, the Drug Enforcement Administration, the United States Attorneys, and many more. Its employment page gives you information on the kinds of jobs available in its many sections plus easy links to the postings through the OPM's USAJobs.

Lawenforcementjob.com

lawenforcementjob.com

This is a wonderful collection of employment information and job leads for those looking for work in law enforcement. This site even has online practice exams developed in cooperation with several agencies. Those who think they might be interested in law enforcement as a career or who have questions about the job-search process can participate in the many message boards operating here.

Security Jobs Network

http://securityjobs.net

This is a nice resource for security and law enforcement professionals. Access to the job listings requires a paid subscription, but the site also offers great research links to additional security and law enforcement resources online.

Fire and Protective Services

National Directory of Emergency Services

firejobs.com

This site is a good source of information for job leads and training for people interested in careers in fire fighting or police work. Access to the job leads is by paid subscription, but you can search the database of training academies for free. Persons interested in career opportunities in these areas should check out the demo database search and see what info is returned before making any decisions. At the time of review, the information provided in a job listing included the hiring organization, contact info, statistics for the department and locality, salary ranges, specialized areas (canine units, emergency medical technicians, etc.), and a link to the hiring organization's website if available.

National Fire Protection Association (NFPA)

nfpa.org

This website puts you in contact with fire departments, building code regulators, emergency services, fire and safety associations, and anyone else you can think of who would have a part in fire protection and safety regulation in the United States and abroad. Many of these organizations and fire protection departments have information on job openings or job lines for you to call. In addition, the NFPA's free Career Center lists jobs for fire protection engineers, inspectors, technicians with monitoring firms, and other professionals in this field.

Military and the Defense Industry

The Defense Industry

http://members.home.net/marylandcareers/intel.html

This guide to employment information and opportunities in the defense industry is sponsored by Maryland Careers, an online source for employment information in Maryland provided by Tom Coates, a local career consultant. The links here include industry information, recruiters, associations, and other job sources for the defense industry, and they connect to national as well as local resources and associations for the Washington, DC, area.

DefenseLink

defenselink.mil/other_info/careers.html

DefenseLink, the official website of the U.S. Department of Defense, was developed to serve as the starting point for finding U.S. military information online. Under "Defense Sites" are links to the listings for civilian job opportunities as well as the recruiting sites for all branches of the military. There are several sources for these listings, so this serves as a nice central resource. To learn more about the Department of Defense, its organization, and the three military departments within it, review the Defense Almanac, found under the Publications link (defenselink.mil/pubs/almanac).

Military Career Guide Online, The Defense Manpower Data Center

militarycareers.com

If you are considering some time in the military before pursuing a career in the private sector, this site will be useful to you. The Military Career Guide describes itself as the "leading career information resource for the military world of work. It gives you details on 152 enlisted and officer occupations, one by one. Because most military occupations are comparable to one or more civilian occupations, you are given the civilian counterpart for every applicable military occupation. In addition, this site describes training, advancement, and educational opportunities within each of the major services—Army, Navy, Air Force, Marine Corps, and Coast Guard."

United States Armed Services

Connect to each service's website for more information on military service opportunities, benefits of a military career, and recruiter locations:

Opportunities with the U.S. Navy

navyjobs.com

You can click on "Ask a Question" to get answers to the most frequently asked questions about serving in the Navy, or enter your zip code to find your nearest recruiter. For more information, check out the Navy's official website (navy.mil).

U.S. Air Force

airforce.com

It is easy to learn about careers in the United States Air Force from this site. Look over the list of frequently asked questions and then look for a recruiter near you.

U.S. Army Recruiting Home Page

goarmy.com

The Army's recruiting site includes profiles of current service personnel, information on all 212 MOS (military occupational specialties), and an easy connection to a local recruiter. You can also review the Army's main website (army.mil).

U.S. Coast Guard

uscg.mil

Actually a division of the Department of Transportation, the Coast Guard ensures safe and efficient marine transportation, works to enforce laws and treaties on the seas, protects our nation's borders, and provides for the national defense. Check the website for more information on service or civilian jobs, or call (800) GET-USCG.

U.S. Marines

marines.com

Based on your current situation (high school student, college graduate, etc.) you will be routed to recruiting information relevant to you. The main site for the Marines (usmc.mil) will give you tremendous information about this branch of the service and its training facilities.

Public Administration

American Society for Public Administration (ASPA)

aspanet.org

This professional society includes more than ten thousand public administration practitioners, students, and academics. The website is filled with great information on public administration, and the Careers section includes the ASPA's own job database, The Recruiter Online, which features public administration job openings in government and nonprofit organizations as well as at several universities. It also links to many more useful resources for this field.

ExecSearches.com

execsearches.com/exec

ExecSearches.com is a premier site for nonprofit and public sector employment in higher education, health, advocacy, philanthropy, government, social and human services, and community and economic development. It helps nonprofits, the public sector, socially conscious businesses, and other search firms and third-party recruiters to find middle-, executive-, and director-level fund-raising, finance, operations, human resources, communications, administrative, program, and other key personnel. Search the job listings or post a profile for employers to review.

Public Policy Institutions

Brookings Institute

brook.edu

The Brookings Institute is America's oldest policy think tank. This site contains information about the institution and its work. Information about employment opportunities, fellowships, and internships is accessible from the home page.

The Heritage Foundation

heritage.org

The Heritage Foundation is "a research and educational institute—a think tank—whose mission is to formulate and promote conservative public policies based on the principles of free enterprise, limited government, individual freedom, traditional American values, and a strong national defense." The foundation sponsors a free Job Bank for conservative job seekers and prospective employers, with a convenient online application form.

International Monetary Fund (IMF)

imf.org

The IMF is "an international organization of 183 member countries, established to promote international monetary cooperation, exchange stability, and orderly exchange arrangements; to foster economic growth and high levels of employment; and to provide temporary financial assistance to countries to help ease balance of payments adjustment." Jobs with the IMF include positions for experienced economists, specialized professionals, research assistants, and other support-level personnel. Although some programs like the Summer Intern Program have fixed annual recruitment cycles, the IMF accepts inquiries and applications at any time of the year. You can learn more about current openings through the "Vacancies at the IMF" link on the front page.

National Institute for Research Advancement Think Tank Information

nira.go.jp/ice/index.html

The National Institute for Research Advancement (NIRA) is a policy research organization established to conduct research from an independent standpoint and contribute to the resolution of various complex issues facing contemporary society. Research topics reflect the trends of the times and span a wide range, including politics, economics, international issues, social issues, technology, and local government systems. This no-frills page provides links to think tanks and other policy research resources worldwide plus the latest edition of the institute's World Directory of Think Tanks.

RAND

rand.org

Created as a research and development tool and initially sponsored by the Air Force, RAND is "a nonprofit organization that helps improve policy and decision making through research and analysis." The website includes opportunities for employment in research and analysis, research support, administrative support, and corporate services areas.

State and Local Governments

Careers in Government

careersingovernment.com

Careers in Government is a clearinghouse of information, resources, and jobs available in public sector organizations in the United States and abroad. It provides access to all kinds of jobs in government and the public sector, including positions with many county and municipal agencies. Search by keyword and other criteria, or by employer and location. Register to have job postings of interest automatically E-mailed to you or to submit your resume. Also included is a helpful list of related associations.

GovtJob.Net

govtjob.net

Sponsored by the Local Government Institute (LGI), GovtJob.Net provides a centralized online source of jobs available in local governments nationally. In the contents frame, click on the job descriptor that interests you and view the employment opportunities in the frame on your right.

govtjobs.com

govtjobs.com

Govtjobs.com is devoted to helping individuals find the jobs they are seeking in the public sector. Agencies listing positions with govtjobs.com include cities, counties, states, executive search firms, advertising agencies, and other governmental jurisdictions. In addition to job listings, the site has links to agencies, executive search firms, and resources for locating more opportunities.

The Internet Job Source

statejobs.com

The Internet Job Source links to government jobs in most states, dozens of agencies within the federal government, and many Fortune 500 companies. Search for a job by major industry or state, or click to check out the major newspapers, magazines, and other news and government resources available through this site.

JOB LISTINGS FROM THE STATE GOVERNMENTS

Following is a list of state government job pages. Unlike the state job banks noted in Chapter 11, these are jobs working for the state government. You may find other career resources for states, counties, and municipalities in Chapter 11.

Alabama

personnel.state.al.us

Alaska

http://teak.state.ak.us/wa/mainentry.nsf/?OpenDatabase

Arizona

state.az.us/employment.html

Arkansas

arstatejobs.com

California

spb.ca.gov

Colorado

state.co.us/jobinfo.html

Connecticut

das.state.ct.us/HR/HRhome.htm

Delaware

http://delawarepersonnel.com

District of Columbia

dc.gov/gov/index.htm

Florida

myflorida.com/myflorida/jobopportunity.html

Georgia

gms.state.ga.us

Hawaii

state.hi.us/hrd

Idaho

dhr.state.id.us

Illinois

state.il.us/cms/persnl/default.htm

state.il.us/gov/officeinternships.htm (internships)

Indiana

in.gov/jobs/stateemployment/jobbank.html

Iowa

iowajobs.org

Kansas

http://da.state.ks.us/ps/aaa/recruitment

Kentucky

state.ky.us/agencies/personnel/pershome.htm

Louisiana

dscs.state.la.us

Maine

state.me.us/statejobs

Maryland

http://dop.state.md.us

Massachusetts

mass.gov

Michigan

state.mi.us/mdcs

Minnesota

doer.state.mn.us

Mississippi

spb.state.ms.us

Missouri

oa.state.mo.us/stjobs.htm

Montana

http://jsd.dli.state.mt.us

Nebraska

wrk4neb.org

Nevada

state.nv.us/personnel

New Hampshire

state.nh.us/das/personnel

New Jersey

state.nj.us/personnel

New Mexico

state.nm.us/spo

New York

cs.state.ny.us

North Carolina

osp.state.nc.us

North Dakota

state.nd.us/cpers

Ohio

state.oh.us/das/dhr/emprec.html

Oklahoma

state.ok.us/~opm

Oregon

dashr.state.or.us

Pennsylvania

http://sites.state.pa.us/jobpost.html

http://sites.state.pa.us/Internopp/index.html (internships)

Rhode Island

det.state.ri.us

South Carolina

state.sc.us/jobs

South Dakota

state.sd.us/bop/jobs.htm

Tennessee

state.tn.us/personnel

Texas

twc.state.tx.us/jobs/gvjb/gvjb.html

Utah

dhrm.state.ut.us

Vermont

state.vt.us/pers

Virginia

dpt.state.va.us

Washington

http://hr.dop.wa.gov

Washington, D.C.
See "District of Columbia."

West Virginia

state.wv.us/admin/personel

Wisconsin

http://jobs.der.state.wi.us/static

Wyoming

http://personnel.state.wy.us

You can find even more information for jobs with state and local governments through these resources:

Library of Congress Information on State and Local Governments

http://lcweb.loc.gov/global/state/stategov.html

National Association of State Chief Information Officers (NASCIO)

https://www.nascio.org

State and Local Government on the Net

statelocalgov.net

The State Web Locator from the Center for Information Law and Policy

infoctr.edu/SWL

10

Entry-Level
and Summer
Employment,
Internships,
and Co-ops

If you are a college student, your first stops for cooperative and internship information should be your department head and college career center. However, in the event that you do not find an opportunity that interests you through those avenues, we have gathered a few leads that might help you find a position. In addition to these resources, use the virtual libraries and other resources and procedures outlined in Chapter 1 to identify other organizations in your major field, and contact them about possible work. Use the search engines to search keywords including *intern, internship, co-op, cooperative education*, and *summer* or *temporary* for some other possibilities. Another tip: check college and university web servers in the region where you would like to work to see if they have any possible leads from local organizations. Many resources in Chapter 11 may also provide contacts. The major job-listing sites included in Chapter 3 can yield good leads as well, so be sure to search their databases, paying special attention to any areas set aside for college students or entry-level personnel.

Entry-Level Positions and Internet Resources for New Graduates

College Grad Job Hunter

collegegrad.com

Search the entry-level job or internship databases by keyword, or review the entire list of openings. You can also limit your search by state and look for selected opportunities only, or you can ask the career specialist a question.

Monster.com's Campus

http://campus.monster.com

This zone from Monster.com provides even more help for recent graduates. You'll find career advice and planning tools, as well as help in creating the right resume and acing the job interview. Research the companies for which you're interested in working, and sign up for the site's free newsletter.

Youth Resource Network of Canada

youth.gc.ca

Created to help prepare young people for the workplace and the job hunt, Youth Resource Network is a partnership among several agencies of the Canadian government and the private sector. The site provides self-assessment tools and career resources, along with job opportunities and resources for starting your own business. This site is available in both English and French.

Internships, Co-Ops, Work Exchanges, and Study Abroad

Action Without Borders

idealist.org

This site matches idealistic job seekers with nonprofit and public-service organizations. You can search for jobs, internships, and volunteer opportunities by country or specialty.

Best Bets for Student Work Exchange

cie.uci.edu/iop/work.html

Put together by the Center for International Education at the University of California, Irvine, this page contains links to work-abroad websites, as well as "listings of some of the better-known programs that exist." It is intended to "assist students to find these exchange programs, as opposed to permanent career positions abroad."

California Polytechnic State University

careerservices.calpoly.edu

California Polytechnic's Career Services page has information about part-time, summer, and cooperative education positions along with some good career resources. Registered students and alumni can use the "Web Walkup" (WWU) login page to sign up for hundreds of job opportunities.

Career and Community Learning Center

http://oslo.umn.edu

The Career and Community Learning Center provides experiential learning opportunities for students at the University of Minnesota through its internship, career services, and field learning and community service program. The site also links to other great internship sites for students nationwide.

Case Western Reserve University Career Planning and Placement

cwru.edu/stuaff/careers

Find information on Case-sponsored internships. There are also links to summer job sites.

Council on International Education Exchange

ciee.org

If you are considering international studies or internships, you may want to check out the programs and services offered by this organization. No, they will not find you a job nor provide housing if you are enrolling in a university program, but they will help you fill out the forms, give you lists of housing locations and potential employers, and support you in other ways. They charge a fee for their services, but the facilitation should be well worth it.

GoAbroad.com

goabroad.com

GoAbroad.com is filled with information geared to college students, but it covers almost anything you might want to find out about going overseas. Search for internships, volunteer opportunities, teaching opportunities, study opportunities, travel information, and much more. The site has featured programs under each area but below that offers a full directory search starting with a target country.

Internship Programs.com

http://internships.wetfeet.com/home.asp

This site offers listings with thousands of internship opportunities from around the world. To begin, choose to search by company or region. We did note that many of the organizations posting here don't list actual internships but say you should contact them about opportunities. People aiming for internships in major metropolitan areas will also want to scan the city interns area, with links to local information for many U.S. cities.

MonsterTrak.com

monstertrak.com

As noted in Chapter 3, your college or university must be a member of MonsterTrak for you to gain access to the job postings here. If your institution is listed as a member, you can call your career center and ask for the password. This site has some tremendous resources. Those who cannot access the job listings might be able to target the companies listed to ask about opportunities. This is the former JobTrak and is still offering the same services.

New England Board of Higher Education (NEBHE)

nebhe.org

The NEBHE website has a nice collection of resources for high school students, college students, and beyond. Search the links of interest to you.

Russian and Eastern European Internship Opportunities from REEIWeb

indiana.edu/~reeiweb/indemp.html

The REEIWeb lists internships available in Eastern European countries, along with academic and nonacademic positions. Check this site for information on funding of related studies and additional links. This site is sponsored by the Russian and East European Institute at Indiana University.

Sistahs in Science

mtholyoke.edu/courses/sbrowne/sistahs/final/index.html

Founded by a Mount Holyoke professor and a chemistry student, Sistahs in Science exists to help minority women excel in science. The site features links to internships and other opportunities in the hard sciences, for students ranging from high school to postcollege.

Studyabroad.com

studyabroad.com

Studyabroad provides links and contact information for thousands of opportunities in dozens of countries. Search by country, or use the menu for language programs, internships, or summer jobs. Consult the "Study Abroad Handbook" for tips on living abroad, or check off the "Pre-departure Checklist." Contact the specific sites for more information about their programs.

Government-Sponsored Student Work Opportunities and Political Internships

The Corporation for National Service

nationalservice.org

Established in 1993, the Corporation for National Service engages more than a million Americans each year in service to their communities—helping to solve community problems. The Corporation's three major service initiatives are AmeriCorps (including AmeriCorps*VISTA and AmeriCorps*NCCC), Learn and Serve America, and the National Senior Service Corps. The Corporation offers its own opportunities for fellowships and internships in its offices across the United States, and anyone interested in any of the AmeriCorps programs can learn about these programs and apply for any through that section of the website.

Peace Corps

peacecorps.gov

You'll find background information on the organization and access to a transition service for RPCVs (returned Peace Corps volunteers) at this site provided by the Peace Corps. Check out the database for current positions, and then send in your application using the guidelines outlined on the web page. The College Students Guide lists opportunities in the Masters International Program.

Project Vote Smart

vote-smart.org

This national nonpartisan nonprofit organization researches federal and state candidates and elected officials to provide factual information to the public regarding their voting records and stands on issues. Ninety percent of the Vote Smart workforce consists of volunteers or college students, many selected through its National Internship Program. Generous scholarships are available. Print out the site's application for an internship, or contact the organization for more information via E-mail at intern@vote-smart.org or by telephone at (888) VOTE SMART.

Studentjobs.gov

studentjobs.gov

Studentjobs.gov is a site from the U.S. Office of Personnel Management and the U.S. Department of Education's Student Financial Assistance Office. As they say, "this website is designed to be your one stop for information you need to find the job you want in the federal government. Whether you're in high school, college, or graduate school, you could be eligible for a variety of special opportunities for students in the federal government." Most federal agencies are required to post vacancies in this database, but Studentjobs.gov has gathered information on the agencies that aren't under Other Job Opportunities, "giving you the most comprehensive access to federal job opportunities available. Learn about co-ops, internships, summer employment, the Outstanding Scholars Program, volunteer opportunities, and plenty of temporary and permanent part-time and full-time jobs." You can search for jobs, post a profile to allow auto-matching with posted jobs, store your resume here, and learn about the many government agencies and departments.

Washington Intern Foundation

http://interns.org

The Washington Intern Foundation is a nonprofit organization that assists individuals in locating and successfully completing internships in the Washington, DC, area and on Capitol Hill. View the dozens of currently available internships listed on the website, both on "the Hill" and off, or post your resume for free.

The White House Fellowships

whitehousefellows.gov

The White House Fellows program spans multiple fields and provides gifted young Americans firsthand experience in the process of government, either in the Office of the President or in one of the cabinet-level agencies. You'll find information about applying here.

Volunteer Opportunities

Missions Opportunities Database

globalmission.org/go.htm

Are you looking for an opportunity to serve others throughout the world in a variety of ways? This searchable database lists hundreds of openings in countries and areas where help is needed. Many assignments are unpaid voluntary positions, but some provide a small salary or stipend. This service is provided by the EFC Task Force for Global Mission, a Canadian Christian organization.

Teach for America

teachforamerica.org

The national teacher corps is looking for new graduates who will commit two years to teach in rural and urban public schools in need. Teacher certification is not required in order for you to participate.

VolunteerMatch

volunteermatch.org

If you are looking for something to do with your time and talent that can benefit your community and yourself, then plug in your zip code and get a list of organizations nearby that need you. You can even specify how far you can travel, when you can start, and whether you want a one-time or ongoing opportunity. Each listing includes a profile of the organization plus a rundown of all activities associated with the group. You can even "Express interest in this activity" online by simply filling out the form provided, which will then be forwarded to the sponsoring organization.

Places to Check for Miscellaneous Opportunities and Seasonal Work

Back Door Jobs—Exciting Career Adventures

backdoorjobs.com

This is a companion to the book *The Back Door Guide to Short-Term Job Adventures* by Michael Landes (Ten Speed Press), where you can take a look at some of the short-term exciting or adventurous job experiences included in the full book. Even better, Landes uses this site to keep his material current. For a younger person, this could open some interesting doors. For an older person, it could be an interesting break from the suit and tie and that chance to follow your childhood dream of riding the range.

CollegePro Painters

collegepro.com

You've seen the signs—these people are painting houses all over the country! Job and internship descriptions plus information about the availability of local franchises are here online.

Cool Works

coolworks.com

Check out the loads of seasonal jobs at this website. Ranch jobs, ski jobs, and cruise jobs are a click away! Search by state, or use the menu of job categories. Cool Works links you to information about the job and the organization's web page, if available, along with contact information so you can follow up on the lead.

Great Summer Jobs

http://gsj.petersons.com

Brought to the Internet by Peterson's, the publisher of college catalogs, this site is filled with jobs in summer camps. To search the job listings, select a type of position and a location (if you have a preference). You are not required to register a resume in order to use this service, but they really encourage it to make applying for jobs easier and to make it possible for employers to find you.

My Summers

mysummers.com

This is a source for summer jobs, mostly in summer camps. The free registration is required, and you must be eighteen or older and a high school graduate to participate. Once you are registered (which includes filling in a bit of an application), your information will be forwarded to all of the camps that subscribe to this service (pretty much the same list you see advertising in Campfinders.com). You can also search the job postings and apply to any jobs that look interesting.

Project America Home Page

http://project.org

Project America is a nonprofit organization designed to promote community involvement. Read "Get Involved by Volunteering in Your Community" to find links to specific community project sites.

Seasonal Employment

seasonalemployment.com

Seasonal Employment lists jobs for specific times of the year, which means they are usually in or about various recreational facilities. Pick a season (summer or winter), a location (by state or choose Canada), or employer, and review the information on available job openings.

Summer Jobs

summerjobs.com

Search these summer jobs by keyword or geographic location, or link to other job sites and career or training resources. There are listings for all over the world, and you'll find many opportunities to exchange your skills for several weeks in locations such as the Caribbean.

More Possibilities

The following two sites are unique in their attention to colleges, careers, and the entry-level employment scene. Take a look around. Check out the "real-life tales from the world of work," or send a question to a career professional. Contact your career counselor if you need help in using the linked resources. Both sites are sponsored by NACE, the National Association of Colleges and Employers.

The Catapult

jobweb.com/catapult

NACEWeb: The National Association of Colleges and Employers

naceweb.org

You can also search America's Job Bank (ajb.org) plus the individual state job banks linked from the sites for local opportunities.

State and Local Resources for the United States

The growth of niche and geography-specific resources on the Internet continues as we enter a new millennium. This chapter will give you an idea of how vast the local resources are. Every listing is specific to a city, state, region, or territory of the United States, including Guam and Puerto Rico.

These local resources or portal sites include state and local governments, regional sites organized by grassroots initiatives or with help from libraries or other local institutions, and grant-funded community networks. And today, even the smallest local newspapers publish their help-wanted ads online. Many add value by including career advice or articles or company profiles. Many others are linking to prepackaged career services such as Employment Wizard or CareerBuilder to offer extra value to their readers. In addition, all of the state-sponsored job service sites are online, and individual states continue to develop additional resources for job seekers and career changers.

We did not include the hundreds of U.S. colleges and universities in this list, except for noting a few of the career service centers offered by some of them for their students or alumni. You can easily find any of the educational institutions through Yahoo! (yahoo.com) or by using a search engine like Google (google.com). You can also use any of the college directories listed in Chapter 14. Colleges and universities usually collect information pertinent to their local communities and list their own employment opportunities on their websites.

Because most state governments post their employment opportunities online, we've provided a convenient list of them in Chapter 9, which covers government job sites. This chapter presents some of the larger county or municipal job sites, as well as other state job resources, including the offerings of the Job Service partnership with America's Job Bank.

Community information networks frequently carry local job listings and provide all kinds of information for a region, including available housing and lists of local businesses. Although each community net is organized differently, you can generally find helpful career information in the listings of government resources and services, community centers, libraries, or business resources. The business or commercial resources may also cite the names of companies or people to contact about potential work opportunities.

To access hundreds of the nation's top newspapers on the Web, go to NewsLink (newslink.org), U.S. Newspapers (usnewspaperlinks.com), or Editor & Publisher (editorandpublisher.com). You'll also find many other newspaper sites in this chapter.

States are presented in alphabetical order, with state job banks listed first. All other resources within the state are listed alphabetically after that. When you are looking at the many resources online, check those listed for neighboring states, as they may frequently cover your area too. This is particularly important for anyone living near a state line, but it could apply to other areas too.

While we have a lot of information here, it's possible that we still don't have exactly what you need. In that case, use the resources and strategies in Chapter 1 to help you find more local sources for employment. The general resources at the beginning of this chapter also will serve you well.

General Resources

America's Job Bank (AJB)

ajb.org

Part of America's Workforce Network (usworkforce.org) and the federal government's continuing effort to provide quality resources for American job seekers and career changers, AJB includes the job listings for all of the state employment services (and those of Guam, Puerto Rico, and other U.S. territories). America's Job Bank is simple to use and offers several ways for you to search, including military specialty codes so that people leaving the military can match their skills to jobs in the nonmilitary marketplace. You'll also find links to the other parts of the Network; America's Career InfoNet (acinet.org), a comprehensive source of occupational information; America's Learning eXchange (alx.org), a free electronic marketplace connecting people with the training and education they need; and America's Service Locator (servicelocator.org) with its listings of service providers relevant to employment and training, ranging from one-stop career centers to child care providers and transportation services. These resources and the individual state employment services job banks have incredible lists of opportunities waiting for you. You support these with your tax dollars, so use them!

Library of Congress Meta-Indexes for State and Local Government Information

http://lcweb.loc.gov/global/state/stategov.html

The Library of Congress maintains these listings of state and local government resources.

National Association of State Chief Information Officers (NASCIO), formerly NASIRE

nascio.org/stateSearch

Representing chief information officers of the states, NASCIO's unique "StateSearch" organizes state government information by subject and now features more than two thousand links.

State and Local Government on the Net

statelocalgov.net

This continues to be an outstanding collection of links to state government resources! Dana Noonan updates this list as the state and local governments announce new services, so check with this site for the latest information. State and local government servers can be fantastic sources of information! Beyond providing information about themselves, they often list businesses within the state, educational institutions, and other bits of helpful information for job hunters.

Yahoo!

yahoo.com

http://dir.yahoo.com/Regional/U_S__Metros

As we reviewed resources for this edition of the *Guide*, we found that Yahoo! now offers portals or gateway collections for cities in every state with the exception of Delaware, New Hampshire, and New Jersey. Scroll down the opening page to reach links to the Yahoo! websites for the largest metropolitan areas of the United States. Use the second URL to go to the regional directory, organized alphabetically by state, and then by community.

Alabama

Alabama's Job Bank

ajb.org/al

dir.state.al.us/es/default.htm

The easiest way to search the Job Bank is to select a job category and enter your zip code in the Occupation Search. You can also search by keyword, military code, or job number. The second URL leads to the Internet Job Search System of the Alabama State Employment Service, which offers job leads, a listing of job fairs, and other resources for Alabama job hunters.

Alabama Career Information Network System (ACINS) formerly SOICC

adeca.state.al.us

adeca.state.al.us/soicc/soicc/WebSTAR3.0/soicc/default.html

Start at the Alabama Department of Economic and Community Affairs or use the second URL to go to ACINS directly. ACINS offers information about specific careers, links to job leads, financial aid resources, and educational opportunities, including a listing of Alabama colleges by programs of study.

Alabama Development Office

ado.state.al.us

The mission of the Development Office is to create jobs. It also provides a great deal of helpful information about the state economy and labor force, an Industrial Directory organized by Standard Industrial Classification (SIC) number, and a link to the Alabama Industrial Development Training (AIDT) site, which provides job-specific and on-the-job training programs.

Alabama Live

al.com

al.com/careers

Brought to you by Advance Internet, Alabama Live is a comprehensive interactive electronic source for news, community resources, business information, and classifieds. Use the second URL to go directly to the Alabama Careers site. Use the relocation tools, or search for jobs in the Birmingham, Huntsville, and Mobile newspapers. Register to post your resume, use the power search, or receive job listings via E-mail.

Alabama Works!

alabamaworks.org

Alabama Works! is a public-private partnership whose mission is to attract jobs to the state and to assist the people of Alabama in obtaining the necessary skills to compete in today's workplace. Job leads are accessible through a link to Brass Ring.

AlaWeb

state.al.us/2k1

Alabama's official website offers facts and figures about the state, with links to local community resources, state agencies, and educational institutions. Click on the state Employment Service link to reach the job postings and career-related information.

Jefferson County Personnel Board (Birmingham)

bham.net/pbjc/index.html

Click on a job title to view more detailed information about it. Applications for these county government jobs are accepted on official forms only. Call (205) 325-5515, or send E-mail to jcpersonnel@jcpb.co.jefferson.al.us to request an application for a specific job when it is announced (multiple requests are accepted).

Shoals *Times Daily*

timesdaily.com

timesdaily.com/classified/classif2.htm

The *Times Daily* serves Muscle Shoals and several other small communities in northwest Alabama. The second URL goes directly to a listing of job-related categories such as sales, jobs wanted, or help wanted. Click on the keyword most appropriate to your situation to view the current postings.

Alaska

Alaska Job Center Network

jobs.state.ak.us

http://146.63.75.43/akjb

The Alaska Job Center Network, "where people and jobs connect," brings together all of the state's resources for job hunters. You'll find training and continuing education, apprenticeship opportunities, a job fair calendar, detailed information about local communities and social services, and links to job leads and search tips. The second URL goes directly to the job-search page. Use the map of the state or pull-down menu to select a region, choose a job category, and click on the search button to view the results.

Alaska Department of Labor and Workforce Development

labor.state.ak.us

The Department of Labor maintains this page for job seekers, workers, and employers. You'll find job opportunities, employment and unemployment services, labor statistics, and information about the laws and regulations dealing with the workplace.

Alaska Jobs Center (AJC)

ilovealaska.com/alaskajobs

When we reviewed the site, AJC was soliciting ideas from its users for a new name. Suggestions include Employment Goldmine, mulletjobs.com, and the Alaska Job Locator. We wish them well in their endeavor! The AJC bills itself as the "most comprehensive directory of employment resources in Alaska," and it does offer quite an array of links! Among its offerings are business and organization websites, newspapers, educational institutions, government agencies, and seasonal job opportunities.

Alaska State Troopers

dps.state.ak.us/Ast/recruit

The state troopers are actively recruiting candidates for law enforcement divisions, rescue operations, and fish and wildlife protection programs.

Anchorage Daily News

adn.com

Click on Alaska Jobs to get to the employment section and hundreds of jobs. Browse the ads by category, or search by keyword. You can also link to the Jobs Network database to post your resume or read the career advice columns.

The Capitol City Home Page

juneau.lib.ak.us

Juneau's public libraries have developed this comprehensive collection of local information. Although the site offers a great deal of helpful information, it can be difficult to navigate unless you're using a newer browser.

Fairbanks Alaska Internet Resources Network for Education and Training (FairNet)

fairnet.org

Fairbanks's electronic community network features links to agencies and organizations, educational resources, training programs, and government information. Easiest access is through the site map. Select Employment Resources in the Alaska Info section to view the job and career information.

Finding Work in Alaska

labor.state.ak.us/esd_alaska_jobs/ak_over.htm

Created for the individual in the lower forty-eight who dreams of starting all over in Alaska, this site contains a lot of helpful information about the state and its resources. If you're thinking of starting a new life in Alaska, check out this site!

Juneau Empire

http://juneauempire.com

Juneau's daily newspaper provides a handy guide to Juneau and several other communities. Choose the Classifieds link to access the job resources. Select Employment from the pull-down category menu to browse all the current postings.

SLED: Alaska's Statewide Library Electronic Doorway

http://sled.alaska.edu

Developed by the State Library and the University of Alaska, SLED provides free, easy, equitable, and nicely organized access to electronic information. Choose the Alaska Communities link to view all kinds of information about the state and its local communities, or look over the business links. Click on Job & Employment Resources to go directly to a comprehensive page of career information.

Workplace Alaska

http://notes.state.ak.us/wa/mainentry.nsf/?OpenDatabase

Workplace Alaska is the state's online recruitment system. You'll find loads of good links here!

Arizona

Arizona's Job Bank

ajb.org/az

The easiest way to search the Job Bank is to select a job category and enter your zip code in the Occupation Search. You can also search by keyword, military code, or job number.

Arizona Central

azcentral.com

The *Arizona Republic*'s answer to electronic access! Click on Jobs in the Classifieds menu to go to the employment resources. Select a job category, add keywords (optional), and click on Search to view the results. Helpful features include community information and links to other career resources.

Big Deal Classified (formerly StarNet Electrifieds)

bigdealclassifieds.com

Brought to you by Arizona's *Daily Star* newspaper, the Employment section of the Big Deal Classifieds contains job leads for the area.

Phoenix ComputerJobs

phoenix.computerjobs.com

Headquartered in Atlanta, ComputerJobs.com is the leading Internet-based job-search source for computer and information technology professionals.

Arkansas

Arkansas Job Bank

ajb.org/ar

The easiest way to search the Job Bank is to select a job category and enter your zip code in the Occupation Search. You can also search by keyword, military code, or job number.

Arkansas Business

arkansasbusiness.com

The site of the business weekly features up-to-date news about the state's business community, small-business resources, and links to Arkansas businesses on the Web.

Arkansas Career Development Network (ACDN)

accessarkansas.org/onestop

Arkansas Employment Security Department (AESD)

accessarkansas.org/esd

accessarkansas.org/esd/employment.htm

Together these sites equal an Arkansas all-purpose job-and-career-resources page. ACDN (formerly known as ONE-STOP) offers a single point of contact for support services, education and training, and career development. Click on the map to find the center near you. The AESD site provides information about the labor market, colleges and training opportunities, job postings, and other career resources. Use AESD's second URL to reach the collection of job links.

Arkansas Employment Register

arjobs.com

A biweekly newspaper devoted solely to employment, the *Arkansas Employment Register* is distributed on alternate Mondays. At this site, you can search for a job, visit the Reading Room, or link to other good career resources.

Arkansas Online

ardemgaz.com

The online version of the *Arkansas Democrat-Gazette*'s newspaper offers business and technology news and a handy "Biz" directory. Much of the content is accessible without registering, but to view the classified ads, you must register (free). Browse through the employment categories, or use keywords to search for a job.

Workforce Excellence: Community Assistance Network (WE CAN)

onestop.org/homepage.htm

The WE CAN website is the electronic equivalent of the One-Stop Career Centers, offering information about employment and community services throughout the state. You can search for jobs locally or statewide, or you can use a national database to look beyond Arkansas. Use the free resume-posting service or locate helpful educational resources. You will find lots of good information here.

California

California's Job Bank

ajb.org/ca

The easiest way to search the Job Bank is to select a job category and enter your zip code in the Occupation Search. You can also search by keyword, military code, or job number.

BayAreaCareers.com

bayareacareers.com

Check out this comprehensive list of links to hundreds of company employment websites, newspapers, and recruiters within the greater San Francisco region. BayAreaCareers.com connects candidates directly to the job opportunities of the employers of their choice. Search by resource or region, or use one of its partner websites for other California jobs:

Los Angeles	lacareers.com
North Bay	northbaycareers.com
Orange County	orangecountycareers.com
San Diego	sandiegocareers.com

California ComputerWork

http://california.computerwork.com

Find more jobs in the IT sector! This is one of dozens of local sites that ComputerWork maintains for professionals in the information technology field.

California Online Job Network (COJN)

cajobs.com

COJN is your electronic doorway to community employment resources. Click on the community icons to access job leads, major local employers, and information about the regions served. Register to post your resume online and have job postings sent to you via E-mail. You'll find a separate selection of work-at-home opportunities. The Network includes these sites:

Los Angeles	losangelesjobs.com
Oakland	oaklandjobs.com
Orange County	orangecountyjobs.com
Riverside	riversidejobs.com
Sacramento	sacramentojobs.com
San Diego	sandiegojobs.com
San Francisco	sanfranciscojobs.com
San Jose	sanjosejobs.com

California State Government

ca.gov

ca.gov/state/portal/myca_homepage.jsp

California continues its leadership in bringing information to the people. You'll find education and training resources, government agencies, employment information, and more. You can now personalize the website, with links to resources you use most often. Also new this edition is a wireless and E-mail information delivery service that will bring you lottery results, press releases, and other California information of interest.

California State University Employment Board

http://csueb.sfsu.edu/csueb/pages/index.html

The Employment Board maintains a list of all available faculty and administrative positions for the twenty-three campuses of California State University, searchable by campus and discipline.

California WorkNet

sjtcc.ca.gov/sjtccweb/one-stop

WorkNet is the electronic version of California's One-Stop Career Center system. It serves as your entrée to education, job training, and employment-services information, along with support services that are available to residents of the state.

Employment Development Department (EDD)

edd.cahwnet.gov

CalJOBS

caljobs.ca.gov

For more than sixty years, the EDD has been linking Californians with jobs. At this site, you'll find labor market information, links to training resources, and job opportunities. Use the second URL to go directly to the CalJOBS system, which matches potential employers with job candidates. You must register (free) to access the database.

JobStar Central

jobstar.org

Celebrating its fifth year of providing employment assistance online, JobStar remains one of the best career offerings on the Web! Cybrarian Mary-Ellen Mort, aka Electra and a noted expert in this field, brings you the most comprehensive listing of salary surveys available, along with resume-writing tips and a guide to the hidden job market. Search for jobs in specific California regions, or "Ask Electra" for career advice. JobStar is slowly expanding to include new regions (JobStar New Jersey was available at the time of review) plus additional assistance with national and international job searching.

Los Angeles and Southern California ComputerJobs

la.computerjobs.com

Headquartered in Atlanta, ComputerJobs.com is the leading Internet-based job-search source for computer and information technology professionals.

Los Angeles Times

latimes.com

latimes.com/class/employ/workplace

The *Times* Business section has a Work & Career page featuring articles about labor conditions and the world of work. The educational and technology pages could also provide you with helpful information. Scroll down the opening page and click on the Workplace/Jobs link or use the second URL to go directly to the job leads. Post your resume, look through the company profiles, or try some of the other features. To start your Mega Job Search, select a location, click on a job category, and type in additional keywords to refine your search. Select "Search Now" to view the results.

NewsChoice Online Newspaper Network

newschoice.com/default.asp

The dozens of newspapers represented on this site include many from California. Check out the classified ads from the *Alameda Times-Star, Long Beach Press-Telegram, Pasadena Star-News, Oakland Tribune, San Mateo County Times,* and more! Use the Classified link to go directly to the ads, and then click on the state link to view the alphabetical list of California classified pages. Select Employment, choose the appropriate categories and keywords, and view the job postings!

Palo Alto Weekly Online Edition

paweekly.com

Palo Alto Online

PaloAltoOnline.com

The first URL leads to the weekly newspaper from Palo Alto. Read the current edition or access issues back to 1994. The second URL leads directly to Palo Alto's community network, which is supported by the newspaper and features loads of information about the area. Find helpful phone numbers and services, or use the handy guide for getting around the region. Browse the job postings in the Classified Marketplace Online or link to WorkbasePA (see listing later in this section).

The *Sacramento Bee*

sacbee.com

sacbee.com/ib/careers

The Business section features technology news, a local business calendar, and a few career-related links. Visit Our Town to view the community calendar and a Residents' Guide containing contact information for helpful local resources. Scroll down the opening page to the Jobs link, or use the second URL to go there directly. To start your Mega Job Search, select a location, click on the job category that interests you, and type in additional keywords to refine your search. Select Search Now to view the results.

San Bernardino County Employment Opportunities

co.san-bernardino.ca.us/hr/jobs/mainjobs.htm

You'll find all the information you need to apply for a job in San Bernardino County at this site. The jobs are in two categories: those with deadlines and those for which the employers recruit regularly. You'll also find a link to jobs in superior court. For the latest job information, you can also call (909) 387-5611.

San Francisco Bay Area Volunteer Information Center

volunteerinfo.org

Don't overlook this site if you're interested in working in the nonprofit sector—where there are volunteer positions, there might be job possibilities as well! Here you'll find loads of volunteer opportunities, along with information about the organizations that participate in the Information Center. Many organizations also make the information available via telephone, (800) CARE123.

San Francisco Cityspan Information Center

ci.sf.ca.us/info.htm

"Bridging government and citizens through technology," Cityspan offers loads of information about living in San Francisco. You'll find community facts and services, tips for business start-up, and links to agency websites. Click on Employment to access links to current openings in municipal and county government. Some jobs are never posted, so call the hot line (updated on Thursday evenings) at (415) 557-4888 to hear about other employment opportunities.

San Jose Mercury

bayarea.com

http://careers.bayarea.com

The *Mercury* offers business, technology, and lifestyle sections, along with helpful yellow pages for the Bay Area. Click on Find a Job, or use the second

URL to go directly to the San Jose newspaper's CareerBuilder page. Post your resume, read career-related articles, or view the company profiles. Click the Go button for a quick list of job opportunities, or use the form to conduct a more focused search.

SF Gate

sfgate.com

Brought to you by the *San Francisco Chronicle* and *Examiner* newspapers, SF Gate offers the latest news along with housing, business, and technology information. Scroll down the opening page and click on the Jobs link to access the employment resources. Specify the day of the week in which you're interested, and add keywords (optional) to search for employment. Or save your precious time and sign up for an E-mail Alert that will inform you of job leads. New this edition is the Bay Recruiter E-recruiting service. Register to have your skills matched with potential employers.

Silicon Valley ComputerJobs

siliconvalley.computerjobs.com

Headquartered in Atlanta, ComputerJobs.com is the leading Internet-based job-search source for computer and information technology professionals.

WorkBasePA (Palo Alto)

workbase.com/palo_alto/index.html

Looking for work? Fill in one simple online form so that potential employers in the Palo Alto area can find you.

Colorado

Colorado's Job Bank

ajb.org/co

The easiest way to search the Job Bank is to select a job category and enter your zip code in the Occupation Search. You can also search by keyword, military code, or job number.

Boulder Community Network

http://bcn.boulder.co.us

http://bcn.boulder.co.us/oscn

The Boulder Community Network connects you to information about the region and its educational and business opportunities, community organizations, social services, and more. The second URL takes you directly to the One Stop Career Network, a collection of links to employment opportunities and career resources in the Boulder area and throughout the state.

Boulder County

co.boulder.co.us

Search here for employment opportunities with Boulder County government. You can also call the twenty-four-hour Job Line at (303) 441-4555 or correspond with them via E-mail at jobs@co.boulder.co.us.

Colorado Virtual Library

aclin.org

The Virtual Library, maintained by the Access Colorado Library and Information Network (ACLIN), a statewide network of libraries and information resources, offers access to a wealth of community, business, and consumer information. You'll also find information about state government and its many services. The "Best Websites for Coloradans" page features links to the state Job Bank and other resources for job seekers and career changers.

Denver ComputerJobs

denver.computerjobs.com

Headquartered in Atlanta, ComputerJobs.com is the leading Internet-based job-search source for computer and information technology professionals.

The *Denver Post* Online

denverpost.com

employmentwizard.com

Use the second URL to take you to the Employment Wizard. The Wizard accesses job listings in the *Post-News Classified, Denver Post, Rocky Mountain News*, and some other newspapers throughout the state. You'll find additional postings from newspapers as far away as Florida and Alaska. It is important for you to specify the area in which you're interested in order to obtain the best results. Register to post your resume or take the online personality quiz.

State of Colorado Employment

state.co.us/jobinfo.html

The Colorado page links to jobs in state government, the Colorado Department of Labor and Employment, and other career resources. You'll find labor statistics and other traditional job services provided for both job seekers and employers.

Connecticut

Connecticut's Job Bank

ajb.org/ct

The easiest way to search the Job Bank is to select a job category and enter your zip code in the Occupation Search. You can also search by keyword, military code, or job number.

Connecticut Works

ctdol.state.ct.us

The Connecticut Department of Labor, whose motto is "Working with you for a better future," does just that for individuals and businesses alike. This website makes it easy for businesses to post jobs, and easy for job seekers to access the Job Bank and other resources. You'll find a calendar of free career-related workshops that are offered in a CW office near you, job market news, labor statistics, and more!

Hartford Courant Newspaper

http://courant.ctnow.com/classifieds/careers

Use the Connecticut website directory or the local business directory. To start your Mega Job Search, select a location, click on the job category that interests you, and type in additional keywords to refine your search. Select Search Now to view the results.

jobfind.com

jobfind.com

Jobfind is a great one-stop resource for New England jobs! Post your resume free in the Resume Port, check out the career articles or the handy calendar of events, or research company profiles. To find a job, enter a keyword or phrase into the Job Search box and press the Go button to view the results.

Delaware

Delaware's Job Bank

ajb.org/de

The easiest way to search the Job Bank is to select a job category and enter your zip code in the Occupation Search. You can also search by keyword, military code, or job number.

DelAWARE

lib.de.us

DelAWARE: The Digital Library of the First State is a joint project of the state's libraries and the Technical and Community College. Use the DelaWeb links to access educational resources, governmental agencies, and business information. The Jobs and Careers page includes links to jobs in Delaware and a listing of employment sites by category.

Delaware Online, a service of the *Wilmington News Journal*

delawareonline.com

This site presents all of the usual features of a daily newspaper, plus yellow pages for Delaware businesses. Click on the Jobs link to access the career resources. Register to post your resume, or check out the featured employers. Search for a job by keyword in the local or national databases, or browse the leads by employer.

Delaware Virtual Career Network

vcnet.net

The state of Delaware's one-stop employment and training delivery system puts you in charge! Use the self-help job search and career resources, get bus schedules, access child care referrals, or locate information about training and educational opportunities.

MBNA Career Services Center (CSC), University of Delaware

udel.edu/csc/students.html

The University of Delaware's CSC has developed this wonderful resource for students and alumni of the school. You can explore career opportunities or get sound advice for interviewing or developing your resume. The Major Resource Kits link connects academic majors to career alternatives and offers sample job titles, information on developing your own career path, and listings of jobs in your field. New to this edition are the Web presentations. You will need to download RealPlayer in order to hear them.

District of Columbia

District of Columbia's Job Bank

ajb.org/dc

The easiest way to search the Job Bank is to select a job category and enter your zip code in the Occupation Search. You can also search by keyword, military code, or job number.

CapAccess: Greater Washington's Community Network

capaccess.org

You'll find helpful information about the local communities and links to libraries and educational institutions. You'll also find business resources and government agencies, although there are very few career resources listed.

DC Metro ComputerJobs

dc.computerjobs.com

Headquartered in Atlanta, ComputerJobs.com is the leading Internet-based job-search company for computer and information technology professionals.

Washington, DC, ComputerWork

http://dc.computerwork.com

Find more jobs in the IT sector! This is one of dozens of local sites that ComputerWork maintains for professionals in the information technology field.

The *Washington Post*

washingtonpost.com

Click on WashingtonJobs to access the career page. Post your resume or check out the career advice in Job Central. Search by category, employer, job location, and keyword. Use several keywords and join them with *and* (e.g., residential *and* property *and* manager) or use quotes to delineate a phrase (e.g., *property manager*). You can also add *not* for any term you want to exclude (e.g., *not night* will exclude jobs with graveyard shifts).

Florida

Florida's Job Bank

ajb.org/fl

The easiest way to search the Job Bank is to select a job category and enter your zip code in the Occupation Search. You can also search by keyword, military code, or job number.

Florida Agency for Workforce Innovation (AWI)

http://www2.myflorida.com/awi

Newly created by the Florida legislature in the year 2000, AWI offers interviewing and resume-writing tips, along with links to Florida job leads.

Florida Board of Education Division of Colleges and Universities Position Vacancies

borfl.org/EmploymentOps

The Florida State University Job Board includes job postings for all the state's universities. Listings are for faculty, administration, and support personnel. Select a school to access the job information. You'll also find salary information and application details.

Florida ComputerJobs

florida.computerjobs.com

Headquartered in Atlanta, ComputerJobs.com is the leading Internet-based job-search company for computer and information technology professionals.

Florida ComputerWork

http://florida.computerwork.com

Find more jobs in the IT sector! This is one of dozens of local sites that ComputerWork maintains for professionals in the information technology field.

MyFlorida.com (formerly Government Services Direct)

myflorida.com

myflorida.com/myflorida/employment/index.html

MyFlorida.com offers information about a range of resources and services available to Florida residents. You'll find a listing of continuing education opportunities, business forms, organization contact information, and local community links. Click on Employment, or use the second URL to access the job page. Visit the High-Tech Employment Center, search for Florida government jobs, or link to county, municipal, and other job offerings.

Tallahassee Free-net

freenet.tlh.fl.us

Tallahassee's network offers a great deal of helpful information. You'll find links to business information and directories, government agencies, community and educational resources, and some interactive forums or communities. On the opening page, scroll down to Employment to access the job and career resources. The job resources listed as Local & Florida are among the most extensive we have seen for the state.

Workforce Florida

wages.org/wages/wfi/index.html

At the time of review, Workforce was under construction. It intends to be the "online gateway to workforce information and resources" for the state of Florida.

Georgia

Georgia's Job Bank

ajb.org/ga

The easiest way to search the Job Bank is to select a job category and enter your zip code in the Occupation Search. You can also search by keyword, military code, or job number.

AccessAtlanta.com

accessatlanta.com

In partnership with the *Atlanta Journal-Constitution* and other media outlets, AccessAtlanta offers consumer information, an entertainment calendar, and resources of interest to community residents. Click on Find a Job to reach the employment page. Browse by category or date, or link to the *Journal-Constitution* job leads.

Atlanta ComputerJobs

atlanta.computerjobs.com

Headquartered in Atlanta, ComputerJobs.com (computerjobs.com) is the leading Internet-based job-search company for computer and information technology professionals. More than four thousand companies post jobs to ComputerJobs, which serves nineteen metropolitan markets. You'll find industry, training, and career information for computer professionals, plus an events schedule. Post your resume and check out the hundreds of job listings.

Atlanta Journal-Constitution

ajc.com

ajcclassifieds.com

The *Atlanta Journal-Constitution* offers this online version of the newspaper. Click on the AJCclassified link or use the second URL to access the jobs. Research Atlanta employers, learn more about ajcjobsTV, a local television program featuring information of interest to area job seekers and career changers, or check out the calendar of events for job fairs and networking possibilities. Search for employment by job category.

City of Atlanta Home Page

ci.atlanta.ga.us

You'll find information about the community here, including links to local events, government information, and services for residences and businesses. Click on the Employment link for a list of current job opportunities and instructions for applying for a position. You can also call the Job Line at (404) 330-6456 or send E-mail to cityjobs@ci.atlanta.ga.us for up-to-date information.

Fulton County, Georgia, Personnel Department

fulton.ga.us/personnel/joblistings.html

New job opportunities are posted at this site as they become available. Call (404) 730-6700 or send E-mail to fcrecruiting@co.fulton.ga.us for more information.

Georgia Department of Education

doe.k12.ga.us

Scroll down the Department of Education page to the Employment link. You'll find jobs within the department and with the public schools of Georgia. Teacher certification information, directories of educational institutions, and continuing education resources are all accessible through this website.

Georgia Department of Labor

dol.state.ga.us

Georgia One-Stop Career Network

g1careernet.com

The department of labor provides links to state agency recruitment sites, labor market information, welfare-to-work resources, and other assistance for job seekers and career changers. Link to the One-Stop system from the DOL website or use the second URL to go there directly. The One-Stop site offers support services, job information, and career resources, all in one handy location.

Guam

Guam's Job Bank

ajb.org/gu

The easiest way to search the Job Bank is to select a job category and enter your zip code in the Occupation Search. You can also search by keyword, military code, or job number.

Government of Guam Official Departments

gov.gu/government.html

This page leads to all of Guam's government agencies, including the Department of Labor and the University of Guam. Some of the agencies offer their employment opportunities online.

Guam's One-Stop Career Service Center

http://onestopcareer.gov.gu

Post your resume, explore career options, or find training or financial aid information. Additional links include information about transportation and child care, business start-up and development resources, and . . . job leads!

JobsonGuam.com

jobsonguam.com

Search by job title or by company.

Hawaii

Hawaii's Job Bank

ajb.org/hi

The easiest way to search the Job Bank is to select a job category and enter your zip code in the Occupation Search. You can also search by keyword, military code, or job number.

Career Giant

careergiant.com

Research the company profiles or explore the helpful resources in the Career Communities. Browse through all of the jobs, or search for a specific job title.

Hawaii.com

hawaii.com

hawaii.net

Hawaii.com serves as a portal or single point of entry into the state of Hawaii's websites. You'll find lifestyle links and information about doing business in the fiftieth state. Scroll down the opening page to the Business link to access a helpful business directory and the employment resources. The job leads are from area newspapers, government agencies, and other career websites. If you're thinking of relocating to Hawaii, be sure to check out the moving guide to assist you in making the transition.

Hawaii Department of Labor and Industrial Relations (DOLIR)

http://dlir.state.hi.us

http://dlir.state.hi.us/wdd

The DOLIR page links to career resources developed by the state, current labor market information, and information supplied by the federal government. Link to the One-Stop Career Centers or use the second URL to go there directly. The Workforce Development Division (WDD) of the Labor Department is the lead agency for job placement and training in Hawaii.

Maui Island Guide

mauimapp.com

mauimapp.com/community/resourcesa.htm

The use of frames makes this site difficult to navigate, but you'll find links to a calendar of events, along with some business, community, and government information. There are no job listings here, although the second URL links directly to a directory of phone numbers that includes employment assistance.

Online Hawaii

hcc.hawaii.edu/hspls/onlhaw.html

hcc.hawaii.edu/hspls/hjobs.html

Brought to you by the Hawaii State Public Library System, Online Hawaii offers business information and directories, government information, and community resources. The second URL takes you directly to the Job Listings page.

Idaho

Idaho's Job Bank

ajb.org/id

The easiest way to search the Job Bank is to select a job category and enter your zip code in the Occupation Search. You can also search by keyword, military code, or job number.

Idaho Department of Labor

doe.state.id.us

Idaho Works: Idaho's Workforce Development System

idahoworks.state.id.us

The Idaho Department of Labor is part of the Workforce Development System, a partnership of state and local agencies whose mission is the continuing development of an educated workforce in the state. The DOL created and maintains Idaho Works, which assists businesses in solving employment challenges and helps individuals with career transitions. Use the second URL to go directly to Idaho Works.

Illinois

Illinois's Employment Opportunities and Job Bank

ides.state.il.us/general/jobs.htm

ajb.org/il

This is your one-stop source for skills matching, job opportunities in state government, and the Illinois Job Bank. The second URL takes you directly to the Job Bank. Searching is easiest when you select a job category and enter your zip code in the Occupation Search. You can also search by keyword, military code, or job number.

Champaign-Urbana News Gazette

newsgazette.com

Find a job; find a place to stay! The *News Gazette* offers a searchable database of more than one thousand housing units maintained by the Champaign County Apartment Association. Scroll down the opening page to access the Link2Careers or @Work resources. You can submit your resume, but keep in mind that the service is not confidential, and anyone with access to the Internet can view it.

Chicago ComputerJobs

chicago.computerjobs.com

Headquartered in Atlanta, ComputerJobs.com is the leading Internet-based job-search company for computer and information technology professionals.

Chicago ComputerWork

http://chicago.computerwork.com

Find more jobs in the IT sector! This is one of dozens of local sites that ComputerWork maintains for professionals in the information technology field.

Chicago Sun-Times

suntimes.com/classified/Employment.html

The *Sun-Times* offers career advice, along with technology and business information. To start your job search, choose a category, add keywords if you wish, and click on the search button to view the results. You can also browse through all of the job leads or link to a consortium of other newspapers that includes the *Pioneer Press, Daily Southtown, Star Newspapers,* and *Post-Tribune.*

Chicago Tribune

http://chicagotribune.com

http://chicagotribune.com/careers

The Business page features helpful articles, recommended websites, and a business adviser for small-business owners. Click on the Jobs link or use the second URL to go directly to the career page and assemble a professional resume. Check out the high-tech news and job leads in the Silicon Prairie or the always helpful advice of Carol Kleiman.

ChicagoJobs.org: the Definitive Chicago Area Job and Career Guide

chicagojobs.org

Maintained by librarians at the Skokie Public Library and supported in part by the North Suburban Library System, ChicagoJobs continues as a quality guide to resources for local job seekers and career changers. You'll find links to job postings, salary surveys, recruiters, networking opportunities, career advice, and more. ChicagoJobs is part of NorthStarNet (northstarnet.org), the comprehensive community information network for the northern suburbs of Illinois.

City of Chicago

cityofchicago.org

From the Chicago home page, you can link to all the city's agencies and services. Scroll down the page to the Job Opportunities link. Browse through the job leads online or call the twenty-four-hour job hot line: (312) 744-1369. If you find a position in which you're interested, apply at the Application Service Center at City Hall, 121 North LaSalle, room 100, Chicago, IL 60602. The city also offers "Looking for Work?" a cable television program (stations 23 and 49) that features career advice, job leads, and live interviews with Chicago-area job seekers. Job seekers interested in appearing on the program should send a resume to City Hall, room 1100.

Illinois Department of Commerce and Community Affairs (DCCA)

commerce.state.il.us

The DCCA site provides a lot of good information about starting a new business and managing it successfully, as well as resources for updating your skills to compete in today's job market. You'll also find up-to-date community profiles and a calendar of events.

Midwest ComputerWork

http://midwest.computerwork.com

Find more jobs in the IT sector! This is one of dozens of local sites that ComputerWork maintains for professionals in the information technology field.

State Journal-Register Online

sj-r.com

Find jobs in the state's capital city! Scroll down the page to the Employment link to access the career resources. You can browse the job leads by category.

Indiana

Indiana's Job Bank

ajb.org/in

The easiest way to search the Job Bank is to select a job category and enter your zip code in the Occupation Search. You can also search by keyword, military code, or job number.

Access Indiana, the Official Website of the State of Indiana

ai.org/index.html

state.in.us

Indiana's official website is an interactive system that provides convenient access to loads of good information. Either URL will take you to the main page. State agencies, educational resources, social services, and community and business information are all just a click away!

HoosierNet

bloomington.in.us

HoosierNet pulls together a wealth of community information for the Bloomington area, including educational and business resources. You'll also find links to libraries and IRIS, a searchable database of local social service organizations. Click on the Employment link to reach the career resources.

Indiana Career and Postsecondary Advancement Center

http://icpac.indiana.edu

The Indiana Career and Postsecondary Advancement Center website provides timely, useful education, financial aid, and career information. It's a great resource! Complete the interactive Career Interest Checklist to see what careers fit your interests. New since the last edition of this book are the College Profiles, which contain helpful information about more than twenty-eight hundred colleges and universities nationwide.

Indiana Department of Workforce Development (DWD)

in.gov/dwd

in.gov/dwd/joblistings.shtm

DWD maintains this website and free access to job banks, career-planning assistance, unemployment assistance, a calendar of career fairs, and more! The second URL goes directly to the job listings and to DWD's Customer Self Service System (CS3), an interactive service that provides access to statewide job-matching and labor market information.

Indianapolis Online (IO)

indianapolis.in.us

Choose a category, or search the website for helpful job and career information. Billing itself as the "Community Network for Indianapolis," IO provides access to lots of good resources—housing and relocation information, government agencies, educational institutions, business directories and assistance, plus several local and state job links.

Indico: Indiana Digital County Network

indico.net

Community Information Networks (CINs) offer a great deal of helpful local information, and residents of Indiana have Indico to provide the framework that connects all of the state's CINs. The business, government, education, and community links could be helpful in your job search.

Star/News Online

starnews.com

The *Star News* provides a helpful Community section and offers business information that could assist you in your search. Choose the Classifieds link on the opening page to access the career information. Research the major employers or search for employment opportunities in the *Star News* classifieds or WorkAvenue.com. You must register (free) to post your resume or to develop your profile for the Job Agent.

Iowa

Iowa's Job Bank

ajb.org/ia

The easiest way to search the Job Bank is to select a job category and enter your zip code in the Occupation Search. You can also search by keyword, military code, or job number.

Iowa Jobs

state.ia.us/jobs/index.htm

Browse or search for full-time or part-time work in the public or private sector. As you browse, be sure to click on the sort-by-date option to ensure that the newest jobs are listed first. You'll also find links to other job and career resources.

Iowa Workforce Development (IWD)

iowaworkforce.org

The organization whose motto is "Putting Iowa to Work" links job placement, skill development, and lifelong learning through programs and services created for workers, job seekers, and employers. From the IWD website, you can search the job bank or find labor statistics, career information, or the local Workforce office nearest you.

Kansas

Kansas Job Bank

ajb.org/ks

The easiest way to search the Job Bank is to select a job category and enter your zip code in the Occupation Search. You can also search by keyword, military code, or job number.

AccessKansas.com

accesskansas.org

The official website for the state of Kansas offers access to government and community information, assistance in doing business in Kansas, and links to educational organizations. Click on Working in Kansas to open a helpful page of information and links to government jobs, resources organized by profession, and a salary calculator.

Kansas City Star

kcstar.com

kansascity.com

http://careers.kansascity.com

Browse the newspaper online, or use the second URL to link to the Kansas City Community page. KC's yellow pages, business and community resources, and other helpful information are all available at the touch of a keyboard. Use the third URL to access the career resources. Check out the employer profiles or salary information, submit your resume, or look over some of the career articles. To start your Mega Job Search, select a location, click on the job category that interests you, and type in additional keywords to refine your search. Select "Search Now" to view the results.

Kansas Department of Human Resources (KDHR)

hr.state.ks.us

kansasjobs.org

The KDHR links to training and career resources, along with information about the employment services offered to Kansans. Use the second URL to go directly to the Employment and Training page and the Kansas Job Link.

Kansas Job Link

kansasjoblink.com

New this edition is the Kansas Job Link (KJL), which matches employers with job candidates. When we reviewed KJL, we experienced a number of Java errors, which made it difficult to navigate the website.

Topeka Capital-Journal

cjonline.com

http://cjonline.com/jobfetcher

Under the heading of Marketplace, select JobFetcher from the pull-down menu to access the career resources or use the second URL to go there directly. Use JobFetcher's employment tools to research a potential employer, get helpful career advice, or create a cover letter. To start your job search, click on Job Search and select a specific category. The job listings include those from many other newspapers, so be sure that you select the Topeka newspaper.

Wichita Area Chamber of Commerce

wichitakansas.org

wichitakansas.org/wichitanationjob/index.html

Click on the Chamber of Commerce link to get into the site. The resources include a searchable membership directory. You'll also find several helpful resources under the Member Services section. These include a job database, Wichita NationJob Network, which is updated daily. Use the second URL to go there directly. You can view all current job leads or browse by company name.

Kentucky

Kentucky's Job Bank

ajb.org/ky

The easiest way to search the Job Bank is to select a job category and enter your zip code in the Occupation Search. You can also search by keyword, military code, or job number.

Kentucky Cabinet for Workforce Development

http://kycwd.org

desky.org

"Kentucky's Key to Employment" offers education, training, and employment information for job seekers and employers. Use the second URL to go directly to Job Services, which matches available workers with potential employers. You will also find current labor market information, learn about the One-Stop Career Centers, or locate the nearest service center.

Louisville Courier-Journal

courierjournal.com

The *Courier-Journal* has teamed up with *USA Today* to offer helpful articles and their "Ask a Counselor" service. Just click on LouisvilleJobs to get to the employment offerings. To start your "Kentuckiana" job search, type in keywords, select a job category, and click the Search button. You can then browse through the results or refine your search and try again.

Louisiana

Louisiana's Job Bank

ajb.org/la

The easiest way to search the Job Bank is to select a job category and enter your zip code in the Occupation Search. You can also search by keyword, military code, or job number.

The *Baton Rouge Advocate*

theadvocate.com

lajobmarket.com

Easiest access to the job section is through the Classified Ads. Scroll down the page and click on the Help Wanted icon to view the jobs. You could also link to the Louisiana Job Market from here. Use the second URL to go there directly, although when we reviewed the site, it didn't offer nearly as many job leads as the *Advocate*'s classified section did.

Louisiana Works

ldol.state.la.us

ldol.state.la.us/jobspage.htm

Downloadable forms, career resources, and job services are all at your fingertips! Users can access occupation and labor information, statistics, and more from the Louisiana Occupational Information System (LOIS). Click on Jobs or use the second URL to go directly to the job-search page. To start the search, answer the question, "Where would you like to work?"

NOLA Live with the *Times-Picayune*

nola.com

nola.com/careers

Learn all about New Orleans and the music and traditions of Mardi Gras. Use the handy yellow pages to find businesses in the area or the Community Connection to access information about local organizations. Click on Find a Job or use the second URL to go directly to the career resources. Access the Career Wise columns or the relocation tools. To initiate a Quick Search, select a category and follow the directions. You must register (free) to post your resume or to have job postings sent to you via E-mail.

Maine

Maine's Job Bank

ajb.org/me

The easiest way to search the Job Bank is to select a job category and enter your zip code in the Occupation Search. You can also search by keyword, military code, or job number.

jobfind.com

jobfind.com

Jobfind is a great one-stop resource for New England jobs! Post your resume free in the Resume Port, check out the career articles or the handy calendar of events, or research company profiles. To find a job, enter a keyword or phrase into the Job Search box and press the Go button to view the results.

Maine State Government

state.me.us

mainecareercenter.com

The state of Maine offers a wealth of resources through its server. Link to communities statewide, access the HealthWeb for up-to-date health information, visit libraries and educational institutions, or find loads of information about starting or growing a business. Click on Business to reach the Employment links, which include state jobs and the CareerCenter, or use the second URL to go directly to the resources.

MaineToday.com/*Press Herald* Online

portland.com

http://business.mainetoday.com

http://careers.mainetoday.com

The *Press Herald* is your gateway to tons of business and career resources! You can also go directly to either section using the alternative URLs. Access the small-business articles, or get savvy career advice. Find a job three ways: fill out your career profile and have your skills matched with potential employers, search the classified ads of the *Portland Press Herald, Maine Sunday Telegram, Morning Sentinel,* and/or *Kennebec Journal,* or browse the employer profiles.

Maryland

Maryland's Job Bank

ajb.org/md

The easiest way to search the Job Bank is to select a job category and enter your zip code in the Occupation Search. You can also search by keyword, military code, or job number.

HometownAnnapolis.com

hometownannapolis.com

HometownAnnapolis.com includes a directory of local businesses and organizations on the Web. Easiest navigation is through the Site Map. To find employment, select Classifieds from the menu, then select from among the *Capital,* the *Maryland Gazette,* or the *Washingtonian* Online. Use keywords to refine your search, or browse all of the offerings.

Maryland Careers

http://members.home.net/marylandcareers

Maryland Careers pulls it all together in a comprehensive and easy-to-use website for job seekers and career changers! You'll find association and business links, a handy page of job hot lines, career resources from around the state, and information about "how hiring is actually done in Maryland."

Maryland's CareerNet

careernet.state.md.us

Maryland's CareerNet provides employment and training services for job seekers and employers in locations throughout the state. CareerNet on the Internet is a nicely organized page of links accessible by county or by topic. Self-assessment tools, career exploration and planning resources, and job leads are all available here. The Professional Outplacement Assistance Center (POAC) provides information and services for individuals in the professional, technical, and managerial occupations. Use the POAC Meta List to access all kinds of helpful resources.

Sailor: Maryland's Online Public Information Network

sailor.lib.md.us

Developed by the libraries of Maryland, Sailor connects its communities with state and local information and library databases. It also links to select Internet sites. To access the career resources, select the Business/Employment link or choose E for Employment in the Maryland A to Z section. You'll also find education, government, and community information, and more!

SunSpot.net from the *Baltimore Sun*

sunspot.net

SunSpot is an online service of the *Baltimore Sun*, a newspaper with a more than 160-year history of serving its readers. As Maryland's Online Community, this is a great starting point for opportunities in the state. You can search the more recent two weeks of job classifieds here, compliments of the *Sun* and CareerBuilder. To find your dream job, just select a major Maryland area and the job category that interests you.

Massachusetts

Massachusetts Job Bank

ajb.org/ma

The easiest way to search the Job Bank is to select a job category and enter your zip code in the Occupation Search. You can also search by keyword, military code, or job number.

Boston ComputerWork

http://boston.computerwork.com

Find more jobs in the IT sector! This is one of dozens of local sites that ComputerWork maintains for professionals in the information technology field.

The *Boston Globe*'s Boston.com

boston.com

http://digitalmass.boston.com

http://bostonworks.boston.com

Read the latest about area businesses or find an apartment. Use the second URL to visit DigitalMASS, featuring news about the computer industry and current IT job opportunities. Click on Boston Works, or use the third URL to go directly to the career page. Check out the employer profiles, post your resume, or access a job fair schedule. Boston.com claims to have the largest database of New England–region jobs. Online-only listings are added daily, while the *Boston Sunday Globe* listings are updated every Monday. To search, choose a category, add keywords, and click on the Search button.

Boston Online

boston-online.com

Boston Online maintains this collection of links to business and educational resources, communities, libraries, and more! You'll find the tongue-in-cheek "Wicked Good Guide" to Boston English along with reasons why Boston is better than Atlanta. Click on the Boston Links to reach the career resources.

BostonComputerJobs

boston.computerjobs.com

Headquartered in Atlanta, ComputerJobs.com is the leading Internet-based job-search source for computer and information technology professionals.

BostonSearch.com

bostonsearch.com

You can search for jobs, look up employers, and post your resume on this site specific to the Boston area.

Commonwealth of Massachusetts Home Page

state.ma.us

state.ma.us/job.htm

When we reviewed the site, the new and improved Massachusetts "Portal Power to the People" home page (mass.gov) was under construction. When it is completed, Mass.gov will offer even *more* services online. Currently, you can download forms or pay or apply for services online. You'll find links to the local communities and information of interest to experienced entrepreneurs and new business owners alike. The Employment link offers an interesting assortment of mostly government job opportunities. Use the second URL to go there directly.

jobfind.com

jobfind.com

Jobfind is a great one-stop resource for New England jobs! Post your resume free in the Resume Port, check out the career articles or the handy calendar of events, or research company profiles. To find a job, enter a keyword or phrase into the Job Search box and press the Go button to view the results.

Massachusetts Tech Corps

masstechcorps.org

The Tech Corps was created in 1995 to take advantage of the technical expertise available within the community. At the time of review, Massachusetts was home to more than twenty-seven hundred software companies employing more than one hundred thousand individuals. Volunteers from the Tech Corps use their skills to work with public schools throughout the commonwealth, helping to teach young folks about technology or working on projects to enhance technology in the classrooms. More volunteers are needed, and this could be a good way to get that much-needed hands-on experience, develop your network, or keep active by sharing what you know with others.

New England ComputerWork

http://newengland.computerwork.com

Find more jobs in the IT sector! This is one of dozens of local sites that ComputerWork maintains for professionals in the information technology field.

Tango! from the *Telegram & Gazette*

telegram.com

eworcester.com

eworcester.com

Catch the news and up-to-date business information from southern Worcester County and northern Connecticut. Select from among the tabs at the top of the page to access the information you need. Eworcester.com offers community information. You'll also find a yellow pages directory. Select Employment from the Classifieds menu to start your job search.

Town Online

townonline.com

townonline.com/working

"Building community" in eastern Massachusetts, Town Online offers news and information about and for the dozens of towns represented here. Among the offerings are community calendars, yellow pages, and other information of local interest. Use the second URL to delve into the employment resources. Check out the advice columns or ask an expert a question about work. Job leads are provided through jobfind.com.

Michigan

Michigan Talent Bank

http://michworks.org

Michigan Works maintains the Talent Bank and supplies job seekers and employers with the help they need via a statewide system of service centers. Users have access to a wide range of training opportunities, employment support services, and job leads. Register your skills and post your resume. To start your job search, choose the area of the state map in which you're interested, and click on the Close button. Next, enter a job title or keywords and click on the Search button to view the results.

MEL: Michigan Electronic Library

http://mel.lib.mi.us

http://mel.lib.mi.us/michigan/MI-business.html

http://mel.lib.mi.us/michigan/MI-employment.html

A joint project of the state's libraries, MEL is an excellent one-stop answer for your Michigan information needs, including businesses (potential employers) and job resources. The Michigan link leads to helpful local information. Use the second URL to access a searchable directory of Michigan businesses and the third to go directly to the Michigan career resources.

Michigan Department of Career Development (MDCD)

state.mi.us/career

The MDCD website reflects the department's mission to provide resources and support services that increase the skill levels of Michigan workers. These services include Michigan Works, the Michigan Talent Bank, Work First (Welfare-to-Work), and other workforce development resources. New this edition is the Talent Freeway that offers career exploration and planning tools for youth, retirees, college-age job seekers, and others navigating the world of work.

Minnesota

Minnesota's Job Banks

ajb.org/mn

mnworks.org

The first URL leads to the usual menu of Job Bank options. The easiest way to search the Job Bank is to select a job category and enter your zip code in the Occupation Search. You can also search by keyword, military code, or job number. The second URL links to Minnesota's other Job Bank. Register and create your profile so that you can save searches or have new job leads E-mailed to you.

METRONET

metronet.lib.mn.us/mn/mn.html

metronet.lib.mn.us/mn/mn-bizb.html

METRONET is a multitype library organization serving academic, public, and special libraries in the Twin Cities (Minneapolis and St. Paul). Use the second URL to go to the business-to-business resources that include employment information. You'll find additional links in the Minnesota Web Directory to education, media, government, association, and business resources, which could prove helpful in navigating the hidden job market.

Minnesota Workforce Center System

mnworkforcecenter.org

iseek.org

mnworkforcecenter.org/cjs/cjs_site/index.htm

Minnesota continues to deliver cutting edge service to its job seekers and career changers! The first URL leads to the full range of career-related resources provided by the state of Minnesota. New this year is a state-of-the-art Mobile Career Development Van that goes wherever job seekers and employers need it most. Use the second URL to use the Internet System for Education and Employment Knowledge (ISEEK), a tool for career exploration that links to educational offerings, training programs, occupations, skill requirements, and job openings. Use the third URL to access the Creative Job Search online guide (CJS), which teaches the skills necessary for conducting a successful job search. These are wonderful resources!

Star Tribune WorkAvenue

startribune.com/workavenue

Minneapolis–St. Paul Star Tribune online features links to WorkAvenue and Internet System for Education and Employment Knowledge (ISEEK) career resources. The Quick Search allows searching by job category, job title, or keyword. Use the Advanced Search to narrow your results to a specific location and preferred rate of pay. To receive new job postings via E-mail or post your resume, you'll need to register (free).

Mississippi

Mississippi's Job Bank

ajb.org/ms

The easiest way to search the Job Bank is to select a job category and enter your zip code in the Occupation Search. You can also search by keyword, military code, or job number.

Mississippi Employment Security Commission (MESC)

mesc.state.ms.us

Scroll down the opening page to get to labor market information, job fair schedules, and the state Job Bank.

State of Mississippi

state.ms.us

The state of Mississippi page serves as a gateway to resources throughout the state. Use the Business link to view the employment links, jobs in state government, and information about the business community. You'll also find links to Mississippi's schools and colleges and to local, state, and federal government information.

Missouri

Missouri's Job Bank

ajb.org/mo

The easiest way to search the Job Bank is to select a job category and enter your zip code in the Occupation Search. You can also search by keyword, military code, or job number.

Department of Labor and Industrial Relations (DOLIR)

dolir.state.mo.us

DOLIR links to all of the agencies and services created for Missouri's job seekers and career changers. There are a few job leads.

Kansas City, Missouri

kcmo.org

Check here for information about the "City of Fountains," municipal services, and a calendar of upcoming events. Click on Job Opportunities to review the employment listings along with information about the application process, or use the twenty-four-hour job hot line: (816) 513-1127.

Missouri State Government Web

state.mo.us

oa.state.mo.us/stjobs.htm

The state website links to the usual government agencies and services. Click on State Jobs, or use the second URL, to go to a nice assortment of Missouri job links. These include the universities, individual agency postings, and jobs in St. Louis.

Missouri WORKS!

works.state.mo.us

Missouri WORKS! is about employment, job development, and training. Job seekers can register and post their resumes online. The Resource Center offers labor market statistics, information on veterans' benefits, details of federal training programs, and more. Start your search for job opportunities by selecting the area of the state map in which you're interested.

St. Louis ComputerJobs

stlouis.computerjobs.com

Headquartered in Atlanta, ComputerJobs.com is the leading Internet-based job-search company for computer and information technology professionals.

St. Louis Employment Links

http://members.tripod.com/~Jablon/assess.html

Moira Jablon-Bernstein created this alphabetical listing of links for St. Louis job seekers. It features mostly businesses along with a few government, school, and organization websites.

St. Louis, Missouri, Community Information Network (CIN)

http://stlouis.missouri.org

http://stlcin.missouri.org/citypers/jobs.cfm

The St. Louis CIN features a Community Resources database that includes more than thirty organizations that offer employment assistance. You'll find other useful links including information about the neighborhoods and local and state governments. Use the second URL to go directly to the current city job opportunities.

Stlouisatwork.com

stlouisatwork.com

Stlouisatwork.com represents a public-private partnership that matches candidates to jobs through "My e-Recruiter" matching service. You'll also find profiles of leading employers as well as training and educational opportunities. View all jobs or search by category, level of educational attainment, job title, salary, and other qualifiers.

STLtoday.com

stltoday.com

stltoday.com/jobs

Brought to you by the *St. Louis Post-Dispatch*, STLtoday.com offers business news and searchable business yellow pages. Click on the Jobs link or use the second URL to go to the Job Search page. Link to the Stlouisatwork.com database or search the *Post-Dispatch* and *Suburban Journal* job leads. Select today's ads, Sunday's ads, or those for the past seven days. Add keywords to limit your results.

Montana

Montana's Job Bank

ajb.org/mt

The easiest way to search the Job Bank is to select a job category and enter your zip code in the Occupation Search. You can also search by keyword, military code, or job number.

Billings Gazette Online

billingsgazette.com

Explore the community, business, and technology links or check out the Work Week section. Click on the Classifieds icon to access the job opportunities. To browse the current offerings, select the day of the week and the Employment page.

Discovering Montana

discoveringmontana.com

The official website for the state of Montana features agency and education information, tourist resources, and helpful guides to working, living, and doing business in Montana. Navigation is easiest using the site map. The Employment Guide includes links to the state's Job Service, Montana Job Network, state government offerings, and opportunities in teaching and the health professions.

Montana Job Service

http://jsd.dli.state.mt.us

Check the Montana Job Service for all kinds of job opportunities throughout the state. New this edition are the Natural Resource Education Youth Summer Camps designed to educate Montana's future natural resource managers. You'll also find additional material devoted to youth services, job-hunting advice, and labor market information.

Nebraska

Nebraska's Job Bank

ajb.org/ne

The easiest way to search the Job Bank is to select a job category and enter your zip code in the Occupation Search. You can also search by keyword, military code, or job number.

Access Omaha

accessomaha.com

The local chamber of commerce maintains this website featuring a business directory searchable by company name or industry. Click on Area Jobs or use the pull-down menu to reach the employment resources and web links. These include hot lines, employer information, career fair schedules, and job leads.

Career Link

careerlink.org

The Applied Information Management (AIM) Institute maintains this database of Nebraska career opportunities organized by field. Most jobs are in the information technology, education, engineering, and health care fields.

Lincoln Journal Star

journalstar.com

workforyounebraska.com

The *Lincoln Journal Star* newspaper now offers its job listings through the Employment Wizard. Use the second URL to go there directly. The job listings include those from the *Journal Star* and many other newspapers, so be sure that you select the Lincoln newspaper.

lincolnjobs.com

lincolnjobs.com

Maintained by the Lincoln Partnership for Economic Development, lincolnjobs.com offers a bit of career advice, links to several local employers, and a place to create and store your resume.

Nebrask@Online

nol.org

The official website for the state offers links to communities, libraries, government agencies, and more. Look for the job listings in the Business & Employment section of the site, where you will also find assistance for business start-up, directories of businesses, and information about specific industries. Nebrask@Online also includes links to state educational resources and information about child care alternatives.

Nebraska University (NU) Career Services

unl.edu/careers

At the time of review, NU Career Services was under construction but offering tons of helpful information nonetheless! NU's site includes information about internships, explores specific career paths, offers career keys for helping you make sound career decisions, and provides information about jobs in particular fields. The Husker Hire Link is available to students and alumni only and matches job candidates with potential employers.

Nebraska Workforce Development

dol.state.ne.us

Nebraska Workforce Development leads the state's job-creation and training efforts by providing services, tools, and information for job seekers and employers. Click on Worker Services to find a job or access other resources for job hunters.

Omaha.com

omaha.com

The *Omaha World-Herald* maintains this online edition of the newspaper. As with Lincoln's *Journal Star*, the job listings include those from many other newspapers, so be sure that you select Omaha's job ads.

Nevada

Nevada's Job Bank

ajb.org/nv

The easiest way to search the Job Bank is to select a job category and enter your zip code in the Occupation Search. You can also search by keyword, military code, or job number.

Las Vegas Review-Journal

lvrj.com

Search for a nonprofit organization under Community Link. To start your job search, click on the Classifieds link. Select Employment to browse through all the job listings, or browse through the featured job-training opportunities.

Lasvegas.com

lasvegas.com

lasvegas.com/features/jobs.html

You'll find information about visiting, living in, or moving to Las Vegas. Use the second URL to go directly to the job listings, which include opportunities in the city of Las Vegas, the University of Nevada at Las Vegas, and many other local employers.

Nevada Department of Employment Training & Rehabilitation (DETR)

http://detr.state.nv.us

Locate workshops, the Nevada Talent Bank, and a Career Information System open to Nevada residents only. You'll also find a listing of service locations and loads of other DETR resources.

NevadaNet

nevadanet.com

Developed and maintained by Reno's *Gazette-Journal*, the NevadaNet guide offers a taste of life in northern Nevada. Separate links on the home page take you to the newspaper, calendars of special events, and other items of interest. Click on the Career Finder link to go to the classifieds. Select the Search button to browse all available employment opportunities. To refine your search, choose a category or add keywords.

New Hampshire

New Hampshire Works and Job Bank

nhworks.state.nh.us

nhworks.state.nh.us/jobs/jobs.htm

Updated daily, New Hampshire Works features career resources, job leads, regional economic and labor market information, and links to other New Hampshire resources. New this edition is NHetwork, designed for individuals in need of more detailed information about careers and the world of work. Use the second URL to go directly to the Job Bank.

jobfind.com

jobfind.com

Jobfind is a great one-stop resource for New England jobs. Post your resume free in the Resume Port, check out the career articles or the handy calendar of events, or research company profiles. To find a job, enter a keyword or phrase into the Job Search box and press the Go button to view the results.

NH.com

nh.com

NH.com has the New Hampshire news, information, and directories you need. Click on NH JOBFINDER to start your job search. Select a job category and location to view the results.

The *Telegraph* on the Web

nashuatelegraph.com

The *Nashua Telegraph*, an NH.com partner, maintains this online version of the newspaper. Check out the community profiles, or keep up with local business and high-tech news. To explore the employment opportunities, click on the NH Jobfinder to reach the job leads, then enter your location and/or occupation.

WEBSTER: the New Hampshire State Government Online Information Center

state.nh.us

Maintained by the New Hampshire State Library, WEBSTER is the official website for the state. WEBSTER offers information about the cities and towns of the state, plus resources for living in, working in, and doing business in New Hampshire. You'll find additional links to the state's schools and colleges as well as other resources of interest. Use the Working in NH link to access the list of job resources.

New Jersey

New Jersey's Job Bank

ajb.org/nj

The easiest way to search the Job Bank is to select a job category and enter your zip code in the Occupation Search. You can also search by keyword, military code, or job number.

IN Jersey

injersey.com

http://jobs.injersey.com

From the opening page, New Jersey's "Home on the Internet" offers access to several of the state newspapers, including the *Asbury Park Press*, *Home News Tribune*, and *Courier News*. You'll also find a helpful Community Guide, featuring information compiled by the local newspapers. Click on Jobs or use the second URL to go directly to the employment page. Search one of the five classified pages listed, investigate the employer profiles, or post your resume.

New Jersey Home Page

state.nj.us

New Jersey's official website provides access to a multitude of services online, as well as resources statewide. Information about the state, its agencies, its counties, and its municipalities is at your fingertips. You'll also find dozens of links to business resources, local child care information, and education websites. The Ride/Fly/Drive page saves the time of the user by providing the information needed to travel anywhere in the state. Click on Work Here to reach an extensive collection of employment opportunities and other career resources. This is a wonderful example of tax dollars well spent!

New Jersey Online

nj.com

nj.com/careers

New Jersey Online offers business links, news from several of the state's newspapers, and handy yellow pages. The HomeTown section provides directories searchable by locale along with community resources. Click on Find a Job or use the second URL to reach the employment page. Consult the Career Calendar, learn more about local businesses, or use the relocation tools. Find a job in the *Express Times*, *Jersey Journal*, *Star Ledger*, or other newspapers. Search separately or simultaneously. Register (free) to create a profile and post your resume.

NJ Jobs

njjobs.com

NJ Jobs updates the job leads once a week. Use the search engine or browse the employment opportunities, which are listed in alphabetical order, by job title. You can browse through this week's jobs (A–M or N–Z) or look through the previous week's offerings. Use the Find feature of your web browser to look for keywords. Contact the employer or agency directly to apply for a listed position.

Philadelphia Online/Philly Jobs

philly.com

http://careers.philly.com

The online home of the *Inquirer* and the *Daily News*, Philadelphia Online serves the greater Philadelphia/South Jersey area as the "Region's Home Page." Use the handy search engine to access the community yellow pages, recent news articles, or the news archives. New this edition is Philly 101, which offers all the advice you need to manage as a full-time student and still have a great time. The Community and Education links offer helpful information about area schools and nonprofit organizations. To start your job search, select the Careers link, or use the second URL to go directly to the job page. Answer the question, "Where do you want to work?" then follow the directions, and view the results.

Workforce New Jersey Public Information Network (WNJPIN)

wnjpin.state.nj.us

Workforce New Jersey has developed this comprehensive one-stop career center featuring career resources, social services, and employer information. The site offers excellent information on conducting a job search and additional information about New Jersey communities, events, and activities. You'll also find help in starting your own business and dozens of helpful resources for students entering the world of work.

New Mexico

New Mexico's Job Bank

ajb.org/nm

The easiest way to search the Job Bank is to select a job category and enter your zip code in the Occupation Search. You can also search by keyword, military code, or job number.

ABQjournal: *Albuquerque Journal* **Online**

abqjournal.com

Check out the AP wire and business sections for up-to-date news and other issues that affect individuals and businesses in New Mexico. Classified ads are all just a click away! To search for job leads, select Employment and hit the Search button. Add a keyword to focus your search.

New Mexico Department of Labor (DOL)

http://www3.state.nm.us/dol/dol_home.html

http://www3.state.nm.us/dol/nmworks/front.asp

The DOL's mission is to promote economic development by matching the needs of employers with the skills of job seekers. Click on the NMWorks icon or use the second URL to access the online One-Stop Career Center. At this site, you'll also find information about training programs plus links to other useful New Mexico websites.

New York

New York's Job Bank

ajb.org/ny

The easiest way to search the Job Bank is to select a job category and enter your zip code in the Occupation Search. You can also search by keyword, military code, or job number.

Brooklyn Public Library Education and Job Information Center (EJIC)

brooklynpubliclibrary.org/central/ejic.htm

The librarians at the EJIC have developed a great resource that provides information about careers, education, test preparation, and businesses. Luckily, much of it has been made available here online! Other resources are accessible when you visit the Central Library in Brooklyn.

daVinci Times

davincitimes.org

DaVinci offers New Yorkers science and engineering news, links to additional engineering resources, internship opportunities, links to local technical schools, plus a bit of humor. Click on a specific discipline to locate the companies that typically need those skills. Select Careers to browse all of the current engineering and technical job opportunities. Registered users can post a resume and develop a profile for potential employers.

New York ComputerJobs

newyork.computerjobs.com

Headquartered in Atlanta, ComputerJobs.com is the leading Internet-based job-search company for computer and information technology professionals.

New York ComputerWork

http://newyork.computerwork.com

Find more jobs in the IT sector! This is one of dozens of local sites that ComputerWork maintains for professionals in the information technology field.

New York State Department of Labor

labor.state.ny.us

http://nycareerzone.org

The first URL takes you directly to the Department of Labor home page, whose mission is "Putting New Yorkers to Work." It's an outstanding resource for job seekers and career changers (and for the next generation entering the world of work). You'll find the Job Bank and labor statistics, plus links to other career resources. You'll also find additional links to business start-up information and the e-bizNYS resource page. Find information for the kids at the Youth Careers page. Link to or use the second URL to go directly to the CareerZone interactive career information system.

New York Times on the Web

nytimes.com

Although access to the *Times* is free, the publisher of "all the news that's fit to print" asks that you register before you use the paper. Check out the technology and company information, the business links on the Web, and other business resources. The Find a Job link leads to the Job Market page and thousands of listings. To start your job search, select a category, or enter a keyword.

Newsday.com

newsday.com

This site is the online home of *Newsday*, the newspaper for Long Island and Queens. There are handy yellow pages and guides for the two communities. Click on the Jobs link to reach the classified ads. To start your search for your dream job, answer the question, "Where do you want to work?" Next, select a category or enter a keyword, and view the results.

NYC.gov: The Official New York City Website

http://home.nyc.gov

New this edition is the "I Want To . . ." directory of commonly requested services. Whether it's about parking tickets, child care referrals, restaurant inspections, or jobs, you can get to the information you need from the opening page. You'll find the newly updated Business-to-Business directory, information about starting and growing a business in New York City, and anything else you could want to know about the "Big Apple." The Job Opportunities link offers an examination schedule, application procedures, and job leads.

RochesterCareers.com (formerly SmartDog)

rochestercareers.com

Now part of the *Democrat and Chronicle* online, RochesterCareers.com still features SmartDog, who offers his reasons why you should relocate to Rochester and a better life. Browse the company profiles or search the job listings. You must register (free) to post your resume, apply online, or use the Intelligent Agent to notify you via E-mail when a job matching your profile is posted.

Syracuse.com

syracuse.com

Syracuse.com, operated in partnership with The Herald, Inc., offers interactive forums, up-to-date business information, and a WebGuide featuring organizations, educational institutions, government agencies, and other resources in Central New York. Click on Find Jobs to access the educational and career resources. To start your Quick Search, select a job category, and follow the directions to view the results. Read the "Career Wise" articles or check out the Relocation Tools. Register (free) to post your resume or use the Power Search.

WNYWired.net

wnywired.net

Western New York Jobs (WNYJOBS)

wnyjobs.com

WNYWired.net offers a selection of helpful community resources that are browsable by topic or searchable sitewide. Education, business, and organization information are at your fingertips. Click on Employment or use the second URL to go directly to WNYJOBS and opportunities in the Buffalo, Jamestown, Niagara Falls, and Rochester areas. Job leads are updated daily. You can also register to post your resume and to be notified electronically by e-JOBS when new positions become available.

North Carolina

North Carolina's Job Bank

ajb.org/nc

The easiest way to search the Job Bank is to select a job category and enter your zip code in the Occupation Search. You can also search by keyword, military code, or job number.

Carolina ComputerJobs

carolina.computerjobs.com

Headquartered in Atlanta, ComputerJobs.com is the leading Internet-based job-search company for computer and information technology professionals.

Charlotte.com

charlotte.com

http://careers.charlotte.com

Here you'll find access to the *Charlotte Observer* online, searchable phone and E-mail directories, and links to schools, businesses, and local organizations. Click on Careers to reach the employment resources.

Employment Security Commission (ESC) of North Carolina

esc.state.nc.us

Here you'll find access to all the services and information provided by the ESC for North Carolinians. The ESC also serves as a gateway to other agency services and resources such as social services, transportation, child care, and child development resources. You'll also find job fair schedules, labor statistics, economic data, the Job Bank, and other employment-related resources.

The *News and Observer* Classifieds

newsobserver.com

nando.net

trianglejobs.com

One of the first newspapers online, the *News and Observer* site remains a good one. Read the annual survey of the Triangle's top technology companies. Stay on top of local news and business information, or use the second URL to go to the Nando Times News Watcher for updated headlines every fifteen minutes. New this edition is mobile access—get the latest headlines, movies, and more sent to you via your personal digital assistant. The third URL goes directly to the giant database of jobs from the Research Triangle, Chapel Hill, Raleigh, and Durham areas. Browse by job category, or use keywords to focus your results.

Public Library of Charlotte and Mecklenburg County

bizlink.org

Charlotte's librarians have gathered an outstanding selection of business resources for the Bizlink website. Whether it's researching a company or starting a new business, you'll find the information you need at this website. Link from the opening page to the Career Corner, which features resume assistance, career exploration tools, and local and regional job postings.

North Dakota

North Dakota's Job Bank

ajb.org/nd

The easiest way to search the Job Bank is to select a job category and enter your zip code in the Occupation Search. You can also search by keyword, military code, or job number.

GrandForks.com

grandforks.com

GrandForks.com features up-to-date news from the *Grand Forks Herald* and *AgWeek*. Click on Careers to access the job leads. Answer the question, "Where do you want to work?" to start your job search. Register (free) to post your resume.

Job Service North Dakota

state.nd.us/jsnd

Customer Resource Information System for North Dakota (CRISND)

http://crisnd.com/cris/home.html

Link to education and training resources, or access the helpful interviewing techniques and other strategies for putting your best foot forward. You'll also find a listing of upcoming job and career fairs. Use the second URL to access CRISND, part of the One Stop Delivery System that empowers its users and provides easy access to programs and services in North Dakota.

North Dakota Education Vacancies

state.nd.us/jsnd/education/update.vac.daily.htm

Job Service North Dakota maintains this handy collection of teaching job links for educators from kindergarten through twelfth grade to the community college level.

Ohio

Ohio's Job Bank

ajb.org/oh

The easiest way to search the Job Bank is to select a job category and enter your zip code in the Occupation Search. You can also search by keyword, military code, or job number.

CareerBoard

careerboard.com

CareerBoard is designed to bring together local jobs with the residents of Greater Cleveland and Akron, Ohio. You can access information about both traditional and online training opportunities or research local companies. Search the job database by category. Add keywords to focus your results. Register (free) to create and post your resume or have job postings sent to you via E-mail.

Cincinnati.com

http://cincinnati.com

http://careerfinder.cincinnati.com

Cincinnati's home page, sponsored by the *Enquirer* and *Post* newspapers, includes links to the newspapers, up-to-date traffic maps, and a community guide to more than one hundred Cincinnati-area neighborhoods. The Web Directory features all kinds of helpful community links. Click on the Jobs link or use the second URL to go directly to the Careerfinder. You'll find job-search tips, hints for preparing your resume, and strategies for cover letters and interviews. To search newspaper classified ads, enter a keyword or select a category, and press the Search button to view the results.

Columbus Dispatch

dispatch.com

columbusjobs.com

The award-winning Ohio newspaper features a business directory, links to local organizations and agencies, and a section detailing new technology and the Internet. Use the Classifieds link or the second URL to access the Employment page. You'll find job-hunting tips, company profiles, and the job leads, which are updated daily. On the Search page, choose one or more of the job categories (hold the control key to select more than one). Select a location, type in keywords to refine your search, and click on Search to view the results.

Ohio ComputerJobs

ohio.computerjobs.com

Headquartered in Atlanta, ComputerJobs.com is the leading Internet-based job-search company for computer and information technology professionals.

Ohio Department of Job and Family Services (ODJFS)

state.oh.us/odjfs/index.stm

state.oh.us/odjfs/jobsearch

The organization whose credo is "Helping Ohioans" certainly does just that. Information on child care referrals, health care, transportation, and more are simply a click away. You'll find career counseling, education and training, labor market information, assistance in preparing a resume and in conducting your job search, and job leads. Use the second URL to go directly to the job opportunities.

Ohio Works!

ohioworks.com/prod

Answer the question, "What do you need?" as you enter the site. You'll find tons of good information about the labor market. Register (free) to take part in the skill-matching service or to post your resume.

State of Ohio Government

ohio.gov

The state's "front page" offers links to agencies and helpful services, educational institutions, health and social services, and forms for transacting business or accessing services online. New this edition is the Dolphin Project, a service of the Ohio Bureau of Workers' Compensation (BWC) to assist employees in coping with workplace injuries. You'll also find links to resources for doing business in the state, employment services, and an easily accessible link to state government jobs.

Oklahoma

Oklahoma's Job Bank

ajb.org/ok

The easiest way to search the Job Bank is to select a job category and enter your zip code in the Occupation Search. You can also search by keyword, military code, or job number.

City of Oklahoma City Hall

okc-cityhall.org

Click on the Departments link to reach Personnel or Workforce Development. Workforce Development administers the Job Training Partnership Act (JTPA) and offers skills assessment and counseling services, while Personnel handles the city's human resources functions for more than forty-five hundred employees. A list of current job openings and an application you can download are available with a click, or call the Job Information Line at (405) 297-2419.

Oklahoma Employment Security Commission (OESC)/Oklahoma's Job Net

oesc.state.ok.us

oesc.state.ok.us/OKJobNet

The OESC provides programs and services for job seekers and employers throughout the state. Labor market statistics, training opportunities, veterans' services, and downloadable forms are all available at this site. You'll also find a link to Oklahoma's Universal Computerized Assistance Network (OKUCAN), an interactive online network that supplies referrals for social service needs in the state, and Job Net, the state skills-matching service. Use the second URL to go directly to Job Net, where your skills and experience are coded and matched with job openings listed with the Oklahoma State Employment Service (OSES).

NewsOK.com

newsok.com

The Internet edition of the *Daily Oklahoman* offers searchable yellow pages focused on specific sections of the site and also available in its entirety. Click on JobsOK to reach the Chamber Job Search, which accesses the resources of both the Greater Oklahoma City Chamber of Commerce and the *Oklahoman*, the state's largest newspaper. Use the Relocation Wizard or Salary Calculator, read the latest news for job hunters, or post your resume. Start your job search by selecting a category. Add keywords to refine your search, and click the Submit button to view the results. You can then perform an additional search on the newspaper classified ads.

Oregon

Working in Oregon/Oregon Jobs

emp.state.or.us

emp.state.or.us/emplsvcs

The Employment Department's Child Care Division oversees a system of safe, affordable, and high-quality child care services, including the Child Care Resource & Referral Programs. New this edition to Working in Oregon is RealJobFairs.com, an ongoing series of virtual job fairs featuring area employers and their current offerings. Apply online when you find the company you want. Click on Jobs or use the second URL to go directly to Oregon's job-search page. From the menu on the left, choose from among apprenticeships, government jobs, or the Oregon Jobs link. Browse them by job category and location, or search by keywords, location, or order number.

CascadeLink

cascadelink.org

businessinportland.org

Created for the global community of Portland, CascadeLink continues to lead the way in providing access to helpful local and regional information. Volunteers can match themselves with organizations that need them. Individuals can access the community profiles or COOL (Community Organizations OnLine), the database of community organizations maintained by the Multnomah County Library. New this edition is BusinessInPortland.org (second URL), which offers start-up and business development resources, along with information about doing business with government and best business practices. Click on the Jobs link to view the career resources.

Medford Mail Tribune

mailtribune.com

mailtribune.com/jobnet/index.htm

Southern Oregon's online newspaper offers news and business information along with a nice selection of Southern Oregon government, business, and education websites. Click on the icon or use the second URL to reach the Job Network, an online service that matches potential employers and job candidates. Visit the Education & Resource Center, or access the job resources. To start your job search, select an employment category, and choose a location and the dates of the classified ads you want to view. Note: the resume-posting service is no longer free.

Oregon Live

oregonlive.com

The *Oregonian*, the newspaper that bills itself as "practically indispensable," brings you Oregon Live, featuring up-to-date news and consumer and lifestyle information. Read the Tech NW pages and other business news. Click on the Find a JOB menu item to reach the career resources. To search for a job in the *Oregonian* or *Hillsboro Argus*, select a job category (or categories) from the menu and follow the directions. Register (free) to post your resume or have current job leads sent to you via E-mail.

Oregon OnLine

state.or.us

The official website for the state, Oregon OnLine offers helpful information that is easy to find. Choose a link from the menu on the left to access specific agency websites or city and county links, including State of Oregon government job offerings. The business resources include links to job leads throughout the state.

Portland Metropolitan Chamber of Commerce

pdxchamber.org

portlandchamber.com/jobbank

Here you'll find information about the community of Portland, Oregon, along with a searchable database of local businesses and a relocation guide. The second URL leads to employment assistance and the job leads.

Welcome to Oregon

el.com/to/oregon

This collection of Oregon links is part of the well-organized Essential Links website (el.com). The community resources and the Internet Essential Links provide a wealth of information about the state, its educational resources, cities and counties, local government, and the business community. There are no separate listings of job leads, but many of the hundreds of links include them.

Pennsylvania

Pennsylvania's Job Bank

ajb.org/pa

The easiest way to search the Job Bank is to select a job category and enter your zip code in the Occupation Search. You can also search by keyword, military code, or job number.

Carnegie Library of Pittsburgh

clpgh.org

clpgh.org/clp/JCEC

The library whose credo is "Free to the People" has developed and linked to some especially helpful sites for its users. The Business Department maintains a website that includes company research guides and resources for small-business start-up. You can also sign up for Biznews, an E-mail update of business programming and services. Drop by the highly regarded Job and Career Education Center if you're in the neighborhood—it could be just the boost you need to jump-start your career! Or use the second URL to visit the JCEC home page via the Internet. You'll find a great deal of assistance, including interview and resume tips, links to financial aid information, and other career resources. And yes, job leads!

JobNet.com

jobnet.com

Check out the employment and business news or the job fair schedule accessible via the website. Register (free) to post your resume to the database. To start your job search, type in keywords, or browse through up to fifty leads at a time.

LibertyNet

libertynet.com

LibertyNet provides online regional information to the Philadelphia area. Resources include community organizations, government agencies, and educational institutions.

PA-Today: The Best of Pennsylvania's Newspapers Online

pa-today.com

PA-Today links to the home pages of dozens of Pennsylvania newspapers. To start your search for gainful employment, click on the individual newspaper's icon and follow the links. Read the directions to search the help-wanted ads and get to the job leads.

PHILA.GOV

phila.gov

phila.gov/departments/personnel/announce/current/index.htm

The home page of the "City of Brotherly Love" offers online access to all of its departments and services. Click on Philadelphia Business to access the helpful resources for starting and growing a business in the community. Scroll down the Business page to get to the Employment Opportunities page, which includes federal and state job leads, census information, labor market statistics, and a link to City of Philadelphia jobs. Use the second URL to go there directly.

Philadelphia ComputerJobs

philadelphia.computerjobs.com

Headquartered in Atlanta, ComputerJobs.com is the leading Internet-based job-search company for computer and information technology professionals.

Philadelphia Online/Philly Jobs

philly.com

http://careers.philly.com

The online home of the *Inquirer* and the *Daily News*, Philadelphia Online serves the greater Philadelphia/South Jersey area as the "Region's Home Page." Use the handy search engine to access the community yellow pages, recent news articles, or the news archives. New this edition is Philly 101, which offers all the advice you need to manage as a full-time student and still have a great time. The community and education links offer helpful information about area schools and nonprofit organizations. To start your job search, select the Careers link, or use the second URL to go directly to the CareerBuilder page. Answer the question, "Where do you want to work?" Follow the directions, and view the results.

PhillyBurbs.com

phillyburbs.com

phillyburbs.com/jobsearch/home.html

Maintained by the *Intelligencer-Record* and the newspapers of Bucks and Burlington Counties, PhillyBurbs.com features news, information, and entertainment. Scroll down the page to access a special Community Guide that offers in-depth profiles of the neighborhoods. Select Job Search from the menu or use the second URL to go directly to the employment page. Choose the employment category that interests you, add or exclude keywords, and decide how far you're willing to commute. Click on the Search button to view the results.

PhillyJobs.com

phillyjobs.com

PhillyJobs.com serves as a gateway connecting companies and recruiters with the qualified talent they need. Look here for permanent jobs or independent contractor positions.

PhillyWorks

phillyworks.com

Since 1995, PhillyWorks has been providing information for Philadelphia-area job seekers and career changers. You'll find a good mix of helpful links here.

Career counseling and training sites, chambers of commerce, resources for minorities, and links to businesses and newspapers in metropolitan Philadelphia are all featured here.

Team Pennsylvania

teampa.com

pacareerlink.state.pa.us

Team Pennsylvania represents a partnership of the public and private sectors whose mission is to create and retain jobs within the state. You'll find information for entrepreneurs and a link to career resources. The second URL takes you directly to CareerLink, the online equivalent of the state's one-stop services for job seekers and employers. Get help in managing your career or in preparing your resume. You'll also find support services and training programs, and soon you will be able to take advantage of the eLearning Institute's online educational opportunities. Click on Job Seeker Services to start your job search.

Three Rivers Free-Net

http://trfn.clpgh.org

Another great resource supported by Carnegie Library of Pittsburgh, Three Rivers is a community information network that provides free access to local information and the world of the Internet. Click on the Subject Guide to get to a comprehensive collection of informative resources covering business, education, government, and social services. Use the Employment link to get to the career resources. Click on Job Postings to start your search for work in the area. The site is easy to navigate and chock-full of great resources!

Puerto Rico

Puerto Rico Clasificados Online

clasificadosonline.com

Look here for business yellow pages and real estate offerings in Puerto Rico. Click on Empleos to access the job opportunities.

Puerto Rico Trade Virtual Center

http://camcom.bc.inter.edu/index.html

The region's chambers of commerce maintain this site as a means of providing information about Puerto Rico and promoting trade. Search the trade leads database or the chamber members' interactive directory to find information about Puerto Rico's business community.

WEPA!

wepa.com

WEPA! is a nicely organized collection of Puerto Rican links. Use the Communication links to view the newspapers, and use the Business links for industry news, directories, and information about individual businesses. Learn more about the local community or the neighboring Caribbean islands. Click on Employment to access the job leads, although when we reviewed the website, some links were clearly out of date.

Rhode Island

Rhode Island's Job Bank

ajb.org/ri

The easiest way to search the Job Bank is to select a job category and enter your zip code in the Occupation Search. You can also search by keyword, military code, or job number.

jobfind.com

jobfind.com

Jobfind is a great one-stop resource for New England jobs! Post your resume free in the Resume Port, check out the career articles or the handy calendar of events, or research company profiles. To find a job, enter a keyword or phrase into the Job Search box and press the Go button to view the results.

Projo.com

projo.com

Maintained by the *Providence Journal-Bulletin*, Projo.com offers many helpful links in its business section, including the chamber of commerce members' directory, local business news, and the state corporation database. You'll also find helpful information about the community, regional news, and a digital update. Click on CareerBuilder to access the employment resources that include hints for resume writing, interviewing, and the job search. Answer the question, "Where do you want to work?" to start your job search, and follow the directions to view the job leads.

Rhode Island Department of Labor and Training (RIDLT)

det.state.ri.us

Here you'll find jobs in state government and a link to the Professional Regulation Division. New this edition is Find-It! Rhode Island, your key to the agencies and services provided by state government. You'll also find a link to netWORKri, the state's recruitment listings home page, along with the employment resources and job bank.

Swearer Center for Public Service at Brown University

brown.edu/Departments/Swearer_Center

brown.edu/Departments/Swearer_Center/publications/ricomjobjoin.shtml

The Swearer Center views service as an important component of a liberal education. The Center's website offers advice for working within the community, job leads, and volunteer opportunities. Use the second URL to subscribe to the Rhode Island Community Jobs List (RICOMJOB), a public E-mail announcement list that connects Rhode Islanders with jobs in the local nonprofit sector.

South Carolina

South Carolina's Job Bank

ajb.org/sc

The easiest way to search the Job Bank is to select a job category and enter your zip code in the Occupation Search. You can also search by keyword, military code, or job number.

Charleston.Net

charleston.net

Sponsored by the South's oldest newspaper, the *Post and Courier*, Charleston.Net provides links to business and government resources, including local government and chamber of commerce websites. The Net Gateway leads to some interesting local and regional resources, including community organizations, educational links, and government agencies. Click on Jobs to access the Career Center. Select Help Wanted, type in a keyword or select a job category, and click on Begin Search to view the results.

SCIway . . . the South Carolina Information Highway

sciway.net

sciway.net/jobs

"South Carolina's Front Door" offers loads of helpful information about the state and its communities. Use the site search engine or the simple menu structure to find exactly what you need. The home page leads to libraries, maps, a calendar of events, newspapers, and government and education sites. The Directories link takes you to a wonderful assortment of yellow pages for the state, organized by topic and including directories of medical facilities and technical colleges. Many of the entries are accessible by county or city as well as by topic or keyword. To get to the employment links, click on Jobs or use the second URL to go there directly. Private employment services, the state Job Service, listings by location and by type of organization (e.g., nonprofit), and links to other helpful career-related sites are all here. This is a tremendous resource.

South Carolina Employment Security Commission

sces.org

Visit this site to check out the job-related services provided by the state. Learn more about the One-Stop initiative, locate the closest employment office, or gather current labor market information. Link to jobs in state and federal government, or access South Carolina's Job Bank.

State of South Carolina Public Information Home Page

myscgov.com

South Carolina's window on the Internet offers many services online, including forms you can download and interactivity with many of the state agencies. New this edition is the Business One Stop (DORBOS) that provides online access to the information you need to start your business. You'll also find links to the public colleges and universities, community information, and a searchable database of charitable organizations. Look over the state job leads, or link to the Employment Security Commission resources.

South Dakota

South Dakota's Job Bank

ajb.org/sd

The easiest way to search the Job Bank is to select a job category and enter your zip code in the Occupation Search. You can also search by keyword, military code, or job number.

Sioux Falls Chamber of Commerce

siouxfalls.com

The local chamber maintains a nice selection of resources for the community. You'll find information about the area's most important industries, links to educational resources, the city government page, and more. One of the most helpful features is the Chamber of Commerce Directory, searchable by category or business name. Click on Employment to reach the Employment Resource websites.

South Dakota Department of Labor

state.sd.us/dol/dol.htm

The Department of Labor manages all aspects of employment and training for the people of South Dakota. At this site, you'll find information about those services, the *South Dakota Occupational Outlook Handbook*, training and apprenticeship opportunities, and the One-Stop initiative. And, of course, you'll find a link to South Dakota's Job Bank.

South Dakota Popular Internet Places

http://sodapop.dsu.edu

SoDa PoP's designers and maintainers, many of whom are students at Dakota State University, would like to make this a one-stop source for local information and more. At SoDa PoP, "where actual human beings organize sites into categories," you can search for specific information or use the Contents menu to browse by topic. At the time of review only one business was listed under the employment category, but links to newspapers, business directories, and other resources make this a very helpful resource for job seekers and career changers. Among the other offerings are links to colleges and universities, vocational education and community colleges, and community information.

Tennessee

Tennessee's Job Bank

ajb.org/tn

The easiest way to search the Job Bank is to select a job category and enter your zip code in the Occupation Search. You can also search by keyword, military code, or job number.

Knoxville News-Sentinel Online

knoxnews.com

knoxcareers.com

The *News-Sentinel* features business and community links that could be helpful in your job search. Scroll down the opening page to access the easy-to-use yellow pages. Click on Careers or use the second URL to access the KnoxCareers page. Use the community and relocation information accessible via the Career Guides page or register (free) to post your resume. To start your Job Finder search, select a category and date and be sure you select Knoxville or Tennessee as your target location (the search box includes many other communities). Click on the Search button to view the results.

Memphis Commercial Appeal

gomemphis.com

gomidsouthjobs.com

Recognizing the contributions made by both men, the *Commercial Appeal* maintains extensive photo and information archives for Martin Luther King Jr. and Elvis Presley, accessible from the opening page. The *CA* also offers a handy city guide and Apartment Browser. To access the career resources, choose the GoMidSouthJobs link from the easy-access menu or use the second URL to go there directly. To start your job search, select a category or enter a keyword, choose the newspaper publication date, and be sure to select Memphis or Tennessee as your target location. Click on the Search button to view the results.

Metropolitan Government of Nashville and Davidson County

nashville.org

Nashville's city and county governments maintain this website featuring links to local agencies and services. New this edition is the Newcomers Information page designed to help you get the information you need, make the necessary connections, and establish yourself in the community. You'll also find information about business start-up, downloadable forms, and a link to the chamber of commerce. If you're interested in working for county government, click on the Job Opportunities link.

Nashville Area Chamber of Commerce

nashvillechamber.com

nashvillejobslink.com

The chamber of commerce maintains a searchable database of local businesses. You'll also find information about starting and growing a business in Nashville, local demographics, and helpful information about the community. To look for employment, click on the Job Opportunities link or use the second URL to go directly to the career resources. Post your resume, find an internship, volunteer for a community service, or find a job.

Tennessee Department of Employment Security (DES)

state.tn.us/labor-wfd/esdiv.html

From here, you can link to the Job Bank or check out the other services provided by the DES. Among the many offerings is the Source, which features career, demographic, and labor market information in an easily accessible format.

Tennessee Today

tntoday.com

The Tennessee Press Association brings together all of the state's newspapers in one handy website. Browse by city, county, or newspaper title. You'll find additional links to state government, educational institutions, and high school and college newspapers.

Texas

Texas's Job Bank

ajb.org/tx

The easiest way to search the Job Bank is to select a job category and enter your zip code in the Occupation Search. You can also search by keyword, military code, or job number.

Austin City Connections

ci.austin.tx.us

Choose City Jobs from the menu on the left to search for job opportunities with the City of Austin government. You can also call the twenty-four-hour Employment Information Line at (512) 499-3301 or download the Job Bulletin. Other resources include a helpful collection of employment FAQs.

Austin 360: Austin Starts Here

austin360.com

Brought to you by the *American-Statesman*, Austin360 offers entertainment and lifestyle information, plus links to other good information. Search or browse the business yellow pages, or explore the community information. Select Austin-area Jobs to access the job opportunities. Search by keyword and location, or browse by job category and date of publication. Scroll down the page to access organizations, agencies, job fairs, and other helpful resources.

Express-News Online

expressnews.com

http://mysa.com

sajobsearch.com

This is San Antonio's contribution to online news services. Use the handy yellow pages to search for a specific business, or browse the listings by broad category. Click on SA JobSearch or use the third URL to access the JobSearch page. Search by keyword or browse through the job categories that interest you.

Galveston County Daily News

galvnews.com

Texas's oldest newspaper now offers GALVNEWS.com E-mail Extra!, a daily newsletter featuring the latest news and available to you via E-mail. To look for work, click on Classifieds on the Services menu. Scroll down the list of categories (professional, medical, etc.) to view only those leads in your area of interest.

Governor's Job Bank

twc.state.tx.us/jobs/gvjb/gvjb.html

The Governor's Job Bank (GVJB) offers access to state agency job openings in Texas. Search the database by location, job category, education level, and so on.

HIRE TEXAS

http://m06hostp.twc.state.tx.us/jobmatch/jobseeker/htapp.html

This searchable labor-exchange system matches employers and job applicants. HIRE TEXAS will match up to fourteen of your skills with potential employers. You can also list up to nine locations that interest you.

Houston Chronicle Interactive

chron.com

chron.com/class/jobs/index.html

Find a person, find a business, or get maps or directions in the handy Directory Center. Read the latest technology or business news, or access the hundreds of government agencies and business, nonprofit, and social service organizations detailed in the Community section. Click on the Classifieds link or use the second URL to access the ChronicleJobs.com page. Job Smart offers advice on managing your career, resume and interviewing tips, and salary and relocation information. Search by keyword or browse by employment categories, or register (free) to have the Houston e-Recruiter send job leads to you via E-mail.

State of Texas Home Page

state.tx.us

texas.gov

Either URL will reach the site, and you'll find links to state and local agencies along with loads of information about the state. New this edition is TexasOnline, a website designed to facilitate online interactions with government agencies and services. You'll find the information you need to start your business, educational resources, and information about all the communities of the state. The Employment link is prominently displayed in the center of the opening page. This site is easy to navigate, with interesting information.

Texas ComputerJobs

texas.computerjobs.com

Headquartered in Atlanta, ComputerJobs.com is the leading Internet-based job-search company for computer and information technology professionals.

Texas ComputerWork

http://texas.computerwork.com

Find more jobs in the IT sector! This is one of dozens of local sites that ComputerWork maintains for professionals in the information technology field.

Texas Workforce Commission

twc.state.tx.us

The Texas Workforce Commission provides access to all the government-supported career resources and services in the state, including the Governor's Job Bank, HIRE TEXAS, and the TWC Express. You'll find lots of good tips for the job search and career-planning advice. Additional information about job training, employment laws, the labor market, and child care services is also at your fingertips.

TWC Job Express

twc.state.tx.us/jobs/jobx/express.html

TWC Job Express includes private sector jobs listed with the Texas Workforce Commission. Search by job category and location. Many of the jobs listed include contact information for the employers so that you can contact them directly.

Utah

Utah's Job Bank

ajb.org/ut

The easiest way to search the Job Bank is to select a job category and enter your zip code in the Occupation Search. You can also search by keyword, military code, or job number.

Deseret News

http://deseretnews.com/dn

Salt Lake City's *Deseret News* offers up-to-date business and technology news. New this edition is the Local Grocer, which allows you to compare prices in area groceries and develop your shopping list online. The Utah County links include the chamber of commerce, local government, schools, and higher education. Select Jobs from the menu on the left to access the employment page. Click on the Employment Wizard icon to start your job search. Enter keywords in the Swift Search box and press Go to view the results.

Herald Extra

harktheherald.com

Provo's *Daily-Herald* newspaper maintains "Utah County's Information Source" online. Click on the Classifieds link to start your job search; choose Help Wanted to browse the listing of current job opportunities.

Utah Department of Workforce Services: Utah's Job Connection

dws.state.ut.us

The Department of Workforce Services (DWS) is the lead agency for job and career-related services in the state. You'll find job-search guides, career-outlook data, and child care resources. DWS also links to employers who are currently hiring, the Job Bank, and the Electronic Job Board. Check back from time to time—Utah's Job Connection is growing as it adds services requested by job seekers and employers alike.

Working in Utah

state.ut.us/working/employment.html

The state of Utah has pulled together some great resources here. You'll find all the information you need for living, learning, doing business, and working in the state. From this page, you can link to the Job Bank and the other resources provided by Workforce Services, get answers to your frequently asked questions about Utah employment, and link to the state's newspapers, major employers, and universities. Lots of Utah job leads are accessible from this website.

Vermont

Vermont's Job Bank

ajb.org/vt

The easiest way to search the Job Bank is to select a job category and enter your zip code in the Occupation Search. You can also search by keyword, military code, or job number.

Addison County Independent

addisonindependent.com

Middlebury, Vermont's, twice-weekly newspaper offers news of interest and a community calendar for residents of Addison County. Click on Help Wanted to browse the current job leads. Use the Find function of your browser to get to jobs of interest.

Department of Employment and Training

det.state.vt.us

Vermont's easy-to-navigate employment page links to the Job Bank and other job referrals, as well as to Vermont's Talent Bank. There are additional links to training and education information, apprenticeships and job opportunities with state government, and other employment resources and agencies. This is a must-see for Vermont job hunters.

jobfind.com

jobfind.com

Jobfind is a great one-stop resource for New England jobs! Post your resume free in the Resume Port, check out the career articles or the handy calendar of events, or research company profiles. To find a job, enter a keyword or phrase into the Job Search box and press the Go button to view the results.

State of Vermont Home Page

state.vt.us

Your entrée to the "Green Mountain State" features the most up-to-date information about local ski conditions, along with maps, agency links, and ServiceNet, a guide to community services. Link to the great career resources at the Department of Employment and Training, or check out the job possibilities with state government.

Virginia

Virginia's Job Bank

ajb.org/va

The easiest way to search the Job Bank is to select a job category and enter your zip code in the Occupation Search. You can also search by keyword, military code, or job number.

CareerConnect

careerconnect.state.va.us

Designed by the commonwealth of Virginia to function as an electronic one-stop workforce development system, CareerConnect does just that. You'll find training and education opportunities, apprenticeships, financial aid information, career-preparation assistance, and job listings from the Virginia

Employment Commission job bank. In addition, the site lists community resources for those who are in need of child and elder care support, health information, transportation, and housing.

Gateway Virginia

gatewayva.com

http://careers.timesdispatch.com

The *Richmond Times-Dispatch Gateway* pulls together a wealth of resources for the area, including a searchable yellow pages and directories of schools and colleges. Easily accessible from the opening page are links to other Virginia newspapers with separate links to their classified ads. New this edition is Cosmo Community, which offers free websites, a calendar, and a message board for community organizations. Access Virginia offers links to cities, counties, universities, government information, and more. Click on the Classified link or use the second URL to go directly to the employment opportunities advertised in the *Richmond Times-Dispatch*. Register (free) to post your resume. To start your job search, answer the question, "Where do you want to work?" Select a job category or add keywords, and click Go! to view the results.

Guide to Career Prospects in Virginia

ccps.virginia.edu/career_prospects

The Guide is a database of information about careers that are important to Virginia (and almost every other state). For each career, you'll find a written analysis that includes required educational levels, skills, earnings, and job outlook, along with a set of statistical tables covering wages and job outlook at the Virginia regional as well as national levels. While most of the salary data is specific to Virginia, descriptions of each career area are general enough to be relevant to all and are very well done. Search by keyword or browse the careers by job family.

Pilot Online

pilotonline.com

HamptonRoads.com

hamptonroads.com

http://jobs.hamptonroads.com

The Hampton Roads–based *Virginian-Pilot* maintains this online newspaper and the HamptonRoads.com community network. Use the yellow pages to find businesses by type or by name or to explore the community resources. Click on the CareerConnection link to access the employment resources. You'll find another link to community information, a well-stocked career-resource center, and help in posting your resume. Search for jobs four ways: by "super-category," by category, by keyword, or by posting your resume.

Virginia ComputerWork

http://virginia.computerwork.com

Find more jobs in the IT sector! This is one of dozens of local sites that ComputerWork maintains for professionals in the information technology field.

Virginia Employment Commission

vec.state.va.us

vec.state.va.us/seeker/listing.htm

The Job Bank and other job seeker services of the state's Employment Commission (VEC) are all accessible from this page. You'll also find lots of great career-management tools. Get help developing your resume, assessing your career direction, and fine-tuning your interviewing style. Don't overlook the Automated Labor EXchange system (ALEX), which offers a self-directed job search.

The *Washington Post*

washingtonpost.com

Click on WashingtonJobs to access the career page. Post your resume or check out the career advice in Job Central. Search by category, employer, job location, and keyword. Use several keywords and join them with *and* or use quotes to delineate a phrase. You can also add *not* for any term you want to exclude (e.g., *not night* will exclude jobs with graveyard shifts).

Washington

Washington's Job Bank

ajb.org/wa

The easiest way to search the Job Bank is to select a job category and enter your zip code in the Occupation Search. You can also search by keyword, military code, or job number.

Access Washington

http://access.wa.gov

Use the easy-to-use menu system or the "Ask George" search engine to explore Washington's gateway to the Internet. You'll find considerable content, including a selection of online services, education directories and resources, an index to agencies by service, and more. In addition, there are links to state, local, and federal agencies and services, as well as to business and consumer resources. Click on Employment to access information for teens entering the world of work, training resources, jobs in state government, and the Job Bank.

CityofSeattle.net

cityofseattle.net

Named the "Best Local Government Website" by *Government Technology* magazine, the official website for the city serves as a public network for Seattle. Search by keyword, by service, or by agency, or browse using the simple menu structure. You'll find all the information you need to live in Seattle, start a business, get around the city, or access online services. Click on the Employment icon to reach the career resources and job leads, including jobs with city government and King County and University of Washington job opportunities.

Seattle Community Network

scn.org

This is one of Seattle's helpful public networks. You'll find information about the neighborhoods, local businesses, and organizations here. Click on the Employment link to access job hot lines, career events and resources, and job leads.

The *Seattle Times*

seattletimes.com

nwsource.com

http://classifieds.nwsource.com/job

The Pulitzer Prize–winning *Seattle Times* has developed an outstanding online presence. New this edition are the Portable City Guide and Wireless Web news headlines services, available to you for downloading to your personal digital assistant. You'll also find a School Guide, featuring information on more than six hundred area schools, and business resources for the entrepreneur. The second URL goes directly to NWSource, a service of the *Times* that provides a wealth of information about Seattle and the Pacific Northwest. Scroll down the opening page to the Jobs link or use the third URL to go directly to the career resources. Read the helpful career advice of Carol Kleiman or register (free) to post your resume. To look for job opportunities, select a category, add keywords, and click on the Search button to view the results.

SpokaneNet

spokane.net

Spokane's community information network offers free web hosting for community organizations. You'll also find handy yellow pages, a service that matches volunteers with specific opportunities, and a virtual town hall. Scroll down the page and click on JobSmart to access the career resources, which include a resume generator and plenty of useful job-hunting tips and career-development tools.

TRIBnet

tribnet.com

southsoundjobs.com

Brought to you by the *Tacoma News Tribune*, this online news source offers links to municipal government pages and selected community resources within the region. Click on the Classifieds link or use the second URL to reach the job leads. To find that dream job, select a category, or search by keyword.

WorkSource Washington

http://work.wa.gov

The Employment Security Department sponsors WorkSource, an online collection of the services and programs offered by the state of Washington for job seekers and career changers. Get help creating your resume and posting it to the state's talent bank, or find training and educational opportunities. Ask your personal Internet Career Counselor for help, look over the opportunities in dozens of local governmental units, or access the handy collection of the state's newspaper classified ads neatly arranged on one web page.

Washington, DC

See "District of Columbia."

West Virginia

West Virginia's Job Bank

ajb.org/wv

The easiest way to search the Job Bank is to select a job category and enter your zip code in the Occupation Search. You can also search by keyword, military code, or job number.

Charleston Gazette Online

wvgazette.com

Click on the Jobs link to access the career resources. To start your search with the Job Finder, select a category (sales, restaurants, etc.), add a keyword, and be sure to select Charleston or West Virginia as your target location.

Dominion Post Online

dominionpost.com

The *Dominion Post* dates back to 1864, about the time the state was created, and this online version bills itself as the "most comprehensive news site" in the state. To start your quest for work, click on the Employment link on the front page. Select the date of publication to browse through all of the ads. You can also search using keywords. Click on the Search button to view the results.

State of West Virginia Home Page

state.wv.us

The official website of the state of West Virginia offers a simple menu system and easy-to-navigate access to all of the state's agencies. The Communities link to city and county information and the Education link to school and college directories and to job-training resources are particularly helpful for job seekers and career changers. Scroll down the opening page to view the Employment links. They include West Virginia teaching jobs, state government jobs, and the Search for Work link to the Employment Service website.

West Virginia Jobs

wvjobs.org

Read the company profiles or post your resume. Browse all of the job listings or select a specific category to view.

Wisconsin

Wisconsin's Job Bank

ajb.org/wi

The easiest way to search the Job Bank is to select a job category and enter your zip code in the Occupation Search. You can also search by keyword, military code, or job number.

City of Madison

ci.madison.wi.us

If you'd like to live in the "City of Lakes," click on the Employment link or tune in to Madison City Channel 12 to learn about current job opportunities. New job listings are posted weekly.

madison.com

madison.com

The owners of the *Wisconsin State Journal* and the *Capital Times* operate Madison.com. The *Capital Times* offers a helpful collection of local links that include the chamber of commerce, area communities and organizations, and yellow pages that you can browse or search by name or category. New this edition is the Answer Book, featuring answers to all your questions about living in Madison, and Plugged In, your guide to getting the most out of your computer. Click on Jobs to access the employment page. You can search the classified ads by category and keyword or browse by classification. Madison.com also provides access to the Employment Wizard career resources. To start that job search, select a category and keywords, and be sure to select Madison or Wisconsin as your targeted location. Click on the Search button to view the results.

Milwaukee Journal Sentinel

jsonline.com

onwisconsinjobs.com

If you're a fan, check out the Packer and Badger links while you're here. There's an archive of information about your favorite teams and photographs, too. New this edition is OnWisconsin.com, your guide to food, fun, and festivals in the state. The business section offers a helpful feature entitled WorkPlace & Careers. Click on Jobs or use the second URL to access the employment page. Enter a keyword to start your job search, or scroll down the page to access the other career resources.

State of Wisconsin Information Server

wisconsin.gov

You'll find a wealth of information here, with links to information about the state and to all aspects of state government, including the employment services. This server also has links to economic development and municipal, county, and community websites, along with the University of Wisconsin and other educational resources. New this edition are the separate job banks for some professions, including teachers, so be sure to check the separate agency listings as well as the main Employment in Wisconsin database.

Wisconsin Department of Workforce Development (DWD)

dwd.state.wi.us

dwd.state.wi.us/jobnet

The DWD website provides access to all of the services and programs available to Wisconsin job seekers and career changers. These include apprenticeship and training opportunities, child care referrals, labor market data, seasonal job listings, and guidance for job seekers entering the world of work as well as those who are changing careers. Click on JobNet or use the second URL to go directly to the database of job leads. To start your job search, identify an area of the state you're targeting. You can browse the job leads by category or search by employer or keyword.

Wyoming

Wyoming's Job Bank

ajb.org/wy

The easiest way to search the Job Bank is to select a job category and enter your zip code in the Occupation Search. You can also search by keyword, military code, or job number.

Wyoming Job Network

http://onestop.state.wy.us

Individuals using the system can perform a quick search using keywords or browse the job offerings. By registering, you will be notified when a job matching your skills set becomes available, and you will also be included in the state talent bank. New in this edition is the Teacher Tips link, which provides access to a separate database of teaching jobs. Teachers can search or browse the positions, or they can register (free) to have their skills matched with available positions.

Wyoming Works

http://wydoe.state.wy.us

The Wyoming Department of Employment is responsible for all of the services and programs offered by the state to job seekers and employers. You'll also find labor statistics, occupational health and safety information, and workforce development tools. Resources here include the state's job bank, employment offices, job openings in the state government, job-hunting tips, and links to other career resources. Note: don't let the acronyms at the top of the page scare you. Simply use the menu on your left to access the job-seeker services.

12

International
Opportunities

This chapter features Internet resources for locating global offerings or employment opportunities outside of the United States in North America, Latin and South America, Europe, Africa, the Middle East, and the Pacific Rim. We have arranged it by region and then alphabetically by country in order to facilitate searches in neighboring countries. Keep in mind that many international recruiters based in one country work to place employees in other countries, so you may want to check neighboring countries for references.

The growth of websites with a regional focus continues. Yahoo! offers several sites focused on particular countries or regions of the world and many more designed to cover U.S. metropolitan areas. These focused web resources offer links to embassies, government agencies, and other information about foreign countries, as well as access to foreign newspapers. In addition, Northwestern University Library maintains a listing of links to foreign government websites (library.nwu.edu/govpub/resource/internat/foreign.html) that could prove helpful in your job search.

Among the Web-based job and career resources, Monster.com (monster.com) continues to lead in terms of globalization and the development of job and career resources worldwide. There are also other, lesser-known efforts, and the result is good for job hunters. When possible, we have included these regional resources so that job seekers can focus their efforts on a particular region instead of wasting time looking through the millions of websites now accessible via the Internet.

Many of the larger Internet job sites in Chapter 3 carry international postings, including America's Job Bank. Elsewhere in the book, some international sites listing jobs in a given specialty have been placed with that specialty, such as mining and academe.

Services with Listings for Multiple Countries and Regions

Addresses of International Organizations

psc-cfp.gc.ca/intpgm/epb7_e.htm

In partnership with Foreign Affairs and International Trade Canada, the Public Service Commission of Canada maintains this listing of international agencies' websites arranged alphabetically by organization name.

Dave's ESL Cafe Job Board

http://eslcafe.com/joblist

Dave Sperling's ESL Cafe is still a great resource for students and teachers of English as a second language and English as a foreign language. In addition to the listing of current international positions for teachers, he offers live chats and a forum for discussion.

Escape Artist

escapeartist.com

Since 1995, Escape Artist has offered advice to overseas job seekers, "escaping" Americans, adventurers, and other individuals who are relocating outside the United States. Among its offerings are detailed country profiles, relocation information, offshore investment resources, and job opportunities.

Headhunters International

avotek.nl

Avotek supports this directory and guide to international jobs. Many of the links lead to advertisements for guides in print that Avotek is selling, but there are resources such as the international jobs page that do provide free job and career information. Try the fast, free IQ test or one of the other personality tests available on the site, or check out the list of international recruiters on the Web. Avotek also has lists of recruiters based in various countries available for purchase. These can be used to create E-mail campaigns.

International Career Employment Center

internationaljobs.org

For a decade, International Careers has published a weekly international employment newspaper for subscribers only. Several categories of job listings are also accessible via the website to nonsubscribers. These include the "hot jobs" that employers are urgently seeking to fill, which can also be sent to you via E-mail.

International Chamber of Commerce (ICC)

iccwbo.org

The official site for the ICC features links to member countries and additional resources helpful to you in researching the employment outlook in specific countries.

International Herald Tribune Education Marketplace

iht.com/misc/education.htm

The Education Marketplace of the *International Herald Tribune* website features listings of upcoming career fairs and educational events in Europe. Continuing education opportunities are accessible by region. The Business and Technology pages offer up-to-date news about the international community.

International Rescue Committee (IRC)

intrescom.org/jobs/index.cfm

Founded by Albert Einstein in 1933, the IRC is the leading nonsectarian voluntary organization providing emergency relief and resettlement assistance for refugees worldwide. Individuals are encouraged to send their resumes and register for the Emergency Response Roster so that they can be considered for employment as it becomes available.

JobPilot AG (Formerly Jobs & Adverts)

jobpilot.com

jobpilot.net

Since its inception, JobPilot has expanded to fifteen European countries and regions of Asia and Australia. To start your job search, select a region and industry. Click on the Search button to view the results. You can also browse by company name or explore the career resources. Register to post your resume or have job listings sent to you via E-mail. At the time of review, the countries and regions included in the JobPilot series were North America, the Middle East, Asia and the Pacific Rim, Australia, Austria, Germany, Poland, Belgium, Hungary, Spain, the Czech Republic, Italy, Sweden, Denmark, the Netherlands, Switzerland, France, Norway, and the United Kingdom.

JobShark

jobshark.com

JobShark has now expanded beyond Canada, Ireland, and the United Kingdom into Central and South America. Select the country of choice to start your job search: Canada, the United Kingdom, Ireland, Mexico, Peru, Venezuela, Colombia, Brazil, Chile, Argentina, and Uruguay.

Monster International

http://international.monster.com

Monster is in the process of adding countries to its job site and essentially blazes the overseas careers trail with global offerings and work-abroad features. Click on Jobs or use the Global Gateway (http://globalgateway.monster.com) to get from where you are to "where you want to be." Select the country you want to work in to see all of the job offerings. You can refine your search by adding *not* to a keyword and submitting a subsearch. Additional career articles, tips and tools, a guide to salaries, and forums for communicating with other job seekers are accessible through the Career Center. The global search includes Australia, Belgium, Canada, Denmark, Spain, France, Hong Kong, Ireland, India, Italy, the Netherlands, New Zealand, Singapore, and the United Kingdom.

OverseasJobs.com

overseasjobs.com

Part of the AboutJobs.com Network, this website is easy to use—simply click on the tabs to access any area of the site. Select the Jobs tab to browse the international offerings. Following the international listings are jobs for specific countries or regions of the world. Get help with your resume or link to other career resources.

Les Pages Emploi

http://emploi.hrnet.fr

les-pages-emploi.com

The main page of this site is written in French primarily and provides access to Internet job sites located throughout the world. Click on Le Répertoire to browse by country, or view the pages with an English translation provided by AltaVista.

PlanetRecruit.com's International Channel

planetrecruit.com

This site includes mostly jobs in the United Kingdom and Ireland, but it does feature jobs from around the globe. You can search without registering, but you need to register in order to apply online. PlanetRecruit.com is simple to navigate and search, and using the + or – options will produce better search results.

Top Jobs on the Internet

topjobs.net

Top Jobs is an international employment resource that features company profiles, career resources, and a job agent to send job announcements to you via E-mail or cell phone. Access your specific country's website from the listing on the opening page: Ireland, the Netherlands, Norway, Poland, Spain, Sweden, Switzerland, the United Kingdom, or Thailand.

Yahoo!

yahoo.com

At the time of review, we found separate Yahoo! portals set up for Argentina, Brazil, Canada, and Mexico in the Americas; Denmark, France, Germany, Italy, Norway, Spain, Sweden, and the United Kingdom and Ireland in Europe; and Australia and New Zealand, China, Hong Kong, India, Japan, Korea, Singapore, and Taiwan in Asia and the Pacific Rim. There are also American Yahoo!s written in Chinese and Spanish. Simply scroll down the opening page to reach the Yahoo! for your country or region of the United States.

North America

Resources for the United States are included in Chapter 11.

CANADA

Sites with resources for the whole country are at the beginning of this section. Those for specific provinces (Alberta, British Columbia, Manitoba, Ontario, and Quebec) follow, in alphabetical order. Most but not all sites in Canada have versions in French and English with easy links to both versions from the front page.

ActiJob.com

actijob.com

ActiJob.com features job listings for some of the major cities in Canada. Search by province or job category.

AtlanticCanadaCareers.com

atlanticcanadacareers.com

These job listings and career resources are focused on the Atlantic region provinces (Nova Scotia, New Brunswick, Newfoundland, and Prince Edward Island). Browse by province, job category, or what's new in the database. You'll find a few jobs from other Canadian regions posted here.

Campus WorkLink: NGR

connect.gc.ca/en/270-e.htm

The National Graduate Register (NGR) and the Canadian Association of Career Educators and Employers (CACEE) have partnered to offer the redesigned Campus WorkLink: NGR. Campus WorkLink is a bilingual database that matches the skills of young Canadian job seekers with suitable employers. Students must register to access the job database and the full range of resources.

Canada WorkinfoNET

workinfonet.ca

The bilingual WorkinfoNET is the primary source of career and training information for Canadians. You'll find help with the job search, job postings, employment trends, and other resources for job seekers, career changers, and people who wish to be self-employed. This is an excellent resource. An exciting new feature is "What's New?" which highlights current job trends and resources. You can gather results from all over the country or search the individual provinces. Simply click on the regional map, or go directly to the province website of your choice:

Alberta (ALIS): alis.gov.ab.ca

British Columbia (BCWIN): http://workinfonet.bc.ca

Manitoba (MBWIN): mb.workinfonet.ca

New Brunswick (NBWIN): nb.workinfonet.ca

Newfoundland and Labrador (NLWIN): gov.nf.ca/nlwin

Northwest Territory (NorthWIN): workinfonet.ca/northwin

Nova Scotia (NSWIN): ns.workinfonet.ca

Ontario (ONWIN): on.workinfonet.ca

Prince Edward Island (InfoPEI): gov.pe.ca/infopei/Employment/index.php3

Quebec: qc.info-emploi.ca (French) or qc.info-emploi.ca/english/main.cfm (English)

Saskatchewan (SaskNetWork): sasknetwork.gov.sk.ca

Yukon (YUWIN): yuwin.ca/english/index.cfm

Canadian Association of Career Educators and Employers (CACEE)

cacee.com

The Canadian Association of Career Educators and Employers (CACEE) website offers information for students, members, and the general public alike. You'll find career fair contacts, a searchable database of Canadian internship opportunities, tools for researching potential employers, and links to other good career resources.

CanadianCareers.com

canadiancareers.com

CanadianCareers covers all facets of the job hunt. You'll find information about occupations, job opportunities, career fair schedules, and internship details. This site is very nicely done.

CanJobs.com

canjobs.com

From the opening page, you can select a job category and province and perform a quick search to view recent job opportunities. You can also browse all jobs by province or link to other resources of interest. Register to post your resume, use the job agent, apply for jobs online, or receive the free newsletter.

Career Edge

careeredge.org

Career Edge is a national, nonprofit organization whose mission is to improve youth employability. It does this by connecting recent graduates with internships that provide them with career-related work experience and bring them into the world of work.

CareerPlace

careerplace.com

An initiative of the Native Women's Association of Canada, CareerPlace maintains this database of Aboriginal women seeking employment. Through its network of support and mentoring programs, CareerPlace assists Aboriginal women in finding and keeping jobs and advancing their careers.

Charity Village

charityvillage.com

charityvillage.com/charityvillage/main.asp

Developed as an information resource for Canadian nonprofit organizations, Charity Village includes hundreds of job listings and continuing education opportunities for the sector. Use the second URL to get past the splash page, and scroll down to the Jobs link. Browse the jobs by the posting date or search by keyword. Some learning opportunities are online, and you'll find a schedule for other Canadian training programs and events.

Electronic Labour Exchange

ele-spe.org

"Where Employers and Workers Connect," the Electronic Labour Exchange (ELE) is part of the Human Resource Development Canada initiative (see HRDC-DRHC) and Canada's only automatic, skills-based matching service. Individuals looking for a job supply a work profile that will be compared with the skills needed by employers who are part of the Exchange. ELE is simple to use, prompting you for each step, and uses a uniform vocabulary to match employers and job seekers, which produces more accurate results.

EmployCanada.com

employcanada.com

The launch date for EmployCanada.com was May 21, 2001. When we reviewed the site, a short survey of user preferences was being taken. Features will include new and improved resume posting, job listings, and links to resources throughout the country.

HRDC-DRHC (Human Resources Development Canada)

hrdc-drhc.gc.ca

jobbank.gc.ca

The Canadian government sponsors this site and other HRDC-DRHC (Developpement des ressources humaines Canada) sites in the individual provinces. It features a full range of career and human services. Among the items of special interest to job seekers and career changers are the career-planning and self-assessment tools and the training and self-employment resources. The second URL goes directly to the Job Bank. To start the job search, select a region. You can then perform a quick search or search only jobs that have been posted within the past forty-eight hours.

Monster Canada

monster.ca

This division of the popular Monster.com job bank was set up specifically for opportunities in Canada.

Positionw@tch Internet Recruitment

positionwatch.com

Now part of RecruitAd's career services, Positionw@tch is an online IT recruiter. Search the entire database by keyword, search by company, or use the quick search to see the most up-to-date postings only.

Public Service Commission (PSC) of Canada

http://jobs.gc.ca

PSC is responsible for the appointment of qualified individuals to Canadian federal government positions. Search here for jobs, training opportunities, student work experience, and internships with the Canadian government.

Strategis

http://strategis.gc.ca

Industry Canada supports this wide-ranging business resource. You'll find company directories, business information by industry, and labor statistics. Plus, get the information you need to start a new business. Training and employment resources, consumer information, and the latest business news are also accessible here.

Workopolis.com

workopolis.com

New this edition is Workopolis.com, which offers a great deal of helpful content for Canadian job seekers and career changers. Workopolis.com represents a partnership between the Toronto Star Newspapers and Globe Interactive and offers thousands of job postings, including all career listings from major Canadian newspapers. You'll also find humor, good career advice, and a forum for discussions.

WorkSearch/ProjetEmploi

http://worksearch.gc.ca

WorkSearch/ProjetEmploi is a new Internet interface developed by Human Resources Development Canada to assist Canadians in finding work and developing a career. You'll find strategies for evaluating your next steps in the career process, online budget assistance, and a career assistant that allows you to develop a resume, store your test information, or receive job postings via E-mail. Immigrants to Canada will find a special area titled "Looking for Work in Canada" that includes links to immigration information and other resources designed to assist you in joining the workforce.

Youth Employment Information

youth.gc.ca

Created by Youth Resource Network of Canada (YRNC), this site offers information for Canadian young adults about the world of work. Career assessment and planning tools, training and education resources, job opportunities, and other tools for preparing youth to enter the workforce are at your fingertips.

Alberta

Alberta WorkinfoNET (ALIS)

alis.gov.ab.ca

This is the local section of WorkInfoNET specifically set up and maintained for Alberta.

Calgary Community Pages

calcna.ab.ca/calgary/calgary.html

The Calgary Community Network provides access to these business, education, and government links and more. Within the business section, you'll find the Employment Opportunities and hundreds of job-related links, from local businesses to international listings.

Career and Placement Services (CaPS)

ualberta.ca/~caps

A service of the University of Alberta for its students, CaPS offers onsite counseling, self-assessment tools, and other career resources. Online, you'll find a wonderful collection of career-related tip sheets, schedules for career fairs and workshops, and the Electronic Job Bank, updated each Tuesday and Thursday by noon.

JOB SEARCH TIP:

Don't forget the Freenets! Several great Freenets have been established all over Canada. Use Peter Scott's Directory of Freenets and Community Networks (another great Canadian product) to find them and put them to good use. Look for "Business" or similar headings at lights.com/freenet.

Edmonton FreeNet

freenet.edmonton.ab.ca

Click on Community Awareness to reach the heart of the community information resources, and then explore the Careers & Employment link for job opportunities. Check out the business listings for information about local companies, browse the newspapers for job postings, or look at the government and education sections to learn more about the nonprofit sector.

Government of Alberta Home Page

gov.ab.ca

Here you'll find everything you need to know about the government of Alberta—phone numbers, news briefings, legal information, and more. The Employment link includes Bulletin Online, the Alberta Government Job Board. You'll also find rules for the workplace, labor statistics, and other career resources.

British Columbia

BC Ministry of Employment and Investment

gov.bc.ca/ei

The Ministry is considered the lead agency for economic development, job creation, and doing business in British Columbia. Scroll down the opening page to the Employment Opportunities link. You'll find positions in provincial government, the "BladeRunners" career information program for youth, and other resources for BC job seekers and career changers.

British Columbia Chamber of Commerce

bcchamber.org

Use the business directory or the handy collection of business links.

British Columbia WorkinfoNet (BCWIN)

http://workinfonet.bc.ca

This is the local section of WorkInfoNET specifically set up and maintained for British Columbia.

CareerClick

careerclick.com

Brought to you by the *Vancouver Sun* and *Province* newspapers, CareerClick offers career advice, resume posting, and job postings from many of Canada's major city newspapers. Search for jobs by company, or do the advanced search by location and keyword. You can also register to have job postings sent to you via E-mail.

Greater Victoria Chamber of Commerce

http://gvcc.org

Search the membership database by category, or browse through the business links for job listings and information about the local business community.

Prince George Public Library

lib.pg.bc.ca

Scroll down the main page to the Online Resources link. This will take you to the Education and Employment page with its numerous links to Canadian job and career information.

Vancouver CommunityNet

vcn.bc.ca

Use the search engine to find specific information, or browse the community resources by topic. The Employment and Labour page has extensive links to local and regional job and career resources, and the Education, Business, and other community links could provide additional help to you in your job hunt.

Manitoba

Manitoba WorkinfoNet (MBWIN)

mb.workinfonet.ca

This is the local section of WorkInfoNET specifically set up and maintained for Manitoba.

Winnipeg Free Press Online

winnipegfreepress.com/news/index.html

Scroll down the page and click on Careers. From the Careers page you can either start with broad categories or search by keyword for specific job opportunities.

Working in Manitoba

gov.mb.ca/working.html

The provincial government offers this wonderful website, with everything you ever wanted to know about Manitoba at your fingertips. The URL listed here takes you directly to the Jobs page, but the menu on the left of the website allows you to easily go to other resources on the site. You'll find jobs in government, other job offerings in the province, apprenticeships, and resources for youth entering the world of work. The Business section includes a Companies Database, featuring more than one thousand Manitoba businesses searchable by sector, market, company name, and more.

Ontario

HALINET

hhpl.on.ca

hhpl.on.ca/library/jobs.htm

The government and education information are accessible from the main menu, as is the Community Information page, which includes a searchable database of local organization information. Use the second URL to go directly to the Job Search Resources, which are nicely annotated and provide links to many good employment sites. Scroll down to the bottom of the Job Search Resources page to link to the HALINET Business Resources.

Ontario WorkinfoNet (ONWIN)

on.workinfonet.ca

This is the local section of WorkInfoNET specifically set up and maintained for Ontario.

Sheridan College Career Centre

sheridanc.on.ca/career

Sheridan provides a number of resources for choosing or reevaluating your career, researching an employer, or searching for a job. The Career Services page offers helpful links that include resume tips, career-planning assistance, and listings of employers. Additional links to community information are also accessible from the Career Services page.

Student Development Centre

sdc.uwo.ca/career

The University of Western Ontario maintains this Student Development Centre for both students and alumni, although the information offered is helpful to any job seeker or career changer in the area. Resources include a Job Search Clinic and listings of local employers.

Toronto Free-Net, Inc. (TFN)

freenet.toronto.on.ca

The Business and Economy link leads to the job, career, and business offerings on TFN. If you click on Canadian Jobs, you'll reach a listing of dozens of job-opportunity and career-resource websites. A few of the links are focused exclusively on Toronto or Ontario, although most appear to be national in scope.

Toronto Star

http://thestar.workopolis.com

New this edition is the Workopolis career website, which partners with several Canadian websites and newspapers to provide access to job postings and career assistance. Because all of the Canadian jobs are accessible, you must search by geographical area to get to the Toronto jobs.

University of Waterloo Career Services

careerservices.uwaterloo.ca

Work your way up the pyramid of the award-winning Career Development Manual. Starting with "Self-Assessment," you'll learn about your strengths and weaknesses and get valuable tips for the job hunt and helpful advice for successfully building your career. There are lots of good resources here.

Quebec

Montreal Gazette

montrealgazette.com

The *Gazette* links to the CareerClick job resource. When we reviewed the site, a few positions were also listed in the Classifieds section.

The Montreal Page

toutmontreal.com (French)

toutmontreal.com/english/index.html (English)

The main page is in French, but you can select the English version (the second URL) if that is your preference. Montreal Page has nicely organized categories of information about living and working in the city. Click on the Businesses and Services link to access the job and career resources.

Quebec WorkInfoNET

qc.info-emploi.ca (French)

qc.info-emploi.ca/english/main.cfm (English)

This is the local section of WorkInfoNET specifically set up and maintained for Quebec.

Latin America and South America

Bolsa de Trabajo

bolsadetrabajo.com

Here you'll find employment opportunities and resumes for Spanish-speaking professionals. You must register to access the job openings or post your resume.

JobShark

jobshark.com

JobShark has now expanded beyond Canada, Ireland, and the United Kingdom into Central and South America. Select the country of choice to start your job search.

Latin American Jobs

latinamericanjobs.com

You must register before you have full access to the job listings. Business news from some of the Latin American countries is available without registering.

LatPro.com

latpro.com

LatPro is a comprehensive online career center for Spanish- and Portuguese-speaking professionals. Use the Quick Picks for "Latin Wall Street Jobs," H1B visa job postings, or jobs in specific countries. Use the customized search to sort jobs by location and job category, or have job listings sent to you via E-mail. LatPro.com also offers free by subscription the *Latin Career News (LCN)* or *Latin Tech Weekly,* online newsletters for Spanish- and Portuguese-speaking professionals.

United States–Mexico Chamber of Commerce (USMCOC)

usmcoc.org

The USMCOC maintains this resource featuring a calendar of events and other links of interest to individuals doing business in Mexico.

Europe

REGIONAL RESOURCES

EuroPages: the European Business Directory

europages.com

A directory of European businesses in thirty different countries, EuroPages is searchable by company name or service, or you can simply browse through the category links. You'll also find a collection of European yellow pages plus additional links to information about companies and the economy of Europe.

EURopean Employment Services (EURES)

http://europa.eu.int/comm/employment_social/elm/eures/index.htm

EURES is the result of labor agreements made by European Union (EU) members about issues that affect all member nations. As members, they are subject to EU regulations that affect labor mobility and work and residence permits. There are no jobs here, but the site index includes dozens of links regarding current employment issues and regulations.

European Governments Online

http://europa.eu.int/abc/governments/index_en.html

The European Union maintains this list of links to its member nations and other European countries. It offers a profile of the countries included, plus links to news and official websites. Job resource availability and information offered depends on the country.

JobPilot AG (Formerly Jobs & Adverts)

jobpilot.com

JobPilot has expanded to fifteen European countries and regions of Asia and Australia. To start your job search, select a region and industry. Click on the Search button to view the results. You can also browse by company name or explore the career resources. Register to post your resume or have job listings sent to you via E-mail.

Monster.com

monster.com

Several European countries are represented here. Access jobs in other countries, and view the highly regarded Monster content.

France, Belgium, Italy, and Spain

Association Bernard Gregory

abg.asso.fr

Check here to find job postings for scientists in France and other material of interest to the profession. Click on ABG-Jobs to get to the employment page. All listings are in French.

FDAssociates

fdassociates.com

FDAssociates is a recruiter for high-tech positions in France.

French National Center for Scientific Research (CNRS)

cnrs.org/cw/fr/band/autr/emploi.html

The CNRS includes information about its own job offerings plus links to other scientific job sites.

FrogJobs—Employment in France

To subscribe: listproc@list.cren.net

Message: subscribe frogjobs yourname

The French Scientific Mission in Washington, DC, sponsors this mailing list intended to help young French scientists pursuing a Ph.D. or help postdoctorates abroad prepare for their professional return to France or Europe. FrogJobs provides a network of support, with complete information on scientific employment, job opportunities, and contacts in public and private research centers.

Le Monde

lemonde.fr

http://emploi.lemonde.fr

The French newspaper of record offers all the news that's fit to print. Use the second URL to go directly to the career page. Search by job function or location.

newmonday.com (Formerly Jobworld.co.uk)

newmonday.com

Newmonday.com is rapidly expanding its geographical boundaries and is now assisting in all aspects of career development rather than focusing exclusively on IT and the financial industry. Use the Professional Selection Service to develop your profile and have your skills matched with job opportunities. Browse by industry sector, or search by job title or location.

Prospective Management Overseas (PMO) Vacant Positions Overseas

pmo.be

PMO specializes in the selection, recruitment, and management of experts such as technicians, engineers, or administrators for international projects. Click on the Positions icon to browse the listing of job possibilities. You can also choose to view only the newest postings or submit your CV.

Réseau Européen pour l'Emploi

reseau.org/emploi

You'll find many job listings at this site. Submit your resume or CV, or check out the list of online recruiters for France. You also have the option of receiving job postings via E-mail.

Trabajo.org

trabajo.org

Here you'll find listings for jobs in Spain. Check out the "hot jobs," search by region and/or job category, and post a resume. There is also a nice advice section. Trabajo.org is available only in Spanish.

Germany and Austria

Breitbach Unternehmensberatung

breitbach.com

Breitbach is a German IT recruiter and consulting company. Select English or German language, and click on Jobs to access a brief description of opportunities available in Germany.

newmonday.com (Formerly Jobworld.co.uk)

newmonday.com

Newmonday.com is rapidly expanding its geographical boundaries and is now assisting in all aspects of career development rather than focusing exclusively on IT and the financial industry. Use the Professional Selection Service to develop your profile and have your skills matched with job opportunities. Browse by industry sector, or search by job title or location.

Ireland

IrishJobs.ie

irishjobs.ie

exp.ie

Ireland's longest-established recruiting website, IrishJobs.ie has its job-search form readily accessible on the opening page. You can register to post your resume or to have job listings that match your profile waiting for you when you log in. Other features include resources for executives and new graduates.

NIjobs.com

nijobs.com

A recruiter for jobs in Northern Ireland, NIjobs.com has its job-search form readily accessible on the opening page. You can register to post your resume or to have job listings that match your profile waiting for you when you log in.

Netherlands

Avotek Headhunters

avotek.nl/dutchpag.htm

Avotek Publishers maintains a Dutch jobs page at this URL. Many of the links access information about print publications that Avotek is selling, but others do contain information for job hunters in the Netherlands.

newmonday.com (Formerly Jobworld.co.uk)

newmonday.com

Newmonday.com is rapidly expanding its geographical boundaries and is now assisting in all aspects of career development rather than focusing exclusively on IT and the financial industry. Use the Professional Selection Service to develop your profile and have your skills matched with job opportunities. Browse by industry sector, or search by job title or location.

QuoteJobs.nl

quotejobs.nl

The Netherlands' edition of the international Top Jobs website (topjobs.com) features company profiles, career resources, and a job agent to send job announcements to you via E-mail or cell phone.

Scotland

JobsinEdinburgh.com

jobsinedinburgh.com

This is one of four related sites dedicated to employment openings all over Scotland. The group also includes JobsinNewcastle.com, JobsinGlasgow.com., and JobsinAberdeen.com. Job seekers can post their resumes here for free and sign up to have matching jobs sent to them via E-mail.

Switzerland

StepStone

swisswebjobs.ch/sok

Formerly called SwissWebJobs, this area of StepStone features hundreds of job listings, employers, recruiters, and other career resources. You can also post your resume. This site is mostly in German.

TeleJob

telejob.ethz.ch

TeleJob is the electronic job exchange board for the Association of Assistants and Doctoral Students of the technological institutes of Zurich (AVETH) and Lausanne (ACIDE). Choose from the five languages offered, then select a field of interest to you and view the listing of jobs. Register with the Push-Service to have job announcements sent to you electronically.

United Kingdom

The British Council

britcoun.org/eis

The British Council facilitates the development of partnerships and the exchange of information with other cultures. Their Education Information Service provides this "Virtual Campus," a helpful tour of the resources available for students working in Britain. You'll also find answers to the most frequently asked questions. This is a great resource!

CityJobs

cityjobs.com

CityJobs specializes in finance, IT, accountancy, media, and legal sector positions in the United Kingdom. The keyword search on the opening page allows you to get results quickly. Use as few terms as possible for best results. You must register to post up to five resumes on the site. Be aware that the registration process requires you to enter your date of birth.

JobPilot AG (Formerly Jobs & Adverts)

jobpilot.co.uk

JobPilot has expanded to fifteen European countries and regions of Asia and Australia. This URL takes you directly to jobs in the United Kingdom. Click on "Go to Jobs" to start your job search. You can also browse by company name or explore the career resources. Register to post your resume or have job listings sent to you via E-mail.

JobServe

jobserve.com

JobServe is one of the largest sources of information technology jobs in the United Kingdom. At the time of review, it included hundreds of jobs overseas and a few for telecommuters as well. JobServe is simple to navigate, and you can browse jobs by agency or view the most recent postings only. You can subscribe to the newsletter or have job postings that fit your specifications sent to you by E-mail.

London Times

thetimes.co.uk

thetimes-appointments.co.uk

Go to the *London Times* for world headlines and business news. Services here include the Mobile Times, which downloads the headlines to your cellular phone, and the Student Weekly, which includes headlines, articles, and issues of interest to students. Select the Times Services icon to reach the Appointments (jobs) link, or use the second URL to go there directly. Search the jobs by industry or keyword, or register to post your CV.

MediaWeek

mediaweek.co.uk

mediamoves.co.uk

MediaWeek Online brings you this website featuring media industry news, program information, industry directories, and jobs. Click on Jobs to search the Mediamoves job and career resource, or use the second URL to go there directly. Register to use the CV template and post your resume or to receive job postings via E-mail.

newmonday.com (Formerly Jobworld.co.uk)

newmonday.com

Newmonday.com is rapidly expanding beyond the United Kingdom, primarily into Belgium, France, and the Netherlands. In addition to extending the geographical range of the service, newmonday.com is also assisting in all aspects of career development rather than focusing exclusively on IT and the financial industry. Use the new Professional Selection Service to develop your profile and have your skills matched with job opportunities. Browse by industry sector, or search by job title or location.

NISS: National Information Services and Systems

niss.ac.uk

vacancies.ac.uk

NISS serves as a portal for the academic community in the United Kingdom. The website provides news of interest, links to colleges and universities, and employment opportunities at the universities in the Commonwealth countries (United Kingdom, Canada, Australia, etc.). To initiate a job search, click on the Common Room link and look for the NISS Vacancies Service, or use the second URL to go directly to the search page. Search by keyword, browse the newest postings, or browse the listings by discipline.

PeopleBank: the Employment Network

peoplebank.com

PeopleBank has operated its Web-recruitment and job-matching service since 1995. Guests can search or browse the job ads without registering, but to get the most out of the service, you will need to register and obtain a password. You can then submit your resume to PeopleBank or have job ads sent to your E-mail account.

Reed Personnel Services

reed.co.uk

Register your skills at no cost at this site, which features jobs in a variety of fields and where "the right job looks for you." Check out the regional salary calculator for the United Kingdom. Register to try Reed's free tutorials, post your CV, or have the latest job postings sent to you via E-mail or text message to your mobile phone.

THES: The *Times* Higher Education Supplement

thesis.co.uk

jobs.thes.co.uk

The *Times* Higher Education Supplement (THES) chronicles the latest developments in higher education and provides a forum for issues that affect the world of academe. For print subscribers only, THES makes available a searchable archive of articles going back to 1994 and free access to the British Library's journal search service. New academic job opportunities appear every Tuesday. Browse them by broad category, search by keyword, or sign up for an E-mailed job alert. Use the second URL to go directly to the Jobs page.

Eastern Europe

REGIONAL RESOURCES

CrossroadsEurope

crossroadseurope.com

CrossroadsEurope was developed for teachers of English as a second language who are interested in working in Central Europe. You'll find listings of language schools, embassy addresses, information about visas and work permits, plus a nice selection of helpful links.

European Internet Resources (EIN)

europeaninternet.com

EIN offers a range of resources to individuals living in Central Europe and the Balkans. From the opening page, you can access the Russian and other country-specific pages. Most (classifieds, discussion boards, etc.) of the sites are free; however, the news section is available only to subscribers.

JobPilot AG (Formerly Jobs & Adverts)

jobpilot.com

JobPilot has expanded to fifteen European countries and regions of Asia and Australia. To start your job search, select a region and industry. Click on the Search button to view the results. You can also browse by company name or explore the career resources. Register to post your resume or have job listings sent to you via E-mail.

Czechoslovakia

Czechjobs.cz

czechjobs.cz

A recruiter for jobs in Czechoslovakia, Czechjobs.cz has its job-search form readily accessible on the opening page. You can register to post your resume or to have job listings that match your profile waiting for you when you log in.

Russia

American Chamber of Commerce in Russia

amcham.ru

The AmCham website includes both a directory of its membership, searchable by industry and company, and a directory for the St. Petersburg chapter. You'll also find a calendar of events and advice for doing business in Russia.

Bucknell University List of U.S. Firms in Russia

departments.bucknell.edu/russian

The Russian Program at Bucknell maintains this database of U.S. firms operating in the former Soviet Union. It's accessible from the menu on the left. Click on the Jobs link, and the database is the first of many job and career resources listed.

Human Resources Online

hro.ru

This site includes mostly Russian positions, although it features a few opportunities in other countries. Click on the Jobs icon to reach the collection of flags. Select the flag for the country you're interested in to browse those job listings.

Russia Donors Forum

donorsforum.ru/donorsforum/news.nsf

The Russia Donors Forum is an informal coalition of more than twenty-five foundations, grant makers, and governmental agencies working in Russia. Click on the News and Announcements link to get to the jobs.

Russian and East European Institute Employment Opportunities

indiana.edu/~reeiweb/indemp.html

Indiana University offers this resource for individuals seeking jobs in Russia or Eastern Europe or for those with expertise in the languages, history, or cultures of these areas. Loads of up-to-date links are here, and the Find a Job page includes helpful advice for job searchers as well as links to other employment resources.

Russian International Job Agency

job.ru/start.htm

To start your Russian job search, select a job category and specify a location. This site is available in Russian only.

The Scandinavian Countries

REGIONAL RESOURCES

Jobfinder

jobfinder.se

Headquartered in Sweden, Jobfinder offers services for individuals throughout the Nordic region. Its target groups include the IT sector, engineers, and finance professionals. Choose a job category, then select the location, and click on the Search button to view the results.

JobPilot AG (Formerly Jobs & Adverts)

jobpilot.com

JobPilot has expanded to fifteen European countries and regions of Asia and Australia. To start your job search, select a region and industry. Click on the Search button to view the results. You can also browse by company name or explore the career resources. Register to post your resume or have job listings sent to you via E-mail.

Denmark

Job-Index

jobindex.dk

Since 1996, Job-Index has maintained this Web collection of job opportunities in Denmark. Browse the jobs by category, register to have job announcements sent to your E-mail account, post your CV, or take a break and explore the shopping links.

Finland

Helsingin Sanomat

helsinginsanomat.fi

This online edition of Finland's largest newspaper features hundreds of job ads searchable by keyword or category.

Ministry of Labour, Finland

mol.fi

Maintained by the Finnish government, this website is a good starting place for a job search in Finland. Try the search engine "Avoimet tyopaikat" with categories and keywords. Included here are listings for thousands of job opportunities all over Finland with additional links to job openings in Scandinavia and the rest of Europe.

Sweden

JobPilot

jobpilot.se

When we reviewed the site, there were more than nine hundred opportunities throughout Sweden. Register to personalize your JobPilot and to receive E-mail notification of job possibilities.

Swedish Employment Service

ams.se

Developed by the Swedish National Labour Market Administration (AMV), this resource includes information about the labor market, employment services available for citizens of Sweden, and living and working in Sweden. To start your job search, select German or English language, click on the Working/ Studying link, and select "How to find a job." You'll find links to the nation's top newspapers and online career resources, plus a Swedish yellow pages.

Africa and the Middle East

Africa

Escape Artist Africa

escapeartist.com/jobs8/africa.htm

This section of the Escape Artist website for "escaping" Americans, adventurers, and others relocating outside the United States includes resources for living and working in Africa.

South Africa

Daily *Mail & Guardian* work@za

mg.co.za/mg/work

mg.co.za/jump/jump.html

Work@za is the *Mail & Guardian* newspaper's free South African online job shop for primarily professional and academic positions. Click on the Job Search icon to bring up all of the current job offerings. The second URL takes you to JumpStart, a comprehensive collection of South African Web resources. The government and education links could be especially useful to you as you pursue your job hunt.

Employnet

employnet.co.za

This site offers an opportunity for recruiters and potential employers to see your CV.

Hampton Consultancy

hampton.co.za

Based in South Africa, Hampton Consultancy posts current IT job opportunities from businesses in the community. Choose either Contract or Permanent to view the job postings.

The Personnel Concept

personnel-concept.co.za

The Personnel Concept recruits in the areas of IT, electronics, and finance. Browse the job postings by broad category or search by keyword.

Israel and the Middle East

Association of Americans and Canadians in Israel (AACI) Jobnet

jobnet.co.il

AACI brings you this online service—updated daily—with the financial help of the Ministry of Science and the Samis Foundation. Use the Search Index to browse by job category or by employer, or search for jobs using keywords. The Job Basket allows you to mark all the positions in which you're interested and then print them or send them to your E-mail address at the end of your session.

JobPilot Mideast

mideast.jobpilot.com

This division of the JobPilot site is set up specifically for opportunities in the Middle East.

Asia and the Pacific Rim

REGIONAL RESOURCES

Asia-Net

asia-net.com

Asia-Net serves the Asia/Pacific Rim business communities by matching job candidates with potential employers. This online recruitment service provides current job postings for professionals who are Asian nationals or have close ties to the Asian community. You can search the job database or let the jobs find you. Simply fill in your E-mail address and check the language and type of listings you would like to receive, and you will be notified when a job meeting your specs is posted.

Asiadragons Asia Employment Center

asiadragons.com/employment/home.shtml

Asiadragons provides access to job opportunities throughout Asia and beyond. Browse through the listings of all current job offerings, or scroll down the page to view by country. Post your resume for free.

JobAsia

jobasia.com

To get the full benefit of this free job site you must register, and your browser must be Java enabled. Use the simple search or PowerSearch for jobs, or look up companies by industry or name, and attach your results to a clipboard to print out or view later. You can also develop your job-search profile and have JobAsia find jobs for your personalized list. Select one of the three templates to create a quick resume and use it to instantly apply for positions online.

Monster Work Abroad

http://international.monster.com

Monster Work Abroad includes hundreds of job listings for this region in its database. Click on the Jobs link and select your destination to view them.

Australia

APN EdOnline (Formerly *Campus Review*)

edonline.com.au

When we reviewed it, EdOnline was not yet fully operational. The site by the publisher of *Campus Review*, *Nursing Review*, and *Education Review* will include an online interactive career resource and study guides. Our hope is that when it is completed, EdOnline will be on a par with its successful predecessor, the *Campus Review* job site.

Australian Career Directory

careers.gov.au

jobsearch.gov.au

You'll find everything you need to make decisions about your career, research companies, look for educational alternatives, or explore the world of work. The Career Directory offers a tremendous array of resources for the Australian job hunter. To start the job search, click on Job Hunt and select the job category or location of interest, or use the second URL to go directly to the Job Search page. Register to post your resume or develop your profile. This site is a must-see for Australian job seekers and career changers.

Careers Online

careersonline.com.au/menu.html

Developed by a former Australian career adviser, Careers Online is a full-service career site with links to resume-writing and interviewing tips and other helpful career resources. Careers Online is simple to use, with plenty of quality links.

Department of Education, Training, and Youth Affairs (DETYA)

deetya.gov.au

http://jobsearch.deetya.gov.au

jobsearch.gov.au

DETYA's mission is to support the lifelong learning needs of all Australians, and it provides a wealth of information in that pursuit. Navigation is simplest using the Site Index. Get career advice, learn about training opportunities, or find out what's happening on the Australian job front. Search for a job in the Commonwealth database by location or occupation, or link to other helpful resources. Use either of the other URLs to go directly to the JobSearch page.

Employment Opportunities in Australia

employment.com.au

The Adcorp Group maintains this online recruitment website for job opportunities in Australia. Adcorp's website offers job postings and a variety of helpful tools for job hunters. This is another great resource for Australian job hunters.

JobNet Australia

jobnet.com.au

educateit.com.au

JobNet offers a comprehensive range of information technology career services to Australian job hunters and recruiters. Browse the thousands of IT job leads by geographical area. Use Educate IT to locate training and educational opportunities. Register for the daily E-mail job alert or to post your resume.

Monster Australia

monster.com.au

This division of the popular Monster.com job bank is set up specifically for opportunities in Australia.

PeopleBank: The Employment Network

peoplebank.com.au

This site is the Australian version of the United Kingdom's free service for information technology professionals.

Sydney Morning Herald

smh.com.au

mycareer.com.au

To start your job search, select Jobs on the menu or use the second URL to go directly to the Job Search page. Choose a sector or type in a keyword. Refine the search by region or job type (full-time, part-time, etc.). You can specify today's ads only. Register to create your job folder, to have job postings that meet your specifications delivered to you via E-mail, or to post your resume.

Workplace Connect

workplaceconnect.org.au

Established in 1982, Workplace Connect matches individuals with trainee and apprentice positions, enabling them to get firsthand experience in the world of work and learn job-related skills at the same time. It also offers certification for a number of disciplines and provides fee-for-service training for corporations and government agencies.

China

Career Wise at DragonSurf

globalvillager.com/careerwise/index.cfm

Career Wise provides job postings for work with companies in China, Korea, the United States, and beyond. You must register to use the site.

Wang & Li Asia Resources

wang-li.com

Wang & Li matches Asian returnee and Asian-American professionals with corporations operating or doing business in the greater China region.

India

CareerMosaic India

careermosaicindia.com

Part of the original CareerMosaic Gateway, CM India now represents a partnership between Careerbuilder and TMI Network, a recruitment advertising agency. Most of the job offerings are management or IT related.

Naukri

naukri.com

Maintained by Info Edge of New Delhi, Naukri has fast become one of the best resources for job hunters in India. Search for a job by keyword or location, or browse the entire list by category. Register to post your resume or to receive E-mail notification of current opportunities.

Japan/Hong Kong/Korea/Malaysia

CareerCross Japan

careercross.com

New to this edition is CareerCross, a bilingual recruitment resource serving the English-Japanese business community. Learn about living and working in Japan, and find jobs in Japan and overseas. First select either English or the Japanese language. Browse the latest jobs, or search by job category, location, or other qualifiers. Leave the fields blank to see all of the jobs. Register to receive E-mail updates or to post your resume.

Jobs in Japan

jobsinjapan.com

The self-proclaimed "mother lode of Japan job info" features free do-it-yourself job and resume posting. The jobs listed are up-to-date and eclectic, including a mix of IT, teaching, waitressing, and acting positions.

KyushuNet Japan Association for Language Teaching (JALT)

kyushu.com/jalt/index.html

KyushuNet JALT offers resources for teachers of English as a foreign language, such as a notice board and an events calendar. The Finding a Job section features advice for living and working in Japan along with links to job opportunities.

O-Hayo Sensei, The Newsletter of (Teaching) Jobs in Japan

ohayosensei.com

O-Hayo Sensei is a free-subscription electronic newsletter that lists teaching positions at dozens of schools and companies in Japan. Have the newsletter E-mailed to you, or download it from the website. You'll also find information about living and working in Japan.

New Zealand

career.co.nz

http://career.co.nz

The Adcorp Group maintains this online recruitment website for job opportunities in New Zealand. Following the lead of CareerMosaic, Adcorp's website offers job postings and a variety of helpful tools for job hunters. This is a must-see for New Zealand job seekers and career changers.

JobNet

jobnet.com.au

educateit.com.au

JobNet's career site for IT professionals includes hundreds of jobs in New Zealand. To access them, browse the job leads by geographical area. Use Educate IT (the second URL) to find training and educational opportunities. Register for the E-mail job alert or to post your resume.

Jobstuff (Formerly InfoTech Weekly Online JobNet NZ)

jobstuff.co.nz

Established in 1995 by Independent Newspapers Limited (INL), Jobstuff is part of Stuff, a news and information portal for New Zealand. Search the diverse collection of job postings by keyword and geographical area, or browse by category. Register for the Job Alert to have job leads that match your specifications automatically E-mailed to you. Stuff's InfoTech and Business pages (stuff.co.nz) feature timely news about the economy.

Monster New Zealand

monster.co.nz

This division of the popular Monster.com job bank is set up specifically for opportunities in New Zealand.

Singapore and Thailand

Department of Employment (DOE), Thailand

doe.go.th

This is a good source of job leads for Thailand. The DOE supervises Thai nationals working overseas as well as foreign nationals working in Thailand.

Singapore Economic Development Board

sedb.com

Look here for detailed information about specific industries in Singapore. You'll also find helpful tips for living, working, and starting a business in Singapore, business statistics, and educational resources.

13

Resources for Diverse Audiences

This chapter comprises a small collection of websites offering information and, in some cases, job leads targeted to specific audiences. They are certainly not the only places online to look for job listings, but users can be assured that the employers and recruiters advertising at these sites are concerned about equality and diversity in their organizations. In many cases, sites not offering job leads will have advertisers, information to point you toward potential employers, or good information for your career in general.

General Diversity Sites

Diversity/Careers in Engineering & Information Technology

diversitycareers.com

The print publication focuses on minority/diversity technical professionals and features career articles and job announcements. The website includes the online magazine and carries a full list of employers placing advertisements in the latest print issue, linking to each employers' website for job announcements.

Diversity Employment

diversityemployment.com

This site "seeks to become a centralized employment resource for individuals of diverse ethnicities." It's easy to search the job database by keyword or to scan the regional listings.

Diversity Link

diversitylink.com

Diversity Link includes job listings and resume postings targeted for diversity candidates (women, persons from varied ethnic backgrounds, people with disabilities, etc.).

Equal Opportunity Publications, Inc.

eop.com

The EOP website includes information on the company's family of publications, *Equal Opportunity*, *Woman Engineer*, *Minority Engineer*, *CAREERS & the disABLED*, and *Workforce Diversity for Engineering and IT Professionals*. EOP also publishes *Information Technology Career World*, a career/recruitment magazine for nondiversity entry-level and professional job seekers in the field of information technology. The same list of job opportunities can be found under each magazine title (except for *ITCW*), but the list of employers changes for each. At the time of review, all of these subscriptions were free except for *CAREERS & the disABLED*.

Hire Diversity

hirediversity.com

This national diversity recruitment service links qualified candidates from entry level to senior level with Fortune 500 companies and the government. It has separate news channels of interest to each different population, but the jobs listed are all in one job bank. This site is owned by Hispanic Business, Inc. (see the listing under Hispanic-Americans).

IMDiversity.com

imdiversity.com

IMdiversity.com is an excellent resource for all minority and diversity candidates. It is set up in "villages" for African-Americans, Asian-Americans, Hispanic-Americans, Native Americans, and women. The resources and information in each village are specific for each group, and those without a specific village will find information for their needs in the Global Village. Job listings here are updated frequently and are easy to access. Formerly known as Minorities Job Bank, this site was conceived by *The Black Collegian* magazine (see its listing under African-Americans). The sponsors are committed to serving all professionals of color, and they are doing a great job.

NAACP Diversity Career Fair

http://naacpjobfair.com

This site brings career resources, resume postings, company profiles, job listings, and much more to a diverse population. You can also check the schedule for career and job fairs in your area. The job search connects to BestDiversityEmployers.com, but it is really an integral part of this site.

National Diversity Newspaper Job Bank

http://newsjobs.com

This is the nation's most comprehensive Internet listing of business-side and newsroom openings dedicated to increasing diversity in the newspaper industry. You must submit a resume in order to get a login/password to view the job listings. It is free, but this first step is required.

Older/Disadvantaged Workers

Experience Works!

experienceworks.org

Established as Green Thumb, Experience Works! is a nationwide staffing service dedicated to providing temporary and permanent employment opportunities to older individuals, dislocated workers, welfare participants, and other adults seeking employment and needed income. Job seekers must register with their local office to be considered for openings in their area. A list of those offices plus contact information is included.

NSCERC Online: the National Senior Citizens' Education and Research Center, Inc.

nscerc.org

NSCERC is a not-for-profit company working to provide employment for seniors through the Senior AIDES Program, the Senior Environmental Employment Program, and Mature Staffing Systems. These and other programs NSCERC administers are funded by grants from the Department of Labor, the Environmental Protection Agency, and the Department of Education, and you can learn about programs and opportunities in your area through the website.

Senior Job Bank

seniorjobbank.com

Senior Job Bank is a nonprofit referral service working to match seniors who want to work with opportunities. All services are paid for through the advertising on the site. To search the job bank, you must first select a state. At the time of review, we did not find many jobs here, but we hope this service will become an active resource for this community.

ThirdAge

thirdage.com

ThirdAge defines itself as a website for those entering their third age of life, usually someone in her or his forties or fifties, someone starting to question who he or she really is and what is really desired from life. The site is filled with health, life, financial, and other information. The Money area includes "Your Next Job," a section filled with articles and information on self-employment, changing careers, and even early retirement. Job listings are provided in partnership with Monster.com.

Women

Advancing Women

advancingwomen.com

This is a nice business site dedicated to women. It subdivides into sections for younger women, some diversity groups among women, work and leisure, and money issues. The job and career information is provided in partnership with Careerbuilder.net.

Business Women's Network Interactive (BWNI)

bwni.com

BWNI provides businesswomen with information and resources they need to stay competitive and growing in their businesses. It also serves as a medium for businesses to target the fast-growing and powerful women's market. The website includes a career section in co-partnership with JobOptions (joboptions.com/bwni).

Feminist Career Center

feminist.org/911/jobs/911jobs.asp

This service of the Feminist Majority Foundation Online is intended to increase awareness of a wide variety of feminist issues and to help feminist employers and job seekers find each other. The jobs are listed by geographic region, and while they are updated on a regular basis, some older position announcements are in the list. Check the dates, and contact the posting agency to be sure a position is still open. Other services available here are the Positions Wanted database (submit your resume for free; it will be listed for six months), Internships (arranged by organization name), and links to additional job boards.

iVillage

ivillage.com

At iVillage, you can find interactive services and support in many areas of interest to women, including working from home and entrepreneurship. Look in the Work area for information on salaries, careers, work-from-home ideas, and jobs. For job listings, iVillage partners with CareerBuilder.com.

WITI: Women in Technology International

witi.com

WITI's services to members include mentors, networking opportunities, and jobs for qualified women in technology. The group's purpose is to encourage women to reach the upper administrative levels in all industries and encourage more women to pursue technical careers. It is a great professional and support organization. The job database includes more than just technology jobs, but most positions are in various high-tech companies.

Womans-Work

womans-work.com

This site lists alternative and flexible opportunities for women, including part-time, work-from-home, flextime, telework, and freelance opportunities. It gives salary information by geographic location or job title. Although no posting dates are listed, the webmaster says that no job is more than sixty days old, and new jobs are added almost daily.

WomensFinance

womensfinance.com

WomensFinance is filled with lots of financial advice for women. The advice is divided into various topics, including life events (marriage, divorce, and widowhood), investing, credit and debt, and jobs and careers. The job listings are provided in partnership with CareerBuilder.com.

WWWomen

wwwomen.com

This is a subject directory similar to Yahoo!, and it is a good place to look for links to information by and for women and minorities. Many career-related sites are included, along with a huge list of professional and trade associations for women.

Transitioning Military Personnel

Career Command Post

careercommandpost.com

This site helps bring active-duty military personnel and their spouses as well as veterans of the armed forces together with civilian employers. There is a wide variety of positions listed with salaries ranging from $20,000 to $90,000 per year.

Career Development

cdc-va.com

This firm is one of the leading placement companies for junior military officers in the United States. Based in Alexandria, Virgina, this group has been working since 1972 and has placed more than six thousand former military officers in positions in more than six hundred companies across the United States. There is no fee for applicants, and the company does not even want you to work with its representatives exclusively. Career Development provides a list of positions around the country that it is working to fill, along with a profile of the ideal qualities for successful candidates. It looks like a very good firm.

Corporate Gray Online

greentogray.com

This site targets job seekers transitioning from military to civilian careers, connecting you with military-friendly companies nationwide. The premise comes from the popular Corporate Gray books for finding jobs in the private sector after a military career—*From Army Green to Corporate Gray*, *From Navy Blue to Corporate Gray*, and *From Air Force Blue to Corporate Gray*—all distributed by Competitive Edge. All users are required to fill out the free registration form in order to search the job database.

The Destiny Group

destinygrp.com

The Destiny Group connects corporations with the military community. The site includes resume-writing and job-hunting information. The job postings are at all levels of expertise and experience. You must register to use this site, but all services are free to the job seeker.

Military.com

military.com

Military.com claims to be the largest online site for the military, those in transition, and their families. It is sponsored by Military Advantage, which includes military, academic, and businesspeople. The site has a lot of interesting information in addition to job opportunities, but free registration is required to view the job listings.

Transition Assistance Online (TAO)

taonline.com

This is a cooperative effort by DI-USA, Inc., and the Army Times Publishing Company launched in January 1997. There is no charge for service members to submit their resumes or to search the wide variety of employment opportunities. TAO provides information on second-career strategies, starting one's own business, continuing/distance-education programs, and relocation assistance. You'll also find information on veterans' benefits, reserve matters, and transition resources. You might want to scan the list of all jobs by employer to get a good overview of what is offered. Many of these openings seem well geared for the specialties we see more in the military and less in the civilian market. Don't skip the calendar of military career fairs, complete with descriptions of what type of employment openings will be available and how to make sure you are on the list.

Use Your Military Experience and Training (UMET)

http://umet-vets.dol.gov

This is a great site with information on licensing and certification for all kinds of civilian jobs in each state. In addition, it helps you translate military experience to civilian experience and includes tuition-assistance services.

VetJobs.com

vetjobs.com

This site is not just for senior officers but includes all transitioning military personnel as well as longtime veterans. Users will find general career information, a resume database, and entry-level as well as middle management positions posted here.

Workforce Transition Program (WTP) from CWA/NETT

cwanett.org/military.asp

This is a distance-learning program that provides state-of-the-art training in computer and internetworking technology. Course curriculum is accessed over the Internet. Training is offered in computer technology (A+) and to become a Cisco-certified network associate (CCNA) through WTP's educational partner, Stanly Community College of North Carolina, which is fully accredited by the Southern Association of Colleges and Schools. Through arrangements with the Department of Labor, the Communications Workers of America National Education and Training Trust (CWA/NETT) provides training to veterans and those on active duty in the military. The training offered addresses the needs of candidates looking to enter the industry and workers wanting to update their skills to keep current with changing technologies. Employment referral is also available through this site.

Disabled Workers

Able to Work

abletowork.org

This is a consortium of business leaders that reads like a *Who's Who in Business*, managed by the National Business and Disabilities Council (business-disability.com). Their goal is to increate awareness of, and employment for, persons with disabilities through the coordinated effort of "North America's largest employers." College graduates with disabilities may post resumes here, and there is a variety of information available for job applicants.

DisabilityDirect.gov

disabilitydirect.gov

Created by the Presidential Task Force on Employment of Adults with Disabilities in July 2000, this site provides one-stop career centers, job and resume banks, personal assistance services, veterans' employment programs, welfare-to-work information, temporary employment opportunities, and much more. It is an easy-to-use, excellent site.

Disability Resources Monthly

disabilityresources.org

This is operated by a nonprofit organization that "monitors, reviews, and reports on resources" every day to empower the disabled. It disseminates information to libraries, disability organizations, health and social service professionals, consumers, and family members. Scroll down the menu on the right side to get to the Employment area, a collection of links to sites and services ready to assist you in your job search.

DO-IT (Disabilities, Opportunities, Internetworking, and Technology), University of Washington

washington.edu/doit

"DO-IT is people with disabilities successfully pursuing academics and careers, programs to promote the use of technology to maximize the independence, productivity, and participation of people with disabilities, and resources for you." Here you also have links to resources and services with suggestions for pursuing your dream career.

JobAccess

jobaccess.org

Started as a joint project of Headhunter.net and *Ability* magazine, JobAccess enables people with disabilities to enhance their professional lives by providing them with a dedicated system for finding employment with business, government, and nonprofit employers. The database is easy to search by geographic area, field of interest, job category, or company. Job listings are dated, but you can also select just those listings posted in the past three days.

African-Americans

BET.com

bet.com

BET.com is a huge portal to African-American life, including information on families, lifestyles, music, technology, and careers. It was founded in 1999 by several major companies, including Microsoft, and it is "tailored to the preferences and needs of the African-American and urban communities." Job listings here are provided in partnership with Monster.com.

The Black Collegian

black-collegian.com

The print publication for college students and professionals of color has set up this extensive online information resource. The website includes job resources, resume information, career guidance, and all kinds of other great articles and resources for everyone. *The Black Collegian* also sponsors IMDiversity.com (see listing at the beginning of this chapter).

Black Voices

blackvoices.com

This is another large site addressing the needs of African-Americans for news, entertainment, sports, shopping, job fairs, and careers. The career center is where you post your resume and review job listings provided by the CareerBuilder.com network. A really special feature here is the Engineering & Technology Virtual Career Fair. Participants send their resumes directly to the hiring managers.

Blackworld

blackworld.com

Blackworld is an enormous international Internet directory designed primarily, but not exclusively, for black communities around the world. The Job Seeker Resource Center is especially extensive and offers everything from resume services to continuing education sources.

National Black MBA Association (NBMBAA)

nbmbaa.org

This group is "a business organization which leads in the creation of economic and intellectual wealth for the African-American community." NBMBAA has a nice employment network to handle job listings and resumes for African-American professionals. You are encouraged to register your resume first because all communication between the job seeker (that's you) and the employer will take place online. You can search the job database without registering, but when you find a listing you like, you will have to register your resume in order to apply.

NetNoir

netnoir.com

NetNoir describes itself as "a Black interactive online community . . . we believe there are fundamental Black cultural values that have to be reflected in the programming of our service." In addition to the cultural and business news provided here, NetNoir sponsors BlackJobs, a database of professional jobs for African-Americans. The site's services are free, but you must register in order to access the job listings.

Hispanic-Americans

DiversiLink Employment Web Site: The Site for Hispanic Engineers

diversilink.com

This site, sponsored by the Society for Hispanic Professional Engineers (SHPE), is dedicated to assisting its members in finding work, preparing resumes and cover letters, and exploring their career options. SHPE (shpe.org) is a "leading social-technical organization whose primary function is to enhance and achieve the potential of Hispanics in engineering, math, and science . . . SHPE promotes the development of Hispanics in engineering, science, and other technical professions to achieve educational excellence, economic opportunity, and social equity." The job listings, student opportunities, and virtual career fairs are open to all to view. A private resume database and mailing list for job announcements are also available and are open to anyone wishing to participate. This site is a very good source of jobs and information, and if you are not a member and get ahead by using the services provided here, please repay the group's generosity by joining. You can sort the jobs by geographic area, posting date, company name, and job title.

Hispanic Business, Inc.

hispanicbusiness.com

Hispanic Business provides a wealth of business information to the Spanish-speaking community. The site includes feature articles from the print magazine of the same name along with job listings. Hispanic Business also operates Hire Diversity for people of different backgrounds (see the listing at the beginning of this chapter).

Hispanic Online

hisp.com

Hispanic Online is a leading Web and America Online forum for Latinos living in the United States. The site offers job listings (in partnership with CareerBuilder), chat rooms, message boards, and news, events, and issues of interest to the Latino community based on *Hispanic* magazine, a monthly for and about Latinos, with a national circulation of 250,000 and a readership of more than one million. Back issues and articles are available on both the America Online and public websites.

Saludos

saludos.com

This site, dedicated exclusively to promoting Hispanic careers and education, is supported by *Saludos Hispanos* magazine. Information here includes the Career Center, Education Center, Resume Pool, Article Archive with recent articles from *Saludos Hispanos*, and Hispanic Resource Index with links to additional resources of interest to the Hispanic community. In addition to the bilingual career opportunities, this site offers a free newsletter. Most ads are general pointers back to employer websites, but many are specific and dated at the bottom of the page. This is a very nice resource.

Asian-Americans

Asian American Economic Development Enterprises, Inc. (AAEDE)

aaede.org

This organization began in 1977 to help Chinese immigrants acclimate to their new environment and obtain financial security. It has since grown into a full-service nonprofit organization dedicated to economic self-help for Asian-Americans and others. David Woo, founder and president, says that "AAEDE exists to help people find employment; to assist them in getting the expanded education they may need to ensure their promotion and competence; and to assist them on the road to building a successful enterprise which will then, in turn, employ more Asian Americans." The jobs are listed by company name. There is a fee to post your resume here.

Career Cross Japan

careercross.com

This is a bilingual recruitment source for Japanese jobs in many countries, including the United States and Japan. Of special interest is the information about living and working in these various countries.

National Association of Asian American Professionals (NAAAP)

naaap.org

NAAAP is an "all-volunteer organization whose mission is to promote the personal and professional development of the Asian American community."

Native North Americans

American Indian Science and Engineering Society

aises.org

This is the website of a national nonprofit organization dedicated to the "building of community by bridging science and technology with traditional Native values." It helps American Indian and Native Alaskan students prepare for careers in science, technology, engineering, and business. It also provides professional development activities to teachers to enable them to work more effectively with this population. Scholarships, federal internships, and networking opportunities are available here. Its quarterly magazine *Winds of Change* focuses on careers and education and is available by subscription. This also includes the annual college guide issue. Some content from the current issue is available on the website.

CareerPlace

careerplace.com

CareerPlace, an initiative of the Native Women's Association of Canada, is helping aboriginal women in Canada succeed through exciting and rewarding employment opportunities. Services include matching you with employers who are looking for someone with your skills, contacting the companies, identifying career opportunities, negotiating the position for you, and mentoring. There is an extensive list of links to many websites of interest to women in general and aboriginals in particular.

National Indian Council on Aging (NICOA)

nicoa.org

NICOA has operated as a national sponsor of the Senior Community Services Employment Program (SCSEP) under Title V of the Older Americans Act. Its mission is "to bring about improved, comprehensive services for American Indian and Alaska Native elders." Through the SCSEP grant, NICOA provides part-time work experience, training, and an opportunity for persons to transition into private or public sector jobs. You must be fifty-five years or older and meet low-income guidelines to participate in this program.

NativeWeb

nativeweb.org

NativeWeb "exists to utilize the Internet to educate the public about indigenous cultures and issues, and to promote communications between indigenous peoples and organizations supporting their goals and efforts." NativeWeb has an employment database under Community Center that provides "a service to native or indigenous owned/run businesses, or organizations or businesses seeking to fill positions related to the native and indigenous community." Under Resources—Business & Economy, you will find a section for Jobs and Opportunities that contains links to more locations for jobs.

The Tribal Employment Newsletter

nativejobs.com

This is a recruitment tool for employers who want to increase their efforts to hire diverse populations. For the job seeker, it is easy to access job announcements, but because the jobs are not dated, it is difficult to tell if they are still active listings. There are other resources here that will be of interest to Native Americans.

Gay/Lesbian

GAYWORK.com

gaywork.com

The site sponsor explains, "GAYWORK.com is a job-search/job-listing service for truly equal opportunity employers. Employers may place job listings and search our database of resumes for the best and brightest applicants." The job database is easy to search and is filled with good positions. You can post your resume for free, and it will be displayed for sixty days. You can update, edit, or delete it at any time within that period. This database is for everyone, but the site encourages job postings only from truly equal opportunity employers. The employer profiles are searchable by such terms as "domestic partner benefits," and many of the profiles link to employer websites. At the time of review we found many good companies and nonprofits posting very good jobs here along with many links to similar sites, making this an excellent gateway to these resources.

GoGay.net

gogay.net

GoGay.net is dedicated to informing the gay/lesbian/bisexual/transsexual community on the gay-friendly status of private and public organizations and companies. They give you a company's record on sexual orientation issues, and if your company is not found in their database, they will research it and add it. You can also link from here to glvReports.com, a private company that rates more than five hundred leading companies based on a survey covering such issues as health care benefits for domestic partners, diversity training, and written nondiscrimination policies. These two sites along with all the other resources they link to will be of great assistance in evaluating current and potential employers.

ProGayJobs.com

progayjobs.com

ProGayJobs is dedicated to the career needs of gay and lesbian job seekers and to the inclusion of sexual orientation in the equal opportunity agenda. The employers posting here express the belief in supporting diversity of sexual orientation and in providing an open work environment. The site is free to the job seeker, but registration is required before you can use it.

Religious Affiliations

Christian Career Center

christiancareercenter.com

Professional career counselors interested in helping job seekers to "integrate their faith with career/life planning and find work that fits their God-given design" operate the Christian Career Center. There is a lot of job-hunting help, including career-consultation services, a resume bank, and career resources and guides.

Christian Jobs Online

christianjobs.com

This site is intended as "a place where Christian job seekers and employers can meet." The service posts job openings, positions wanted, and resumes. Many of the organizations posting here are Christian-based nonprofits with a variety of needs (e.g., social workers, architects with experience designing churches). There is a fee for resume posting (180 days). Job listings are posted for one month.

Hillel: the Foundation for Jewish Campus Life

hillel.org

Hillel was founded in 1923 to strengthen Jewish life on college campuses. The website includes the directory "Guide to Jewish Life on Campus/Campus Contacts," information about internships, study opportunities, grants, awards and scholarships, and career opportunities with the national organization.

14

Lifelong Career Planning

In 1999, the National Career Development Association (NCDA) released the results of the Fourth NCDA/NOICC/Gallup Survey of Working America prepared with the assistance of the Gallup Organization. Among other findings, the researchers noted that most adults reported they liked their current job very much (50 percent) or quite a bit (31 percent). But at the same time, seven out of every ten adults surveyed (69 percent) said that if they were starting over, they would try to get more information about the job and career options open to them than they got the first time. [If you are interested in reviewing the full report, contact NCDA through their website at ncda.org, or call (866) 367-6232.]

Whether or not you want to admit it, your work is critical to your happiness and your life. It affects your standard of living, your lifestyle, and how you spend most of your waking hours. Decisions that affect your career affect your life, and those decisions are not limited to asking for a raise, accepting a promotion, or changing employers. They include ideas such as changing jobs, changing occupations, moving to a new place because the opportunities there are better, or going back to college because you can get further with the degree than you can without it. Career planning is not just what happens when you are finishing high school or college. It is a lifelong process of exploration and decision making that affects your life and the lives of those around you.

As you go through life and encounter decision points (either by choice or by force), you need tools to help you explore options, make decisions, plan actions, and execute those plans. This chapter outlines a little bit of that process and provides you with a select list of resources designed to help you every time you feel the need to work through even a small part of your career planning. It includes help for the job search, tips on interview preparation, career guides to let you explore occupations, information on how to get any additional training and education you might need, and much more. However, this is just a small fraction of the good things available online. Even more listings can be found through The Riley Guide (rileyguide.com).

General Resources for Lifelong Career Planning

All of the sites listed here include numerous resources and information sources to help you with planning and managing your career, from the start to the end and even your life after work.

CareerJournal from the *Wall Street Journal*

http://careerjournal.com

Check out the Salary and Hiring Info section for several articles and resources reviewing hiring activity, salaries, and other trends nationwide. You'll also want to look over the Job-Hunting Advice with its information on resumes, interviewing, changing careers, using the Internet, and much more.

The Catapult, Career Service Professionals Home Page

jobweb.com/catapult

The Catapult is the springboard to the frequently visited places of career service professionals and other great souls. The National Association of Colleges and Employers maintains the Catapult, and it contains more than two hundred links to career and employment resources, including assessment and exploration resources.

Minnesota Careers 2001

mncareers.org

"What do I want to do with my life? What do the numbers say? Where do I go from here?" This guide from the Minnesota Department of Employment Security is here to help you answer these questions and plan your career path. While they start by talking to young persons just out of high school, older and more experienced people will also find this guide to be extremely helpful. It's not just for Minnesotans!

USNews.com: Education

usnews.com/usnews/edu/eduhome.htm

The publisher of *U.S. News and World Report* has produced one of the most outstanding guides to education and career information on the Web. Dedicated sections of this site focus on college, graduate school, financial aid, and careers, and each is filled with the quality news, information, and resources you expect from this publication. This is an excellent resource for anyone who is considering what career to pursue, wanting to change careers, or wanting to get ahead in a current career.

Career Planning Processes

Career Planning Process, Bowling Green State University

bgsu.edu/offices/sa/career/process

Developed by Pam Allen and Ellen Nagy, this site guides you through various steps to evaluating yourself and your career options.

CareerSearch from the College Board Online

http://cbweb9p.collegeboard.org/career/bin/career.pl

How do you select a career? What if you already know what you want to do but need to find out how to accomplish this dream? This site can help. It has descriptions of hundreds of occupations (including training and education requirements and salary expectations) and a wonderful career questionnaire that can help you in narrowing your choices.

nextSteps.org

nextsteps.org

This is a great guide to career planning, exploration, and decision making for young persons ages fifteen to twenty-four with interactive tools you can use as you work through the various steps and exercises tied to great resources. NextSteps.org is a service of the Calgary Youth Employment Center, Canada.

The Parachute Library for Job Hunters and Career Changers from JobHuntersBible.com

jobhuntersbible.com/library/hunters/library.shtml

Richard Bolles, one of the great leaders in career exploration, has produced a very attractive and informative guide to help job hunters and career changers find the best career sites on the Internet. This particular section contains several articles written by Bolles covering life/work planning; an overview of job hunting; what (would you most love to do?), where (would you most love to do it?), and how (do you find such a job?); and he also looks at what happens after you get the job. JobHuntersBible.com supplements Bolles's book *What Color Is Your Parachute?* and includes helpful information from that as well as from his Net Guide to the online job search.

University of Waterloo Career Services Career Development Manual

careerservices.uwaterloo.ca/manual-home.html

Try this six-step process for career- and life-planning success. The first step is self-assessment, but the other five steps will take you through the job-search process right up to choosing which job offer to accept.

Counseling

APA Help Center

http://helping.apa.org

Through this site, the American Psychological Association offers useful facts, information, and advice on how psychological services can help people cope with problems such as stress, depression, family strife, or chronic illness. The site provides sections devoted to psychology in the workplace, the health implications of the mind-body connection, family and personal relationships, and psychology in daily life. In addition, you may order a free print brochure, "How to Find Help for Life's Problems," learn how and when to choose a psychologist, and obtain a referral to a psychologist in your area. A detailed site map and an easy-to-use keyword search facility aid navigation of these helpful pages.

Counselor Licensure Legislation: Protecting the Public (American Counseling Association)

counseling.org/resources/licensure_legislation.htm

"One might think that the answer to the question, 'Who is qualified to provide counseling services?' would be a simple one. In actuality, this is a confusing issue for those persons seeking services." This short article helps explain the laws governing counselors in all states, making it easier for you to review the services of persons in your area.

Jewish Vocational Service Agencies in the United States, Canada, and Israel

jvsnj.org/affiliates.html

The Jewish Vocational Service (JVS) is a comprehensive vocational, educational, and technical training agency providing a broad range of services on a nonsectarian basis. You can check this list provided by the JVS of MetroWest (New Jersey) to find the JVS affiliate closest to you.

National Board of Certified Counselors (NBCC)

nbcc.org

The NBCC is a national certification agency for counselors, including career counselors. Certification from this group or from a local licensing or certification board gives you the assurance that a counselor has met certain professional standards. The NBCC will send you a list of board-certified counselors in your area at no charge. Another feature you will find on the NBCC website is a list of the state credentialing boards for counselor certification. This list, found under the heading for State Credentialing, lists the contact information for all states requiring counselors to go through their own certification process before they are allowed to practice as counselors. You can also contact these agencies for lists of certified counselors in your area who may not hold national certification.

National Career Development Association

ncda.org

This association is the career-counseling arm of the American Counseling Association (counseling.org), a group that has been instrumental in setting professional and ethical standards for the counseling profession. While it does not provide assistance in locating counselors in your area, it does offer its "Consumer Guidelines for Selecting a Career Counselor" along with a list of frequently asked questions about career counselors and career counseling.

Self-Assessment

Sometimes a self-assessment test can help you to understand yourself better, but sometimes it can lead to more questions, best answered with the assistance of a counselor.

Campbell Interest and Skill Survey

http://assessments.ncspearson.com/assessments/tests/ciss.htm

If you are interested in a career that requires some post-secondary education, the CISS® (Campbell Interest and Skill Survey) assessment can help point you in the right direction. Developed by David Campbell, Ph.D., the CISS uses targeted questions and analysis to help you understand how you fit into the world of work. This survey has been a popular tool with career counselors, and NCS Pearson is now making it available to the public through the Internet for a fee. The report you receive upon completion of the survey compares your results to the results of people who are successfully employed in the same fields you're interested in. Nearly sixty occupations are covered in your personalized report, and it also includes a comprehensive career planner to help you interpret your results and plan for your new career.

Career Interests Game

http://career.missouri.edu/holland

This game is designed to help match your interests and skills with similar careers. University of Missouri-Columbia has created a separate web page for each of the six Holland groups: realistic, artistic, investigative, social, enterprising, and conventional. These groups were developed by Dr. John Holland and are based on his theory that people and work environments can be loosely classified into six different groups. Each occupation links to the full description available at the Occupational Outlook Handbook website (http://stats.bls.gov/oco).

Career Tests and Resources from Queendom.com

queendom.com/portals/career.html

This site, dedicated to self-exploration, has a huge collection of tests along with some other stuff, but it is pretty much all devoted to helping you learn more about yourself. The career tests include evaluation of things like coping skills, sales personality, assertiveness, and success likelihood. There is also a list of counselors who provide services via E-mail, but be sure to check for licensing and/or certification.

Keirsey Temperament Website

keirsey.com

This is the official website for the test developed by David Keirsey. Based on the Myers-Briggs Type Indicator (MBTI), the Keirsey Temperament Sorter helps people discover their basic personality type as indicated by their preferences and personality. You can take the Keirsey Temperament Sorter and the Keirsey Character Sorter online at no cost and learn basic information about your type and how it might affect your career choices and work style. Some of the tests are available in languages other than English.

Test Your IQ, Personality, or Entrepreneurial Skills on the Web

2h.com

This is a great collection of self-assessment tests on the Internet, many of which come from Europe. Skip the IQ tests and focus on the personality (including many career-assessment tests) and entrepreneurial tests.

Career Exploration

If you are considering a career change, these sources can help with finding information and options, including how to transfer your current skills to new occupational areas and industries.

INFORMATION AND RESOURCES FROM THE U.S. GOVERNMENT

America's Career InfoNet

acinet.org

This service, part of America's Career Kit and sponsored by the U.S. Department of Labor, provides information on hundreds of occupations and what you need in order to do each job. The Career Information link shows you wage and trend reports, occupational requirements, and much more. The Career Tools link helps you check your employability, explore careers, look for employers, and review occupational licensing information for various states. You will also find a financial aid adviser, ready to help you find ways to pay for the training or education you may need or want in order to move to the next best gig.

Career Guide to Industries

bls.gov/oco/cg

The Career Guide to Industries provides information on available careers by industry, including the nature of the industry, working conditions, employment, occupations in the industry, training and advancement, earnings and benefits, employment outlook, and lists of organizations that can provide additional information. It is a nice way to find out who's needed by various industries and see if you fit the bill. This is another great guide from the Bureau of Labor Statistics.

The *Occupational Outlook Handbook (OOH)*

bls.gov/oco

This is the current edition of the printed guide produced by the U.S. Bureau of Labor Statistics. You can use keyword searching in this valuable handbook to find out where your interests fit in the top 250 occupations in the country. You can also use the index to explore various occupations, or you can select an occupational cluster to see what is included within each group. In addition to this information, you'll find well-written articles on how to find a job and evaluate a job offer, where to find career information, and what tomorrow's jobs look like. This is a great source for employment and career information.

Occupational Outlook Quarterly (OOQ)

bls.gov/opub/ooq/ooqhome.htm

Published quarterly by the Bureau of Labor Statistics, this magazine features articles with practical information on jobs and careers. The topics cover a wide variety of career- and work-related topics such as new and emerging occupations, training opportunities, salary trends, and results of new studies from the Bureau of Labor Statistics. The Grab Bag section includes short news alerts, and "You're a What?" looks at unusual occupational fields and is quite fun for younger persons to read.

O*NET OnLine

http://online.onetcenter.org

O*NET OnLine was created to provide broad access to the O*NET database of occupational information, which includes information on skills, abilities, work activities, and interests associated with occupations. O*NET includes information for more than 950 occupations. You'll like searching this by keyword or code and will enjoy seeing what occupations are similar to yours and which ones use the skills you already have.

RESOURCES FROM OTHER ORGANIZATIONS

Career Exploration Links

uhs.berkeley.edu/students/careerlibrary/links/careerme.htm

The Career and Educational Guidance Library, part of the Counseling and Psychological Services housed within University Health Services at the University of California at Berkeley, provides this well-organized set of links to career resources in a large number of occupational fields. The sponsors are proud to say what this site includes—no jobs, just information.

Career Guides from JobStar

jobstar.org/tools/career/index.htm

This site is one of the most comprehensive collections of career information, including career tests, places to look to find trends, career guides you can find in libraries, and links to descriptive information for hundreds of occupational fields. Other sections of this website cover job information and salaries.

Careers OnLine Virtual Careers Show

careersonline.com.au/show/menu.html

This enormous directory of more than one thousand job and occupational descriptions comes from the Australian Department of Education, Employment, Training, and Youth Affairs. Search by keyword, browse by interest group, or scan the list alphabetically. Please note that the information here is written for citizens and residents of Australia. While it can point you toward some interesting career options, you will need to check other resources more specific to your country for relevant education and training information.

Guide to Career Prospects in Virginia

ccps.virginia.edu/career_prospects

The Guide is a database of information about careers that are important to Virginia (and almost every other state!). For each career, you'll find a written analysis that includes required educational levels, skills, earnings, and job outlook, along with a set of statistical tables covering wages and job outlook at the Virginia regional level as well as the national level. While most of the salary data is specific to Virginia, descriptions of each career area are general enough to be relevant to all and are very well done. Search by keyword or browse the careers by job family.

Major Resource Kit

udel.edu/csc/mrk.html

The Career Services Center at the University of Delaware developed these "kits" as a tool to help undergraduates at the school. The Major Resource Kits link academic majors to career alternatives by providing information on career paths, sample job titles, and a short bibliography of printed materials available in many libraries. Each kit includes information such as entry-level job titles that previous University of Delaware graduates in that program have attained, brief job descriptions, and major employers for that field, along with additional materials.

The *Princeton Review* Online: Career

review.com/career/index.cfm

The *Princeton Review* has created a wonderful guide to careers and the job search for all users. The Career Search database brings together practical career information about daily life, the future outlook, and organizations to contact. You can also take the free Princeton Review Career Quiz to learn more about your most likely interests and work style and what careers would likely suit you.

Self-Employment

The Contract Employee's Handbook

cehandbook.com

Here is an excellent guide to the world of the contract worker. While it is written more for the technical consultant, anyone thinking of becoming a private consultant should read it over. There are links to additional resources throughout.

Inc. Magazine

inc.com

inc.com/500

Inc. is *the* magazine for the small business! *Inc.* magazine dedicates many issues to topics that hit the heart and pocketbook of the entrepreneur. Use the second URL to go directly to the Inc. 500, which includes a benchmarking form so you can see how your business ranks against the best.

The Online Women's Business Center

onlinewbc.org

This site is a learning resource and guide for anyone considering starting a business and is sponsored by the Office of Women's Business Ownership at the Small Business Administration. It is a real one-stop shop where you can find information about everything from how to start your business to how to operate in the global marketplace.

Small and Home-Based Business Links

bizoffice.com

This website was designed to be an Internet one-stop source for small and home-based business owners or for people who want to start their own small or home-based businesses. The collection includes franchise information, home business resources, and search tools. It's very nicely done.

Starting Your Business from the Small Business Administration (SBA)

sba.gov/starting

This resource from the SBA takes you through the process of starting your own business, beginning with the basic question of "Do I have what it takes to own/manage a small business?" You want to look through everything here, especially the frequently asked questions (FAQs) and the Startup Kit.

Startup Journal

http://startupjournal.com

From the *Wall Street Journal* comes a site dedicated to the self-employed or the wanting-to-be-self-employed. Like everything else the *Wall Street Journal* does, it is a great resource with listings of business ventures and franchises, a database of venture capital firms (the Kennedy directory, but you must pay to see your results), HR issues for small businesses, articles from the *WSJ*, and a free online business plan creation and evaluation tool—the MiniPlan from Palo Alto software. Use the MiniPlan to define your mission, analyze markets, and much more.

Industry and Hiring Trends

Employment Projections from the Bureau of Labor Statistics (BLS)

bls.gov/emp

This section of the BLS website provides many reports from the Office of Employment Projections, which develops information about employment trends, the national labor market, and the implications of these data on employment opportunities for specific groups in the labor force. Assessments are also made of the effect on employment of specified changes in economic conditions and/or changes in federal programs and policies. You will find a link from this page to several resources, including the Occupational Employment, Training, and Earnings report, the Occupational Outlook Quarterly, the Career Guide to Industries, and the Occupational Outlook Handbook, all of which also carry information on projected employment trends and earning potential.

Employment Review Magazine

employmentreview.com

This monthly publication includes stories on hiring trends in various industries. Check the News to Peruse for hiring/layoff trends and reports from specific states.

Labor Market Information State by State

rileyguide.com/trends.html#gov

Labor Market Information includes statistics on employment, wages, industries, and other factors affecting the world of work. These links from The Riley Guide take you to labor market information for the individual states so you can see how the industry or occupation you are exploring is doing wherever you want to be. While the Bureau of Labor Statistics and the other federal agencies give us data based on national averages, you might find the state you are targeting to be in a different, uh, state.

Occupational Employment Statistics (OES), U.S. Bureau of Labor Statistics

bls.gov/oes

The OES produces an annual survey of occupational employment and wages for more than 750 occupations. You'll find all kinds of very useful information, from wage and compensation data to occupational descriptions and employment projections.

State Occupational Projections 1998–2008

http://almis.dws.state.ut.us/occ/projections.asp

This site contains projections of occupational employment growth developed for all states and the nation as a whole. Allowing you to review state-level data lets you make a more informed decision about what is going on in your neighborhood rather than trying to guess based on the average for the whole United States. One of the most important uses of the projections is to help individuals make informed career decisions. You can review information on projected employment growth for an occupation and compare this among several states or select several occupations and compare their growth projection in just one state. The projections found here are usually updated on a two-year cycle, so you will see new data regularly added.

Financial Aid

Carnegie Library of Pittsburgh: Financial Aid Pathfinder

carnegielibrary.org/clp/JCEC/aid.html

The librarians at Carnegie Library have created a terrific tool for finding financial aid! Check out their listing of print resources, databases, and Internet resources that offer information for anyone seeking assistance with the costs of higher education.

College Is Possible

collegeispossible.com

This is a resource guide for parents, students, and education professionals from the Coalition of America's Colleges and Universities. This site walks you through preparing for college, choosing a college, and paying for college with simple information as well as links to resources and even more information. Some material is in Spanish, much of the cited resource material can be downloaded online at no cost, and the advice and information given is very good. There is also a section dedicated to those adults who have decided to either return to college after a time away or are now deciding to attend college for the first time. With two out of every five college students now over the age of twenty-five, you will not be alone.

FinAid, The Financial Aid Information Page

finaid.org

Established in 1994, FinAid is a gold mine of information and resources for sources of financial aid for education. There are calculators for figuring out your debt load and payback, and there are facts on scams as well as alerts. If you use only one online financial aid site, make it this one.

Planning and Paying for School from Sallie Mae

salliemae.com/planning/index.html

For more than a quarter-century, Sallie Mae has been helping students achieve their dreams of higher education by providing funds for educational loans, primarily federally guaranteed student loans originated under the Federal Family Education Loan Program (FFELP). The free Planning/Paying service allows students (and parents) to learn about the many ways there are to pay for college. Sallie Mae created Wiredscholar to help students and families prepare for entrance exams, evaluate and select the best college to attend, and apply for and finance the cost of college—entirely from home. Financial Aid 101 will introduce you to key terms and concepts in reviewing various funding options. You can search the Scholarship database or locate a free Paying for College seminar near you. And finally, you can look at debt-management tips and mortgage and consumer loan information.

The Student Guide to Financial Aid

ed.gov/prog_info/SFA/StudentGuide

The Student Guide is the most comprehensive resource on student financial aid from the U.S. Department of Education. Grants, loans, and work-study are the three major forms of student financial aid available through the federal Student Financial Assistance Programs. Updated each award year, the Student Guide tells you about the programs and how to apply for them, and it even includes the online Free Application for Federal Student Aid (FAFSA). The online guide is available in English and Spanish.

USNews.com: Financial Aid

usnews.com/usnews/edu/dollars/dshome.htm

Get help with your financial aid application, check the picks for top financial aid sites online, use the SmartSheets to figure out costs and payments you can afford, and check out the other great stuff.

Education and Training Resources

Don't forget to check USNews.com: Education at the beginning of this chapter. This includes the annual College Rankings and Graduate School Rankings published by *US News and World Report* (usnews.com/usnews/edu/eduhome.htm).

America's Learning eXchange (ALX)

alx.org

In this huge database of classes, degree programs, specialty training opportunities, and more, you can find information on financial aid, certification and accreditation, and licensing for the various states and learn how career information can help your education and training plans. You will also find links to additional training and education information and articles on how to ensure the quality of the training before you sign up for the program. ALX is part of America's Career Kit, along with America's Job Bank, America's Career InfoNet, and America's Service Locator, and you will see some resources carried from one site to another.

College and University Rankings

library.uiuc.edu/edx/rankings.htm

This collection of links and references to print and online rankings of colleges and universities around the world is provided by the Education and Social Science Library at the University of Illinois at Urbana-Champaign. Be sure to read the information on the controversy of ranking services before you start perusing the rankings.

COOL: College Opportunities On-Line

http://nces.ed.gov/ipeds/cool

According to the site sponsors, "College Opportunities On-Line (COOL) is a research tool that allows access to information on more than nine thousand trade schools, colleges, and universities in the U.S. Users may search COOL by geographic region, by state, by city, by type of institution, or by instructional programs, either alone or in combination. COOL is a product of the National Center for Education Statistics (NCES) Integrated Postsecondary Education Data System (IPEDS)."

College and University Directories

CollegeNET

collegenet.com

CollegeNET lets you browse information on colleges by various criteria, including geography, tuition, and enrollment. More than five hundred college applications are available here for you to fill out and submit online. Financial aid and scholarship information can also be found here.

Collegiate.Net, The Center for All Collegiate Information

collegiate.net

Collegiate.Net not only lets you search for colleges and degrees but also lets you tap the manufacturers of collegiate products, alumni associations, and other sites related to the college scene.

GoCollege

gocollege.com

This is another searchable guide to colleges, but GoCollege has teamed up with Cliffs to also help you prepare for the SAT and ACT exams. You can even access the full version of the practice tests for free on specific dates. You'll want to check the site's front page regularly for the dates. Users are told, "Our practice tests are written by testing experts. Your tests are saved under your user ID for future reference." Free registration is required for the test area and to access the scholarship search area.

NCES Global Education Locator

http://nces.ed.gov/globallocator

The National Center for Education Statistics features four keyword search engines: On-Line, National Public School/District Locator, Public Library Locator, and Private School Locator. Use the appropriate one to find information about colleges (including community and technical colleges), public schools or school districts, public libraries that might be around your new home, or private schools located in the United States.

Peterson's

petersons.com

Peterson's, the well-known publisher of guides to colleges, provides this great resource for information on undergraduate and graduate programs, summer work, and professional training and distance-education programs. Some areas and resources are free to all users, while others can be accessed only through a paid subscription.

Web U.S. Higher Education

utexas.edu/world/univ

This page of the University of Texas, Austin Web Central, contains links to web servers at universities and community colleges in the United States. Only one server is listed for each campus: the primary central server. In the absence of a central server, another server is selected. The list is divided into Universities and

Community Colleges. Check the lists by name or state to get to the various schools' home pages.

Yahoo! Colleges and Universities

http://dir.yahoo.com/education/higher_education/colleges_and_universities/index.html

Yahoo!'s list is a great place to browse for all kinds of colleges and universities worldwide. The United States list looks at the colleges by type—public, private, community, and technical colleges; American Indian tribal colleges; historically black colleges; and so on. The Region list will let you browse geographically by international country or states of the United States.

Distance Education

Distance Education and Training Council

detc.org

The Distance Education and Training Council (DETC) is a nonprofit educational association located in Washington, DC. Previously called the National Home Study Council, it serves as a clearinghouse of information about the distance-study/correspondence field and sponsors a nationally recognized accrediting agency called the Accrediting Commission of the Distance Education and Training Council. Through the website, you can find accredited high school and college degree programs, a single directory of all institutions accredited by this group, and a list of study subjects available from the many programs.

Globewide Network Academy (GNA)

gnacademy.org

The Globewide Network Academy is "dedicated to promote the access to educational opportunities for anybody, anywhere. To do this, GNA pioneers and develops distance learning relationships and facilities for the worldwide public to use." Search the catalog for distance-learning opportunities ranging from precollege to postgraduate and anything in between. Once you've found a program that interests you, you will need to contact the listed institution directly for admissions and registration procedures. With more than twenty-three thousand courses in more than two thousand programs worldwide, you can almost certainly find just what you need.

Hungry Minds

hungryminds.com

A division of IDG Books Worldwide, Inc., Hungry Minds is your gateway to online learning. Get job training, develop professional skills, and access thousands of quality academic courses from leading universities, organizations, and experts. Browse the Academic Learning, Professional Development, or Lifelong Learning categories, but even better is the What's Free link to discussion forums, tips, recommended websites, subject experts, and more than seven thousand free online courses.

Vocational and Technical Schools

COOL: College Opportunities On-Line

http://nces.ed.gov/ipeds/cool

According to the site sponsors, "College Opportunities On-Line (COOL) is a research tool that allows access to information on more than nine thousand trade schools, colleges, and universities in the U.S. Users may search COOL by geographic region, by state, by city, by type of institution, or by instructional programs, either alone or in combination. COOL is a product of the National Center for Education Statistics (NCES) Integrated Postsecondary Education Data System (IPEDS)."

RWM Vocational School Database

rwm.org/rwm

This database of private postsecondary vocational schools in all fifty states is organized first by state, then by training occupation. All the schools listed are state licensed or accredited. Not all categories in every state have listings. The information provided is simply a name, address, and telephone number for each school, but you can call the school to request a catalog and further information. At the top of each state is a link to resources for that state from the U.S. Department of Education.

Other Education and Training Options

Apprenticeship Information from the U.S. Department of Labor

doleta.gov/individ/apprent.asp

Apprenticeship is a combination of on-the-job training and related classroom instruction in which workers learn the practical and theoretical aspects of a highly skilled occupation. Apprenticeship programs are sponsored by joint employer and labor groups, individual employers, and/or employer associations. This page will give you information on how to find and apply for apprenticeship programs in the United States.

The Job Corps

jobcorps.org

Here is the online site of the nation's largest residential education and training program for disadvantaged youth between the ages of sixteen and twenty-four. The Job Corps operates more than one hundred centers around the country and in Puerto Rico, with a focus on training the whole person. According to the site source, "Once students have been admitted to the program, they receive their training at a selected Job Corps center. All students receive integrated academic, vocational, and social skills training. With good performance, they can also receive advanced training."

National School-to-Work Learning and Information Center

stw.ed.gov

This website is sponsored by the national School-to-Work Learning Center from the Department of Education. It includes information for employers, educators, young people and their parents, and researchers on how to set up and use School-to-Work programs and establish partnerships and careers. The sponsors explain: "On May 4, 1994, President Bill Clinton signed the School-to-Work Opportunities Act of 1994. This law provides seed money to states and local partnerships of business, labor, government, education, and community organizations to develop school-to-work systems. This law doesn't create a new program. It allows states and their partners to bring together efforts at education reform, worker preparation, and economic development to create a system to prepare youth for the high-wage, high-skill careers of today's and tomorrow's global economy."

Training and Certification Opportunities Through Seminars and Short Courses

These courses may lead to certification or may be used for continuing education or to earn credit toward recertification. Most are relatively short, covering a few hours to a few days. Some of the courses and seminars are offered by colleges and universities, but many are offered by other groups or organizations.

SIS: Seminar Information Service

seminarinformation.com

This is a place to find listings of seminars, but it has a great twist. Select the subject area in which you are interested, and it lists not only the course topics but also the date and location of the next seminar. Select the date and location that interests you, click the Details button, and get all the info on location, cost, and course outline. You can enroll right online using a credit card, purchase order, or your company's info (including the name of who approved the payment).

SmartPlanet

zdnet.com/smartplanet

With SmartPlanet, you won't receive a degree, but you will have access to classes that add to your skill set. It charges by class and also allows you to take a variety of online courses for a monthly fee. Most of the classes are computer and technology related.

ThinQ E-Catalog

thinq.com

The ThinQ E-Catalog includes information on thousands of training programs from more than one thousand providers. The courses cover hundreds of topics from Java/JavaBeans to change management to "How to Handle People with Tact and Skill."

Professional and Trade Associations and Unions

These resources will take you to hundreds of associations and organizations representing many occupations and professions. These groups are good resources for finding out more about the areas they represent. See what they offer in internships and apprenticeships, networking and support, mentoring, certification programs, professional development and training, and publications.

American Society of Association Executives

asaenet.org

The American Society of Association Executives (ASAE) is a terrific resource for anyone trying to locate a professional association for any field or interest. Click on the link for "Find associations, people, businesses," and then pull down the extensive menu of searchable directories on the site. We suggest starting with the Gateway to Associations and then trying other sources.

Labor Unions, from Yahoo!

http://dir.yahoo.com/business_and_economy/labor/unions

Yahoo! maintains a separate list of labor unions covering many occupations and industries.

Organizations, from Yahoo!

http://dir.yahoo.com/business_and_economy/organizations

This is Yahoo!'s entry to its list of organizations, including professional and trade associations.

The Scholarly Societies Project

scholarly-societies.org

You can search or browse this list of scholarly, professional, and labor organizations on the Internet. It is one of the best projects online, maintained by the University of Waterloo Library.

Union Resource Network

unions.org

This is a great resource for finding unions. You can even use the keyword-searchable database.

Salary and Compensation Information

In addition to using the following resources, surveying job listings in the many job banks will provide some salary information. More sources can be found in the resources already cited in this chapter, particularly in the career guides. You can also check The Riley Guide (rileyguide.com/salary.html) for more resources and salary-research ideas.

CareerJournal from the *Wall Street Journal*

http://careerjournal.com

This site's information on salaries and hiring includes great articles plus salary charts for several job functions, occupational areas, and industries. Many will cover the varying levels of experience within a job area from entry-level to senior management positions. You'll also find information on negotiations, region pay and employment trends, and much more.

JobStar Salary Surveys

http://jobstar.org/tools/salary/index.htm

JobStar has put together what many consider to be the finest collection of salary surveys online anywhere. Combined with lists of books to request from your local library and articles from experts such as Jack Chapman, this site will lead you in the right direction for your salary search.

Salary.com

salary.com

This site is much more than just salary resources and an easy-to-remember URL. It is dedicated to total compensation—not only what is in your paycheck but the additional benefits and perquisites you receive as a part of your earnings. The Salary Wizard is fast and easy to use, allowing you to search for base, median, and top-level earnings in hundreds of jobs for many occupational areas, and much of the data applies to your local jurisdiction. Salary.com has a team of compensation specialists working to add value to salary surveys done by others like the Bureau of Labor Statistics, and the team knows what it is doing (and you should take advantage of it). Beyond the Salary Wizard you'll find helpful articles and exercises to help you figure out things like benefits, stock options, bonuses (and how to get them), and even negotiations.

SalaryExpert.com

salaryexpert.com

A free service of Baker, Thomsen Associates, SalaryExpert.com offers compensation information for more than eight hundred of the most common jobs in the United States targeted to your selected region. Not finding your own job? Download the bigger database covering thirty thousand job titles and do a more extensive search. You get a huge pull-down menu of job titles. Just start typing to get to the place you want to be, then add your zip code or commuting area. The Result page has tabs to let you review the salary and total compensation, job description, source of information, methodology, and other places to go for similar information.

Employer Research

Many more resources can be found in The Riley Guide under "Tell Me About This Employer" (rileyguide.com/employer.html).

Hoover's Online

hoovers.com

Hoover's, the well-respected publisher of business almanacs, gives visitors to its website a lot of information on more than ten thousand companies in the United States, and it now has a European directory, too. Additional links to more resources and news expand this information even further.

Research and Reference Gateway: Research Guides: Business

libraries.rutgers.edu/rul/rr_gateway/research_guides/busi/business.shtml

The librarians at Rutgers University Libraries have created a wonderful resource. You'll find the top business-research sources (both print and online) in one easy-to-use place. The collection includes business news, company information, job-searching resources, market research tools, and helpful information about small business start-up and development.

Researching Companies Online

http://home.sprintmail.com/~debflanagan/index.html

This step-by-step, interactive tutorial provides instructions on using more than fifty free online resources for researching companies. Currently, the service focuses on U.S. resources, but it hopes to add international sites in the near future. The person who put this together is a professional trainer, and she has done a very good job.

Vault.com

vault.com

Vault.com offers insider guides to companies, including many anonymous interviews with current and past employees to find out "what it's really like in there." (Under one law firm, the comment is, "support staff so-so.") College students may be familiar with the company's print guides, but you can view nice reports online for free on this site. (Even more detailed reports are available to registered users, another free service at this site.) Scan the alphabetical lists of companies or law firms, or use the industry reports to find out current trends and major employers.

WetFeet.com

wetfeet.com

WetFeet compiles insider guides to companies. The standard company profiles include some basic statistics, company overview, the company's major line of business, contact information, and a link to the major industry category so you can check out some of its competitors. Those companies with extended profiles include a look at culture and lifestyle of the company, what it's like to interview there, extensive statistics including a hiring forecast, and a list of questions and answers called "Inside the Company."

Relocation Research

The Best Place to Live from *Money* Magazine

http://money.cnn.com/best/bplive

At this site, you can check the list of winners, compare the cost of living among cities, and even create your own "best places" list using the screening tool. This source includes a salary calculator.

Chamber of Commerce International Directory

http://chamber-of-commerce.com

Using the International Chamber of Commerce and City-State-Province Directory, you can search the worldwide or the city-state sections for the chamber of commerce in your target location and then contact the office for information on the region.

CIA World Factbook

odci.gov/cia/publications/factbook/index.html

This regularly updated resource is considered one of the best directories of international information anywhere. Each country is described in an in-depth profile covering its geography, people, government, economy, transportation system, military, communications system, and "transnational issues," including disputes with other countries.

Distance Calculator from Indo.com

indo.com/distance

How far is it? This service uses data from the U.S. census and a supplementary list of cities around the world to find the latitude and longitude of two places and then calculates the distance between them (as the crow flies). It could be helpful in deciding whether or not you need to move closer to your new job.

Editor & Publisher

editorandpublisher.com

NewsLink

http://newslink.org

U.S. Newspapers

usnewspaperlinks.com

These three sites feature links to hundreds of electronic newspapers across the United States and around the world. Reading local newspapers can give you a wonderful feel for the area and let you know what is going on.

Homefair.com

homefair.com/index.html

This site proclaims, "Our mission is to provide interactive tools and useful information so that you can stay organized, make the right decisions, and keep more of your own money when buying a home, selling a home, or relocating!" Users will find numerous reports, tools and calculators, and consumer information to use in researching communities, including the Salary Calculator to let you compare the cost-of-living differences among hundreds of U.S. and international cities. Homefair is now part of the Homestore.com network (see next entry).

Homestore.com

homestore.com

Homestore.com has about everything you need to find a new place to live, move there, order new appliances, landscape and decorate, and get the insurance in place. They have listings for homes, apartments and rentals (including senior living), and much more.

MapQuest

mapquest.com

With MapQuest, you can search for addresses and get maps of their location or driving directions from here to there. It also provides some local city maps of businesses centered in a specific area as well as useful travel links.

Monstermoving.com

monstermoving.com

Monstermoving.com can help you look for a new place to live, get mortgage and insurance information and quotes, find a mover or learn how to do it yourself, and much more.

MyWay.com

myway.com

zip2.com

MyWay.com lists more than sixteen million U.S. businesses in its database. It not only looks the business up but also will give you directions on how to get to that office from your office or hotel.

Realtor.com

realtor.com

Realtor.com is brought to you by the National Association of Realtors and allows you to find a home, find a neighborhood, or find a Realtor online. The home search lets you search by state and city, map, or zip code, and there is good advice for sellers as well as buyers here. Realtor.com is connected to Homestore.com (see earlier entry).

State and Local Government on the Net

statelocalgov.net

This extensive guide links to official federal, state, and local government resources for the United States and many territories. From here, you can find all kinds of helpful information on the various locations in which you are interested.

Superpages.com from Verizon

superpages.com

At this site, you can find the business you want or all the businesses in a certain category in a certain location and then have a map show you where they are located and give you driving directions. The site also has white pages, consumer guides, and city pages for you to peruse.

USA CityLink

http://usacitylink.com

The USA CityLink project is a city's interface to the world. This site is the Internet's most comprehensive listing of U.S. states and cities, offering information on travel, tourism, and relocation.

15

Executive Job Searching Online

This chapter contains selected resources directed toward the mid- to senior-level executive engaged in a job search. These were selected because they have been reported to be very useful by users. Many other resources listed throughout the *Guide* also include job listings at this level. The good news is that, yes, executives can search for new job opportunities online. The bad news is that most of the best sources are fee-based, but they are usually worth the expense based on the quality of listings and the confidentiality of your information.

General Services and Resources

CareerJournal from the *Wall Street Journal*

careerjournal.com

As explained in several places throughout this book, this site is an excellent source of good career news and great job leads. The content changes daily and is made up of new articles written for this site as well as relevant articles from the *Wall Street Journal*. While we feel that the articles are the best part of this site, we know many of you will be interested in the job listings. Many of the postings are listings from various search firms, others are direct postings from employers, and still others have been taken from the print version of the *Wall Street Journal*. In addition to providing the jobs listed here, CareerJournal is a partner with the executive search firm Korn/Ferry in its online site, Futurestep (described later in this appendix). CareerJournal also offers a searchable version of the indispensable Directory of Executive Recruiters published by Kennedy Publications (kennedyinfo.com), found under the button labeled "Find a Headhunter" at the top of the page. (More information on Kennedy's is also available later in this appendix.) You can search the directory for free, but you must pay to download the resulting list of search firms. You will be told how many firms match your criteria and how much the list will cost, so you can opt to refine your search before buying. You will also find print copies of the directory in most bookstores as well as public and college library reference collections. But don't stop here. CareerJournal has much more to offer the executive job seeker, including career and job-search advice and salary profiles. Take the time to explore all the offerings.

ChiefMonster.com

chiefmonster.com

ChiefMonster.com is a service of Monster.com. While it is free, it is an exclusive club requiring you to apply for membership. "To become a ChiefMonster member, your credentials must match our pre-set qualification standards." Members get exclusive access to "senior-level opportunities from today's top employers, executive search firms, and Venture Capital Companies. As a member, you'll also have the opportunity to benchmark your skills and compensation against peers, expand your networking circle, and arm yourself with personalized real-time tools and information. Membership is free and completely confidential." If you don't make it here, there's always Monster Management (http://management.monster.com).

Exec-U-Net

execunet.com

Exec-U-Net is a career-management service for executives, offering not just listings of very good jobs but also a resume-review program and face-to-face networking meetings organized around the country. Twice a month, Exec-U-Net publishes the Job Opportunities Report listing approximately seven hundred jobs per issue in the fields of general management, finance, sales, marketing, human resources, operations management, research and development, engineering, and management information systems opportunities. Several levels of membership are offered, each providing a different level of access to information and services; full membership is required for the Job Opportunities Report. Contact information within Canada can also be found on the website. This service has been available for a long time and has always received very good comments from members.

ExecutivesOnly

executivesonly.com

This service offers executives the opportunity to not only review job leads but also to ask for assistance in preparing a resume and to speak with a career-management consultant about the best ways to present yourself plus plan your next career move. The people behind this service have extensive backgrounds in recruiting and outplacement and offer quality service based on what they know. They offer several membership options based on how long you wish to be a member and what services you'd like during your tenure. If you are currently enrolled in an outplacement program or recently ended a program without successfully making a transition to a new opportunity, contact ExecutivesOnly to inquire about discounted membership.

Netshare

netshare.com

Netshare is a fee-based service offering listings of exclusive confidential job leads for senior executives along with a resume database and career-management tools. If you haven't heard of Netshare, don't be concerned. Think of the company as "the quiet guys" who don't do as much general advertising as the competition but have a terrific reputation through word of mouth. The database is updated daily, and Netshare offers varying membership options including an exclusive direct E-mail service (Netshare Direct) for listings that match your profile. A three-month "trial membership" costs only slightly less than the six-month membership fee, so we suggest that, if you're interested, you just go for the six months.

A Short List of Search Firms

You will find additional listings for search firms along with resources targeting specific industries throughout the book. Please remember that recruiters work for the employers who have hired them, not for you. They are not working to help you find a job. They are working to help their client successfully fill a position. While you may submit your resume to them to be considered for their searches, it is unlikely you will be contacted unless you match the qualifications for a search they are currently conducting.

Heidrick & Struggles International

heidrick.com

Heidrick & Struggles is one of the world's largest executive search firms with offices in more than seventy-five locations throughout North and South America, Europe, the Middle East, Africa, and Asia. Senior executives who wish to be included in its database can submit a resume to a Heidrick & Struggles consultant who specializes in your particular industry or functional area. These contacts can be found on the website under Industry Expertise, or you can peruse the Office Locations to find contacts in specific offices around the world. For management and senior-management professionals earning in the $75,000 to $180,000 range, Heidrick & Struggles has created LeadersOnline (leadersonline.com). After registering with LeadersOnline, your profile and resume are matched against available positions, and if a match is found, you'll be contacted with details about the position. You then decide whether you're interested in further pursuing the opportunity. If you are interested, LeadersOnline will do a more extensive evaluation of your qualifications, but you are kept informed of the progress, from initial evaluation to interviews and offers of employment.

Korn/Ferry International

kornferry.com

Korn/Ferry International is a worldwide leader in recruiting and search, covering senior-level searches, middle-management recruitment, and college administration recruitment. Its global network includes more than one hundred offices in forty-one countries in North America, Latin America, Europe, and Asia/Pacific. It offers two different online services for persons wishing to be considered as candidates in the hundreds of searches it performs each year. For the senior executive, there is e-KornFerry (ekornferry.com). This allows candidates to register their resume with the firm, review posted searches, and submit their resume for consideration. Candidates who are found to match current searches will be invited by the consultant handling the search to review a particular search and research the company through links provided by the consultant. For the midlevel executive, there is Futurestep (futurestep.com), its service for management professionals. Futurestep "offers registrants complimentary personalized career feedback from our validated proprietary assessment tools, and the opportunity to be considered for exclusive middle- to upper-management level positions." You can also "Flirt with Opportunities" by reviewing searches currently under way and submitting your information for consideration. With both of these services, Korn/Ferry is establishing a long-term relationship with the client, holding your information in its database and offering you career-management information and advice designed to help you move forward in your career. Both require an extensive registration process that includes more than just a resume, but both are free to the job seeker.

SpencerStuart.com

spencerstuart.com

SpencerStuart.com is the online presence of Spencer Stuart, a leading management consulting firm specializing in senior-level executive search and board director appointments. Spencer Stuart has fifty offices in twenty-four countries around the world. Part of SpencerStuart.com is the Talent Network, a way for executives to register with the firm and receive potential opportunities via E-mail. The Talent Network also offers participants access to a database of current openings the firm is working to fill, self-assessment tools, salary benchmarking reports, and much more.

Additional Sources for Leads and Connections

These are services and resources you can use to locate job leads or present your information to executive search firms. You will find other resources and services listed throughout the book, so don't limit yourself to just these few.

BlueSteps from the Association of Executive Search Consultants

bluesteps.com

The Association of Executive Search Consultants (AESC) represents retained executive search consulting firms worldwide, establishes professional and ethical standards for its members, and provides information to the profession, the media, and the public on the field of executive search. BlueSteps offers two services for executives seeking new career options. First, there is the Executive Profile area where you can submit your resume for consideration by the members of AESC. Second, there is a searchable directory of all AESC members that you can use to make direct contact with firms that handle searches in your industry and functional field. BlueSteps is a fee-based service, with various pricing schemes based on the services you wish to purchase. We recommend that persons consider the joint package, purchasing access to the directory along with the option of posting a profile.

CEO Job Opportunities Update

ceoupdate.com

CEO Job Opportunities Update is a biweekly publication that lists vacancies for senior-level nonprofit opportunities. In addition to accepting announcements from HR professionals and executive search firms, it actively seeks out jobs in newspapers, magazines, websites, specialty publications, and newsletters; checks the status and accuracy of each positing; and verifies that it compensates above $50,000. According to the website, CEO Update "tracks over three hundred searches in a typical two-week publishing cycle." The twenty-eight-page print version of the newsletter is published every other Thursday and contains details about the newest 100 to 150 searches. The print version also features "Who Got the Job" selection announcements along with new and updated information on current searches. Through the subscriber-only portion of the website, subscribers can also access information about an additional 100 to 150 job openings for which employers and recruiters are still actively seeking candidates. This is still a print publication, with the website serving to handle the overflow that did not get into the print publication. Current subscription information can be found on the website.

Imcor

imcor.com

Imcor, a division of Spherion, is "America's Leading Supplier of Portable Executives," offering opportunities for short- to midterm placement in senior management positions. Several current assignments are posted on the web page with date, title, and location information, and you can submit your resume to any Imcor office for consideration in future placements.

6FigureJobs.com

6figurejobs.com

6FigureJobs offers experienced professionals the opportunity to confidentially seek and be considered for some of the most prestigious jobs in the country. The service is free but is definitely for only executive-level placement. The site also offers a free resume database for all experienced persons who would like to be considered for the job listings, but candidates maintain a lot of control over the confidentiality of the information. Once a resume is submitted, a search consultant personally reviews it; candidates with the skills and experience to justify being considered for a senior-level position are admitted into the "Network of Experienced Professionals." These select people are given access to jobs that the firm's clients have marked as "confidential," and they are also given the choice to be automatically notified of newly posted jobs with requirements that match their qualifications. 6FigureJobs explains that this procedure helps people who do not yet have senior-level experience but whom the recruiters feel are qualified for these positions and should be considered. This could be a great way for those who are ready to break into the "c-suite" to get their chance.

Directories of Recruiting Firms

You can use the following resources to locate recruiting firms in your local area as well as those specializing in your target industry or occupation discipline. Many career consultants suggest that you contact the firms to let them know of your interest in being considered for searches that they might be handling and submit a resume for review. If you know the name of an individual search consultant, particularly one a colleague can recommend, then address your approach to this person. If you have never worked with an executive search firm or recruiter before, we suggest checking out some of the articles in the Executive Recruiters section of CareerJournal (see earlier entry) for advice and information to help you understand and work effectively with these firms.

BlueSteps from the Association of Executive Search Consultants

bluesteps.com

Please see its entry earlier in this chapter.

Custom Databanks, Inc.

customdatabanks.com

If you are familiar with the CareerSeach product found in many college career centers and outplacement firms, then you already know Custom Databanks. Custom Databanks provides the database of executive search firms used by CareerSearch, and it also makes this database available to the public for a fee. This is a competitive product to Kennedy's, but in many cases it may provide more contact names for each firm listed. To start your search, click on Download Data, and then select your search criteria. You can search the directories of retained or contingency search firms by industry or position specialty, salary range handled, and cities/states/regions (United States and Canada). The results will tell you how many records have been found and the cost before you buy, but here's another interesting feature: it will tell you how many firms have listed E-mail addresses, fax numbers, or merely postal addresses. You can buy whichever list you want based on your needs and contact plans, but we suggest you don't limit yourself to those firms with E-mail addresses. You are buying a data file that can easily be imported into Excel or any word processor for mail-merge and campaign management. While you are here, check out the other databases, including the Venture Capital Firms and Temporary/Contract Placement Firms.

The Directory of Executive Recruiters from Kennedy Publications

kennedyinfo.com/db/db_der_bas.html

Kennedy's is probably the best-known name in this particular field. It is free to do a search to find out how many records (search firms) match your criteria and how much the resulting list will cost you. Yes, you must pay to see the final list, but this is a very good resource. You have the option of redoing your search to be more specific (and less costly) before you buy. You can find print copies of the directory in most major bookstores as well as in public and business libraries. Many colleges and universities will also have this in their reference collections, and they usually allow the public to use materials in-house. While you are at the site, notice that it offers a separate searchable International Database of Executive Recruiters as well as a searchable database of Hiring Companies. CareerJournal also offers a searchable version of the original directory through its site, but there is no price difference.

Headhunter E-mail Address Lists from Avotek

avotek.nl/emailgds.htm

Based in the Netherlands, Avotek is a marvelous resource for an international job search. It now offers lists of recruiters from several countries, allowing you to contact them directly via E-mail and submit your resume for consideration in searches they are conducting. Each list tells you what country is covered, how many addresses are listed, when the list was last updated, and the cost.

Oya's Directory of Recruiters

i-recruit.com

Oya's is a directory of recruiters arranged by specialty or location. You can also do a keyword search, which produces even better results than the specialty or location listings.

Recruiters by Industry from Myjobsearch.com

myjobsearch.com/cgi-bin/mjs.cgi/recruiters.html

Myjobsearch.com has collected and collated this list of links to recruiters on the Internet. Select your target field or industry, but don't skip the All Industries and All Professions categories.

Recruiters Online Network

recruitersonline.com

You know Recruiters Online Network from our discussion of major job banks in Chapter 3. This network includes more than seven thousand third-party recruiters, making it a great central resource for connecting to these firms. All participants agree to adhere to certain ethical guidelines in recruiting and placement, so we are happy to recommend them.

The Recruiting & Search Report

rsronline.com

These are print directories listing contingency and retained executive search firms that specialize in various industry and functional areas. For an additional fee per directory, they will provide the content of any specific directory on diskette. The file is in ASCII for easy import into Excel or any word-processing program. You can review the list of available directories on the website and then place your order either online or by phone or fax.

RiteSite.com

ritesite.com

This website is the companion to the 2001 edition of John Lucht's book *Rites of Passage at $100,000 to $1 million+*. "Purchase maximum assistance in submitting your resume to the 356 top search firms honored in *Rites of Passage*." These tools include postal mailing data, "one-click" simultaneous E-mailing, fax numbers, website addresses, and what Lucht calls the "Maximum Efficiency" combination list. See Chapter 14 of the book for a full explanation of all the services members will enjoy. There is a fee for membership.

Executive Compensation Information

At some point in a successful search, you will be asked what you expect to receive in compensation. What salary are you asking, and what additional perquisites and benefits might attract you to a particular position? The following resources along with many already listed can help you in preparing your answers and in the negotiation process that will inevitably follow. Many of the resources noted earlier in this appendix will also have information and guides for you. You can find even more information in The Riley Guide (rileyguide.com).

Articles and Reports on CEO Pay from Forbes.com

forbes.com

Forbes publishes several articles plus special surveys on executive compensation throughout the year, including the annual report on Best Paid CEOs. When you connect to the website, look for the Careers section or search the site for "compensation."

BusinessWeek

businessweek.com

BusinessWeek presents frequent articles on pay and perquisites for management and executive professionals throughout the year, and it also publishes an annual survey of CEO pay every April. To start finding this information online, connect to the site and head to the Careers area. Select Pay & Perks from the left menu to gather all of the articles on pay and perquisites published over the past year. Then, use the Search feature to find the keywords "executive pay." Search the entire site, and you will find some reports and articles from more than a year ago. Some content on *BusinessWeek*'s website is for subscribers only, but much of it is open to the public.

CareerJournal from the *Wall Street Journal*

careerjournal.com

CareerJournal's section on Salary and Hiring Info contains articles and charts on pay, perquisites, options, and anything else you need to know before talking money.

DEF 14A Reports from the EDGAR Database of Corporate Information, United States Securities and Exchange Commission (SEC)

sec.gov/edgar.shtml

Compensation for the top executives and members of the boards of directors of every publicly traded company in the United States must be reported to the SEC. While some fee-based EDGAR (Electronic Data Gathering, Analysis, and Retrieval system) services will pull this information out for you, it is not difficult to find it using this free database. Select two or three competitive companies similar in size and industry to your preferred employer, go to EDGAR's "Search for Company Filings," and use the "Quick Forms Lookup" to search EDGAR for the DEF 14A form for each, and then use the Find command in your Web browser (usually control-F) to scan the long document for the word *compensation*. This will not only reveal salary and stock information, but it also may give you some ideas for additional compensation considerations, like cars, travel expenses for your spouse or partner, cell phones, and much more.

Ecomp, the Executive Compensation Database

ecomponline.com

Yes, it's just spitting out the same information you can find yourself by searching the DEF 14 reports filed by each company, but this site does it so much faster. And you can search by company or ticker name if you are looking for a particular organization. If you are more interested in covering a particular state, industry, or industry sector, all those options are also available so you can compare varied locations or organizations in one sector. The information includes name, title, salary and bonuses, and the year that the information represents. What it will not give is a summary of the non-cash perquisites, severance packages, and stock options awarded to the chief executives of each company. This is more likely to be found in the full DEF 14 reports, perhaps as footnotes.

Index of Cited Resources

A/E/C JobBank
    aecjobbank.com, 148
AAEA Employment Service: American Agricultural
    Economic Association
    aaea.org/classifieds, 122
AAFA:American Association of Finance and
    Accounting
    aafa.com, 64
Able to Work
    abletowork.org, 314
ABQjournal: Albuquerque Journal Online
    abqjournal.com, 244
Abracat
    http://abracat.com/abracat/index.jsp, 50
Academic Employment Network
    academploy.com, 82
Academic Physician and Scientist (APS)
    acphsci.com, 133
Academic Position Network (APN)
    apnjobs.com, 82
Academic360.com
    academic360.com, 82
Access America
    accessamerica.gov, 176
Access Indiana
    ai.org/index.html, 224
    state.in.us, 224
Access Omaha
    accessomaha.com, 239
Access Washington
    http://access.wa.gov, 268
AccessAtlanta.com
    accessatlanta.com, 218
AccessKansas.com
    accesskansas.com, 226
Accountemps
    accountemps.com, 65
Accounting.com
    accounting.com, 65
ACPA Ongoing Placement Listings
    http://acpant.acpa.nche.edu/onplace.nsf, 85
ActiJobs.com
    actijob.com, 280
Action Without Borders
    idealist.org, 191
AdAge.com's Career Center
    adagespecials.com/jobbank/careercenter.html,
    68
Addison County Independent
    addisonindependent.com, 265–66
Addresses of International Organizations
    psc-cf-.gc.ca/intgphm/epb7_e.htm, 276
AdminExchange
    adminexchange.com, 73
Adsearch
    adsearch.com, 50
Advancing Women
    advancingwomen.com, 310
AdWeek
    adweek.com, 69
AECT Placement Center
    aect.org, 170
AEJob.com
    aejob.com, 140
AERA Bulletin Board
    aera.net/anews, 82
AeroWorldNet
    aeroworldnet.com, 142
AICPA Online: American Institute for Certified
    Public Accountants
    aicpa.org, 65
Airparts.com
    airparts.com, 146
Alabama
    personnel.state.al.us, 183

Alabama Career Information Network System
    (ACINS)
    adeca.state.al.us, 202
    adeca.state.al.us/soicc/soicc/WebSTAR3.0/soicc/
    default.html, 202
Alabama Development Office
    ado.state.al.us, 202–3
Alabama Live
    al.com, 203
    al.com/careers, 203
Alabama Works!
    alabamaworks.org, 203
Alabama's Job Bank
    ajb.org/al, 202
    dir.state.al.us/es/default.htm, 202
Alaska
    http://teak.state.ak.us/wa/mainentry.nsf/?Open
    DataBase, 183
Alaska Department of Labor and Workforce
    Development
    labor.state.ak.us, 204
Alaska Job Center Network
    http://146.63.75.43/akjb, 204
    jobs.state.ak.us, 204
Alaska Jobs Center (AJC)
    ilovealaska.com/alaskajobs, 204
Alaska State Troopers
    dps.state.ak.us/Ast/recruit, 204
AlaWeb
    state.al.us/2k1, 203
Alberta WorkinfoNET
    alis.gov.ab.ca, 280, 284
Alpha Systems
    jobbs.com, 140, 166
AltaVista
    altavista.com, 9, 16
Amerian Meteorolgoical Society
    ametsoc.org/ams, 132
American Academy of Forensic Sciences
    aafs.org, 130
American Anthropological Association
    aaanet.org, 80
American Arbitration Association
    adr.org, 80
American Association of Cereal Chemists
    scisoc.org/aacc, 126
American Association of Law Libraries
    aallnet.org, 89
American Astronomical Society (AAS) Career
    Services
    aas.org/career/index.htm, 125–26
American Banker.com
    americanbanker.com, 65
American Chamber of Commerce in Russia
    amcham.ru, 297
American Culinary Federation
    acfchefs.org, 103–4
American Dental Association (ADA)
    ada.org, 135
American Fisheries Society Jobs Bulletin
    fisheries.org/jobs.html, 124
American Gas Association
    aga.org, 162
American Indian Science and Engineering
    Society
    aises.org, 318
American Industrial Hygiene Association
    aiha.org, 160
American Institute of Aeronautics and
    Astronautics (AIAA)
    aiaa.org, 142
American Institute of Physics: Employment and
    Industry
    http://aip.org/industry.html,
    132

American Library Association (ALA) Library
    Education and Employment Menu Page
    ala.org/education, 89
American Marketing Association
    ama.org, 76
American Massage Therapy Association
    amtamassage.org, 137
American Mathematical Society
    ams.org, 157
American Planning Association (APA)
    planning.org, 143–44
American Public Works Association (APWA)
    apwa.net, 148
American Society for Public Administration
    (ASPA)
    aspanet.org, 180
American Society for Quality (ASQ)
    asq.org, 75
American Society for Training and Development
    (ASTD)
    astd.org, 77
American Society of Agricultural Engineers
    (ASAE)
    asae.org, 122
American Society of Association Executives
    asaenet.org, 341
American Society of Civil Engineers
    asce.org, 148
American Society of Crime Laboratory Directors
    ascld.org, 130
American Society of Landscape Architects (ASLA)
    asla.org, 144
American Society of Limnology and
    Oceanography (ASLO)
    http://aslo.org/jobs.html, 124
American Society of Payroll Managers
    aspm.org, 65
American Symphony Orchestra League, The
    (ASOL)
    symphony.org, 110
American Water Works Association (AWWA)
    awwa.org, 162–63
American Zoo and Aquarium Association
    aza.org, 15
America's Career InfoNet
    acinet.org, 329
America's HealthCareSource
    healthcaresource.com, 133
America's Job Bank
    ajb.org, 15, 51, 201
America's Learning eXchange
    alx.org, 336
Anchorage Daily News
    adn.com, 204
APA Help Center
    http://helping.apa.org, 326
APA Monitor Classified Advertising: American
    Psychological Association
    apa.org/ads, 96
APN EdOnline
    edonline.com.au, 301
Apparel News, The
    apparelnews.net, 105
Apprenticeship Information from the U.S.
    Department of Labor
    doleta.gov/individ/apprent.asp, 339
Aquatic Network
    aquanet.com, 124
Aquent
    aquent.com, 166–67
Archaeological Fieldwork Server
    cincpac.com/afos/testpit.html, 80
Archaeological Institute of America
    (AIA)
    archaeological.org, 81

360

Architecture.com
  architecture.com, 144
Arizona Central
  azcentral.com, 206
Arizona's Job Bank
  ajb.org/az, 206
Arkansas
  arstatejobs.com, 183
Arkansas Business
  arkansasbusiness.com, 206
Arkansas Career Development Network (ACDN)
  accessarkansas.org/onestop, 206
Arkansas Employment Register
  arjobs.com, 207
Arkansas Employment Security Department
    (AESD)
  accessarkansas.org/esd, 207
  accessarkansas.org/esd/employment.htm, 207
Arkansas Job Bank
  ajb.org/ar, 206
Arkansas Online
  ardemgaz.com, 207
ARLIS/NA JobNet
  arlisna.org/jobs.html, 89
Art Newspaper, The
  theartnewspaper.com, 100
Arts Deadlines List, The
  xensei.com/users/adl, 101
Arts Wire Current
  artswire.org, 101
Artslynx International Dance Resources
  artslynx.org/dance/index.htm, 105
Artslynx Theatre
  artslynx.org/theatre, 101
ASA/CSSA/SSSA Personnel Listings
  asa-cssa-sssa.org/personnel, 122
ASAE CareerHeadquarters
  asaenet.org/careers, 93
ASEE's National Engineering Information Center
    (NEIC)
  asee.org/neic, 83
Asia-Net
  asia-net.com, 15, 51, 300
Asiadragons Asia Employment center
  asiadragons.com/employment/home.shtml,
    301
Asian American Economic Development
    Enterprises, Inc.
  aaede.org, 318
Askjeeves
  ask.com, 10
ASM International
  asm-intl.org, 157
ASME, the American Society of Mechanical
    Engineers
  asme.org, 157
Association Bernard Gregory
  abg.asso.fr, 290
Association for Computing Machinery (ACM)
  acm.org, 166
Association for Facilities Engineers (AFE)
  age.org, 151
Association for Finance Professions (AFP)
  afponline.org, 65–66
Association of American Veterinary Medical
    Colleges
  aavmc.org., 132–33
Association of Americans and Canadians in Israel
    Jobnet
  jobnet.co.il, 300
Association of Higher Education Facilities Officers
  appa.org, 151
Association of Research Libraries (ARL) Career
    Resources Online Services
  http://db.arl.org/careers/index.html, 89
ASTM International Directory of Testing
    Laboratories
  astm.org/labs, 140
Astronaut Selection from NASA
  nasajobs.nasa.gov/jobs/astronauts/index.htm,
    143
At-sea Processors Association
  atsea.org, 152–53
Atlanta ComputerJobs
  atlanta.computerjobs.com, 218
Atlanta Journal-Constitution
  ajcclassifieds.com, 218
  ajc.com, 218

AtlanticCanadaCareers.com
  atlanticcanadacareers.com, 280
Austin City Connections
  ci.austin.tx.us, 262
Austin360: Austin Starts Here
  austin360.com, 262
Australian Career Directory
  careers.gov.au, 301
  jobsearch.gov.au, 301
AutoCAD Job Network
  acjn.com, 158
Aviation Employee Placement Service (AEPS)
  aeps.com, 146
AVJobs.com
  avjobs.com, 146
Avotek Headhunters
  avotek.nl/dutchpag.htm, 292

Back Door Jobs—Exciting Career Adventures
  backdoorjobs.com, 195
Backstage Online
  backstage.com, 101–2
Bakery-Net
  bakery-net.com, 104
BakingBusiness.com Job Center
  http://jobcenter.bakingbusiness.com/jobcenter/,
    104
Bankjobs.com
  bankjobs.com, 66
Baseball Links
  baseball-links.com, 113
Baton Rouge Advocate, The
  lajobmarket.com, 228
  theadvocate.com, 228
BayAreaCareers.com
  bayareacareers.com, 208
BC Ministry of Employment and Investment
  gov.bc.ca/ei, 285
Beardsley Group, The
  beardsleygroup.com, 167
BeautySchool.com
  beautyschool.com, 106
BenefitNews.com
  benfitnews.com, 71
BenefitsLink
  benefitslink.com, 71
Berry List of Actuarial Resources
  geocities.com/wallstreet/1602, 68
Best Bets for Student Work Exchange
  cie.uci.edu/iop/work/html, 191
Best Places to Live from Money Magazine
  http://money.cnn.com/best/bplive, 344
BestFuture.com
  bestfuture.com, 98
BestJobsUSA.com
  bestjobsusa.com, 51
BET.com
  bet.com, 315
Big Deal Classified
  bigdealclassifieds.com, 206
Billings Gazette Online
  billingsgazette.com, 238
Bio.com Career Center
  http://career.bio.com/pages/index.cfm, 126
BioSpace.com
  biospace.com, 120
Black Collegian, The
  black-collegian.com, 51, 315
Black Voices
  blackvoices.com, 316
Blackworld
  blackworld.com, 316
Bloomberg Online
  bloomberg.com, 66
Blue Line: Police Opportunity Monitor, The
  theblueline.com, 177
BlueSteps from the Association of Executive Search
    Consultants
  bluesteps.com, 353–54
Bolsa de Trabajo
  bolsadetrabajo.com, 288
Bookbinders Guild of New York Job Bank,
    The
  bbgny.com/guild/jb.html, 112
Bookbuilders of Boston
  bbboston.org, 112
Boston ComputerWork
  http://boston.computerwork.com, 231

Boston Globe's Boston.com
  http://bostonworks.boston.com, 231–32
  http://digitalmass.boston.com, 231–32
  boston.com, 231–32
Boston Online
  boston-online.com, 232
BostonComputerJobs
  boston.computerjobs.com, 232
BostonSearch.com
  bostonsearch.com, 232
Boulder Community Network
  http://bcn.boulder.co.us, 212–13
  http://bcn.boulder.co.us/oscn, 212–13
Boulder County
  co.boulder.co.us, 213
Boulware & Associates
  boulwareinc.com, 93
BrassRing.com
  brassring.com, 167
Bread Bakers Guild of America
  bbga.org, 104
Breitbach Unternehmensberatung
  breitbach.com, 292
Britannica
  britannica.com, 8, 13
British Columbia Chamber of Commerce
  bcchamber.org, 285
British Columbia WorkinfoNET
  http://workinfonet.bc.ca, 280, 285
British Council, The
  britcoun.org/eis, 293
Broadcast Employment Services
  http://tvjobs.com, 115
Brookings Institute
  brook.edu, 181
Brooklyn Public Library Education and Job
    Information Center (EJIC)
  brooklynpubliclibrary.org/central/ejic.htm,
    245
BUBL Information Service
  http://bubl.ac.uk, 90
Bucknell University List of U.S. Firms in Russia
  departments.bucknell.edu/russian, 297
Builder Online
  builderonline.com, 148–49
Business Women's Network Interactive
  bwni.com, 311
BusinessWeek
  businessweek.com, 358
BuyingJobs.com
  buyingjobs.com, 74

C. Berger and Company: Library Consultants
  cberger.com, 90
Calgary Community Pages
  calcna.ab.ca/calgary/calgary.html, 284
California
  spb.ca.gov, 183
California ComputerWork
  http://california.computerwork.com, 208
California Online Job Network (COJN)
  cajobs.com, 208
California Polytechnic State University
  careerservices.calpoly.edu, 191
California State Government
  ca.gov, 208–9
  ca.gov/portal/myca_homepage.jsp, 208–9
California State University Employment Board
  http://csueb.sfsu.edu/csueb/pages/index.html,
    209
California WorkNet
  sjtcc.ca.gov/sjtccweb/one-stop, 209
California's Job Bank
  ajb.org/ca, 207
CalJOBS
  caljobs.ca.gov, 209
CallCenterCareers.com
  callcentercareers.com, 70
Campbell Interest and Skill Survey
  http://assessments.ncpearson.com/assessments/
    tests/ciss.htm, 328
Campus WorkLink: NGR
  connect.gc.ca/en/270-e.htm, 280
Canada WorkinfoNET
  workinfonet.ca, 280–81
Canadian Association of Career Educators and
    Employers
  cacee.com, 281

CanadianCareers.com
  canadiancareers.com, 281
CanJobs.com
  canjobs.com, 281
CapAccess: Greater Washington's Community
    Network
  capaccess.org, 216
Capitol City Home Page, The
  juneau.lib.ak.us, 205
Career and Community Learning Center
  oslo.umn.edu, 191
Career and Placement Services
  ualberta.ca/caps, 284
Career Command Post
  careercommandpost.com, 312
Career Cross Japan
  careercross.com, 318
Career Development
  cdc-va.com, 312
Career Edge
  careeredge.org, 281
Career Espresso
  sph.emory.edu/studentservice/Career.html, 138
Career Exploration Links
  uhs.berkeley.edu/students/careerlibrary/links/
    careerme.htm, 330
Career Giant
  careergiant.com, 220
Career Guide to Industries
  bls.gov/oco/cg, 329
Career Guides from JobStar
  jobstar.org/tool/career/index.htm, 331
Career Interests Game
  http://career.missouri.edu/holland, 328
Career Link
  careerlink.org, 239
Career Magazine
  http://vertical.worklife.com/onlines/careermag,
    51
Career Paradise's Colossal List of Links
  emory.edu/CAREER/Main/CareerLinks.html,
    60
Career Planning Proccess, Bowling Green State
    University
  bgsu.edu/offices/sa/caree/process, 325
Career Resource Homepage, The
  careerresource.net, 61
Career Resource Library from N. Y. State
    Department of Labor
  labor.state.ny.us/working_ny/finding_a_job/
    career_resource.html, 29
Career Tests and Resources from Queendom.com
  queendom.com/portals/career.html, 328
Career Wise at DragonSurg
  globalvillager.com/careerwise/index.cfm, 303
CareerBoard
  careerboard.com, 249
CareerBuilder
  careerbuilder.com, 15, 52
CareerCity
  careercity.com, 52
CareerClick
  careerclick.com, 285
Career.com
  career.com, 51
CareerConnect
  careerconnect.state.va.us, 266–67
career.co.nz
  career.co.nz, 304
CareerCross Japan
  careercross.com, 304
CareerExchange
  careerexchange.com, 52
CareerJournal from the Wall Street Journal
  careerjournal.com, 30, 52, 324, 342, 350, 358
CareerMart
  careermart.com, 52
CareerMosaic India
  careermosaicindia.com, 303
CareerPlace
  careerplace.com, 282, 319
Careers in Business
  careers-in-business.com, 64
Careers in Government
  careersingovernment.com, 182
Careers Online
  careersonline.com.au/menu.html, 302
Careers OnLine Virtual Careers Show
  careersonline.com.au/show/menu.html,
    331

CareerSearch from the College Board Online
  http://cbweb9p.collegeboard.org/career/bin/
    career.pl, 325
Careersite
  careersite.com, 52–53
Careers.Org, Career Resource Center
  careers.org, 61
CareerWeb
  careerweb.com, 53
CareGuide
  careguide.com, 103
Carnegie Library of Pittsburgh
  http://org/clp/jcec, 254
  clpgh.org, 254
Carnegie Library of Pittsburgh: Financial Aid
    Pathfinder
  carnegielibrary.org/clp/JCEC.aid.html, 334
Carolina ComputerJobs
  carolina.computerjobs.com, 247
CascadeLink
  businessinportland.org, 252
  cascadelink.org, 252
Case Western Reserve University Career Planning
    and Placement
  cwru.edu/stuaff/careers, 191
Casino Careers Online
  casinocareers.com, 108
Casino Employment Guide
  casinoemployment.com, 108
Catapult, Career Service Professionals Home Page,
    The
  jobweb.com/catapult, 325
Catapult, The
  http://ww.jobweb.com/catapult, 61
  jobweb.com/catapult, 197
CATIA Job Network
  catjn.com, 158
CEO Job Opportunities Update
  ceoupdate.com, 354
CEO Pay from Forbes.com
  forbes.com, 357
CFD (Computational Fluid Dynamics) Jobs Databse
  cfd online.com/Jobs, 152
CFO.com
  http://cof.com, 66
Chamber of Commerce International Directory
  http://chamber-of-commerce.com, 344–45
Champaign-Urbana News Gazette
  newsgazette.com, 222
Champion Personnel System
  championjobs.com, 73
Charity Channel
  charitychannel.com, 93
Charity Village
  charityvillage.com, 282
  charityvillage.com/charityvillage/main.asp,
    282
Charleston Gazette Online
  wvgazette.com, 270
Charleston.Net
  charleston.ent, 258
Charlotte.com
  http://careers.charlotte.com, 247
Chemistry & Industry Jobs On-line
  chemind.org/jobs.html, 126–27
ChemistryJobs.com/ChEJobs.com
  chemistryjobs.com, 127
Chicago ComputerJobs
  chicago.computerjobs.com, 222
Chicago ComputerWork
  http://chicago.computerwork.com, 222
Chicago Sun-Times
  suntimes.com/classified/Employment.html,
    222
Chicago Tribune
  http://chicagotribune.com, 223
  http://chicagotribune.com/careers, 223
ChicagoJobs
  chicagojobs.org, 15
ChicagoJobs.org: the Definitive Chicago Area Job
    and Career Guide
  chicagojobs.org, 223
ChiefMonster.com
  chiefmonster.com, 350–51
Chimney Safety Institute of America
  csia.org, 147
Christian Career Center
  christiancareercenter.com, 321
Christian Jobs Online
  christianjobs.com, 321

Chronicle of Higher Education's Career Network
  http://chronicle.com/jobs, 83
Chronicle of Philanthropy Career Network
  philanthropy.com/jobs, 95
CIA World Factbook
  odci.gov/cia/publications/factbook/index.html,
    345
Cincinnati.com
  http://careerfinder.cincinnati.com, 249–50
  http://cincinnati.com, 249–50
City of Atlanta Home Page
  ci.atlanta.ga.us, 218–19
City of Chicago
  cityofchicago.org, 223
City of Madison
  ci.madison.wi.us, 271
City of Oklahoma City Hall
  okc-cityhall.org, 251
CityJobs
  cityjobs.com, 294
CityofSeattle.net
  cityofseattle.net, 269
Classified Advertising for JAMA, American Medical
    News, and the Archives Journals
  ama-assn.org/cgi-bin/webad, 133–34
Clearinghouse, The
  clearinghouse.net, 8, 13
CLP Resources
  clp.com, 149
C.O.A.C.H.
  coachhelp.com, 113
College and University Rankings
  library.uiuc.edu/edx/rankings.htm, 336
College Grad Job Hunter
  collegegrad.com, 53, 190
College Is Possible
  collegeispossible.com, 334–35
College of Food, Agricultural, and Environmental
    Sciences Career Information, Ohio State
    University
  http://cfaes.ohio-state.edu/career, 122
College Pro Painters
  collegepro.com, 154, 196
CollegeNET
  collegenet.com, 336–37
Collegiate.Net, The Center for All Collegiate
    Information
  collegiate.net, 337
Colorado
  state.co.us/jobinfo.html, 183
Colorado Virtual Library
  aclin.org, 213
Colorado's Job Bank
  ajb.org/co, 212
Columbus Dispatch
  columbusjobs.com, 250
  dispatch.com, 250
Comforce Corporation
  comforce.com, 53
Commarts.com Network
  commarts.com, 69
Commonwealth of Massachusetts Home Page
  state.ma.us, 232
  state.ma.us/job.htm, 232
Community Career Center
  nonprofitjobs.org, 93
Compterwork.com
  computerwork.com, 167
ComputerJobs.com
  computerjobs.com, 167
ComputerWorld
  computerworld.com, 15, 170
Computing Research Association (CRA)
  http://cra.org, 170
Congressional Quarterly (CQ)
  cq.com, 177
Connecticut
  das.state.ct.us/HR/HRhome.htm, 183
Connecticut Works
  ctdol.state.ct.us, 214
Connecticut's Job Bank
  ajb.org/ct, 214
ConstructionOnly.com
  constructiononly.com, 149
ConstructionWebLinks.com
  constructionweblinks.com/index.html, 149
Contract Employee's Handbook
  cehandbook.com, 332
ContractJobHunter
  cjhunter.com, 140

COOL: College Opportunities On-Line
http://nces.ed.gov/ipeds/cool, 336, 339
Cool Jobs
cooljobs.com, 53
Cool Works
coolworks.com, 113–14, 196
Core77 Design Magazine and Resource
core77.com, 155
Corporate Gray Online
greentogray.com, 312–13
CorporateInformation
corporateinformation.com, 13
Corporation for National Service, The
nationalservice.org, 193
Council for Advancement and Support of
Education (CASE) Job Classifieds
case.org/jobs, 85
Council on International Education Exchange
ciee.org, 191–92
Counselor Licensure Legislation: Protecting the
Public
counseling.org/resources/licensure_legisltion
.htm, 327
Counter Offer, from Fritoe & Carleton
adjob.com/counter.htm, 31
Criminal Justice Links, Florida State University
School of Criminology and Criminal Justice
criminology.fsu.edu/cjlinks, 177
C&RL News Classified Advertising, Association of
College and Research Libraries
ala.org/acrl/advert3.html, 90
CrossroadsEurope
crossroadseurope.com, 296
CTOnline Classifieds
counseling.org/ctonline/classified.htm,
96
Custom Databanks, Inc.
customdatabanks.com, 355–56
Customer Resource Information System for
North Dakota (CRISND)
http://crisnd.com/cris/home.html, 249
Cyber-Sierra's Natural Resources Job Search
cyber-sierra.com/nrjobs/index.html, 123
CyberDance: Ballet on the Net
cyberdance.org, 105
Cyburbia, the Planning and Architecture Internet
Resource Center
cyburbia.org, 144
Czechjobs.cz
cezchjobs.cz, 296

Daily Mail & Guardian work@za
mg.co.za/jump/jump.html, 299
mg.co.za/mg/work, 299
Daily News—The Independent Source for Wireless
Industry News
rcrnews.com, 164
Dave's ESL Cafe Job Board
http://eslcafe.com/joblist, 276
daVinci Times
http://ww.davincitimes.org, 245
DBWorld Mailing List Archives
http://groups.yahoo.com/group/dbworld,
171
DC Metro ComputerJobs
de.computerjobs.com, 216
DEF 14A Reports from EDGAR Database of
Corporate Information
sec.gov/edgar.shtml, 358
Defense Industry, The
http://members.home.net/marylandcareers/intel
.html, 178
DefenseLink
defenselink.mil/other_info/careers.html,
179
DelAWARE
http://lib.de.us, 215
Delaware
http://delawarepersonnel.com, 183
Delaware Online, Wilmington News Journal
delawareonline.com, 215
Delaware Virtual Career Network
vcnet.net, 215
Delaware's Job Bank
ajb.org/de, 214
Denver ComputerJobs
denver.computerjobs.com, 213
Denver Post Online, The
denverpost.com, 213
employmentwizard.com, 213

Department of Education, Training, and Youth
Affairs
http://jobsearch.deetya.gov.au, 302
http://jobsearch.gov.au, 302
deetya.gov.au, 302
Department of Employment, Thailand
doe.go.th, 305
Department of Justice
usdog.gov, 177
Department of Labor and Industrial Relations
(DOLIR)
dolir.stat.mo.us, 236
Department of Labor and Training (Vermont)
det.state.vt.us, 266
Deseret News
http://deseretnews.com/dn, 264–65
Destiny Group, The
destinygrp.com, 313
Developers.Net
www.developers.net, 167
Dice.com
dice.com, 167–68
Directory of Executive Recruiters from Kennedy
Publications
kennedyinfo.com/db/db_der_bas.html, 356
Disability Resources Monthly
disabilityresources.org, 314–15
DisabilityDirect
disabilitydirect.gov, 314
Discovering Montana
discoveringmontana.com, 238
Distance Calculator from Indo.com
indo.com/distance, 345
Distance Education and Training Council
detc.org, 338
District of Columbia
dc.gov/gov/index.htm, 183
District of Columbia's Job Bank
ajb.org/dc, 215
DiversiLink
diversilink.com, 141, 316–17
Diversity/Careers in Engineering & Information
Technology
diversity.com, 308
Diversity Employment
diversityemployment.com, 308
Diversity Link
diversitylink.com, 308
DO-IT (Disabilities, Opportunities,
Internetworking, and Technology)
washington.edu/doit, 315
Dogpile
metacrawler.com, 10
Dominion Post Online
dominionpost.com, 270–71
Drilling Research Institute
drillers.com, 158–59

E-Architect, the American Institute of Architects
e-architect.com, 144
E Jobs
ejobs.org, 127
E-JOE
inomics.com/query/show?what=ejoe, 81
Earthworks
earthworks-jobs.com, 127–28
Ecological Society of America Career and Funding
Opportunities
http://esa.sdsc.edu/opportunity.htm, 128
Ecomp, Executive Compensation Database
ecomponline.com, 358–59
Ed Jobs U Seek
http://jobs.coled.umn.edu, 86
Edgar
sec.gov/edgar/shtml, 13
Editor & Publisher
editorandpublisher.com, 9, 115, 345
Edmonton FreeNet
freenet.edmonton.ab.ca, 285
Education in Forensic Science from Forensic DNA
Consulting
http://forensicdna/index.htm, 130
EDUCAUSE Job Posting Service
educause.edu/jobpost/jobpost.html, 85
EE-Link: The Environmental Education Web Server
eelink.net, 128
EE Times.com
eet.com, 150
EFLWEB
eflweb.com, 87

Electronic Blue Book, The
the bluebook.com, 149
Electronic Labour Exchange
ele-spe.org, 282
Electronic News On-Line
http://electronicnews.com, 150
ELECTRICJob.com
electricjob.com, 163
Email.com
email.com, 22
EmployCanada.com
employcanada.com, 282
Employee Relocation Council (ERC)
erc.org, 75
Employers Online
employersonline.com, 53
Employment Development Department (EDD)
edd.cahwnet.gov, 209
Employment Opportunities: Bionet.jobs.offered
bio.net/hypermail/EMPLOYMENT, 126
Employment Opportunities at
Northwest Fisheries Science Center
(NWFSC) and in Fisheries or Related
Fields
http://research.nwfsc.noaa.gov/staff/jobopportu
nitiesmenu.html, 124
Employment Opportunities in Australia
employment.com.au, 302
Employment Opportunities in Women's Studies
and Feminism
inform.umd.edu/EdRes/Topic/WomensStudies/
Employment, 83
Employment Projections from the Bureau of Labor
Statistics
bls.gov/emp/, 333
Employment Review Magazine
employmentreview.com, 333
Employment Security Commission (ESC) of
North Carolina
esc.state.nc.us, 247–48
Employment Wanted: Bionet.jobs.wanted
hypermail/EMPLOYMENT-WANTED, 126
Employnet
employnet.co.za, 299
Energyjobs.com
http://www.energyjobs.com, 163
Engineering Job Source
engineerjobs.com, 141
Engineering News-Record (ENR)
enr.com, 149–50
EngineeringJobs.com
engineeringjobs.com, 141
Ensemble
ensemble.org, 110
EntertainmentCareers.Net
entertainmentcareers.net, 102
Entomological Society of America
entsoc.org, 129
Entry-Level Jobs in Hospitality, Long-Term Care,
and Child Care
urban.org/employment/brochure1/index.htm,
103
Environmental Sites on the Internet
lib.kth.se/lg/envisite.htm, 129
Environmental Careers Organization
eco.org, 129
EnvironmentalCareer.com
environmental-jobs.com, 128–29
Equal Opportunity Publications, Inc.
eop.com, 308
Equimax—Where Jobs and Horse People Find Each
Other
equimax.com, 125
Equipment Leasing Association Online
elaonline.com, 70
EquiSearch.com
equisearch.com, 125
ERP Jobs
erp-jobs.com, 168
Escape Artist
escapeartist.com, 277
Escape Artist Africa
escapeartist.com/jobs8/africa.htm,
299
Escoffier On Line
escoffier.com, 104
eScribe
escribe.com, 22
ESL Cafe's Job Center
http://eslcafe.com/jobs, 87

EuroPages: the European Business Directory
europages.com, 289
EURopean Employment Services
http://europa.eu.int/comm/employment_social/
elm/eures/index.htm, 289–90
European Governments Online
http://europa.eu.int/abc/governments/index_en.
html, 290
European Internet Resources
europeaninternet.com, 296
Evaluating a Job Offer, from the *Occupational
Outlook Handbook*
bls.gov/oco/oco20046.htm, 31
eworcester.com
eworcester.com, 233
Excite
excite.com, 9
Excite Careers
http://directory.excite.com/careers/, 53
Excite Classifieds
classifieds2000.com, 54
Excite Free eMail
excite.com, 22
Exec-U-Net
execunet.com, 351
ExecSearches.com
execsearches.com, 93–94
execsearches.com/exec, 181
Execu-Search Group
execu-search.com, 66
Executive-Placement Services
execplacement.com, 108
Executive Search International
esihbc.com, 74
ExecutivesOnly
executivesonly.com, 351
Experience Works!
experienceworks.org, 309–10
Experimental Medicine Job Listings
medcor.mcgill.ca/EXPMED/DOCS/jobs.html,
134
Express-News Online
http://mysa.com, 262
expressnews.com, 262
sajobsearch.com, 262

FacilitiesNet
facilitiesnet.com, 152
Fairbanks Alaska Internet Resources Network for
Education and Training (FairNet)
fairnet.org, 205
Fargo Enterprises Inc.: Gateway to the Camera
Repair Industry
fargo-ent.com/index.html, 147
Farms.com AgCareers
farms.com/careers, 123
FashionCareerCenter.com
fashioncareercenter.com, 106
FDAssociates
fdassociates, 290
Federal Computer Week
fcw.com, 174
Federal Jobs Digest
jobsfed.com, 174
Federal Jobs Net
http://federaljobs.net, 174
Federal Judiciary
uscourts.gov, 88
Federal Web Locator from The Center for
Information Law and Policy
inoctr.edu/FWL, 176
FEDIX
http://content.sciencewise.com/fedix, 174
FedWorld Federal Job Search
fedworld.gov/jobs/jobsearch.html, 175
Feminist Career Center
feminist.org/911/jobs/911jobs.asp, 311
FinAid, The Financial Aid Information Page
finaid.org, 335
Financial Job Network
fjn.com, 66
FinancialJobs.com
financialjobs.com, 67
Fincareer.com
fincareer.com, 67
Find a Pilot
findapilot.com, 146
Find Executive and Technical Search
find-gis.com, 131

Finding Work in Alaska
labor.state.ak.us/esd_alaska_jobs/ak_over.htm,
205
FindLaw Career Center
http://careers.findlaw.com, 88
Finishing.com
finishing.com, 152
FirstGov
firstgov.gov, 176
FishJobs
fishjobs.com, 153
Fitness Professional's Center, The
http://fitnesslink.com/fitpro, 114
FitnessManagement.com
fitnessmanagement.com, 114
FlipDog
flipdog.com, 54
Florida
myflorida.com/myflorida/jobopportunity.html,
184
Florida Agency for Workforce Innovation (AWI)
http://www2.myflorida.com/awi, 216
Florida Board of Education Division of Colleges
and Universities Position Vacancies
borfl.org/EmploymentOps, 217
Florida ComputerJobs
florida.computerjobs.com, 217
Florida ComputerWork
http://florida.computerwork.com, 217
Florida's Job Bank
ajb.org/fl, 216
FoodIndustryJobs.com
foodindustryjobs.com, 104
Footwear Industries of America
fia.org, 154
Forensic Resources from the Law Office of Kim
Kruglick
kruglaw.com/forensic, 131
Forty Plus of Northern California
fortyplus.org, 31–32
4Work
http://4work.com, 54
French National Center for Scientific Research
cnrs.org/cw/fr/band/autr/emploi.html, 290
Fristoe & Carleton, Inc.
adjob.com, 69
FrogJobs—Employment in France
listproc@list.cren.net, 291
Fulton County, George, Personnel Department
fulton.ga.us/personnel/joblistings.html,
219
FuneralNet
funeralnet.com, 107
Futurestep from Korn/Ferry
futurestep.com, 54

Gaines International
gainesintl.com, 145
Galveston County Daily News
galvnews.com, 263
Gateway Virginia
http://careers.timesdispatch.com, 267
gatewayva.com, 267
GAYWORK.com
gaywork.com, 320
GeoJobSource
geojobsource.com, 131
GeoPlace
geoplace.com, 131
Georgia
gms.state.ga.us, 184
Georgia Department of Education
doe.k12.ga.us, 219
Georgia One-Stop Career Network
g1careernet.com, 219
Georgia's Job Bank
ajb.org/ga, 218
GIS Jobs Clearinghouse
gjc.org, 131
Globewide Network Academy
gnacademy.org, 338
GoAbroad.com
goabroad.com, 192
GoCollege
gocollege.com, 337
GoGay.net
gogay.net, 320
Google
google.com, 9

Google Groups
http://groups.google.com, 22
Government of Guam Official Departments
gov.gu/government.html, 219
Government of Alberta Home Page
gov.ab.ca, 285
Governor's Job Bank
twc.state.tx.us/jobs/gvjb/gvjb.html, 263
GovExec.com Careers
govexec.com/jobs, 175
GovtJob.Net
govtjob.net, 182
govtjobs.com
govtjobs.com, 182–83
GrandForks.com
grandforks.com, 248
GrantsNet
grantsnet.org, 120
Great Summer Jobs
http://gsj.petersons.com, 196
Greater Victoria Chamber of Commerce
http://gvcc.org, 286
Guam's Job Bank
ajb.org/gu, 219
Guam's One-Stop Career Service Center
http://onestopcareer.gov.gu, 220
Guide to Career Prospects in Virginia
ccps.virginia.edu/career_prospects, 267, 331
Guide to Philosophy on the Internet,
The earlham.edu/peters/philinks.htm#jobs, 111

H-Net Job Guide for the Humanities and Social
Sciences
matrix.msu.edu/jobs, 100
Hair-news.com
hair-news.com/pto/html, 106
HairWorld
hairworld.com, 106
HALINET
hhpl.on.ca, 287
hhpl.on.ca/library/jobs.htm, 287
Hall Kinion International (HKI), Asia-Pacific
tkointl.com, 168
Hampton Consultancy
hampton.co.za, 300
HamptonRoads.com
http://jobs.hamptonroads.com, 267
hamptonroads.com, 267
Handling Questionable Questions in Job
Interview
rileyguide.com/dob/html, 30
Harry's Job Search Inernet Hot List
http://jobinfo.freeyellow.com/index.html, 166
Hartford Courant Newspaper
courant.ctnow.com/classifieds/careers, 214
Hawaii
state.hi.us/hrd, 184
Hawaii Department of Labor and Industrial
Relations (DOLIR)
http://dlir.state.hi.us, 220–21
http://dlir.state.hi.us/wdd, 220–21
Hawaii.com
hawaii.com, 220
hawaii.net, 220
Hawaii's Job Bank
ajb.org/hi, 220
Headhunter E-mail Address Lists from Avotek
avotek.nl/emailgds.htm, 356356
Headhunters International
avotek.nl, 277
Health Care Job Store
healthcarejobstore.com, 134
Health Careers Online
healthcareers-online.com, 134
HealthWeb
http://healthweb.org, 134
Heidrick & Struggles International
heidrick.com, 352
Helsingin Sanomat
helsinginsanomat.fi, 298
Herald Extra
harktheherald.com, 265
Heritage Foundation, the
heritage.org, 181
HerpDigest
herpdigest.org, 125
Hieros Gamos, Comprehensive Law and
Governmental Portal
hg.org, 88

HigherEd Jobs
  higheredjobs.com, 83
Hillel: the Foundation for Jewish Campus Life
  hillel.org, 321
Hire Diversity
  hirediversity.com, 309
HIRE TEXAS
  http://m06hostp.twc.state.tx.us/jobmatch/jobsee
    ker/htapp.html, 263
HireKnowledge
  hireknowledge.com, 107, 168
Hispanic Business, Inc.
  hispanicbusiness.com, 317
Hispanic Online
  hisp.com, 317
Hollywood Creative Directory Online
  hcdonline.com, 102
Home Page of Malachy
  execpc.com/maltoal, 54
Homefair.com
  homefair.com/index.html, 345
Homestore.com
  homestore.com, 346
HometownAnnapolis.com
  hometownannapolis.com, 230230
HoosierNet
  bloomington.in.us, 224
Hoover's Online
  hoovers.com, 9, 13, 16, 343
Hospitality Net Virtual Job Exchange
  hospitalitynet.org, 108
HotBot
  hotbot.lycos.com, 9
Hotel Online
  http://hotel-online.com, 109
HotJobs
  hotjobs.com, 54–55
HotMail
  hotmail.com, 21
Houston Chronicle Interactive
  chron.com, 263
  chron.com/class/jobs/index.html, 263
HR Careers from TCM.com
  tcm.com/hr-careers, 71
HR Opportunities from Shaker Advertising
  shaker.com/hropps.html, 71
Human Resources Development Canada
  hrdc-drhc.gc.ca, 282–83
  jobbank.gc.ca, 282–83
Human Resources Online
  hro.ru, 297
Hungry Minds
  hungryminds.com, 338–39
Huntington Group, The
  hgllc.com, 55
HVACJob
  hvacjob.com, 154

IBEW Construction Jobs Board
  ibew.org/jobs_board.htm, 165
Idaho
  dhr.state.id.us, 184
Idaho Department of Labor
  doe.state.id.us, 221
Idaho Works: Idaho's Workforce Development
    System
  idahoworks.state.id.us, 221
Idaho's Job Bank
  ajb.org/id, 221
IDEAS Job Network
  ideasjn.com, 158
IEEE Computer Society's Career Service Center
  http://computer.org/careers, 150–51
IEEE Job Site
  http://jobs.ieee.org, 151
Illinois
  state.il.us/cms/persnl/default.htm, 184
  state.il.us/gov/officeinternships.htm, 184
Illinois Department of Commerce and Community
    Affairs (DCCA)
  commerce.state.il.us, 223
Illinois's Employment Opportunities and
    Job Bank
  ajb.org/il, 222
  ides.state.il.us/genera/jobs.htm, 222
Imcor
  imcor.com, 55, 354
IMDiversity
  imdiversity.com, 55, 309

IN Jersey
  http://jobs.injersey.com, 242
  injersey.com, 242
IName.com
  iname.com, 22
Inc. Magazine
  inc.com, 332
  inc.com/500, 332
Independent School Management Career Corner
  isminc.com/pubs/mart/mm.html, 86
Indiana
  in.gov/jobs/stateemployment/jobbank.html, 184
Indiana Career and Postsecondary Advancement
    Center
  http://icpac.indiana.edu, 224
Indiana Department of Workforce Development
    (DWD)
  in.gov/dwd, 225
  in.gov/dwd/joblistings.shtm, 225
Indianapolis Online
  indianapolisonline.in.us, 225
Indiana's Job Bank
  ajb.org/in, 224
Indico: Indiana Digital County Network
  indico.net, 225
InfoCurent
  infocurrent.com, 90
InfoMine
  infomine.com, 15, 159
InPharm.com
  inpharm.com, 137
Instructional System Technology Jobs
  http://education.indiana.edu/ist/studens/jobs/
    joblink.html, 77
Instructional Systems Technology: Employment
    Opportunities
  http://education.indiana.edu/ist/students/jbos/
    joblink.html, 168
Insurance National Search, Inc.
  insurancerecruiters.com, 72
Intenational Monetary Fund (IMF)
  imf.org, 181
International Association of Assembly Managers,
    Inc.
  http://iaam.org, 73
International Association of Business
    Communicators
  iabc.com/homepage.htm, 69
International Career Employment Center
  internationaljobs.org, 277
International Chamber of Commerce
  iccwbo.org, 277
International Economic Development Council
    (IEDC)
  iedconline.org, 81
International Foundation of Employee Benefit
    Plans
  ifebp.org, 71
International Herald Tribune Education
    Marketplace
  http://222.iht.com/misc/education.htm, 277
International Market Recruiters
  goimr.com, 67
International Pharmajobs
  pharmajobs.com/index.html, 137
International Purchasing Service Staffing
  ipserv.com, 75
International Rescue Committee
  intrescom.org/jobs/index.cfm, 277–78
International Seafarers Exchange
  jobxchange.com, 156
International Services Agencies (ISA)
  charity.org, 94
Internet Career Connection
  iccweb.com, 55
Internet Job Source, The
  statejobs.com, 183
Internet NonProfit Center
  nonprofits.org, 94
Internet Scoping School
  scopeschool.com, 98
InternetWeek
  internetweek.com, 171
Internship Programs.com
  http://internships.wetfeet.com/home.asp,
    192
Interview Tips from Monster.com
  http://content.monster.com/jobinfo/interview,
    30

Iowa
  iowajobs.org, 184
Iowa Jobs
  state.ia.us/jobs/index.htm, 226
Iowa Workforce Development (IWD)
  iowaworkforce.org, 226
Iowa's Job Bank
  ajb.org/ia, 225
IrishJobs.ie
  http://exp.ie, 292
  irishjobs.ie, 292
ISAJobs.org
  isajobs.org, 155
ITCareers.com
  itcareers.com, 169
iVillage
  ivillage.com, 311
Ixquick
  ixquick.com, 10

J-Jobs Journalism Job Bank
  http://www.journalism.berkeley.edu/jobs, 116
Jacobson Associates
  jacobson-associates.com, 72
Jefferson County Personnel Board (Birmingham)
  bhma.net/pjbjc/index.html, 203
Jewish Vocational Service Agencies in the United
    States, Canada, and Israel
  jvsnj.org/affiliates.html, 327
Job Corps, The
  jobcorpos.org, 340
Job Finders Online
  http://jobfindersonline.com, 61
Job Hunting in Planning, Architecture, and
    Landscape Architecture
  lib.berkeley.edu/ENVI/jobs.html, 145
Job-Hunt.org
  job-hunt.org, 61
Job-Index
  jobindex.dk, 298
Job Links for Lawyers
  http://home.sprynet.com/ear2ground, 88
Job Opportunities in Entomology
  colostate.edu/Depts/Entomology/jobs/jobs.html,
    129
Job Resources from the University of Illinois at
    Urbana-Champaign (UIUC)
  lis.uiuc.edu/gslis/resources/jobs.html, 90
Job Search from Library Journal
  libraryjournal.com/classifieds/index.asp, 91
Job-Search Links, Columbia Business School
  columbia.edu/cu/business/career/links, 64
Job Service North Dakota
  state.nd.us/jsnd, 248
Job Sleuth
  jobsleuth.com, 56
JobAccess
  jobaccess.org, 315
JobAsia
  jobasia.com, 301
JobBankUSA.com
  jobbankusa.com, 56
jobfind.com
  jobfind.com, 56, 214, 229, 232–33, 241, 257,
    266
Jobfinder
  jobfinder.se, 298
JobHunt
  job-hunt.org, 15
JobHuntersBible.com
  jobhuntersbible.com, 15, 29, 61–62
JobJunction Executive Search and Recruiting
    Services
  jobjunction.com, 145
JobLink from The Independent Sector
  independentsector.org/members/job_postings
    .htm, 94
JobNet Australia
  educateit.com.au, 302
  jobnet.com.au, 302
JobNet (New Zealand)
  educateit.com.au, 305
  jobnet.com.au, 305
JobNet.com
  jobnet.com, 254
JobOptions
  joboptions.com, 56
JobPilot
  jobpilot.se, 299

JobPilot AG
jobpilot.com, 278, 290, 294, 296, 298
jobpilot.net, 278
JobPilot Mideast
mideast.jobpilot.com, 300
Jobpilot.com
jobpilot.com, 57
Jobs from AIR: Association for Institutional
Research
airweb.org/jobs.html, 85
Jobs in Japan
jobsinjapan.com, 304
Jobs in Linguistics
linguistlist.org/jobsindex.html, 92
Jobs in Philosophy
sozialwiss.uni-
hamburg.de/phil/ag/jobs/main_english.
html, 111
Jobs in Russia and the NISE
departments.bucknell.edu/russian/jobs.html, 92
JobServe
jobserve.com, 294
JobShark
jobshark.com, 278, 289
Jobs4HR
jobs4hr.com, 71
JobsinEdinburgh.com
jobsinedinburgh.com, 293
JobsInFashion.com
http://jobsinfashion.com, 106
JobsInLogistics.com
jobsinlogistics.com, 155
JobsintheMoney.com
jobsinthemoney.com, 67
JobsonGuam.com
jobsonguam.com, 220
JobSpectrum.org from the American Chemical
Society (ACS)
jobspectrum.org, 127
JobStar
http://jobstar.org, 15, 62
JobStar Central
jobstar.org, 209
JobStar Salary Surveys
http://jobstar.org/tools/salary/index.htm, 342
Jobstuff
jobstuff.co.nz, 305
JobWeb from National Association of Colleges and
Employers
jobweb.com, 30
JOE-Job Opportunities for Economists
eco.utexas.edu/joe, 81
Journalism and Women Symposium (JAWS) Job
Bank, The
jaws.org/jobs/shtml, 116
Joyce Lain Kennedy's Careers
sunfeatures.com, 29
Juneau Empire
http://juneauempire.com, 205

Kansas
http://da.state.ks.us/ps/aaa/recruitment, 184
Kansas City, Missouri
kcmo.org, 236
Kansas City Star
http://careers.kansascity.com, 226–27
kansascity.com, 226
kcstar.com, 226
Kansas Department of Human Resources (KDHR)
http://kansasjobs.org, 227
hr.state.ks.us, 227
Kansas Job Bank
ajb.org/ks, 226
Kansas Job Link
kansasjoblink.com, 227
Keirsey Temperament Website
keirsey.com, 328–29
Kentucky
state.ky.us/agencies/personnel/pershome.htm,
184
Kentucky Cabinet for Workforce Development
http://kycwd.org, 228
http://www.desky.org, 228
Kentucky's Job Bank
ajb.org/ky, 227
Kforce.com
kforce.com, 57
Knoxville News-Sentinel Online
knoxcareers.com, 260–61
knoxnews.com, 260–61

Kolok Enterprises
kolok.net, 155–56
Korn/Ferry International
kornferry.com, 352–53
KyushuNet Japan Association for Language
Teaching
kyushu.comn/jalt/index.html, 304

Labor Market Information State by State
rileyguide.com/trends.html#gov, 333–34
Labor Unions, from Yahoo!
http://dir.yahoo.com/business_and_economy/
labor/unions, 341
LandSurveyors.com
landsurveyors.com, 164
Las Vegas Review-Journal
lvrj.com, 240
Lasvegas.com, 241
lasvegas.com, 241
lasvegas.com/features/jobs.html, 241
Latin American Jobs
latinamericanjobs.com, 289
LatPro.com
latpro.com, 289
Lawenforcementjob.com
lawenforcementjob.com, 178
Layoff Lounge, the
layofflounge.com, 32
Le Monde
http://emploi.lemonde.fr, 291
lemonde.fr, 291
LeadersOnline
leadersonline.com, 57
Les Pages Emploi
http://emploi.hrnet.fr, 279
les-pages-emploi.com, 279
Liberal Arts Job Search, The
http://riceinfo.rice.edu/projects/careers/students
/getting-a-job/liberal-arts.shtml, 100
LibertyNet
libertynet.com, 254
LIBJOBS
ifla.org/II/lists/libjobs.htm, 91
Library Job Postings on the Internet
http://webhost.bridgew.edu/snesbeitt/libraryjobs
.html, 91
Library of Congress Information on State and
Local Governments
http://lcweb.loc.gov/globa/state/stategov.html,
186
Library of Congress Meta-Indexes for State and
Local Government Information
http://lcweb.loc.gov/global/state/stategov.html,
201
Lincoln Journal Star
journalstar.com, 239
workforyounebraska.com, 239
Lincolnjobs.com
lincolnjobs.com, 239
Link Staffing Services
linkstaffing.com, 156
Lisjobs.com
lisjobs.com, 91
Live Online from *Washington Post*
washingtonpost.com, 31
London Times
thetimes-appointments.co.uk, 294
thetimes.co.uk, 294
Los Angeles and Southern California
ComputerJobs
la.computerjobs.com, 210
Los Angeles Times
latimes.com, 210
latimes.com/class/employ/workplace,
210
Louisiana
dscs.state.la.us, 184
Louisiana Works
ldol.state.la.us, 228
ldol.state.la.us/jobspage.htm, 228–29
Louisiana's Job Bank
ajb.org/la, 228
Louisville Courier-Journal
courierjournal.com, 228
LucasCareers.com
lucascareers.com, 57
Ludwig & Associates, Inc.
ludwig-recruit.com, 76
Lycos
lycos.com, 10

madison.com
madison.com, 271–72
Maine
state.me.us/statejobs, 184
Maine State Government
maincareercenter.com, 229
state.me.us, 229
Maine's Job Bank
ajb.org/me, 229
MaineToday.com/Press Herald Online
http://business.mainetoday.com, 230
http://careers.mainetoday.com, 230
portland.com, 230
Major Resource Kit
udel.edu/csc/mrk.html, 331
Manitoba WorkinfoNET
mb.workinfonet.ca, 280, 286
Manpower
manpower.com, 57–58
Manufacturing Marketplace
manufacturing.net, 156
MapQuest
mapquest.com, 346
MarketingJobs.com
marketingjobs.com, 76
Maryland
http://dop.state.md.us, 184
Maryland Careers
http://members.home.net/marylandcareers, 230
Maryland's CareerNet
careernet.state.md.us, 230231
Maryland's Job Bank
ajb.org/md, 230
Massachusetts
mass.gov, 184
Massachusetts Job Bank
ajb.org/ma, 231
Massachusetts Tech Corps
masstechcorps.org, 233
MaterialsJobs.com
materialsjobs.com, 57
Maui Island Guide
mauimapp.com, 221
mauimapp.com/community/resourcesa.htm, 221
MBNA Career Services Center (CSC), University of
Delaware
udel.edu/csc/students.html, 215
Medford Mail Tribune
mailtribune.com, 252
mailtribune.com/jobnet/index.htm, 252
MedHunters
medhunters.com, 134
MediaWeek
mediamoves.co.uk, 294
mediaweek.co.uk, 294
Medical Device Link
devicelink.com, 147
Medimorphus.com
medimorphus.com, 135
MedZilla
medzilla.com, 120
MEL: Michigan Electronic Library
http://mel.lib.mi.us, 234
http://mel.lib.mi.us/michigan/MI-business.html,
234
http://mel.lib.mi.us/michigan/MI-employment-
html, 234
Memphis Commercial Appeal
gomemphis.com, 261
gomidsouthjobs.com, 261
Mental Health Net
http://mentalhelp.net, 136
Mental Health Net Joblink: Openings
http://mentalhelp.net/joblink, 96
MentorNet
mentornet.net, 141
MetaCrawler
metacrawler.com, 10
METRONET
metronet.lib.mn.us/mn/mn-bizb.html, 235
metronet.lib.mn.us/mn/mn.html, 235
Metropolitan Government of Nashville and
Davidson County
nashville.org, 261
Michigan
state.mi.us/mdcs, 184
Michigan Agriculture Migrant and Seasonal Farm
Worker Program
michaglabor.org/index_agriculture2.jsp,
130

Michigan Department of Career Development (MDCD)
  state.mi.us/career, 234
Michigan Talent Bank
  http://michworks.org, 234
Midwest ComputerWork
  http://midwest.computerwork.com, 223
MidwifeJobs.com from the American College of Nurse-Midwives
  midwifejobs.com, 136
Migrant and Seasonal Farmworkers Sites
  http://wdsc.doleta.gov/msfw/html/msfwlink.asp, 129
Military Career Guide Online, The Defense Manpower Data Center
  militarycareers.com, 179
Military.com
  military.com, 313
Milwaukee Journal Sentinel
  jsonline.com, 272
Mining Journal, The
  mining-journal.com, 159
Mining USA
  mingusa.com, 159
Ministry of Labour, Finland
  mol.fi, 298
MinistryConnect
  ministryConnect.org, 92
MinistryLink: Employment Opportunities in Church Ministry
  csbsju.edu/sot/MinistryLink/Default.htm, 92–93
Minnesota
  doer.state.mn.us, 184
Minnesota Careers 2001
  mncareers.org, 325
Minnesota Workforce Center System
  iseek.org, 235
  mnworkforcecenter.org, 235
  mnworkforcecenter.org/cjs/cjs_site/index.htm, 235
Minnesota's Job Banks
  http://mnworks.org, 234
  ajb.org/mn, 234
Missions Opportunities Database
  globalmission.org/go/htm, 195
Mississippi
  spb.state.ms.us, 185
Mississippi Employment Security Commission (MESC)
  mesc.state.ms.us, 236
Mississippi's Job Bank
  ajb.org/ms, 235
Missouri
  oa.state.mo.us/stjobs.htm, 185
Missouri State Government Web
  oa.state.mo.us/stjobs.htm, 236
  state.mo.us, 236
Missouri WORKS!
  works.state.mo.us, 237
Missouri's Job Bank
  ajb.org/mo, 236
MOLIS (Minority On-Line Information Service)
  http://content.sciencewise.com/molis, 175
Monitor Daily
  monitordaily.com, 70
Monster Australia
  monster.com.au, 302
Monster Canada
  monster.ca, 283
Monster Healthcare
  http://healthcare.monster.com, 135
Monster International
  http://international.monster.com, 278
Monster New Zealand
  monster.co.nz, 305
Monster Work Abroad
  http://international.monster.com, 301
Monster.com
  monster.com, 15, 58, 290
Monster.com's Campus
  campus.monster.com, 190
MonsterHR
  monsterhr.com, 72
Monstermoving.com
  monstermoving.com, 346
MonsterTRAK
  monstertrak.com, 58, 192
Montana
  http://jsd.dli.state.mt.us, 185

Montana Job Service
  http://jsd.dli.state.mt.us, 238
Montana's Job Bank
  ajb.org.mt, 238
Montreal Gazette
  montrealgazette.com, 288
Montreal Page, The
  toutmontreal.com/english/index.html (English), 288
  toutmontreal.com (French), 288
MRI's PrioritySearch.Com
  http://prioritysearch.com, 58
Museum Employment Resource Center
  museum-emplyment.com, 109
Museum Professionals Mailing List
  http://hclist.de/museum/index1.html, 109
Music Library Association (MLA)
  musiclibraryassoc.org, 91
MusicalOnline
  musicalonline.com, 110
My Summers
  mysummers.com, 196
MyFlorida.com
  myflorida.com, 217
  myflorida.com/myflorida/employment/index.html, 217
MyWay.com
  myway.com, 346
  zip2.com, 346

NAACP Diversity Career Fair
  http://naacpjobfair.com, 309
NACE JobWire
  naceweb.org, 96
NACEWeb: The National Association of Colleges and Employers
  naceweb.org, 197
NACORE International, the International Association of Corporate Real Estate Executives
  nacore.com, 75–76
Nashville Area Chamber of Commerce
  nashvillechamber.com, 261
  nashvillejobslink.com, 261
NASW: National Association of Social Workers
  naswdc.org, 97
NASW California Jobs Bulletin
  http://naswca.org/jobbulletin.html, 97
National Association of Asian American Professionals
  naaap.org, 318
National Association of Church Business Administration
  nacba.net, 70
National Association of College and University Business Officers
  nacubo.org, 85
National Association of Insurance Commissioners (NAIC)
  naic.org, 72
National Association of Professional Band Instrument Repair Technicians (NAPBIRT)
  napbirt.org, 160
National Association of Purchasing Management (NAPM)
  napm.org, 75
National Association of State Chief Information Officers
  https://www.nascio.org, 187
  https://www.nascio.org/stateSearch, 201
National Association of Student Personnel Adminstrators
  naspa.org, 86
National Banking and Financial Services Network
  nbn-jobs.com, 67
National Black MBA Association
  nbmbaa.org, 316
National Board of Certified Counselors
  nbcc.org, 327
National Career Development Association
  ncda.org, 327
National Cartoonists Society
  reuben.org, 103
National Chimney Sweep Guild
  ncsg.org, 147
National Civic League, The
  ncl.org, 94
National Directory of Emergency Services
  firejobs.com, 178

National Diversity Newspaper Job Bank
  newsjobs.com, 309
  newsjobs.com/jobs/jobs.html, 116
National Federation of Paralegal Associations
  paralegals.org, 88–89
National Fire Protection Association (NFPA)
  nfpa.org, 178
National Funeral Directors Association (NFDA)
  nfda.org, 107
National Hospice and Palliative Care Organization (NHPCO)
  nhpco.org, 135–36
National Indian Council on Aging
  micoa.org, 319
National Institute for Research Advancement Think Tank Information
  nira.go.jp/ice/index.html, 182
National NurseSearch
  nursesearch.net, 136
National Press Photographers Association
  nppa.org, 112
National School-to-Work Learning and Information Center
  stw.ed.gov, 340
National Society of Professional Engineers (NSPE)
  nspe.org, 141
National Writers Union (NWU) Job Hotline
  nwu.org, 116
NationJob
  nationjob.com, 15
NationJob Network
  nationjob.com, 58
NativeWeb
  nativeweb.org, 319
Nature
  nature.com, 120–21
Naukri
  naukri.com, 303
NCES Global Education Location
  http://nces.ed.gov/globallocator, 337
Nebrask@Online
  nol.org, 239–40
Nebraska
  wrk4neb.org, 185
Nebraska University (NU) Career Services
  unl.edu/careers, 240
Nebraska Workforce Development
  dol.state.ne.us, 240
Nebraska's Job Bank
  ajb.org/ne, 239
Negotiation Clinic, from Salary.com
  salary.com, 31
Net-Temps
  http://net-temps.com, 58
NetNoir
  netnoir.com, 316
Netshare
  netshare.com, 351–52
Networking Do's and Don'ts
  rwn.org/network.html, 30
Nevada
  state.nv.us/personnel, 185
Nevada Department of Employment Training & Rehabilitation (DETR)
  http://detr.state.nv.us, 241
NevadaNet
  nevadanet.com, 241
Nevada's Job Bank
  ajb.org/nv, 240
New Brunswick WorkinfoNET
  nbworkinfonet.ca, 281
New Dimensions in Technology, Inc.
  ndt.com, 169
New England Board of Higher Education (NEBHE)
  nebhe.org, 192
New England ComputerWork
  http://newengland.computerwork.com, 233
New Hampshire
  state.nh.us/das/personnel, 185
New Hampshire Works and Job Bank
  nhworks.state.nh.us, 241
  nhworks.state.nh.us/jobs/jobs.html, 241
New Jersey
  state.nj.us/personnel, 185
New Jersey Home Page
  state.nj.us, 243
New Jersey Online
  nj.com, 243
  nj.com/careers, 243

New Jersey's Job Bank
ajb.org/nj, 242
New Mexico
state.nm.us/spo, 185
New Mexico Department of Labor (DOL)
http://www3.state.nm.us/dol/dol_home.html,
244
http://www3.state.nm.us/dol/nmworks/front
.asp, 244
New Mexico's Job Bank
ajb.org/nm, 244
New Mobility's Interactive CafE ACU
newmobility.com, 16
New Scientist Jobs
newscientistjobs.com, 121
New York
cs.state.ny.us, 185
New York ComputerJobs
newyork.computerjobs.com, 245
New York ComputerWork
http://newyork.computerwork.com, 245
New York State Department of Labor
http://labor.state.ny.us, 245
http://nycareerzone.org, 245
New York Times on the Web
nytimes.com, 245–46
New York's Job Bank
ajb.org/ny, 244
Newfoundland & Labrador WorkinfoNET
gov.nf.ca/nlwin, 281
newmonday.com
newmonday.com, 291, 292–93
News and Observer Classifieds, The
nando.net, 248
newsobserver.com, 248
trianglejobs.com, 248
NewsChoice Online Newspaper Network
newschoice.com/default.asp, 210
Newsday.com
newsday.com, 246
NewsLink JobLink
http://newslink.org/joblink, 116
NewsOK.com
newsok.com, 251–52
nextSteps.org
nextsteps.org, 326
NH.com
nh.com, 242
NIjobs.com
nijobs.com, 292
NISS: National Information Services and Systems
niss.ac.uk, 294
vacancies.ac.uk, 83–84, 294
NJ Jobs
njjobs.com, 243
NOLA Live with the *Times-Picayune*
nola.com, 229
nola.com/careers, 229
Nonprofit Career Network
nonprofitcareer.com, 94
NonProfit Times
nptimes.com, 95
Nonprofitxpress
npxpress.com, 95
North Carolina
osp.state.nc.us, 185
North Carolina's Job Bank
ajb.org/nc, 247
North Dakota
state.nd.us/cpers, 185
North Dakota Education Vacancies
state.nd.us/jsnd/eduction/update.vac.daily.htm,
249
North Dakota's Job Bank
ajb.org/nd, 248
Northwest Territory WorkinfoNET
workinfonet.ca/northwin, 281
Nova Scotia WorkinfoNET
ns.workinfonet.ca, 281
NSC Crossroads, National Safety Council
crossroads.nsc.org, 161
NSCERC Online: National Senior Citizens'
Education and Research Center, Inc
nscerc.org, 310
NTES: National Technical Employment Services
ntes.com, 169
Nursing Spectrum
nursingspectrum.com, 136
NYC.gov: The Official New York City Website
http://home.nyc.gov, 246

O-Hayo Sensei, The Newsletter of (Teaching) Jobs in
Japan
ohaysensei.com, 304
Occuaptional Employment Statistics
bls.gov/oes/, 334
Occupational Outlook Handbook, The
bls.gov.oco/, 330
Occupational Outlook Quarterly
bls.gov/opub/ooq/ooqhome.htm, 330
Offshore Guides
offshoreguides.com, 159
Ohio
state.oh.us/das/dhr/emprec.html, 185
Ohio ComputerJobs
ohio.computerjobs.com, 250
Ohio Department of Job and Family Services
(ODJFS)
state.oh.us/odjfs/index.stm, 250
state.oh.us/odjfs/jobsearch, 250
Ohio Works!
ohioworks.com/prod, 250
Ohio's Job Bank
abj.org.oh, 249
Oil and Gas Online
oilandgasonline.com, 159
Oklahoma
state.ok.us/opm, 185
Oklahoma Employment Security Commisssion
(OESC)/Oklahoma's Job Net
oesc.state.ok.us, 251
oesc.state.ok.us/OKJobNet, 251
Oklahoma's Job
ajob.org/ok, 251
Omaha.com
omaha.com, 240
1800Drivers.com
http://1800drivers.com, 165
O*NET OnLine
http://online.onetcenter.org, 330
Online Hawaii
hcc.hawaii.edu/hspls/hjobs.html, 221
hcc.hawaii.edu/hspls/onlhaw.html, 221
Online Women's Business Center, The
onlinewbc.org, 332
OnlineSports.com Career Center
onlinesports.com/pages/CareerCenter.html,
114
Ontario WorkinfoNET
on.workinfonet.ca, 281, 287
Open System Consultants
opensystem.com, 164
Operissimo
operissimo.com, 110
Opportunities with the U.S. Navy
navyjobs.com, 179–80
Opportunity NOCs.org
opportunitynocs.org, 95
Optics.org
http://optics.org, 161
Orchestralist
orchestralist.org, 111
Oregon
dashr.state.or.us, 185
Oregon Live
oregonlive.com, 253
Oregon OnLine
state.or.us, 253
Organic Chemistry Resources Worldwide
organicworldwide.net, 127
Organizations, from Yahoo!
http://dir.yahoo.com/business_and_economy/
organizations, 341
Osh.Net
osh.net, 161
Outdoor Network, The
http://wwwoutdoornetwork.com, 114
OverseasJobs.com
overseasjobs.com, 278–79
OWL-Online Writing Lab, Purdue University
http://owl.english.purdue.edu, 48
Oya's Directory of Recruiters
i-recruit.com, 356

PA-Today: The Best of Pennsylvania's Newspapers
Online
pa-today.com, 254
PackagingBusiness.com
packagingbusiness.com, 74
PackagingInfo.com
packaginginfo.com, 74

Packinfo-World
packinfo-world.com/WPO, 74
Palo Alto Online
PaloAltoOnline.com, 210
Palo Alto Weekly Online Edition
paweekly.com, 210
Parachute Library for Job Hunters and Career
Changers from JobHuntersBible.com
jobhuntersbible.com/library/hunters/library
.shtml, 326
PDN Online
pdn-pix.com, 112
Peace Corps
peacecorps.gov, 193
Pennsylvania
http://sites.state.pa.us/Internopp/index.html
(internships), 185
http://sites.state.pa.us/jobpost.html, 185
Pennsylvania's Job Bank
ajb.org/pa, 253
PeopleBank: the Employment Network
peoplebank.com, 295
peoplebank.com.au, 302
Personnel Concept, The
personnel-concept.co/za, 300
Peterson's
petersons.com, 337
Petroleum Place
petroleumplace.com, 160
Pharmacy Week
pharmacyweek.com, 137
Philadelphia ComputerJobs
philadelphia.computerjobs.com, 255
Philadelphia Online/Philly Jobs
http://careers.philly.com, 243, 255
philly.com, 243, 255
PHILA.GOV
phila.gov, 254
phila.gov/departments/personnel/announce/
current/index.htm, 254
Philanthropy News Digest from the Foundation
Center
http://fdncenter.org/pnd/current/index.html,
96
Philanthropy News Network
http://ppnonline.org, 96
PhillyBurbs.com
phillyburbs.com, 255
phillyburbs.com/jobsearch/home.html, 255
PhillyJobs.com
phillyjobs.com, 255
PhillyWorks
phillyworks.com, 255–56
Phoenix Computer Jobs
phoenix.computerjobs.com, 206
Photonics Jobs
photonicsjobs.com, 161–62
Physicians Employment
physemp.com, 135
PhysicsWeb
http://physicsweb.org, 132
PhysLink
physlink.com, 132
Pilot Online
pilotonline.com, 267
PlanetRecruit.com's International Channel
planetrecruit.com, 279
Planning and Paying for School from Sallie Mae
salliemae.com/planning/index.html, 335
Platts Global Energy
platts.com, 163
Playbill
playbill.com, 102
PLUMBjob.com
plumbjob.com, 162
Portfolio Library by Martin Kimeldorf
http://amby.com/kimeldorf/portfolio/, 48
Portland Metropolitan Chamber of Commerce
pdxchamber.org, 253
portlandchamber.com/jobbank, 253
Positions in Christian Higher Education
cccu.org/jobs, 84
Positions in Weed Science (WeedJobs)
nrcan.gc.ca/bcampbel, 123
Positionw@tch Internet Recruitment
postionwatch.com, 283
Post-Docs.com
post-docs.com, 121
PowerMarketers.com
powermarketers.com, 163

PPA's Photcentral
ppa.com, 112
Prince Edward Island WorkinfoNET
gov.pe.ca/infopei/Employment/index.php3, 281
Prince George Public Library
lib.pg.bc.ca, 286
Princeton Review Online: Career
review.com/career/index.cfm, 331–32
Pro/E Job Network
pejn.com, 158
Processfood.com
processfood.com, 153
Professional Brewers' Page
http://probrewer.com, 153
Professional Convention Management Association
pcma.org, 73
Professional Lawn Care Association of America
plcaa.org, 23
Professionals for Nonprofits, Inc.
nonprofit-staffing.com, 95
ProGayJobs.com
progayjobs.com, 320
Project America Home Page
http://project.org, 196
Project Vote Smart
vote-smart.org, 194
Projo.com
projo.com, 257
Prospective Management Overseas (PMO) Vacant
Positions Overseas
http://pmo.be, 291
Public Health Resources on the Internet
lib.berkeley.edu/publ/internet.html, 138
Public Library of Charlotte and Mecklenburg
County
bizlink.org, 248
Public Relations Society of America (PRSA) Career
Resources
http://prsa.org/career, 69
Public Service Commission of Canada
http://jobs.gc.ca, 283
PublicWorks.com
publicworks.com, 150
Publishers Weekly
http://publishersweekly.reviewsnews.com,
113
Puerto Rico Clasificados Online
clasificadosonline.com, 256
Puerto Rico Trade Virtual Center
http://camcon.bc.inter.edu/index.html, 256
Purdue University Center for Career
Opportunities
cco.purdue.edu/student/jobsites.htm, 62

Quebec WorkinfoNET
qc.info-emploi.ca/english/main.cfm (English),
281, 288
qc.info-emploi.ca (French), 281, 288
QuoteJobs.nl
quotejobs.nl, 293

RAND
rand.org, 182
Randstad North America
us.randstad.com/index.html, 59
RCJobs from Roll Call
rcjobs.com, 177
Real Estate Job Store
realestatejobstore.com, 76
Realtor.com
realtor.com, 346
Rebecca Smith's eRsumes & Resources
eresumes.com, 47
Recruiters by Industry from Myjobsearch.com
myjobsearch.com/cig-
bin/mjs.cgi/recruiters.html, 356
Recruiters Online Network
recruitersonline.com, 356–57
Recruiter's Online Network
recruitersonline.com, 59
Recruiting & Search Report
rsonline.com, 357
Reed Personnel Services
http://ww.reed.co.uk, 295
RehabTime.com
rehabtime.com, 137
Research and References Gateway: Research
Guides: Business
libraries.rutgers.edu/rul/rr_gateway/research_
guides/busi/business.shtml, 343

Research Guides, Melvin Gelman Library, George
Washington University
gwu.edu/gelman/guides, 8
Researching Companies Online
http://home.sprintmail.com/debflanagan/index
.html, 344
Réseau Européen pour L'Emploi
reseau.org/emploi, 291
Resort Jobs
resortjobs.com, 109
Resumania
resumania.com, 48
Resume Place, The
resume-place.com, 47–48, 175
RHI Management Resources
rhimr.com, 67
Rhode Island
det.state.ri.us, 186
Rhode Island Department of Labor and Training
(RIDLT)
det.state.ri.us, 257–58
Rhode Island's Job Bank
ajb.org/ri, 257
Right of Way
rightofway.com, 150
Riley Guide, The
rileyguide/employer.html, 16
rileyguide.com, 9, 13, 15, 62
RiteSite.com
ritesite.com, 357
Robert Half Financial Recruitng
roberthalf.com, 68
RochesterCareers.com
rochestercareers.com, 246
Rollins Search Group
rollinssearch.com, 68, 73
Rothrock Associates, Inc. (RAI)
raijobs.com, 156
RRonline.com
rronline.com, 115
Russia and East European Institute Employment
Opportunities
indiana.edu/reeiweb/indemp.html, 297
Russia Donors Forum
donorsforum.ru/donorsforum/news.nsf, 297
Russian and Eastern European Internship
Opportunities for REEIWeb
indiana.edu/reeiweb/indemp.html, 192
Russian International Job Agency
job.ru/start.htm, 297
Rutgers Accounting Web (RAW)
http://accounting.rutgers.edu/raw, 68
RWM Vocational School Database
rwm.org/rwm, 339

Sacramento Bee, The
sacbee.com, 211
sacbee.com/ib/careers, 211
Safestyle.com
safestyle.com, 161
Sailor: Maryland's Online Public Information
Network
sailor.lib.md.us, 231
St. Louis, Missouri, Community Information
Network (CIN)
http://stlcin.missouri.org/citypers/jobs.cfm,
237
http://stlouis.missouri.org, 237
St. Louis ComputerJobs
stlouis.computerjobs.com, 237
St. Louis Employment Links
http://members.tripod.com/Jablon/assess.html,
237
Salary.com
salary.com, 342–43
SalaryExpert.com
salaryexpert.com, 343
Saludos.com
saludos.com, 59, 317
SaludosWeb
saudos.com, 15
San Bernardino County Employment
Opportunities
co.san-bernardino.ca.us/hr/jobs/mainjobs.htm,
211
San Francisco Bay Area Volunteer Information
Center
volunteerinfo.org, 211
San Francisco Cityspan Information Center
ci.sf.ca.us/info.htm, 211

San Jose Mercury
http://careers.bayarea.com, 211–12
Saskatchewan WorkinfoNET
sasknetwork.gov.sk.ca, 281
Scholarly Societies Project
scholarly-societies.org, 9, 342
Science Careers
http://recruit.sciencemag.org, 121
Sciencejobs.com
sciencejobs.com, 121
SCIway...the South Carolina Information Highway
sciway.net, 258–59
sciway.net/jobs, 258–59
Scopists.com
scopists.com, 98
Scout Report, The
http://scout.cs.wisc.edu, 8
Seafarers International Union
seafarers.org, 156–57
Seasonal Employment
seasonalemployment.com, 196–97
Seattle Community Network
scn.org, 269
Seattle Times
http://classifieds.nwsource.com/job, 269
nwsource.com, 269
seattletimes.com, 269
Security Jobs Network
http://securityjobs.net, 178
Semiconbay.com
semiconbay.com, 164
Senior Job Bank
seniorjobbank.com, 310
SF Gate
sfgate.com, 212
Sheridan College Career Centre
sheridanc.on.ca/career, 287
Shoals Times Daily
timesdaily.com, 203
timesdaily.com/classified/classif2.htm, 203
Shoemaking.com
shoemaking.com, 154
ShowBizjobs.com
showbizjobs.com, 102
Silicon Alley Connections
salley.com, 107
Silicon Valley ComputerJobs
siliconvalley.computerjobs.com, 212
Singapore Economic Development Board
sedb.com, 305
Sioux Falls Chamber of Commerce
siouxfalls.com, 259–60
SIS: Seminar Information Service
seminarinformation.com, 340
Sistahs in Science
mtholyoke.edu/courses/sbrowne/sistahs/fina/
index.html, 193
6FigureJobs.com
6figurejobs.com, 354–55
SkiingtheNet
skiingthenet.com, 114
SLED:Alaska's Statewide Library Electronic
Doorway
http://sled.alaska.edu, 205
Small and Home-Based Business Links
bizoffice.com, 332
SmartPlanet
zdnet.com/smartplanet, 341
Snelling Personnel Services
snelling.com, 59
Social Work and Social Services Jobs Online
http://gwbweb.wustl.edu/jobs, 97
Socialservice.com
http://socialservice.com, 97
Society for Human Resource Management
(SHRM)
shrm.org/jobs, 72
Society for Industrial and Organizational
Psychology, The
http://siop.org, 97
Society for Technical Communications
stc.org, 117
Society of Automotive Engineers, The
sae.org, 145
SoftwareJobs.com Home Page
softwarejobs.com, 169
SolidWorks Job Network
swjn.com, 158
South Carolina
state.sc.us/jobs, 186

South Carolina Employment Security Commission
sces.org, 259
South Carolina's Job Bank
ajb.org/sc, 258
South Dakota
state.sd.us.bop/jobs/htm, 186
South Dakota Department of Labor
state.sd.us/dol/dol/htm, 260
South Dakota Popular Internet Places
http://sodapop.dsu.edu, 260
South Dakota's Job Bank
ajb.org.sd, 259
Space Careers
spacelinks.com/SpaceCareers, 143
Space Jobs
spacejobs.com, 143
SpencerStuart.com
spencerstuart.com, 353
SpokaneNet
spokane.net, 269
Sporting Goods Manufacturers Association
(SGMA)
sgma.com, 115
Stagebill
stagebill.com/index.html, 102
Star/News Online
starnews.com, 225
Star Tribune WorkAvenue
startribune.com/workavenue, 235
StarChefs
starchefs.com, 104
Starpoint Solutions
http://starpoint.com, 169
Starting Your Business from the Small Business
Adminstration
sba.gov/starting, 332–33
Startup Journal
http://startupjournal.com, 333
State and Local Government on the Net
statelocalgov.net, 187, 201–2, 346
State Journal-Register Online
sj-r.com, 224
State Occupational Projections 1998-2008
http://almis.dws.state.ut.us/occ/projections.asp,
334
State of Colorado Employment
state.co.us/jobinfo.html, 213
State of Mississippi
state.ms.us, 236
State of Ohio Government
ohio.gov, 250–51
State of South Carolina Public Information Home
Page
myscgov.com, 259
State of Texas Home Page
state.tx.us, 263
texas.gov, 263
State of Vermont Home Page
state.vt.us, 266
State of West Virginia Home Page
state.wv.us, 271
State of Wisconsin Information Server
wisconsin.gov, 272
State Web Locator from the Center for Information
Law and Policy
infoctr.edu/SWL, 187
StepStone
swisswebjobs.ch/sok, 293
Stlouisatwork.com
stlouisatwork.com, 237
STLtoday.com
stltoday.com, 237–38
stltoday.com/jobs, 237–38
Strategis
http://strategis.gc.ca, 283
Student Development Centre
sdc.uwo.ca/career, 287
Student Guide to Financial Aid, The
ed.gov/prog_info/SFA/StudentGuide, 335
Studentjobs.gov
studentjobs.gov, 175–76, 194
Studyabroad.com
studyabroad.com, 193
Summer Jobs
summerjobs.com, 197
SunOasis Jobs
sunoasis.com, 117
SunSpot.net from *Baltimore Sun*
sunspot.net, 231231

SuperPages.com
superpages.com, 16, 347
Susan Ireland
susanireland.com, 47
SWE: The Society of Women Engineers
swe.org, 142
Swearer Center for Public Service at Brown
University
brown.edu/Departments/Swearer_Center, 258
brown.edu/Departments/Swearer_Center/publi
cations/ricomjobjoin.shtml, 258
Swedish Employment Service
ams.se, 299
Sydney Morning Herald
http://mycareer.com.au, 303
smh.com.au, 303
Syracuse.com
syracuse.com, 246

TABS: Association of Boarding Schools
schools.com, 86
Tallahassee Free-net
freenet.tlh.fl.us, 217
Tango! from the *Telegram & Gazette*
telegram.com, 233
TateWeb Optoelectronics Portal
tateweb.com, 162
Tax-Jobs.Com
tax-jobs.com, 68
Teach for America
teachforamerica.org, 87, 195
Teacher Job Links
geocities.com/Athens/Forum/2080, 86
Team Pennsylvania
pacareerlink.stat.pa.us, 256
teampa.com, 256
Tech/Aid
techaid.com, 142
TechEmployment.com
techemployment.com, 142
techies.com
techies.com, 169
Telegraph, The on the Web
nashuatelegraph.com, 242
TeleJob
telejob.ethz.ch, 293
Television and Radio News Research
http://web.missouri.edu/jourvs, 115
Tennessee
state.tn.us/personnel, 186
Tennessee Department of Employment Security
(DES)
stat.tn.us/labor-wfd/esdiv.html, 261
Tennessee Today
tntoday.com, 262
Tennessee's Job Bank
ajb.org/tn, 260
Test Your IQ, Personality, or Entrepreneurial Skills
on the Web
2h.com, 329
Texas
twc.state.tx.us/jobs/gvjb/gvjb.html, 186
Texas ComputerJobs
texas.computerjobs.com, 264
Texas ComputerWork
http://texas.computerwork, 264
Texas Workforce Commission
twc.state.tx.us, 264
Texas's Job Bank
ajb.org/tx/, 262
THES: The *Times* Higher Education Supplement
jobs.thes.co.uk, 295–96
thesis.co.uk, 84, 295–96
ThinQ E-Catalog
thinq.com, 341
ThirdAge
thirdage.com, 310
Thomas Mining Associates
thomasmining.com, 160
Three Rivers Free-Net
http://trfn.clpgh.org, 256
3DSite.com
3dsite.com, 107
Top Echelon
topechelon.com, 59
Top Jobs on the Internet
topjobs.net, 279
Topeka Capital-Journal
cjonlin.com/jobetcher, 227

Topica
topica.com, 22
Toronto Free-Net, Inc.
freenet.toronto.on.ca, 287
Toronto Star
http://thestar.workopolis.com, 287–88
Town Online
townonline.com, 233
townonline.com/working, 233
Trabajo.org
trabajo.org, 291
Transition Assistance Online
tao.com, 313
TransportNews.com
transportnews.com, 165
Tribal Employment Newsletter, The
nativejobs.com, 319
TRIBnet
southsoundjobs.com, 270
tribnet.com, 270
Troops for Teachers
http://voled.doded.mil/dantes/ttt, 87
TWC Job Express
twc.state.tx.us/jobs.jobx/express.html,
264
200 Free Cover Letters for Job Seekers
careerlab.com/letters, 48

UG Job Network
ugjn.com, 158
UK Theatre Web
uktw.co.uk, 102–3
Union Jobs Clearinghouse
unionjobs, 166
Union Resource Network
unions.org, 342
U. S. Air Force
airforce.com, 180
U. S. Army Recruiting Home Page
goarmy.com, 180
U. S. Coast Guard
uscg.mil, 180
U. S. Newspapers
usnewspaperlinks.com, 345
United States-Mexico Chamber of Commerce
usmcoc.org, 289
U.S. Marines
marines.com, 180
University of Delaware Access to Internet and
Subject Resources
http://www2.lib.udel.edu/subj/, 8
University of Waterloo Career Services Career
Development Manual
careerservices.uwaterloo.ca/manual-home.html,
326
University of Waterloo Creer Services
careerservices.uwaterloo.ca/, 288
Update Graphics
updategraphics.com, 08
Update Legal Staffing
updatelegal.com, 89
US Pastry Alliance
uspastry.org, 105
USA CityLink
http://usacitylink.com, 347
USAJobs
usajobs.opm.gov, 176
USA.Net
usa.net, 21
Use Your Military Experience and Training
http://umet-vets.dol.gov, 313
USNews.com: Education
usnews.com/usnews/edu/eduhome.htm,
325
USNews.com: Financial Aid
usnews.com/usnews/edu/dollars/dshome.htm,
335
Utah
dhrm.state.ut.us, 186
Utah Department of Workforce Services: Utah's
Job Connection
dws.stat.ut.us, 265
Utah's Job Bank
ajb.org/ut, 264

Vancouver CommunityNet
vcn.bc.ca, 286
Vault.com@ME:
vault.com, 13, 344

Verbatim Reporters Center
verbatimreporters.com, 98
Vermont
state.vt.us/pers, 186
Vermont's Job Bank
ajb.org/vt, 265
VeterinaryLife.com
http://veterinarylife.com, 133
VetJobs.com
vetjobs.com, 313–14
VetQuest
vetquest.com, 133
Virginia
dpt.state.va.us, 186
Virginia ComputerWork
http://virginia.computerwork.com, 268
Virginia Employment Commisssion
vec.state.va.us, 268
vec.state.va.us/seeker/listing.htm, 268
Virginia's Job Bank
ajb.org/va, 266
Voice of Dance
voiceofdance.com, 105
Volt Services Group
volt.com, 170
VolunteerMatch
volunteermatch.org, 195

Wall Street Research Net
wsrn.com, 13
Wang & Li Asia Resources
wang-li.com, 303
WantedJobs
wantedjobs.com, 60
WardsAuto.com
wardsauto.com, 146
Washington
http://hr.dop.wa.gov, 186
Washington, DC. See District of Columbia
Washington, DC, Computerwork
http://dc.computerwork.com, 216
Washington Intern Foundation
http://interns.org, 194
Washington Post, The
washingtonpost.com, 216, 268
Washington's Job Bank
ajb.org/wa, 268
Web U.S. Higher Educatiaon
utexas.edu/world/univ, 337–38
Webcrawler
webcrawler.com, 10
WEBSTER: the New Hampshire State Government
Online Information Center
state.nh.us, 242
WeedJobs
nrcan.gc.ca/bcampbel, 123
Welcome to Oregon
el.com/to/oregon, 253
WEPA!
wepa.com, 257
West Virginia
state.wv.us/admin/personel, 186

West Virginia Jobs
wvjobs.org, 271
West Virginia's Job Bank
ajb.org/wv, 270
Western New York Jobs (WYNJOBS)
wynjobs.com, 247
WetFeet.com
wetfeet.com, 13, 344
White House Fellowships, The
whitehousefellows.gov, 194
Wichita Area Chamber of Commerce
http://wichitakansas.org/wichitanationjob/index
.html, 227
wichitakansas.org, 227
Winejobs from WineBusiness.com
winebusiness.com/services/industry/jobs.cfm,
153
Winnipeg Free Press Online
winnipegfreepress.com/news/index.html, 286
Winter, Wyman, and Co.
winterwyman.com/boston/index.asp, 60
Wireless Week
wirelessweek.com, 165
Wisconsin
http://jobs.der.state.wi.us/static, 186
Wisconsin Department of Workforce Development
(DWD)
dwd.state.wi.us, 272
dwd.state.wi.us/jobnet, 272
Wisconsin's Job Bank
ajb.org/wi, 271
WNYWired.net
wnywired.net, 247
Womans-Work
womans-work.com, 311
Women in Higher Education
wihe.com, 84
Women in Technology International (WITI)
witi.com, 171, 311
Women's Wear Daily Classified Ads
http://wwd.com/classified/wwdads.htm, 106
WomensFinance
womensfinance.com, 311
WorkBasePA (Palo Alto)
workbase.com/palo_alto/index.html, 212
Workforce Excellence: Community Assistance
Network (WE CAN)
onestop.org/homepage.htm, 207
Workforce Florida
wages.org/wages/wfi/index.html, 217
Workforce New Jersey Public Information Network
(WNJPIN)
wnjpin.state.nj.us, 244
Workforce Transition Program from CWA/NETT
cwanett.org/military.asp, 314
Working in Manitoba
gov.mb.ca/working.html, 286
Working in Oregon/Orgegon Jobs
emp.state.or.us, 252
state.or.us/emplsvcs, 252
Working in Utah
state.ut.us/working/employment.html, 265

Workopolis.com
workopolis.com, 283
Workplace Alaska
http://notes.state.ak.us/wa/mainentry.nsf/?Open
Database, 205
Workplace connect
workplaceconnect.org.au, 303
WorkSearch/ProjetEmploi
http://worksearch.gc.ca, 283–84
WorkSource Washington
http://work.wa.gov, 270
WorldatWork
worldatwork.org, 72
Write Jobs from the Writers Write, The
writerswrite.com/jobs/jobs/htm, 117
WWAR: World Wide Arts Resources
http://wwar.com, 101
WWWomen
wwwomen.com, 312
Wyoming
http://personnel.state.wy.us, 186
Wyoming Job Network
onestop.state.wy.us, 273
Wyoming Works
http://wydoe.state.wy.us, 273
Wyoming's Job Bank
ajb.org/wy, 273

Xlation.com, Resources for Translation
Professionals
xlation.com, 92

Yahoo!
yahoo.com, 16, 279
yahoo.com/Regional/U_S_Metros, 202
Yahoo! Careers
http://careers.yahoo.com, 60
Yahoo! Colleges and Universities
http://dir.yahoo.com/eduction/higher_eduction/
colleges_and_universities/index.html, 338
Yahoo! Employment and Work
http://dir.yahoo.com/business_and_economy/
employment_and_work, 62
Yahoo! Groups
http://groups.yahoo.com, 22
Yahoo! Mail
mail.yahoo.com, 21
Yahoo! Orchestra
http://dir.yahoo.com/Entertainment/Music/
Artists/By_Genre/Classical/Orchestras,
111
Youth Employment Information
youth.gc.ca, 284
Youth Resources Network of Canada
youth.gc.ca, 190
Yukon WorkinfoNET
yuwin.ca/english/index.cfm, 281

ZDNet Careers
zdnet.com/special/filters/techjobs, 170
Zoo and Aquarium Employment Listings
http://resource.aza.org/positions, 125

Subject Index

Aboriginal women, 319
Accounting, 64–68
Acting, 101–3
Actuaries, 68
Administrators, school, 86–87
Advertising, 68–69
Aeronautics/aerospace, 142–43
Africa, 299–300
African-Americans, 315–16
Agre, Phil, 20
Agriculture, 122–24
Alabama, 183, 202–3
Alaska, 183, 204–5
Alberta, 284–85
Animal sciences, 124–25
Anthropology, 80
Arbitration, 80
Archaeology, 80–81
Architecture, 143–45
Arizona, 183, 206
Arkansas, 183, 206–7
Armed services, U.S., 179–80
Arts, general sources for, 100–101
Asia, 300–305
Asian-Americans, 318
Associations, professional or trade, 93–96, 341–42
Astronomy, 125–26
Australia, 301–3
Austria, 292
Automation equipment, 155
Automotive, 145–46
Aviation, 146

Baker, Wayne E., 18
Baroudi, Carol, 22
Belgium, 290–91
Beverage processing, 152–53
Biology, 126
Biomedical engineering, 147
Biotechnology, 147
Blasting services, resume, 45–46
Bolles, Richard Nelson, 5, 18, 24, 29, 46
Britain. See United Kingdom
British Columbia, 285–86
Broadcast media, 115–17
Browsing, 6, 7–9
Business starting points, 64

CAD/CAM skills, 158
California, 183, 207–12
Call centers, 70
Camera repair, 147
Canada, 280–88
Capitol Hill jobs, 176–77
Career Change: Everything You Need to Know to Meet
    New Challenges and Take Control of Your Career
    (Helfand), 5
Career counseling, 326–27
Career counselors, 5
Career exploration, 329–32
Career planning
    lifelong, 324–47
    processes for, 325–26
CareerXRoads (Crispin and Mehler), 29
Cartooning, 103
Certification opportunities, 340–41
Chemistry, 126–27
Child care, 103
Chimney sweeps, 147
China, 303
"Choosing a Job Site" (Joyce), 42
Christian career opportunities, 321
Church business administration, 70
Civil engineering, 148
Co-ops, 191–93

College and university administration, 85–86
College and university directories, 336–38
College and university positions, 82–84
Colorado, 183, 212–13
Communication, 68–69
Compensation information, 342–43
    executive, 357–59
Complete Idiot's Guide to Cool Jobs for Teens, The
    (Ireland), 29
Complete Idiot's Guide to the Internet, The (Kent), 22
Complete Idiot's Guide to the Perfect Cover Letter,
    The (Ireland), 47
Complete Idiot's Guide to the Perfect Resume, The,
    (Ireland), 47
Computer-aided design (CAD), 158
Computer-aided manufacturing (CAM), 158
Computing, 166–71
Connecticut, 183, 213
Construction, 148–50
Control systems, 155
Cool Careers for Dummies (Nemko and Edwards), 5
Copying and pasting resumes, 37
Counseling, 96–97. See also Career counseling
Court reporters, 98
Cover letters, 36
Cover Letters for Dummies (Kennedy), 47
Creating Your High School Resume (Troutman), 47
Criminal justice, 177–78
Criscito, Pat, 46
Crispin, Gerry, 29
Culinary and baking arts, 103–5
Customer relations, 70
Cutting and pasting, privacy and, 37
Czechoslovakia, 296

Damn Good Resume Guide, The (Parker), 47
Dance, 105
Defense industry, 179
Delaware, 183, 213–15
Denmark, 298
Dentistry, 135
Directory of Freenets and Community Networks
    (Scott), 284
Disabled workers, 314–15
Disadvantaged workers, 309–10
Discussion groups, 21–23
Discussion Lists: Mail List Manager Commands
    (Milles), 22
Distance education, 338–39
District of Columbia, 183, 215–16
Diverse audiences, 308–21
Dixon, Pam, 29
Drilling, 158–60

E-resumes. See Electronic resumes (E-resumes)
Earth science, 127–29
Eastern Europe, 296–97
Economics, 81
Education and academe, 82–87
Education and training resources, 336
Education options, 339–40
Edwards, Paul, 5
Edwards, Sarah, 5
Elder care, 103
Electrical engineering, 150–51
Electronic Federal Resume Guidebook (Troutman), 47
Electronic mail (E-mail), common mistakes with,
    17
Electronic Resumes and Online Networking (Smith),
    47
Electronic resumes (E-resumes). See also Resumes
    blasting services for, 45–46
    considerations before sending, 44–45
    copying and pasting, 37
    criteria when sending, 41–44

HTML versions, 35–36
    myth about, 34–35
    preparing plain-text, 38–41
    responding with, 36–37
    using forms for, 37
E-mail. See Electronic mail (E-mail)
Emergency services, 178
Employer preferences, 4
Employer research, 343–44
Employers, finding information on, 11–14
Engineering
    biomedical, 147
    civil, 148
    electrical, 150–51
    facilities, 151–52
    mechanical, 157–58
England. See United Kingdom
English as Second or Foreign Language (ESL/EFL),
    87
Entertainment, 101–3
Entomology, 129
Entry-level positions, 190
Environmental engineering. See Earth science;
    Environmental science; Geographic
    information systems (GIS)
Environmental science, 127–29
Equipment leasing, 70
Europe, 289–99
Event management, 73
Executive compensation information, 357–59
Executive job searching, 350–59
Executive search firms, 352–57

Facilities maintenance, 151–52
FAQs. See Frequently Asked Questions (FAQs)
Farm workers, 129–30
Fashion and beauty, 105–6
Federal government, 174–76
Federal Resume Guidebook, The (Troutman), 47
Finance, 64–68
Financial aid, 334–35
Finishing, 152
Finland, 298
Fire services, 178
Fisheries, 124–25
Flaming, 20
Florida, 184, 216–17
Fluid dynamics, 152
Food processing, 152–53
Footware, 154
Forensics, 130–31
Forestry, 122–24
Foundations, 93–96
France, 290–91
Frank, William S., 47
Freenets, 284
Frequently Asked Questions (FAQs), 10–11, 20
Funeral directors, 107

Gaming, 108
Gays, 320
Geographic information systems (GIS), 131
Georgia, 184, 217–19
Germany, 292
GIS. See Geographic information systems (GIS)
Global Resume and CV Guide, The (Thompson), 47
Government-sponsored student work
    opportunities, 193–94
Graphics, 107–8
Great Britain. See United Kingdom
Guam, 219–20
Gurney, Darrell, 29

Halpern, Nancy, 20
Hawaii, 184, 220–21

Headhunters Revealed! Career Secrets for Choosing and Using Professional Recruiters! (Gurney), 29
Health care, general resources, 133–35
Health sciences, general resources, 120–21
Heating/ventilating/air-conditioning (HVAC), 154
Helfand, David P., 5
Hiring halls, union, 165–66
Hiring trends, 333–34
Hispanic-Americans, 316–17
Holland, 292–93
Hong Kong, 304
Hospice care, 135–36
Hospitality, 108–9
House painting, 154
HTML resumes, 35–36
Human resources, 71–72
Humanities, general sources for, 100
HVAC. *See* Heating/ventilating/air-conditioning (HVAC)

Idaho, 184, 221
Identity, protecting, 16, 37
Illinois, 184, 222–24
India, 303
Indiana, 184, 224–25
Industrial design, 155
Industrial hygiene, 160–61
Industry trends, 333–34
Instrumentation, 155
Insurance, 72–73
International opportunities, 276–305
Internet directories, 7–8
Internet for Dummies, The (Levine, Baroudi, and Young), 22
Internet resumes. *See* Electronic resumes (E-resumes)
Internet Resumes (Weddle), 47
Internships, 191–93
    political, 193–94
Interviewing, resources for, 30
Iowa, 184, 225–26
Ireland, 292. *See also* United Kingdom
Ireland, Susan, 29, 37, 47
Israel, 300
Italy, 290–91

Japan, 304
Jewish career opportunities, 321
Job banks, online, 5
Job-Hunting on the Internet (Bolles), 24, 29
Job lead banks, 50–62
Job listings, 14–16
    evaluating, 24–27
Job offers, evaluating, 31
Job search activities, offline vs. online, 2
Job-search support groups, 31–32
Journalism, 115–17
Joyce, Susan, 37, 41–42, 45
Judiciary jobs, 88–89

K–12 teaching and administration, 86–87
Kansas, 184, 226–27
Kennedy, Joyce Lain, 18, 47
Kent, Peter, 22
Kentucky, 184, 227–28
Keywords, 5
Korea, 304
Kramer, Marc, 18

Landscaping, 122–24
Latin America, 288–89
Law, 88–89
Law enforcement, 177–78
Lesbians, 320
Levine, John R., 22
Librarians, 5
Library and information sciences, 89–91
Linguistics, 92
Listprocs, 21
Listservs, 21
Local governments, 182–87
Local resources, 200–273
Location, 4
Logistics, 155
Louisiana, 184, 228–29

Mailing lists, 21–23
    evaluating, 24

Maine, 184, 229–30
Majordomos, 21
Malaysia, 304
Manitoba, 286
Manufacturing, 155–56
Marine sciences, 124–25
Maritime, 156–57
Marketing, 76
Marler, Patty, 18
Maryland, 184, 230–31
Massachusetts, 184, 231–33
Massage therapy field, 137
Materials, 157
Mathematics, 157
Mattia, Jan Bailey, 18
Mechanical engineering, 157–58
Medicine, general resources, 120–21, 133–35
Meeting management, 73
Mehler, Mark, 29
Mental health, 136
Metacrawlers, 10
Metallurgy, 157
Meteorology, 132
Michigan, 184, 234
Middle East, 300
Midwifery, 136
Military industry, 179
Military personnel, transitioning, 312–14
Milles, Jim, 22
Mining, 158–60
Ministry, 92–93
Minnesota, 184, 234–35
Miscellaneous opportunities, 195–97
Mississippi, 185, 235–36
Missouri, 185, 236–38
Montana, 185, 238
Multimedia, 107–8
Museums and archives, 109
Music, 110–11
Musical instrument repair, 160

Native Americans, 318–19
Natural sciences, general resources, 120–21
Nebraska, 185, 239–40
Nemko, Marty, 5
Netherlands, 292–93
Netiquette, 19–21
Networking, 18–19
Networking, resources for, 30
Networking for Everyone: Connecting with People for Career and Job Success (Tullier), 18
Networking Made Easy (Marler and Mattia), 18
Networking Smart: How to Build Relationships for Personal and Organizational Success (Baker), 18
Nevada, 185, 240–41
New Hampshire, 185, 241–42
New Jersey, 185, 242–44
New Mexico, 185, 244
New York, 185, 244–47
New Zealand, 304–5
Nonprofits, associations, and foundations, 93–96
North Carolina, 185, 247–48
North Dakota, 185, 248–49
Nursing, 136

Occupational safety, 160–61
Occupational therapy field, 137
Occupations, 4
Office support services, 73
Offline job search activities, 2–3
Offshore employment, 158–60
Ohio, 185, 249–51
Oklahoma, 185, 251–52
Older workers, 309–10
Online business directories, 13
Online guides to the job hunt, 60–62
Online job banks, 5
Online job search activities, 2–3
    advantages of, 3–4
    common mistakes in, 16–18
    preparing for, 4–5
    resources for, 29–30
    suggested readings for, 28–29
    time management for, 27–28
Online networking, 18–19

Online recruiting sites and services, 50–60
Online resource guides, 8–9, 13
Online resumes. *See* Electronic resumes (E-resumes)
Ontario, 287–88
Optics, 161–62
Oregon, 185, 252–53

Pacific Rim, 300–305
Packaging, 74
Paralegal jobs, 88–89
Parker, Yana, 47
Pennsylvania, 185, 253–56
Pharmaceutical industry, 137
Philosophy, 111
Photography and photojournalism, 112
Photonics, 161–62
Physical therapy field, 137
Physics, 132
Plain-text resumes, preparing, 38–41
Plumbing, 162
Political internships, 193–94
Power Networking: Using the Contacts You Don't Even Know You Have to Succeed in the Job You Want (Kramer), 18
Privacy, 16, 37
Professional associations, 341–42
Protective services, 178
Psychology, 96–97
Public administration, 180–81
Public health, 138
Public policy institutions, 181–82
Public relations, 68–69
Public utilities, 162–63
Public works, 148–50
Publishing, printing, and bookbinding, 112–13
Puerto Rico, 256–57
Purchasing and procurement, 74–85

Quality control, 75
Quebec, 288

Real estate, 75–76
Recreation, 113–15
Recruiting firms, 352–57
Religious-affiliated careers, 321
Relocation, 75–76
Relocation research, 344–47
Research, 11–14
Resume-distribution services, 45–46
Resumes. *See also* Electronic resumes (E-resumes)
    HTML versions, 35–36
    posting online, 23–24
Resumes in Cyberspace: Your Complete Guide to a Computerized Job Search (Criscito), 46
Rhode Island, 186, 257–58
Rinaldi, Arlene H., 21
Russia, 296

Salary information, 342–43
Sales, 76
Scandinavian countries, 298–99
Scotland, 293. *See also* United Kingdom
Scott, Peter, 284
Search engines, 9–10, 13–14
Search firms, 352–57
Searching, 7, 8–11
Seasonal work, 195–97
Self-assessment, 328–29
Self-employment, 332–33
Semiconductors, 164
Seminars, 340–41
Short courses, 340–41
Singapore, 305
Skills, 4
Smith, Rebecca, 47
Social work, 97
South Africa, 299–300
South America, 288–89
South Carolina, 186, 258–59
South Dakota, 186, 259–60
Spain, 290–91
Sports, 113–15
State governments, 182–87
State resources, 200–273
Student work opportunities, government-sponsored, 193–94

Study abroad programs, 191–93
Summer work, 195–97
Surveying, 164
Switzerland, 293

Teachers
    K–12, 86–87
    recruiting, 87
Technical schools, 339
Telecommunications, 164–65
Tennes*See*, 186, 260–62
Texas, 186, 262–64
Thailand, 305
Thompson, Mary Anne, 47
Time management, for online job searches,
    27–28
Trade associations, 341–42
Training/development, 77
Training options, 339–40
Training resources, 336

Transportation, 165
Troutman, Kathryn Kraemer, 47
Trucking, 165
Tullier, L. Michelle, 18
200 Letters for Job Hunters (Frank), 47

Uniform resource locators (URLs), 11
Union hiring halls, 165–66
United Kingdom, 293–96. *See also* Ireland
United States. *See* Local resources; individual
    states
Universities. *See* College and university
Urban planning, 143–45
URLs. *See* Uniform resource locators (URLs)
Utah, 186, 264–65

Verbatim reports, 98
Vermont, 186, 265–66
Veterinary medicine, 132–33
Virginia, 186, 266–68

Virtual libraries, 7–8
Vocational schools, 339
Volunteer opportunities, 195

Washington, 186, 268–70
Washington, D.C. *See* District of Columbia
Web design, 107–8
Weddle, Peter D., 29, 47
Weddle's Job-Seekers' Guide to Employment Web Sites
    (Weddle), 29
West Virginia, 186, 270–71
What Color Is Your Parachute? (Bolles), 5, 29, 46
Wisconsin, 186, 271–72
Women, 310–12
Work exchanges, 191–93
Writing, 115–17
Wyoming, 186, 273

Young, Margaret Levine, 22
"Your Cyber-Safe Resume" (Joyce), 45